Whether you are looking for the dates
of as renowned a ruler as Charlemagne
or trying to place the Empress Waizero
of Ethiopia, you will find the answer in

KINGS, RULERS AND STATESMEN

And you will learn that the Empress Waizero was
also known as Zauditu, since this book lists sob-
riquets, alternate names and titles.

There is additional information in brief biographical inserts for many key figures of history—and
not only for the best-known ones. Photographs,
works of art, coins and stamps portray the rulers
and statesmen.

INDISPENSABLE AND UNIQUE—
A COMPREHENSIVE ONE-VOLUME
GUIDE TO RULERS AND STATESMEN!

KINGS, RULERS
and STATESMEN

Compiled and Edited by
L. F. Wise and E. W. Egan

A NATIONAL GENERAL COMPANY

KINGS, RULERS AND STATESMEN

*A Bantam Book / published by arrangement with
Sterling Publishing Co., Inc.*

PRINTING HISTORY

*Sterling edition published October 1967
Sterling Revised edition published October 1968*

Bantam edition published December 1969

*Bantam Books are published by Bantam Books, Inc., a National
General company. Its trade-mark, consisting of the words "Bantam
Books" and the portrayal of a bantam, is registered in the United
States Patent Office and in other countries. Marca Registrada.
Bantam Books, Inc., 666 Fifth Avenue, New York, N.Y. 10019.*

PRINTED IN THE UNITED STATES OF AMERICA

THE PLAN OF THIS VOLUME

The information in this book is arranged alphabetically by country. Since the chronologies of some existing countries, e.g., Egypt and Persia, date back to ancient times, ancient and modern states are not arranged in separate sections.

The contents-index basically follows the alphabetical and page order of the book. However, since certain sub-headings relate to more than one general heading, numerous cross-references have been provided.

Headings at the top and bottom of pages are designed to alert the reader to the point in the alphabetical order contained within each two-page spread.

Important modern dependent states included, e.g., Puerto Rico, follow the general alphabetical order. Defunct states with all or most of their territory now part of a single modern state are listed alphabetically within the heading of the modern state. In general these subordinate territories appear alphabetically after the complete chronology of the major state which absorbed them, e.g., Brittany, Burgundy, Champagne, etc., come after the chronology of France from Frankish times to the 5th Republic. These states, along with the names of dynasties and historical periods are listed in the contents, and some are also cross-referenced in the main alphabetical sequence, e.g., *Ukraine, see Russia.*

For convenience, the following are also cross-referenced: former names of countries, e.g., *Siam, see Thailand*; geographical terms for areas formerly composed of many small states not well known to the average reader, e.g., Asia Minor, and countries where there is a geographical link, but not a clear historical and cultural link, e.g., *Mauretania, see Morocco.*

Russian data appear under "Russia," with cross-references for the Soviet Union and the U.S.S.R. Otherwise, popular names, e.g., Holland, appear as cross-references.

Parenthetical notes appear at the beginnings of (and, where needed, throughout) the chronological tables, relating to the origin of the country, changes in its government, and, in the case of defunct states, the circumstances causing its fall.

For the convenience of stamp and coin collectors, names of countries employing the Latin alphabet, where those names differ in the native language from the English form, are translated.

Countries speaking major international languages written in the Latin alphabet are furnished with a translation key, since some monarchs are listed in the text under the English form of their Christian name, others under the native form. These countries are Austria, Belgium, Brazil, France, Germany, Italy, Luxembourg, Monaco, Portugal, and Spain.

Where closely similar correct forms of a name exist in English, e.g., Rumania, Roumania and Romania, it has not been considered necessary to note this in all cases.

No attempt has been made to impart uniformity to names transliterated from Arabic, Chinese, and other languages. Since there is no universally accepted system of rendering these names in English, and since the data contained in this book originated from many different sources, Hussein and Hosein, Abdul and Abd-al, may share the same page.

Decisions had to be made whether to list certain countries separately or under the general heading of another, e.g., Antioch. The fact that the modern city of Antioch is historically part of Syria, but currently part of Turkey, influenced the decision to list the Crusader Principality of Antioch separately.

EDITORS' NOTE

This volume, which contains the most complete listing of kings, rulers and statesmen ever brought together under one cover, is intended to serve the student and researcher by furnishing a starting point and guide and to provide the general reader with information enabling him quickly to find the place of a given historical personage in the chronology of his country. In this book are listed rulers and statesmen representing all modern independent states, some modern dependencies and protectorates of special interest, and significant states of the past, sovereign and semi-sovereign, the records of whose governments have survived. It also lists, in the case of new countries, material that is not yet available elsewhere in book form.

No claim is made that this volume is complete. There are obvious gaps in history which have been recognized by the compilers and there are undoubtedly other gaps which kind readers will call to our attention. An attempt has been made to include all important personages and a large number of lesser ones, with available dates of birth, death and tenure of office. Where the interests of clarity were served by indicating relationships between one person and another, these have been noted.

Biographical inserts appear after many of the entries, to supplement the illustrations. The illustrations themselves have been chosen and placed in the text with an eye to highlighting the less familiar aspects of the man or period, as well as the better-known facts.

Contents

A round table, complete with King Arthur, hangs in Wolvesey Great Hall, Winchester, England. The hall is all that remains of a castle where Queen Mary I once lived. She and the other Tudor monarchs claimed descent from the legendary "King," who was actually an historical personage. He was not a king, but a general who led the 6th-century Britons to war against the Saxon invaders after the Romans abandoned Britain. Recent archaeological finds in southwest England point to that area as his home.

Abyssinia, see Ethiopia

Afghanistan

King Mohammed Zahir Shah
of Afghanistan (1933–   ).

(Belonged to Parthian, Sassanian, Mogul and Persian empires; became an independent
state in 1747)

1747–1773	Amir	Ahmad Shah		b. 1724	d. 1773
1773–1793	,,	Timur Shah, son of Ahmad Shah		b. 1746	d. 1793
1793–1800	,,	Zaman Mirza (Zaman Shah), son of Timur		deposed 1800	
1800–1803	,,	Mahmud Shah, son of Timur		deposed 1803	
1803–1810	,,	Shuja-ul-Mulk, son of Timur			

King Habibullah of Afghanistan (1901–1919), shown operating a film projector, sought to
introduce Western ideas into his country.

1810–1818	Amir	Mahmud Shah			
1818–1826	,,	(Period of anarchy, with various independent khanates)			
1826–1839	,,	Dost Mohammed Khan	deposed 1839	b. 1793	d. 1863
1839	Shah	Shuja		assassinated 1842	
1839–1842	,,	Akbar Khan, son of Dost Mohammed			d. 1849
1842–1863	Amir	Dost Mohammed			d. 1863
1863–1866	,,	Ali Khan, son of Dost Mohammed		b. 1825	d. 1879
1866	,,	Ufzul			d. 1867
1866–1869	,,	Azim			d. 1869
1869–1879	,,	Sher Ali Khan			
1879	,,	Yakub Khan, son of Sher Ali	abdicated 1879	b. 1849	d. 1923
1880–1901	,,	Abdir Rahman Khan, grandson of Dost Mohammed		b. 1845	d. 1901

1901–1919	King	Habibullah, son of Abdir Rahman	b. 1872	assassinated 1919
1919–1929	„	Amanullah Khan	abdicated 1929	b. 1892 d. 1951
1929	„	Habibullah		executed 1929
1929–1933	„	Nadir Shah, cousin of Amanullah	b. 1880	assassinated 1933
1933–	„	Zahir Shah, son of Nadir Shah		b. 1914

Albania (Alb. Shqiperia)

Also see Epirus

*Scanderbeg, National leader of
Albania (1443–1468).*

*King Zog of Albania (1928–
1946).*

1443–1468	National leader	Scanderbeg (Iskender Bey)	b. 1403? d. 1468
		(Under Turkish suzerainty 1468–1912)	
1914	King	Wilhelm Zu Wied	b. 1876 d. 1945
1914	First Minister	Essad Pasha	b. 1863 assassinated 1920
1914–1916	President	Essad Pasha	

(Internal disorders; Italian, Yugoslav, and other foreign intervention; independence
recognized 1921)

1922–1924	Prime Minister	Ahmed bey Zogu	b. 1895 d. 1961
1925–1928	President	Ahmed bey Zogu	
1928–1946	King	Zog I (Ahmed bey Zogu)	
		(Albania occupied by Italy 1939–1944)	
1946–1953	President	Omer Nisani	
1953–	Head of State	Haxhi Leshi	
1945–1953	Prime Minister	Enver Hoxha (Hodja)	b. 1908
1953–	„	Mehmet Shehu	

Algeria Also see Numidia

*Long ruled by Turkey and France,
Algeria became a free nation under the
presidency of Ahmed Ben Bella, following a bitter struggle for independence.*

(Annexed to France in 1842: independent since 1962)

1962–1965	President and Prime Minister	Ahmed Ben Bella	
1965–	„	Houari Boumedienne	b. 1925

Andorra

(Created a principality in 1278)
(Nominal heads of the State: Bishop of Urgel, Spain, and the head of the French government, formerly the King of France, now the President of the French Republic. The two co-princes are represented by *viguiers*)

1966–	Viguier of France	Jean Menant
	Viguier of Spain	Jaime Sansa Nequi

Antioch *Also see Syria, Turkey*

(The Principality of Antioch was founded by the Crusader Bohemond, son of Robert Guiscard)

1098–1111	Prince	Bohemond I	b. 1056	d. 1111
1111–1131	,,	Bohemond II		
1131–1163	Princess	Constance (co-ruler)		d. 1163
1131–1149	Prince	Raymond (co-ruler)		d. 1149
1163–1201	,,	Bohemond III		
1201–1233	,,	Bohemond IV		
1233–1251	,,	Bohemond V		
1251–1268	,,	Bohemond VI		

(Antioch fell to the Egyptian Mamelukes in 1268)

Arabia

*Also see Bahrain, Kuwait, Muscat
and Oman, Qatar, Yemen*

*Stamp issued by the Kingdom
of the Hejaz.*

SAUDI ARABIA
(**WAHHABI DYNASTY**)

1753–1766	Chief	Mohammed Ibn-Saud		
1766–1803	,,	Abd-al-Azis, son of Mohammed Ibn-Saud		
1803–1814	,,	Saud, son of Abd-al-Azis		
	(Turks captured Mecca and Medina in 1812)			
1814–1818	,,	Abd-allah, son of Saud		
1901	Sultan of Nejd	Abd-al-Rahman, descendant of Mohammed Ibn-Saud		d. 1901
1901–1926	,,	Ibn Saud (Abd-al-Azis III)	b. 1880	d. 1953
1926	King of the Hejaz and Nejd	,,		
1932–1953	King of Saudi Arabia	Ibn Saud		
1953–1964	,,	Ibn Saud (Abd-al-Azis IV) son of Ibn Saud	b. 1903	
1964–	,,	Faisal, brother of Ibn Saud		

THE HEJAZ
(Proclaimed an independent kingdom in 1916)

1916–1924	King	Husein ibn-Ali	b. 1856	d. 1931

King Husein ibn-Ali of the Hejaz declared his country independent of Turkey in 1916. Formerly the "sherif" of Mecca, Husein fought at the side of Lawrence of Arabia. His throne did not last long, for by 1926 the Hejaz was annexed to Saudi Arabia.

| 1924–1925 | King | Ali ibn-Husein, | | |
| | | son of Husein ibn-Ali | b. 1878 | d. 1935 |

(Conquered by the Kingdom of Saudi Arabia 1925–1926)

Argentina

(Discovered in 1515 by Spain who ruled it 1553–1816; controlled by junta from 1810)

1826–1827	President	Bernardino Rivadavia	b. 1780	d. 1845
1827–1828	„	Vicente López y Planes	b. 1784	d. 1856
		(Period of anarchy, 1828–1835)		
1835–1852	Dictator	Juan Manuel de Rosas	b. 1793	d. 1877
1854–1860	President	Justo José de Urquiza	b. 1800	d. 1870
1860–1861	„	Santiago Derqui	b. 1846	d. 1891
1861	„	Juan Esteban Pedernera	b. 1796	d. 1886
1862–1868	„	Bartolomé Mitre	b. 1821	d. 1906
1868–1874	„	Domingo Faustino Sarmiento	b. 1811	d. 1888
1874–1880	„	Nicolás Avellaneda	b. 1837	d. 1885
1880–1886	„	Julio A. Roca	b. 1843	d. 1914
1886–1890	„	Miguel Juárez Celmán	b. 1844	d. 1909
1890–1892	„	Carlos Pellegrini	b. 1846	d. 1906
1892–1895	„	Luis Sáenz Peña	b. 1822	d. 1907
1895–1898	„	José Evaristo Uriburu	b. 1831	d. 1914
1898–1904	„	Julio A. Roca		
1904–1906	„	Manuel Quintana	b. 1835	d. 1906
1906–1910	„	José Figueroa Alcorta	b. 1860	d. 1931
1910–1914	„	Roque Sáenz Peña	b. 1851	d. 1914
1914–1916	„	Victorino de la Plaza	b. 1840	d. 1919

Dr. Arturo Illia, President of Argentina (1963–1966), was ousted by a military junta whose members charged him with leniency toward Peronist and leftist elements.

Juan Manuel de Rosas, Dictator of Argentina (1835–1852).

1916–1922	President	Hipólito Irigoyen	b. 1852	d. 1933
1922–1928	„	Marcelo Torcuato de Alvear	b. 1868	d. 1942

1928–1930	President	Hipólito Irigoyen		
1930–1932	,,	José Felix Uriburu	b. 1868	d. 1932
1932–1938	,,	Agustín P. Justo	b. 1878	d. 1943
1938–1941	,,	Roberto M. Ortiz	b. 1886	d. 1942
1941–1943	,,	Ramón S. Castillo	b. 1873	d. 1944
1943–1944	,,	Pedro Ramírez	b. 1884	d. 1962
1944–1946	,,	Edelmiro J. Farrell	b. 1887	
1946–1955	,,	Juan Domingo Perón	b. 1895	
1955	,,	Eduardo Lonardi	b. 1896	d. 1956
1955–1958	,,	Pedro Eugenio Aramburu	b. 1903	
1958–1962	,,	Arturo Frondizi	b. 1908	
1962–1963	,,	José Maria Guido		
1963–1966	,,	Arturo Umberto Illia	b. 1900	
1966–	,,	Juan Carlos Ongania	b. 1914	

Armenia

(Under Median, Persian, Macedonian (331 B.C.), Seleucid (301 B.C.) rule; emerged as independent state *c.* 200 B.C.)

B.C.			
189–	King Artaxias		
?	,, Guras		
?	,, Tigranes I		
c. 100	,, Artavasdes II		
94–56	,, Tigranes II	d. 56	
	(Became vassal of Rome 66 B.C.)		
c. 30	,, Artavasdes III		

Tigranes II, King of Armenia (94–56 B.C.) conquered Syria. This coin was minted at Antioch during his reign.

ARSCACID DYNASTY

(From A.D. 63)

A.D.		
?–216	King Vagarshak	
217– ?	,, Tiridates II	
252– ?	,, Artavasdes (Parthian puppet)	
287– ?	,, Tiridates III	
330–339	King Khosrov II	
428– ?	,, Artaxias IV	
	(Armenia under Byzantines, Persians, Arabs)	

BAGRATID DYNASTY

885–?	King	Ashot I
922– ?	,,	Ashot II the Iron
952–977	,,	Ashot III

(By 1022, Armenia had split into several principalities and came under Byzantine, Seljuk, Mongol, and eventually Ottoman rule. The state of Lesser Armenia, west of the Taurus Mts., remained independent)

LESSER ARMENIA

1092–1100	Prince	Constantine I	
1100–1129	,,	Thoros I	
1129–1139	,,	Leo I	
1145–1168	,,	Thoros II	
1170–1175	,,	Mleh	
1187–1219	King	Leo II	
1219–1226	Queen	Zabel	
1226–1269	King	Hayton	
1320–1342	,,	Leo V	
1342–1344	,,	Guy of Lusignan	
1344– ?	,,	Constantine IV	
? –1374	,,	Constantine V	assassinated 1374

(In 1375, Lesser Armenia fell to the Mamelukes and later to the Ottomans. For modern Armenia, see Russia)

Asia Minor, see Bithynia, Cappadocia, Hittite Empire, Lydia, Pergamum, Pontus, Turkey

Assyria

A 17th-century Dutch coin commemorates Sennacherib's withdrawal from Jerusalem.

(Flourished from about 2500 B.C.; at first ruled by priest-kings)

B.C.			B.C.
1410–1393	King	Ashur-nadir-ahe	
1392–1381	,,	Enib-Adad	
1380–1341	,,	Ashur-yuballidh	
1340–1326	,,	Enlil-nirari	
1325–1311	,,	Arik-den-ili	
1310–1281	,,	Adadnirari I	
1280–1261	,,	Shalmaneser I, great-great-grandson of Ashur-yuballidh	

1260–1232	King	Tukulti-Ninurta I, son of Shalmaneser I	
1231–1214	,,	Ashur nasir pal I	
1213–1208	,,	Ashur-nirari III	
1207–1203	,,	Bel-Kudur-uzur	
1202–1176	,,	Ninurta-apal-ekur I	
1175–1141	,,	Ashur-dan I	
1140–1138	,,	Ninurta-tutulti-Assur	
1137–1128	,,	Mutakkil-Nusku	
1127–1116	,,	Ashur-res-isi	
1115–1103	,,	Tiglath-pileser I	
1102–1093	,,	Ninurta-apal-ekur II	
1092–1076	,,	Ashur-bel-kala I	
1075–1069	,,	Enlil-rabi	
1061–1056	,,	Enriba-Adad	
1055–1050	,,	Shamshi-Adad IV	d. 1039
1049–1031	,,	Ashurnasirpal I	
1030–1019	,,	Shalmaneser II	
1018–1013	,,	Ashur-nirari IV	
1012– 995	,,	Ashur-rabi II	
994– 967	,,	Ashur-res-isi II	
956– 934	,,	Tiglath-pileser II	
933– 912	,,	Assur-dan II	
911– 891	,,	Adadnirari II	
890– 885	,,	Tukulti-Ninurta II, son of Adadnirari II	
884– 860	,,	Ashurnasirpal II	
859– 825	,,	Shalmaneser III, son of Ashurnasirpal II	
824– 812	,,	Shamshi-Adad V, son of Shalmaneser III	
811– 783	,,	Adadnirari III, son of Shamshi-Adad V	
782– 773	,,	Shalmaneser IV	
772– 764	,,	Ashur-dan III	
763– 755	,,	Hadad-nirari IV	
754– 747	,,	Ashur-nirari V	
746– 728	,,	Tiglath-pileser III (Pul)	d. 728
727– 722	,,	Shalmaneser V	d. 722
722– 705	,,	Sargon II	killed 705

The campaigns of King Ashurnasirpal II are very thoroughly documented by contemporary bas-reliefs.

Assyria (continued)

705– 682	King	Sennacherib, son of Sargon II	murdered 682

Sennacherib, after a stormy reign, noted particularly for the destruction of Babylon under his orders, was murdered by his sons.

681– 668	King	Esarhaddon, son of Sennacherib	d. 668
668– 626	,,	Ashurbanipal, son of Esarhaddon	d. 626
632– 629	,,	Ashur-etil-ilani	
629– 612	,,	Sin-sar-iskun, brother of Ashur-etil-ilani	

(The Assyrian capital fell to the Scythians in 612 B.C.)

"The Founding of Australia," by Algernon Talmage, depicts the unfurling of the British flag at Sydney Cove on January 26, 1788, by Captain Arthur Philip, first administrator of New South Wales.

Australia

(No organized government existed in Australia prior to British settlement there. The Commonwealth of Australia was created in 1901)

Colony of New South Wales

(Founded 1788)

1788–1792	Captain-General	Captain Arthur Philip, R.N.		
1792–1794	Administrator	Major Francis Grose		
1794–1795	,,	Captain William Patterson		
1795–1800	Governor	Captain John Hunter, R.N.		
1800–1806	,,	Captain Philip Gidley King, R.N.		
1806–1808	,,	Captain William Bligh, R.N.	b. 1754	d. 1817
1808	Administrator	Lt.-Colonel George Johnston		
1808–1809	,,	Major Joseph Foveaux		
1809	,,	Colonel William Patterson		
1810–1821	Governor	Major-General Lachlan Macquarie		
1821–1825	,,	Major-General Sir Thomas Brisbane	b. 1773	d. 1860
1825	Administrator	Lt.-Colonel William Stewart		
1825–1831	Governor	Lt.-General Ralph Darling		
1831	Administrator	Colonel Patrick Lindesay		

1831–1837	Governor	Sir Richard Bourke
1837–1838	Administrator	Lt.-Colonel Kenneth Snodgrass
1838–1846	Governor	Sir George Gipps
1846	Administrator	Sir Maurice Charles O'Connell
1846–1851	Governor	Sir Charles Augustus Fitz Roy
1851–1855	Captain-General	Sir Charles Augustus Fitz Roy
1855–1861	,,	Sir William Thomas Denison
1861	Administrator	Lt.-Colonel J. F. Kempt
1861–1867	Captain-General	Sir John Young (later Baron Lisgar) b. 1807 d. 1876
1867–1868	Administrator	Sir Trevor Chute
1868–1872	Governor	Earl of Belmore
1872	Administrator	Sir Alfred Stephen
1872–1879	Governor	Sir Hercules Robinson (later Baron Rosmead) b. 1824 d. 1897
1879	Administrator	Sir Alfred Stephen
1879–1885	Governor	Lord Augustus William Spencer Loftus b. 1817 d. 1904
1885	Administrator	Sir Alfred Stephen
1885–1890	Governor	Baron Carrington
1890–1891	Administrator	Sir Alfred Stephen
1891–1893	Governor	Earl of Jersey
1893	Administrator	Sir Frederick Darley
1893–1895	Governor	Sir Robert William Duff
1895	Administrator	Sir Frederick Darley
1895–1899	Governor	Viscount Hampden
1899–1901	,,	Earl Beauchamp

(Entered Commonwealth of Australia in 1901)

Captain William Bligh, shown here in a portrait by Sir Joshua Reynolds, was Governor of New South Wales from 1806 to 1808. Captain Bligh, best known as the victim of the "Bounty" mutiny, was also incarcerated by army mutineers during his governorship.

Colony of Tasmania

(Dependency of New South Wales 1803–1825)

1825–1836	Lieutenant-Governor	Colonel George Arthur
1836–1837	Administrator	Lt.-Colonel Kenneth Snodgrass
1837–1843	Lieutenant-Governor	Sir John Franklin
1843–1846	,,	Sir John Eardley-Wilmot
1846–1847	Administrator	Charles Joseph La Trobe
1847–1855	Lieutenant-Governor	Sir William Thomas Denison

1855–1861	Governor-in-Chief	Sir Henry Edward Fox Young
1861–1862	Administrator	Colonel Thomas Gore Browne
1862–1868	Governor	Colonel Thomas Gore Browne
1868–1869	Administrator	Lt.-Colonel W. C. Trevor
1869–1874	Governor	Charles Du Cane
1874–1875	Administrator	Sir Francis Smith
1875–1880	Governor	Frederick Aloysius Weld
1880	Administrator	Sir Francis Smith
1880–1881	,,	Sir John Henry Lefroy
1881–1886	Governor	Sir George Strahan
1886	Administrator	Chief Justice W. R. Giblin
1886–1887	Administrator	Sir William Dobson
1887–1892	Governor	Sir Robert Crookshank Hamilton
1892–1893	Administrator	Sir William Dobson
1893–1900	Governor	Viscount Gormanston

(Entered Commonwealth of Australia in 1901)

Colony of Western Australia

1829–1832	Lieutenant-Governor	Captain James Stirling, R.N.
1832	Governor	Captain James Stirling, R.N.
1832–1833	Administrator	Captain F. C. Irwin
1833–1834	,,	Captain Richard Daniell
1834	,,	Captain Picton Beete
1834–1839	Governor	Sir James Stirling
1839–1846	,,	John Hutt
1846–1847	,,	Lt.-Colonel Andrew Clarke
1847–1848	,,	Lt.-Colonel F. C. Irwin
1848–1855	,,	Captain Charles Fitzgerald
1855–1862	,,	Arthur Edward Kennedy
1862	Administrator	Lt.-Colonel John Bruce
1862–1868	Governor	John Stephen Hampton
1868–1869	Administrator	Lt.-Colonel John Bruce
1869–1875	Governor	Frederick Aloysius Weld
1875	Administrator	Lt.-Colonel E. D. Harvest
1875–1877	Governor	William C. F. Robinson
1877	Lieutenant-Governor	Lt.-Colonel E. D. Harvest
1877–1878	,,	Sir Harry St. George Ord
1878–1880	Governor	Sir Harry St. George Ord
1880–1883	,,	Sir William F. C. Robinson
1883	Administrator	Henry Thomas Wrenfordsley
1883–1889	Governor	Sir Frederick Napier Broome
1889–1890	Administrator	Sir Malcolm Fraser
1890–1895	Governor	Sir William C. F. Robinson
1895	Administrator	Sir Alexander Campbell Onslow
1895–1900	Governor	Sir Gerard Smith
1900–1901	Administrator	Sir Alexander Campbell Onslow

(Entered Commonwealth of Australia in 1901)

Colony of South Australia

(Colony established in 1836)

1836–1838	Governor	Captain John Hindmarsh, R.N.
1838	Administrator	George Milner Stephen
1838–1841	Resident Commissioner	Lt.-Colonel George Gawler

1841–1845	Governor	Captain George Grey		
1845–1848	Lieutenant-Governor	Lt.-Colonel Frederick Holt Robe		
1848–1854	,,	Sir Henry Edward Fox Young		
1854–1855	Administrator	Boyle Travers Finiss		
1855–1862	Captain-General	Sir Richard Graves MacDonnell		
1862–1868	Governor	Sir Dominick Daly		
1868–1869	Administrator	Lt.-Colonel Francis Gilbert Hamley		
1869–1873	Governor	Sir James Ferguson		
1872–1873	Administrator	Sir Richard Davies Hanson		
1873–1877	Governor	Sir Anthony Musgrave		
1877	Administrator	Chief Justice S. J. Way		
1877	,,	Sir W. W. Cairns		
1877	,,	Chief Justice S. J. Way		
1877–1883	Governor	Sir William Francis Drummond Jervois		
1883	Administrator	Chief Justice S. J. Way		
1883–1889	Governor	Sir William C. F. Robinson		
1889	Administrator	Chief Justice S. J. Way		
1889–1895	Governor	Earl of Kintore		
1895	Administrator	Chief Justice S. J. Way		
1895–1899	Governor	Sir Thomas Fowell Buxton		
1899–1900	,,	Baron Tennyson	b. 1852	d. 1928

(Entered Commonwealth of Australia in 1901)

Colony of Victoria

(Detached from New South Wales 1851)

1851–1854	Lieutenant-Governor	Charles Joseph La Trobe		
1854	Administrator	John Vesey Fitzgerald		
1854–1855	Lieutenant-Governor	Sir Charles Hotham		
1855	Governor-in-Chief	Sir Charles Hotham		
1856	Administrator	Major-General Edward Macarthur		
1856–1863	Governor-in-Chief	Sir Henry Barkly		
1863–1866	Governor	Sir Charles Henry Darling		
1866	Administrator	Brigadier-General G. J. Carey		
1866–1873	Governor	Sir John Manners-Sutton		
1873–1879	,,	Sir George Ferguson Bowen		
1879–1884	,,	Marquess of Normanby		
1884	Administrator	Sir William Foster Stawell		
1884–1889	Governor	Sir Henry Brougham Loch		
1889	Administrator	Sir William C. F. Robinson		
1889–1895	Governor	Earl of Hopetoun	b. 1860	d. 1908
1895	Administrator	Sir John Madden		
1895–1900	Governor	Baron Brassey		
1900–1901	Administrator	Sir John Madden		

(Entered Commonwealth of Australia in 1901)

Colony of Queensland

(Detached from New South Wales 1859)

1859–1868	Governor-in-Chief	Sir George Ferguson Bowen		
1868	Administrator	Sir Maurice Charles O'Connell		
1868–1871	Governor	Colonel Samuel Wensley Blackall		
1871	Administrator	Sir Maurice Charles O'Connell		
1871–1874	Governor	Marquess of Normanby	b. 1819	d. 1890
1874–1875	Administrator	Sir Maurice Charles O'Connell		
1875–1877	Governor	William Wellington Cairns		
1877	Administrator	Sir Maurice Charles O'Connell		

1877–1883	Governor	Sir Arthur Edward Kennedy
1883	Administrator	Sir Arthur Hunter Palmer
1883–1888	Governor	Sir Anthony Musgrave
1888–1889	Administrator	Sir Arthur Hunter Palmer
1889–1895	Governor	Sir Henry Wylie Norman
1895–1896	Administrator	Sir Arthur Hunter Palmer
1896–1900	Governor	Baron Lamington

(Entered Commonwealth of Australia in 1901)

Sir William Slim (1953–1960).

Viscount De L'Isle (1961–1965).

Lord Casey of Berwick (1965–   ).

COMMONWEALTH

1901–1903	Governor-General	Lord Linlithgow, Earl of Hopetoun	b. 1860	d. 1908
1902–1903	Governor-General (acting)	Hallam Tennyson, Baron Tennyson		
1903–1904	Governor-General	Hallam Tennyson, Baron Tennyson	b. 1852	d. 1928
1904–1908	,,	Henry Stafford Northcote, Baron Northcote	b. 1846	d. 1911
1908–1911	,,	Earl of Dudley (William Humble Ward)	b. 1867	d. 1932
1909–1910	Governor-General (acting)	Viscount Chelmsford	b. 1868	d. 1933
1911–1914	Governor-General	Thomas Denman, Baron Denman	b. 1874	d. 1954
1914–1920	,,	Viscount Novar of Raith	b. 1860	d. 1934
1920–1925	,,	Baron Forster of Lepe	b. 1866	d. 1936
1925–1930	,,	Baron Stonehaven	b. 1874	d. 1941
1930–1931	Administrator	Baron Somers	b. 1887	d. 1944
1931–1936	Governor-General	Sir Isaac Alfred Isaacs	b. 1885	d. 1948
1936–1945	,,	Baron Gowrie (Alexander Gore Arkwright Hore-Ruthven)	b. 1872	d. 1955
1938	,,	Baron Huntingfield (in absence of Lord Gowrie)	b. 1883	
1944–1945	,,	Sir Winston J. Dugan	b. 1877	d. 1951
1945–1947	,,	Prince Henry, Duke of Gloucester	b. 1900	
1947	,,	Sir Winston J. Dugan		
1947–1953	,,	Sir William John McKell	b. 1891	
1951	Officer-Administrator	Sir John Northcott	b. 1890	
1953–1960	Governor-General	Sir William Slim	b. 1891	

Field Marshal Viscount Slim took over command of the 14th ("forgotten") Army in Burma in 1943 and led them to victory over the Japanese.

Sir Joseph Cook (1913–1914).

William Morris Hughes (1915–1923).

PRIME MINISTERS

Sir Robert Gordon Menzies (1949–1966).

Harold Holt (1966–1967).

1956	Administrator	Sir John Northcott		
1959	„	Sir Reginald Alexander Dallas Brooks	b. 1896	
1960–1961	Governor-General	William Shepherd, Viscount Dunrossil	b. 1893	d. 1961
1961	Administrator	Sir Reginald Alexander Dallas Brooks		
1961–1965	Governor-General	Viscount De L'Isle	b. 1909	
1965	Administrator	Sir Henry Abel Smith	b. 1900	
1965–	Governor-General	Lord Casey of Berwick	b. 1890	

Statesmen

| 1901–1903 | Prime Minister | Sir Edmund Barton | b. 1849 | d. 1920 |
| 1903–1904 | „ | Alfred Deakin | b. 1856 | d. 1919 |

1904	Prime Minister	J. C. Watson	b. 1867	d. 1941
1904–1905	,,	Sir George Reid	b. 1845	d. 1918
1905–1908	,,	Alfred Deakin		
1908–1909	,,	Andrew Fisher	b. 1862	d. 1928
1909–1910	,,	Alfred Deakin		
1910–1913	,,	Andrew Fisher		
1913–1914	,,	Sir Joseph Cook	b. 1860	d. 1947
1914–1915	,,	Andrew Fisher		
1915–1923	,,	William Morris Hughes	b. 1864	d. 1952
1923–1929	,,	Stanley Melbourne, Viscount Bruce	b. 1883	
1929–1932	,,	James Henry Scullin	b. 1876	d. 1953
1932–1939	,,	Joseph Aloysius Lyons	b. 1879	d. 1939
1939	,,	Sir Earle Page	b. 1880	d. 1961
1939–1941	,,	Sir Robert Gordon Menzies	b. 1894	
1941	,,	Sir Arthur William Fadden	b. 1895	
1941–1945	,,	John Curtin	b. 1885	d. 1945
1945 (1 week)	,,	F. M. Forde	b. 1890	
1945–1949	,,	Joseph B. Chifley	b. 1885	d. 1951
1949–1966	,,	Sir Robert Gordon Menzies		

Few world statesmen of the 20th century held power for as long as Sir Robert Gordon Menzies who became Prime Minister for the first time in 1939 and held the post continuously from 1949 until 1966.

1966–1967	Prime Minister	Harold Holt	b. 1908	d. 1967
1967–1968 (3 weeks)	Acting Prime Minister	John McEwen	b. 1900	
1968–	Prime Minister	John Grey Gorton		

Austria *(Ger. Oesterreich)*

(Austria owes its name and its beginnings to Charlemagne, who set up his easternmost conquests in 788 as the East Mark, later Oesterreich (East Realm))

English versions of the names of rulers of German-speaking states are:

Albert–Adalbert, Albrecht	Frederick–Friedrich	Louis–Ludwig
Charles–Karl	George–Georg	Maurice–Moritz
Ernest–Ernst	Henry–Heinrich	Philip–Philipp
Eugene–Eugen	Joseph–Josef	William–Wilhelm
Francis–Franz	John–Johann	

HOUSE OF BABENBERG

976– 994	Margrave	Leopold I
994–1018	,,	Henry I, son of Leopold I
1018–1055	,,	Adalbert, son of Leopold I
1055–1075	,,	Ernst, son of Adalbert
1075–1096	,,	Leopold II, son of Ernst
1096–1136	,,	Leopold III, the Pious, son of Leopold II canonized 1485
1136–1141	,,	Leopold IV, son of Leopold III
1141–1156	,,	Henry II, brother of Leopold IV b. 1114 d. 1177
1156–1177	Duke	Henry II, grandfather of Leopold VI
1177–1194	,,	Leopold V, son of Henry II
1194–1198	,,	Frederick I, son of Leopold V
1198–1230	,,	Leopold VI, the Glorious, brother of Frederick I b. 1176 d. 1230

Austria (continued)

1230–1246	Duke	Frederick II, brother of Leopold VI
		(To the Empire, 1246–1248)
1248–1250	,,	Hermann von Baden,
		nephew-in-law of Frederick II
		(Anarchy: several claimants, 1250–1253)
1253–1276	King	Ottokar II of Bohemia b. 1230 ? killed 1278

HABSBURG DYNASTY

(Counts of Habsburg in Switzerland, 1023–1276; ruled Austria from 1276–1918)

| 1276–1282 | Duke | Rudolf I, son of Albert IV |
| | | of Habsburg   b. 1218 d. 1291 |

Rudolf I was a comparatively unimportant German count who was made King by the Electors of the Rhine to counter the influence of the King of Bohemia. He and his descendants ruled Austria for 642 years.

1282–1308	Duke	Albert I, son of Rudolf I	b. 1250 ?	murdered 1308
1308–1330	,,	Frederick, son of Albert I	b. 1286 ?	d. 1330
1308–1326	Co-regent	Leopold I, son of Albert I	b. 1290 ?	d. 1326

Leopold III the Pious of Babenberg, Margrave of Austria (1096–1136); later canonized, he became the patron saint of his country.

1330–1358	Duke	Albert II, son of Albert I
1330–1339	Co-regent	Otto, son of Albert I
1358–1365	Duke	Rudolf, son of Albert II
1358–1397	,,	⎰ Albert III, son of Albert II
1365–1379	Co-regent	⎱ Leopold III, son of Albert II b. 1351 killed 1386

(Austria was divided between Albert III and Leopold III in 1379)

LINE OF ALBERT

1379–1395	Duke	Albert III
1397–1404	,,	Albert IV, son of Albert III
1404–1439	,,	Albert V, son of Albert IV
		(Holy Roman Emperor 1438) b. 1397 d. 1439
1440–1457	,,	Ladislaus, son of Albert V

LINE OF LEOPOLD

1379–1386	Duke	Leopold III		
1386–1406	„	William, son of Leopold III		
1386–1411	„	Leopold IV, son of Leopold III		
1406–1424	„	Ernst, son of Leopold III		
1457–1463	„	Albert VI, brother of Frederick		
1457–1493	Archduke	Frederick V, cousin of Ladislaus		
		(Holy Roman Emperor 1440)	b. 1415	d. 1493
1493–1519	„	Maximilian, son of Frederick V	b. 1459	d. 1519
1519–1522	„	Charles, grandson of Maximilian I		
		(Holy Roman Emperor 1519)	b. 1500	d. 1558

Rudolf IV, Duke of Austria
(1358–1365).

Francis Joseph, Emperor of
Austria (1848–1916).

Michael Hainisch, President
of Austria (1920–1928).

1519–1564	Archduke	Ferdinand, brother of Charles		
		(Holy Roman Emperor 1556)	b. 1503	d. 1564
	(See Holy Roman Empire for the periods 1564–1740, 1780–1804)			
1740–1780	Archduchess	Maria Theresa,		
		daughter of Charles VI	b. 1717	d. 1780
1804–1835	Emperor	Francis I		
		(Holy Roman Emperor 1792)	b. 1768	d. 1835
1835–1848	„	Ferdinand I,		
		son of Francis I abdicated 1848	b. 1793	d. 1875
1848–1916	„	Francis Joseph,		
		nephew of Ferdinand I	b. 1830	d. 1916

Francis Joseph was partly educated by Metternich. After revoking the
constitution, he bore the entire responsibility of governing his vast domains
personally. His rule was generally oppressive and absolutist but he genuinely
wanted peace. He experienced tragedy in his personal life, for his wife was
assassinated, and his son Rudolf, committed suicide.

1916–1918	Emperor	Charles I,		
		grand-nephew of Francis Joseph	b. 1887	d. 1922
	(Austria became a republic in 1918)			
1920–1928	President	Michael Hainisch	b. 1858	d. 1940
1928–1938	„	Wilhelm Miklas	b. 1872	d. 1956
	(Annexed by Germany in 1938)			
1938–1939	German	Arthur Jon Seyss-Inquart	b. 1892	hanged 1946
	Governor-General			
	(Second republic established in 1945)			
1945–1950	President	Karl Renner	b. 1870	d. 1950

1951–1957	President	Theodor Körner	b. 1873	d. 1957
1957–1965	„	Adolf Scharf	b. 1890	d. 1965
1965–	„	Franz Jonas	b. 1899	

STATESMEN

| 1753–1792 | Chancellor | Wenzel Anton von Kaunitz | b. 1711 | d. 1794 |
| 1821–1848 | „ | Klemens Wenzel Nepomuk Lothar von Metternich | b. 1773 | d. 1859 |

Metternich had complete control of Austrian affairs for 40 years. He negotiated the marriage between Marie Louise and Napoleon, and presided at the Congress of Vienna. Even during the last 8 years of his life he continued to influence events, though not in office.

1868–1870	Prime Minister	Eduard von Taaffe	b. 1833	d. 1895
1879–1893	„	Eduard von Taaffe		
1919–1920	Chancellor	Karl Renner	b. 1870	d. 1950
1932–1934	„	Engelbert Dollfuss	b. 1892	assassinated 1934
1934–1938	„	Kurt Edler von Schuschnigg	b. 1897	
1945–1953	„	Leopold Figl	b. 1902	d. 1965
1953–1961	„	Julius Raab	b. 1891	d. 1964
1961–1964	„	Alfons Gorbach	b. 1898	
1964–	„	Josef Klaus	b. 1910	

Adolf Scharf, President of Austria (1957–1965).

Josef Klaus, Chancellor of Austria (1964–   ).

Azerbaijan, see Russia

Babylonia

(The Babylonian Empire united the territory of several earlier city-states such as Akkad. The most famous rulers of Akkad were Sargon I (*c.* 2637–2582 B.C.) and Naram-Sin (*c.* 2550 B.C.))

FIRST DYNASTY

B.C.
| 2049–2036 | King | Sumuabi |
| 2035–2000 | „ | Sumu-la-ilu, son of Sumuabi |

1967–1948	King	Sin-muballit
1947–1905	,,	Hammurabi (or Hammurapi or Khammurabi)
1904–1867	,,	Samsu-iluna
1866–1839	,,	Abeshuh
1838–1802	,,	Ammi-ditana
1801–1781	,,	Ammi-zaduga
1780–1750	,,	Samsuditana
		(Unknown dynasty of 11 Kings)

King Naram-Sin of
Akkad
(c. 2550 B.C.).

KASSITE DYNASTY 1746–1171

B.C.

1521–1503	King	Burnaburiash I
1502–1484	„	Kashtiliash II
1483–1465	„	Agum III
1445–1427	„	Karaindash
1344–1320	„	Kurigalza III
1319–1294	„	Nazimaruttash II
1293–1277	„	Kadashman-Turgu
1276–1271	„	Kadashman-Enlil II
1270–1263	„	Kudur-Enlil
1262–1250	„	Sagarakti-Suriash
1249–1242	„	Kastiash III
1232–1203	„	Adad-shum-nasir
1202–1188	„	Melishipah II
1187–1175	„	Merodach (Marduk)-baladan I
1174	„	Zabada-sum-iddin
1173–1171	„	Enlil-nadin-ahe

ELAMITE DYNASTY 1170– 730

B.C.

1170–1153	King	Merodash (Marduk)-shapik-zer	
1152–1147	„	Ninurta-nadin-shumi	
1146–1123	„	Nebuchadnezzar	
1122–1117	„	Enlil-nadin-apli	
1116–1101	„	Merodach (Marduk)-nadin-ahe	
1100–1092	„	Itti-Marduk-balatu	
1091–1084	„	Merodach (Marduk)-shapik-zer-mati	
1083–1062	„	Adad-apal-iddin	
990– 955	„	Nabo-mukin-apli	
954	„	Ninurta-kudur-usur	
953– 942	„	Marbiti-ahe-iddin	
941– 901	„	Samas-mudaminiq	
900– 886	„	Nabo-shum-ukin	
885– 852	„	Nabo-apal-iddin	
851– 828	„	Merodach (Marduk)-zakir-shum	
827– 815	„	Merodach (Marduk)-balatsuiqbi	
814– 811	„	Bau-ahe-iddin	
802– 763	„	Eriba-Marduk	
747– 734	„	Nabonassar	d. 734
734– 733	„	Nadinu	
732– 730	„	Ukin-zer	
729– 728	„	Tiglathpileser III (of Assyria)	
727– 723	„	Shalmaneser V (of Assyria)	
722– 710	„	Merodach (Marduk)-baladan III	d. 710?
710– 705	„	Sargon II (of Assyria)	
705– 682	„	Sennacherib, son of Sargon II (of Assyria)	

B.C.

NEW BABYLONIAN EMPIRE

625– 605	„	Nabopolassar	
605– 562	„	Nebuchadnezzer II, son of Nabopolassar	d. 562
562– 560	„	Evil-Merodach (Amel-Marduk), son of Nebuchadnezzar II	d. 560
559– 556	„	Nergal-shar-usur	
556– 539	„	Nabonidus	d. about 539
539– 538	„	Belshazzar, son of Nabonidus	killed 538
		(Fell to the Persians, 538 B.C.)	

Bahrain

(An Arab state under British protection since 1861, Bahrain is a sheikhdom whose present ruler is the 11th since the dynasty was founded in 1782)

1961–	Sheikh	Isa bin Sulman Al Khalifah	b. 1933

Barbados

(A British colony from 1605 to 1966, Barbados is now an independent Dominion of the Commonwealth)

1959–1966	Governor	Sir John Montague Stow	b. 1911
1966–	Governor-General	Sir John Montague Stow	
1966–	Prime Minister	E. W. Barrow	

Basutoland, see Lesotho

Bechuanaland, see Botswana

Belgium *(Fr. Belgique)*

King Baudouin of Belgium (1951–   ).

English versions of the names of rulers of French-speaking states are:

Baldwin–Baudouin	John–Jean	Philip–Philippe
Francis–François	James–Jacques	Rudolph–Rodolphe
Henry–Henri	Odo–Eudes	Stephen–Etienne
Hugh–Hugues	Peter–Pierre	Theobald–Thibaut
		William–Guillaume

(No authenticated information is available for the period before Baldwin I)

862– 878	Count of Flanders	Baldwin I (Bras de fer)		d. 879
878– 918	,,	Baldwin II, son of Baldwin I		
918– 950	,,	Arnulf I, son of Baldwin II		
950– 961	,,	Baldwin III, son of Arnulf I		
961– 964	,,	Arnulf I (again)		
964– 989	,,	Arnulf II		
989–1035	,,	Baldwin IV		
1036–1067	,,	Baldwin V, son of Baldwin IV		d. 1067
1067–1070	,,	Baldwin VI, son of Baldwin V		
1070–1071	,,	Arnulf III, brother of Baldwin VI		
1071–1093	,,	Robert I, brother of Baldwin VI	b. 1013?	d. 1093
1093–1111	,,	Robert II, son of Robert I		d. 1111
1111–1119	,,	Baldwin VII, son of Robert II	b. 1058	d. 1119
1119–1127	,,	Charles the Good, cousin of Baldwin VII	b. 1083?	murdered 1127

1127–1128	Count of Flanders	William Clito, grandson of William I of England
1128–1157	,,	Didrik of Alsace, grandson of Robert I abdicated 1157 d. 1177
1157–1191	,,	Philip, son of Didrik of Alsace
1171–1195	,,	Baldwin VIII b. 1150 d. 1195
1191	Countess	Margareta (wife of Baldwin of Hainault), sister of Philip
1195–1206	Count	Baldwin IX (Emperor of Constantinople) b. 1171 murdered 1205?
1206–1244	Countess	Joanna, daughter of Baldwin IX
1212–1233	Co-regent	Ferdinand of Portugal, husband of Joanna

King Leopold I of Belgium (1831–1865).

King Leopold II of Belgium (1865–1909).

King Albert (1909–1934) and his consort, Queen Elisabeth, directed Belgian resistance from behind the lines in World War I.

King Leopold III of Belgium (1934–1951) abdicated in the face of public criticism of his leadership during World War II.

1244–1280	Countess	Margaret, daughter of Joanna	b. 1200 ?	d. 1280
1280–1305	Count	Guy de Dampierre, son of Margaret		d. 1305
1305–1322	,,	Robert III of Béthune, son of Guy de Dampierre	b. 1240	d. 1322
1322–1337	Count of Flanders	Louis I de Nevers, grandson of Robert of Béthune	b. 1304?	killed 1346
1336–1345	Governor	Jacob van Artevelde	b. 1290?	d. 1345
1346–1384	Count	Louis II de Male, son of Louis de Nevers	b. 1330	d. 1384

Louis II was wounded at Crécy, where his father was killed fighting with the French against the English under Edward III. His reign was a continuous struggle with the communes and he was aided by the French in subduing the towns.

1384–1405	Countess	Margaret, wife of Philip of Burgundy, daughter of Louis II de Male	b. 1350	d. 1405

(Belgium under Burgundy 1384–1477; under the Habsburgs 1477–1795; see Spanish kings–1714, regents of the Holy Roman Empire 1714–1795; united with France 1795–1814; united with Holland 1815–1830; an independent Kingdom from 1830)

HOUSE of SAXE-COBURG

1831–1865	King	Leopold I, son of Francis Frederick, Duke of Saxe-Coburg-Saalfield	b. 1790	d. 1865
1865–1909	,,	Leopold II, son of Leopold I	b. 1835	d. 1909

Leopold II was a great world-traveller. He financed Stanley's expedition to the Congo, and five years later was granted personal sovereignty over the Congo. His cruel treatment of the Congolese resulted in the Belgian State's annexation of the territory.

1909–1934	King	Albert I, nephew of Leopold II	b. 1875	killed 1934
1934–1951	,,	Leopold III, son of Albert I abdicated 1951	b. 1901	
1951–	,,	Baudouin, son of Leopold III	b. 1930	

Count Hubert Pierlot,
Premier of Belgium
(1944–1945).

Paul-Henri Spaak,
Premier of Belgium
(1947–1949).

Théodore Lefevre,
Premier of Belgium
(1961–1965).

Statesmen

1944–1945	Prime Minister	Hubert Pierlot	b. 1883
1945	,,	Achille Van Acker	b. 1898
1945–1946	,,	Achille Van Acker	
1946	,,	Paul Henri Spaak	b. 1899
1946	,,	Achille Van Acker	

Belgium (continued)

1946–1947	Prime Minister	Camille Huysmans	b. 1871	
1947–1949	,,	Paul Henri Spaak		
1949–1950	,,	Gaston Eyskens	b. 1905	
1950	,,	Jean Duvieusart	b. 1900	
1950–1952	,,	Joseph Pholien	b. 1884	d. 1968
1952–1954	,,	Jean Van Houtte	b. 1907	
1954–1958	,,	Achille Van Acker		
1958	,,	Gaston Eyskens		
1958–1960	,,	Gaston Eyskens		
1960–1961	,,	Gaston Eyskens		
1961–1965	,,	Théodore Lefevre	b. 1914	
1965	,,	Pierre Harmel	b. 1911	
1965–	,,	Paul Vanden Boeynants	b. 1919	

Bhutan

King Jigme Wangchuk of Bhutan (1926–1952).

(Before India became independent in 1947, Bhutan was a British Protectorate. Since that time it has been an Indian Protectorate)

1926–1952	King	Jigme Wangchuk	
1952–	,,	Jigme Dorji Wangchuk	b. 1929
1952–1964	Prime Minister	Jigme Dorjii	assassinated 1964
1964–	,,	Lhendup Durjii, brother of Jigme Dorjii	

Biafra, see Nigeria

Bithynia

(Bithynia lay in western Asia Minor near the Bosporus)

B.C.			B.C.
383– 382	King	Doedalsus	d. 382
381– 378	,,	Botyrus	d. 378
378– 328	,,	Bias	d. 328
328– 281	,,	Zipoetes	d. 281
281– 245	,,	Nicomedes I	d. 245
245– 229	,,	Zelas	d. 229
229– 186	,,	Prusias I	d. 186
186– 149	,,	Prusias II	d. 149
149– 92	,,	Nicomedes II	d. 92
92– 74	,,	Nicomedes III	d. 74

Prusias II.

(Nicomedes III willed his realm to Rome after which it was merged with Pontus)

Bolivia

(Independence declared 1825)

1825–1826	President	Simón Bolívar		b. 1795 d. 1830
1826–1828	,,	Antonio José de Sucre b. 1795		assassinated 1830
1828	President (provisional)	Pedro Blanco		
1829–1839	President	Andrés Santa Cruz		b. 1792 ? d. 1865
1839–1841	,,	José Miguel de Velasco		
1841–1848	,,	José Ballivián		b. 1804 d. 1852

*(Left) Simón Bolívar,
President of Bolivia
(1825–1826).*

*(Right) José Ballivián,
President of Bolivia
(1841–1848).*

1848	President	Eusebio Guilarte	
1848–1855	,,	Manuel Isidoro Belzú	
1855–1857	,,	Jorge Córdoba	
1857–1861	Dictator	José María Linares	b. 1810 d. 1861
1861–1864	President	José María de Achá	
1865–1871	Dictator	Mariano Melgarejo	b. 1818 d. 1871
1871–1872	President	Agustín Morales b. 1810	assassinated 1872
1873–1874	,,	Adolfo Ballivián	b. 1831 d. 1874
1874–1876	,,	Tomás Frías	b. 1804 d. 1882
1876–1880	,,	Hilarión Daza	b. 1840 killed 1894
1880–1884	,,	Narciso Campero	b. 1815 d. 1896
1884–1888	,,	Gregorio Pacheco	
1888–1892	,,	Aniceto Arce	b. 1824 d. 1906
1892–1896	,,	Mariano Baptista	b. 1832 d. 1907
1896–1899	,,	Severo Fernández Alonso	
1899–1904	,,	José Manuel Pando	b. 1848 ? d. 1917
1904–1909	,,	Ismael Montes	b. 1861 d. 1933
1909–1913	,,	Eliodoro Villazón	
1913–1917	,,	Ismael Montes	
1917–1920	,,	José Gutiérrez Guerra	
		(provisional junta, 1920–1921)	
1921–1925	,,	Bautista Saavedra	b. 1870 d. 1939
1925–1926	President (provisional)	Felipe Guzmán	
1926–1930	President	Hernando Siles	b. 1881 d. 1942
1930–1931	President (provisional)	Carlos Blanco Galindo	
1931–1934	President	Daniel Salamanca	b. 1869 d. 1935
1934–1936	,,	José Luis Tejada Sorzano	b. 1881 d. 1938
1936–1937	,,	José David Toro	
1937–1939	,,	Germán Busch	d. 1939
1939–1940	President (provisional)	Carlos Quintanilla	
1940–1943	President	Enrique Peñaranda	b. 1892
1943–1946	,,	Gualberto Villarroel	lynched 1946
1946–1947	President (provisional)	Tomás Monje Gutiérrez	
1947–1949	President	Enrique Hertzog	
1949–1951	,,	Mamerto Urriolagoitia	
1951–1952	,,	Hugo Ballivián Rojas	
1952–1956	,,	Victor Paz Estenssoro	
1956–1960	,,	Hernán Siles Zuazo	
1960–1964	,,	Victor Paz Estenssoro	

1964–	President	Rene Barrientos Ortuño
1965–1966	Co-President	Alfredo Ovardo Candia
1966–	Vice-President	Luis Adolfo Silas Salinas

Bosnia and Herzegovina, see Yugoslavia

Botswana

(Formerly the British Protectorate of Bechuanaland, Botswana became an independent republic in 1966)

1966–	President	Sir Seretse Khama	b. 1921

Brazil

Martin Alfonso da Sousa, Governor-General of Brazil (1549–1553).

(After 3 centuries of Portuguese rule, became an independent empire in 1822 under a member of the Portuguese royal house of Braganza)

English versions of the names of rulers of Portuguese-speaking states are:

Charles–Carlos	Ferdinand–Fernando	John–João
Denis–Diniz	Henry–Enrique	Michael–Miguel
Edward–Duarte	James–Diogo	Peter–Pedro

1549–1553	Governor-General	Martin Alfonso da Souza	
1553–1556	„	Duarte da Costa	
1556–1570	„	Mem de Sá	b. 1500? d. 1572
1570–1572	„	{ Luis de Brito de Almeida { Antônio de Salema	
1572–1577	„	Luis de Brito de Almeida	
1577–1580	„	Lourenço da Veiga	
1580–1583	„	Cosme Rangel	
1583–1587	„	Manuel Teles Barreto	
1587–1591	„	{ Antônio Barreiros { Cristóvão de Barros	
1591–1602	„	Francisco de Souza	
1602–1608	„	Diogo Botelho	
1608–1612	„	Diogo de Menezes e Siqueira	
1612–1617	„	Gaspar de Souza	
1617–1621	„	Luiz de Souza	
1621–1624	„	Diogo de Mendonça Furtado	
1624	„	Mathias de Albuquerque	d. 1646
1624	„	Francisco Nunes Marinho d'Eça	
1624–1626	„	Francisco de Moura Rolim	
1626–1635	„	Diogo Luis de Oliveira	
1635–1639	„	Pedro da Silva	
1639	„	Fernando Mascarenhas, Count of Tôrre	
1639–1640	„	Vasco Mascarenhas, Count of Óbidos	

1640–1641	Governor-General	Jorge Mascarenhas, Marquis of Montalvão (1st Viceroy of Brazil)
1641–1642	"	{ Bispo D. Pedro { Luis Barbalho { Provedor-Mor Lourenço Brito Correia
1642–1647	"	Antônio Teles da Silva
1647–1650	"	Antônio Teles de Menezes, Count of Vila Pouca de Aguiar
1650–1654	"	João Rodrigues de Vasconcelos, Count of Castelo Melhor
1654–1657	"	Jerônimo de Ataíde, Count of Atouguia
1657–1663	"	Francisco Barreto
1663–1667	"	Vasco Mascarenhas, Count of Óbidos (2nd Viceroy of Brazil)
1667–1671	"	Alexandre de Souza Freire
1671–1675	"	Afonso Furtado de Castro de Mendonça, Viscount of Barbacena
1675–1678	"	{ Desembargador Agostinho de Azevedo Monteiro { Alvaro de Azevedo { Antônio Guedes Brito
1678–1682	"	Roque da Costa Barreto
1682–1684	"	Antônio de Souza Meneses
1684–1687	"	Antônio Luís de Souza, Marquis of Minas
1687–1688	"	Mathias da Cunha
1688–1690	"	Manuel da Ressureição
1690–1694	"	Antônio Luiz Gonçalves da Câmara Coutinho
1694–1702	"	João Lencastro
1702–1708	"	Rodrigo da Costa
1708–1710	"	Luis César de Meneses
1710–1711	"	Lourenço de Almada
1711–1714	"	Pedro de Vasconcelos de Souza

Viceroys

1711–1714	Viceroy	Marquês de Angeja (3rd Viceroy of Brazil)
1718–1719	"	Sancho de Faro, Count of Vimieiro
1719–1720	"	{ Sebastião Monteiro de Vide { Desembargador Caetano de Brito e Figueiredo { João de Araújo e Azevedo
1720–1735	"	Vasco Fernandes César de Meneses, Count of Sabugosa
1735–1749	"	André de Melo e Castro, Count of Galveias
1749–1754	"	Luiz Pedro Peregrino de Carvalho Meneses e Ataíde, Count of Atouguia
1754–1755	"	{ José Botelho de Mattos { Manuel Antônio de Cunha Soto Maior { Lourenço Monteiro
1755–1760	"	Marços de Noronha, Count of Arcos
1760	"	Antônio d' Almeida Soares e Portugal, Count of Avintes and Marquis of Lavradio
1760–1763	"	{ Tomás Rubi de Barros Barreto { José Carvalho de Andrada { Barros e Alvim
1763–1767	"	Antônio Alvares da Cunha, Count of Cunha
1767–1769	"	Antônio Rolim de Moura
1769–1778	"	Luiz de Almeida, Marquis of Lavradio

1778–1790	Viceroy	Luiz de Vasconcelos e Souza	
1790–1801	,,	José Luiz de Castro, Count of Resende	
1801–1806	,,	José Fernandes de Portugal e Castro	
1801–1806	,,	José Fernandes de Portugal e Castro	
1806–1808	,,	Marcos de Noronha e Brito, Count of Arcos	
1808–1815	,,	John VI	b. 1769 ? d. 1826
1815–1821	,,	John VI	
1821–1822	Regent	Dom Pedro, son of John VI	b. 1798 d. 1834
1822–1831	Emperor	Pedro I	
1831–1872	,,	Dom Pedro II, son of Dom Pedro I	b. 1826 d. 1891

Dom Pedro II, Emperor of Brazil (1831–1872).

Diogo Antônio Feijó, Regent of Brazil (1835–1837).

Floriano Peixoto, President of Brazil (1891–1894).

Eurico Gaspar Dutra, President of Brazil (1946–1951).

Getúlio Dornelles Vargas, President of Brazil (1930–1945; 1951–1954).

1831	Regent	José Joaquim Carneiro de Campos, Marquis de Caravelas / Nicolau Pereira de Campos Vergueiro / Francisco de Lima e Silva	b. 1785 d. 1853
1831–1835	,,	José da Costa Carvalho, (afterwards Viscount and Marquis of Montalvão) / João Bráulio Muniz / Francisco de Lima e Silva	
1835–1837	,,	Diogo Antônio Feijó	
1837–1840	,,	Pedro de Araújo Lima, (afterwards Viscount and Marquis de Olinda)	
1871–1872	Regent	Isabella	b. 1846 d. 1921
1872–1876	Emperor	Dom Pedro II	
1876–1888	Regent	Isabella	
1888–1889	Emperor	Dom Pedro II	abdicated 1889
		(Became a Republic in 1889)	
1889–1891	President	Manuel Deodoro da Fonseca	b. 1827 d. 1892
1891–1894	,,	Floriano Peixoto	b. 1842 d. 1895
1894–1896	,,	Prudente José de Moraes Barros	b. 1841 d. 1902
1896–1897	,,	Manuel Vitorino Pereira	
1898–1900	,,	Manuel Ferraz de Campos Salles	b. 1846 d. 1913
1900	,,	Francisco de Assis Rosa e Silva	
1900–1902	,,	Manuel Ferraz de Campos Salles	
1902–1906	,,	Francisco de Paula Rodrigues Alves	b. 1848 d. 1919
1906–1909	,,	Affonso Augusto Moreira Penna	b. 1847 d. 1909
1909–1910	,,	Nilo Peçanha	b. 1867 d. 1924

1910–1914	President	Hermes Rodrigues da Fonseca, nephew of Manuel Deodoro da Fonseca	b. 1855	d. 1923
1914–1917	,,	Wencesláo Braz Pereira Gomes	b. 1868	
1917	,,	Urbano Santos da Costa Araujo		
1917–1918	,,	Wenceslóo Braz Pereira Gomes		
1918–1919	,,	Delfim Moreira da Costa Ribeiro		
1919–1922	,,	Epitácio da Silva Pessôa	b. 1865	d. 1942
1922–1926	,,	Arthur da Silva Bernardes	b. 1875	d. 1955
1926–1930	,,	Washington Luiz Pereira de Souza	b. 1869	d. 1957
1930	President elect	Júlio Prestes de Albuquerque		
1930	President	Augusto Tasso Fragoso		
1930–1945	,,	Getúlio Dornelles Vargas	b. 1883	d. 1954
1945–1946	President (provisional)	José Linhares		
1946–1951	President	Eurico Gaspar Dutra	b. 1885	
1951–1954	,,	Getúlio Dornelles Vargas		
1954–1955	,,	João Café Filho		
1955	President (acting)	Carlos Coimbra da Luz		
1955	,,	Nereu de Oliveira Ramos		
1956–1960	President	Juscelino Kubitschek de Oliveira	b. 1922	
1960	,,	Ranieri Mazzilli		
1960–1961	,,	Juscelino Kubitschek de Oliveira		
1961	,,	Jânio de Silva Quadros		
1961–1964	,,	João Belchior Marques Goulart	b. 1918	
1964	,,	Ranieri Mazzilli		
1964–1967	,,	Humberto de Alencar Castelo Branco	b. 1900	d. 1967
1967–	,,	Arthur Costa e Silva	b. 1902	

Juscelino Kubitschek de Oliveira, President of Brazil (1956–1960, 1960–1961).

João Belchior Marques Goulart, President of Brazil (1961–1964).

Humberto de Alencar Castelo Branco, President of Brazil (1964–1967).

Bulgaria

(Right) Ferdinand I, King of Bulgaria (1887–1918).

(Far right) Boris III, King of Bulgaria (1918–1943).

852– 893	Tsar	Boris I (Michael Simeon)	d. 907
893– 927	,,	Simeon I, son of Boris	d. 927

927– 969	Tsar	Peter, son of Simeon I	
969– 972	„	Boris II	

(Conquered by Byzantine Empire 972–1186)

976–1014	Prince	Samuel	
1014–1015	„	Gabriel Radomir	
1015–1018	„	John Vladislav	
1186–1197	Tsar	Peter Asen	d. 1197
1186–1196	(Co-regent)	John Asen I, brother of Peter	d. 1196
1197–1207	Tsar	Kaloyan, brother of Peter	d. 1207
1218–1241	„	John Asen II, son of John Asen I	

John Asen II was the greatest ruler of Bulgaria. He conquered Albania, Epirus, Thrace and Macedonia, assumed the title of tsar of the Greeks and Bulgars, and ruled wisely and well. During his reign, trade, art and industry flourished and many churches and monasteries were founded.

1241–1246	„	Kaliman I	
1246–1257	„	Michael Asen	
1257–1258	„	Kaliman II	
1258–1277	„	Constantine Asen	murdered 1277
1278–1279	„	Ivaljo	
1279–1280	„	Ivan III Asen	

(Feudal anarchy followed extinction of Asen dynasty in 1280)

1280–1292	„	George I Terter	
1292–1300	„	Smilitz	
1300	„	Caka	
1300–1322	„	Theodore Svetoslav	
1322–1323	„	George II Terter	
1322–1330	„	Michael	killed 1330
1330–1331	„	Ivan II Stephen	
1330–1371	„	Ivan I Alexander	
1365–1393	„	Ivan III Shishman	

(Ruled by Turks 1396–1878; made Principality under Turkish suzerainty, 1878)

1879–1886	Prince	Alexander Joseph of Battenberg, nephew of Alexander II of Russia abdicated 1886	b. 1857	d. 1893
1887–1908	„	Ferdinand of Saxe-Coburg-Gotha	b. 1861	d. 1948

(Became independent Kingdom 1908)

1908–1918	King	Ferdinand I		abdicated 1918
1918–1943	„	Boris III, son of Ferdinand I	b. 1894	d. 1943
1943–1944	Regent	Cyril, brother of Boris II	b. 1895	executed 1945
1943–1946	King	Simeon II, son of Boris II	b. 1937	abdicated 1946

(Became Communist republic 1946)

1946–1947	President	Vasil Kolarov	b. 1877	d. 1950
1947–1950	„	Mintso Neitsev	b. 1887	
1950–1959	„	Georgi Damianov	b. 1901	
1960–1964	„	Dimiter Ganev	b. 1898	
1964–	„	Georgi Traikov	b. 1898	

STATESMEN

1887–1894	Prime Minister	Stefan Stambulov	b. 1854	assassinated 1895

The Russians disapproved of Ferdinand, who to appease them adopted a pro-Russian policy. Stambulov resigned, and was murdered in the streets of Sofia by pro-Russian exiles amnestied by the new government.

1919–1923	Prime Minister	Alexander Stamboliski	b. 1879	assassinated 1923
1946–1949	„	Georgi Dimitrov	b. 1882	d. 1949
1950–1956	„	Viko Chervenkov, brother-in-law of Dimitrov		

1956–1962   Prime Minister   Anton Yugov
1962–   „   Todor Zhivkov

Alexander Stamboliski,
Prime Minister of
Bulgaria (1919–1923).

Georgi Dimitrov,
Prime Minister of
Bulgaria (1946–1949).

Vasil Kolarov,
President of Bulgaria
(1946–1947).

Burma

(Separate states united into an empire by Alompra)

1753–1760	King	Alompra (or Alaungpaya)	b. 1711	d. 1760
1853–1878	„	Mindon Min		d. 1878
1878–1885	„	Thibaw (or Theebaw), son of		
		Mindon Min deposed 1885	b. 1858	d. 1916

(Upper and Lower Burma became a province of British India in 1886)

1886–1887	Chief Commissioner	Sir Charles Edward Bernard	b. 1873	d. 1901
1887–1889	„	Charles Haukes Todd Crosthwaite	b. 1835	d. 1915
1889–1890	„	Antony Patrick MacDonnell, later 1st Baron		
		MacDonnell of Swinford	b. 1844	d. 1925
1890–1892	„	Alexander Mackenzie	b. 1842	d. 1902
1892	„	Donald Mackenzie Smeaton	b. 1848	d. 1910
1892–1897	„	Sir Frederick William Richards		
		Fryer	b. 1845	d. 1922
1897–1903	Lieutenant-Governor	Sir Frederick William Richards Fryer		
1903–1905	„	Sir Hugh Shakespear Barnes	b. 1853	d. 1940
1905–1910	„	Sir Herbert Thirkell White	b. 1855	d. 1931
1910–1913	„	Sir Harvey Adamson	b. 1854	d. 1941
1913	„	Sir George Watson Shaw	b. 1858	d. 1931
1913–1915	„	Sir Harvey Adamson		
1915–1917	„	Sir Spencer Harcourt Butler	b. 1869	d. 1938
1917–1918	„	Walter Francis Rice		d. 1941
1918–1922	„	Sir Reginald Henry Craddock	b. 1864	d. 1937
1923–1927	Governor	Sir Spencer Harcourt Butler		
1927–1930	„	Sir Charles Alexander Innes	b. 1874	d. 1959
1930–1931	„	Sir Joseph Augustus Moung Gyi	b. 1872	d. 1955
1932–1935	„	Sir Hugh Lansdowne Stephenson	b. 1871	d. 1941
1935	„	Thomas Couper	b. 1878	d. 1954
1936–1939	„	Sir Archibald Douglas Cochrane	b. 1885	d. 1958

Burma (continued)

1939	Governor	Sir Walter Booth-Graveley	b. 1882
1941–1946	,,	Sir Reginald Hugh Dorman-Smith	b. 1899
		(Invaded by the Japanese in 1941)	
1946–1948	,,	Sir Hubert Elvin Rance	b. 1898
		(Union of Burma founded 1948)	
1948–1952	President	Sao Shwe Thaike	
1952–1957	,,	Ba U	b. 1887
1957–1962	,,	U Win Maung	b. 1916
1962	,,	Sama Duwa Sinwa Nawng	b. 1915
1962–	Chairman of	Ne Win (Maung Shu Maung)	b. 1911
	Revolutionary Council		

U Nu, at left, Prime Minister of Burma for most of the period following World War II, entertains the late Prime Minister Nehru of India (in Burmese dress).

U Thant became Burma's permanent delegate to the United Nations in 1953, and succeeded the late Dag Hammarskjöld as permanent Secretary-General in 1962.

STATESMEN

1948–1956	Prime Minister	U Nu	b. 1907
1957–1958	,,	U Nu	
1958–1960	,,	Ne Win	
1960–1962	,,	U Nu	
1962–	,,	Ne Win	
1962–	Secretary-General of United Nations	U Thant	b. 1909

Burundi

(Formerly a German colony and Belgian trusteeship; an independent state since 1962)

1962–1966	Ruler	Mwambutsa IV, Mwami of Burundi	b. 1912
1966–	,,	Charles, son of Mwambutsa IV	b. 1947
1961–	Prime Minister	Prince Louis Rwagasore, son of Mwambutsa IV	assassinated 1961
1961–1963	,,	Pierre Muhirwa, son-in-law of Mwambutsa IV	
1963–1964	,,	Pierre Ngendandumwe	
1964–1965	,,	Albin Nyamoya	
1965	,,	Pierre Ngendandumwe	assassinated 1965
1965–1966	,,	Joseph Bamina	
		(Republic proclaimed 1966)	
1966–	President	Michel Micombero	b. 1939

Byelorussia, see Russia

Byzantine Empire, see Roman Empire

Caliphate of the East

622–632	Caliph	Mohammed	b. 571	d. 632
632–634	,,	Abu Bekr, father-in-law of Mohammed	b. 573	d. 634
634–644	,,	Omarl, father-in-law of Mohammed	b. 581 ?	assassinated 644
644–656	,,	Othman bin Affan, son-in-law of Mohammed		
			b. 574 ?	assassinated 656
656–661	,,	Ali, cousin and son-in-law of Mohammed		
			b. 600 ?	assassinated 661

OMAYYAD DYNASTY

661– 680	Caliph	Muawiyah	d. 680
680– 683	,,	Yazid I, son of Muawiyah	d. 683
683	,,	Muawiyah II, son of Yazid I	d. 683
684– 685	,,	Marwan I	d. 685
685– 705	,,	Abd al-Melik, son of Marwan I	b. 646? d. 705
705– 715	,,	Walid I, son of Abd al-Melik	b. 675? d. 715
715– 717	,,	Suleiman, son of Abd al-Melik	d. 717
717– 720	,,	Omar II, nephew of Abd al-Melik	d. 720
720– 724	,,	Yazid II, son of Abd al-Melik	d. 724
724– 743	,,	Hisham I, son of Abd al-Melik	d. 743
743– 744	,,	Walid II, son of Yazid II	d. 744
744	,,	Yazid III, son of Walid I	d. 744
744	,,	Ibrahim, son of Walid I	
744– 750	,,	Marwan II, nephew of Abd al-Melik	d. 750
		(end of Arab dynasty)	

ABBASSID DYNASTY (Persian)

750– 754	,,	Abu'l-Abbas, descendant of Abbas, uncle of Mohammed	b. 721 ? d. 754
754– 775	,,	Abu-djafar El-mansur, brother of Abu'l-Abbas	
775– 785	,,	Mohammed al-mahdi, son of Abu-djafar Al-mansur	
785– 786	,,	Musa al-hadi, son of Mohammed al-mahdi	
786– 809	,,	Harun al-Rashid, brother of Musa al-hadi	b. 764? d. 809
809– 813	,,	Mohammed al-amin, son of Harun al-Rashid	
813– 833	,,	Abdullah-al-mamun, son of Harun al-Rashid	
833– 842	,,	El-mutasim-billah, brother of Abdallah-al-mamun	
842– 847	,,	Harun al-wathik-billah, son of Al-mutasim-billah	
847– 861	,,	Djafar al-mutawakkil, brother of Harun al-wathik-billah	
861– 862	,,	Mohammed al-muntasir-billah, son of Djafar al-mutawakkil	
862– 866	,,	Ahmed al-mustain-billah, grandson of Harun al-wathik-billah	
866– 869	,,	Mohammed al-mutazz-billah, son of Djafar al-mutawakkil	
869– 870	,,	Mohammed al-muhtadi-billah, son of Harun al-wathik-billah	
870– 892	,,	Ahmed al-mutamid ala'llah, son of Djafar al-mutawakkil	
892– 902	,,	Ahmed al-mutadid-billah, nephew of Ahmed al-mutamid ala'llah	
902– 908	,,	Ali al-muktafi-billah, son of Ahmed al-mutadid-billah	
908– 932	,,	Djafar al-muktadir-billah, brother of Ali al-muktafi-billah	
932– 934	,,	Mohammed al-kahir-billah, brother of Djafar al-muktadir-billah	
934– 940	,,	Ahmed ar-radi-billah, son of Djafar al-muktadir-billah	
940– 944	,,	Ibrahim al-muttaki-billah, son of Djafar al-muktadir-billah	
944– 946	,,	Al-Mustakfi billah, son of Ali al-muktafi-billah	
946– 974	,,	Al-Muti, son of Djafar al-muktadir-billah	
974– 991	,,	Al-Tai li-amrillah, son of El-Muti	
991–1031	,,	Al-Kadir-billah, grandson of Djafar al-muktadir-billah	
1031–1075	,,	Al-Ka-im, son of Al-Kadir-billah	

The Mosque of Omar is a landmark of Baghdad, Iraq, historic capital of the Caliphate of the East.

1075–1094	Caliph	Al-Muktadi, grandson of Al-Ka-im
1094–1118	„	Al-Mustazhi-billah, son of Al-Muktadi
1118–1135	„	Al-Mustarshir-billah, son of Al-Mustazhi-billah
1135–1136	„	Al-Raschid, son of Al-Mustarshir-billah
1136–1160	„	Al-Muktafi, son of Al-Mustarshir-billah
1160–1170	„	Al-Muktanijd-billah, son of Al-Muktafi
1170–1180	„	Al-Mustadi, son of Al-Mukstanijd-billah
1180–1225	„	Al-Nasir, son of Al-Mustadi
1225–1226	„	Al-Zahir, son of Al-Nasir
1226–1242	„	Al-Munstansir
1242–1258	„	Al-Mustasin-billah
		(Dynasty overthrown by Mongols in 1258)

Cambodia

(The Kingdom of Cambodia reached its peak *c.* A.D. 1000 as the Khmer Empire. In the 15th century a long decline began, and in 1863 Cambodia became a French Protectorate until 1954, when independence was obtained. Below are listed better known monarchs from the period of greatness, and those since independence in modern times)

802? 850	King	Jayavarman II	d. 850
850– 877	„	Jayavarman III	
877– 889	„	Indravarman I	
889– 900	„	Yasovarman I	
928– 942	„	Jayavarman IV	
944– 968	„	Rajendravarman II	
968–1001	„	Jayavarman V	
1002–1050	„	Suryavarman I	
1050–1066	„	Udayadityavarman II	
1066–1080	„	Harshavarman III	
1080–1107	„	Jayavarman VI	
1107–1113	„	Dharanindravarman I	

Royal emblem of Cambodia.

1113–1150	King	Suryavarman II		
1181–1218?	,,	Jayavarman VII	b. 1125?	d. 1218?
1941–1955	,,	Norodom Sihanouk (abdicated)	b. 1922	
1955–1960	,,	Norodom Suramarit (joint ruler)		d. 1960
1955–1960	Queen	Kossamak (joint ruler)		
1960–	Chief of State	Norodom Sihanouk		

Cameroon Republic

(An independent republic since 1960)

1960–	President	Ahmadou Ahidjo
1960–	Vice-President	John Foncha
1960–	Premier	Charles Assale

Canada

Samuel de Champlain explored the St. Lawrence River and the Great Lakes, discovered Lake Champlain, and charted much of the coast of New England and eastern Canada. In 1608 he founded the city of Quebec, and from then until 1635 served as administrator of the French settlements in Canada, except for the period 1629–1633 when he was a captive of the English.

FRENCH CANADA

1608–1629	Lieutenant-Governor of Quebec	Samuel de Champlain	b. 1567?	d. 1635
1629	Governor	Samuel de Champlain		
1633–1635	,,	Samuel de Champlain		
1636–1648	,,	Charles Huault de Montmagny		
1648–1651	,,	Louis D'Ailleboust de Coulonge		
1651–1656	,,	Jean de Lauzon		
1658–1661	,,	Pierre de Voyer, Vicomte D'Argenson		
1661–1663	,,	Pierre Dubois, Baron D'Avaugour		
1663–1665	,,	Augustin de Saffray Mésy		
1665–1672	,,	Daniel de Rémy de Courcelle		
1672–1682	,,	Louis de Buade, Comte de Palluau et de Frontenac	b. 1620	d. 1698

Canada (continued)

1682–1685	Governor	Le Febvre de La Barre		
1685–1689	,,	Jacques-René de Brisay, Marquis de Denonville		
1689–1698	,,	Louis de Buade, Comte de Palluau et de Frontenac		
1699–1703	,,	Louis Hector de Callières Bonnevue	b. 1646	d. 1703
1703–1725	,,	Philippe de Rigaud, Marquis de Vaudreuil	b. 1643	d. 1725
1714–1716	,,	Claude de Ramesay		
1726–1747	,,	Charles Beauharnois, Marquis de La Galissonnière, Rolland		
1749–1752	,,	Jacques Pierre de Taffanel, Marquis de La Jonquière	b. 1680	d. 1753
1752–1755	,,	Duquesne, Marquis de Menneville		
1755–1760	,,	Pierre de Rigaud, Marquis de Vaudreuil-Cavagnal	b. 1698	d. 1765
1760–1763	Head of English Military Government	Jeffrey Amherst	b. 1717	d. 1797

(Became a possession of Great Britain by the Treaty of Paris in 1763)

1763–1768	Governor	James Murray	b. 1721	d. 1794
1768–1778	,,	Sir Guy Carleton, Baron Dorchester	b. 1724	d. 1808
1778–1786	,,	Sir Frederick Haldimand	b. 1718	d. 1791
1786–1796	,,	Sir Guy Carleton		
1797–1807	,,	Robert Prescott		
1807–1811	,,	Sir James Henry Craig	b. 1748	d. 1812
1811–1815	,,	Sir George Prevost	b. 1767	d. 1816
1816–1818	,,	Sir John Coape Sherbrooke	b. 1764	d. 1830
1818–1819	,,	Charles Lennox, Duke of Richmond	b. 1764	d. 1819
1819–1828	,,	George Ramsay, Earl of Dalhousie	b. 1770	d. 1838
1831–1835	,,	Lord Aylmer		
1835–1838	,,	A. A. Gosford		
1838	,,	John George Lambton, Earl of Durham	b. 1792	d. 1840
1838–1839	,,	Sir John Colborne	b. 1778	d. 1863
1839–1841	,,	Charles Edward Poulett Thomson	b. 1799	d. 1841
1841–1843	,,	Sir Charles Bagot	b. 1781	d. 1843
1843–1845	,,	Sir Charles Theophilus Metcalfe	b. 1785	d. 1846
1846–1847	,,	Charles Murray, Earl of Cathcart	b. 1783	d. 1859
1847–1854	,,	James Bruce, Earl of Elgin	b. 1811	d. 1863
1854–1861	,,	Sir Edmund Walker Head	d. 1805	d. 1868
1861–1867	,,	Charles Stanley Monck	b. 1819	d. 1894

(In 1867 Canada was granted a constitution as a Dominion and Monck became the first Governor-General of Canada)

GOVERNORS-GENERAL
Since Confederation 1867

1867–1868	Governor-General	Charles Stanley, Viscount Monck	b. 1819	d. 1894
1868–1872	,,	John Young, Lord Lisgar	b. 1807	d. 1876
1872–1878	,,	Frederick Temple Hamilton Temple Blackwood, Marquis of Dufferin and Ava	b. 1826	d. 1902
1878–1883	,,	John Douglas Sutherland Campbell, Marquis of Lorne	b. 1845	d. 1914
1883–1888	,,	Henry Charles Keith Petty-Fitzmaurice, Marquis of Lansdowne	b. 1845	d. 1927

The Fathers of Canadian Federation met in Charlottestown, Prince Edward Island, in 1864, and as a result of these and later discussions, four provinces united to form the nucleus of a new nation.

1888–1893	Governor-General	Frederick Arthur Stanley, Lord Stanley of Preston	b. 1841	d. 1908
1893–1898	,,	Sir John Campbell Gordon, Earl of Aberdeen	b. 1847	d. 1934
1898–1904	,,	Gilbert John Elliot-Murray-Kynynmound, Earl of Minto	b. 1845	d. 1914
1904–1911	,,	Albert Henry George, Earl Grey	b. 1851	d. 1917
1911–1916	,,	Arthur William Patrick Albert Wettin, Field Marshal H.R.H. Duke of Connaught	b. 1850	d. 1942
1916–1921	,,	Victor Christian William, Duke of Devonshire	b. 1868	d. 1938
1921–1926	,,	Julian Hedworth George Byng, General The Lord Byng of Vimy	b. 1862	d. 1935
1926–1931	,,	Freeman Freeman-Thomas, Viscount Willingdon of Ratton	b. 1866	d. 1941
1931–1935	,,	Vere Brabazon Ponsonby, Earl of Bessborough	b. 1880	d. 1956
1935–1940	,,	John Buchan, Lord Tweedsmuir of Elsfield	b. 1875	d. 1940
1940–1946	,,	Alexander Augustus Frederick William Alfred George Cambridge, Major-General The Earl of Athlone	b. 1874	d. 1957

John Buchan, Baron Tweedsmuir, Governor-General of Canada (1935–1940).

Georges Philias Vanier, Governor-General of Canada (1959–1967).

1946–1952	Governor-General	Harold Rupert Leofric George Alexander, Field Marshal Viscount Alexander of Tunis	b. 1891	
1952–1959	,,	Vincent Massey	b. 1887	d. 1968
1959–1967	,,	Major-General Georges Philias Vanier	b. 1888	d. 1967
1967	,,	Daniel Roland Michener	b. 1900	

PRIME MINISTERS
Since Confederation 1867

L—Liberal   C—Conservative

1867–1873	Prime Minister	Sir John Alexander Macdonald (C)	b. 1815	d. 1891
1873–1878	,,	Alexander Mackenzie (L)	b. 1822	d. 1892
1878–1891	,,	Sir John Alexander Macdonald (C)		
1891–1892	,,	Sir John Joseph Caldwell Abbott (C)	b. 1821	d. 1893
1892–1894	,,	Sir John Sparrow David Thompson (C)	b. 1844	d. 1894
1894–1896	,,	Sir Mackenzie Bowell (C)	b. 1823	d. 1917
1896	,,	Sir Charles Tupper (C)	b. 1821	d. 1915
1896–1911	,,	Sir Wilfrid Laurier (L)	b. 1841	d. 1919
1911–1920	,,	Sir Robert Laird Borden (C)	b. 1854	d. 1937
1920–1921	,,	Arthur Meighen (Unionist)	b. 1874	d. 1960
1921–1926	,,	William Lyon Mackenzie King (L)	b. 1874	d. 1950
1926	,,	Arthur Meighen (C)		
1926–1930	,,	William Lyon Mackenzie King (L)		
1930–1935	,,	Richard Bedford Bennett, (Viscount Bennett, 1941) (C)	b. 1870	d. 1947
1935–1948	,,	William Lyon Mackenzie King (L)		
1948–1957	,,	Louis Stephen St. Laurent (L)	b. 1882	
1957–1963	,,	John Diefenbaker (C)	b. 1895	
1963–1968	,,	Lester Bowles Pearson (L)	b. 1897	
1968–	,,	Pierre Elliott Trudeau (L)	b. 1921	

ALBERTA

1905–1915	Lieutenant-Governor	George Hedley Vicars	b. 1859	d. 1928
1915–1925	,,	Robert George Brett	b. 1851	d. 1929
1925–1931	,,	William Egbert	b. 1857	d. 1936
1931–1936	,,	William Legh Walsh	b. 1857	d. 1938
1936–1937	,,	P. C. Primrose	b. 1864	d. 1937
1937–1950	,,	J. C. Bowen	b. 1872	d. 1957
1950–1959	,,	John James Bowlen	b. 1876	d. 1959
1959–1966	,,	J. Percy Page	b. 1887	
1966–	,,	J. W. Grant MacEwan		

BRITISH COLUMBIA

1858–1864	Governor	Sir James Douglas	
1864–1869	,,	Frederick Seymour	
1869–1871	,,	Anthony Musgrave	
1871–1876	Lieutenant-Governor	J. W. Trutch	
1876–1881	,,	Albert Norton Richards	
1881–1887	,,	Clement F. Cornwall	
1887–1892	,,	Hugh Nelson	
1892–1897	,,	Edgar Dewdney	
1897–1900	,,	Thomas R. McInnes	
1900–1906	,,	Sir Henri G. Joly de Lotbiniere	
1906–1909	,,	James Dunsmuir	
1909–1914	,,	T. W. Paterson	

1914–1919	Lieutenant-Governor	Sir Frank S. Barnard
1919–1920	„	Edward G. Prior
1920–1926	„	Walter C. Nichol
1926–1931	„	R. Randolph Bruce
1931–1936	„	J. W. Fordham Johnson
1936–1941	„	Eric W. Hamber
1941–1946	„	William C. Woodward
1946–1950	„	Charles Arthur Banks
1950–1955	„	Clarence Wallace
1955–1960	„	F. M. Ross
1960–	„	George R. Pearkes

MANITOBA

Lieutenant-Governors of Manitoba since Confederation

1870–1873	Lieutenant-Governor	A. G. Archibald	b. 1814	d. 1892
1873–1877	„	Alex Morris	b. 1826	d. 1889
1877–1882	„	Joseph E. Cauchon	b. 1816	d. 1885
1882–1888	„	James C. Aikins	b. 1823	d. 1904
1888–1895	„	Sir John Schultz	b. 1840	d. 1896
1895–1900	„	J. C. Patterson	b. 1839	d. 1929
1900–1911	„	Sir D. H. McMillan	b. 1846	d. 1933
1911–1916	„	Sir Douglas C. Cameron	b. 1854	d. 1921
1916–1926	„	Sir J. A. M. Aikins	b. 1851	d. 1929
1926–1929	„	Theodore A. Burrows	b. 1857	d. 1929
1929–1934	„	James Duncan McGregor	b. 1860	d. 1935
1934–1940	„	W. J. Tupper	b. 1862	d. 1947
1940–1953	„	R. F. McWilliams	b. 1874	d. 1957
1953–1960	„	John Stewart McDiarmid	b. 1882	d. 1965
1960–1965	„	Errick French Willis	b. 1896	
1965–	„	Richard S. Bowles	b. 1912	

NEW BRUNSWICK

1786–1817	Lieutenant-Governor	Thomas Carleton	b. 1735	d. 1817
1817–1823	„	George Stracey Smythe	?b. 1767	d. 1823
1823–1831	„	Sir Howard Douglas	b. 1776	d. 1861
1831–1837	„	Sir Archibald Campbell	b. 1769	d. 1843
1837–1841	„	Sir John Harvey	b. 1778	d. 1852
1841–1848	„	Sir William Colebrooke	b. 1787	d. 1870
1848–1854	„	Sir Edmund Walter Head	b. 1805	d. 1868
1854–1861	„	Sir John Henry Thomas Manners-Sutton	b. 1814	d. 1877
1861–1866	„	Sir Arthur Hamilton Gordon	b. 1829	d. 1912
1867	„	Sir Charles Hastings Doyle	b. 1804	d. 1883
1867–1868	„	Francis Pym Harding	b. ?	d. 1875
1868–1873	„	Lemuel Allan Wilmot	b. 1809	d. 1878
1873–1878	„	Sir Samuel Leonard Tilley	b. 1818	d. 1896
1878–1880	„	Edward Barron Chandler	b. 1800	d. 1880
1880–1885	„	Robert Duncan Wilmot	b. 1809	d. 1891
1885–1893	„	Sir Samuel Leonard Tilley	b. 1818	d. 1896
1893	„	John Boyd	b. 1826	d. 1893
1893–1896	„	John James Fraser	b. 1829	d. 1896
1896–1902	„	Abner Reid McClelan	b. 1831	d. 1917
1902–1907	„	Jabez Bunting Snowball	b. 1837	d. 1907
1907–1912	„	Lemuel John Tweedie	b. 1849	d. 1917

1912–1917	Lieutenant-Governor	Josiah Wood	b. 1843	d. 1927
1917	,,	Gilbert White Ganong	b. 1851	d. 1917
1917–1923	,,	William Pugsley	b. 1850	d. 1925
1923–1928	,,	William Freeman Todd	b. 1854	d. 1935
1928–1935	,,	Hugh Havelock McLean	b. 1854	d. 1938
1935–1940	,,	Murray MacLaren	b. 1861	d. 1942
1940–1945	,,	William George Clark	b. 1865	d. 1948
1945–1958	,,	David Lawrence MacLaren	b. 1893	d. 1960
1958–1965	,,	J. Leonard O'Brien	b. 1895	
1965–	,,	John Babbitt McNair	b. 1889	

NEWFOUNDLAND

(Discovered by John Cabot, 1497; taken possession of by Sir Humphrey Gilbert, 1583)

1729–1731	Governor	Henry Osborne		d. 1771
1731	,,	Captain Clinton	b. 1686	d. 1761
1732	,,	Captain Falkenham		
1733	,,	Lord Muskerry		d. 1769
1735–1737	,,	Fitzroy Henry Lee		
1738	,,	Captain Vanbrugh		d. 1753
1739	,,	Henry Medley		d. 1747
1740	,,	Lord George Graham		
1741–1743	,,	Thomas Smith		d. 1762
1742	,,	John Byng	b. 1704	d. 1757
1744	,,	Charles Hardy	b. 1716	d. 1780
1746	,,	Richard Edwards		d. 1773
1748	,,	Charles Watson		
1749	,,	George Brydges, Lord Rodney	b. 1719	d. 1792
1750	,,	Francis W. Drake		d. 1780
1753	,,	Hugh Bonfoy		d. 1762
1755–1756	,,	Richard Dorril		d. 1762
1757–1760	,,	Richard Edwards		
1761	,,	James Webb		d. 1761
1762–1764	,,	Lord Thomas Graves	b. 1725	d. 1802
1764	,,	Sir Hugh Palliser	b. 1722	d. 1796
1769	,,	John Byron	b. 1723	d. 1786
1772	,,	Molyneaux, Lord Shuldham		d. 1798
1775	,,	Robert Duff		d. 1787
1776–1778	,,	John Montague	b. 1719	d. 1795
1779	,,	Richard Edwards		d. 1794
1782–1786	,,	John Campbell	b. 1720	d. 1790
1786–1789	,,	Rear Admiral Elliott		d. 1808
1790–1792	,,	Mark Milbanke	b. 1725	d. 1805
1792	,,	Sir R. King	b. 1730	d. 1806
1794–1796	,,	Sir James Wallace	b. 1731	d. 1803
1797	,,	William Waldegrave, Lord Radstock	b. 1753	d. 1825
1800	,,	Sir Charles Morice Pole	b. 1757	
1802	,,	Lord James Gambier	b. 1756	d. 1833
1804	,,	Sir Erasmus Gower		d. 1814
1807–1810	,,	Admiral Holloway	b. 1742	d. 1826
1810–1813	,,	Sir John Thomas Duckworth	b. 1748	d. 1817
1813–1816	,,	Sir Richard Godwin Keats	b. 1757	d. 1834
1817	,,	Sir Francis Pickmore		
1818–1824	,,	Sir Chas. Hamilton	b. 1767	d. 1849
1825–1834	,,	Sir Thos. Cochrane	b. 1789	
1834–1841	,,	Sir H. Prescott	b. 1783	d. 1874

1841–1846	Governor	Sir John Harvey	b. 1778	d. 1852
1847–1852	,,	Sir J. Gaspard LeMarchant	b. 1803	d. 1874
1852–1855	,,	Ker Baillie Hamilton		
1855	,,	Charles Henry Darling	b. 1809	d. 1870
1857	,,	Sir Alexander Bannerman	b. 1783	d. 1864
1864	,,	Sir Anthony Musgrave	b. 1828	d. 1888
1869	,,	Sir Stephen John Hill	b. 1808	d. 1891
1876	,,	Sir John Hawley Glover	b. 1829	d. 1885
1881	,,	Sir Henry Fitz-Harding Maxse	b. 1830	d. 1883
1884	,,	Sir John Hawley Glover		
1886	,,	Sir George W. Des Voeux	b. 1834	d. 1909
1887	,,	Sir Henry A. Blake	b. 1840	d. 1918
1889–1895	,,	Sir Terrence N. O'Brien	b. 1830	d. 1903
1895–1898	,,	Sir Herbert H. Murray	b. 1829	d. 1904
1898–1901	,,	Sir Henry Edward McCallum	b. 1852	d. 1919
1901–1904	,,	Sir Cavendish Boyle	b. 1849	d. 1916
1904–1909	,,	Sir William McGregor	b. 1846	d. 1919
1909–1913	,,	Sir Ralph C. Williams	b. 1848	d. 1927
1913–1917	,,	Sir Walter E. Davidson	b. 1859	d. 1923
1917–1922	,,	Sir Charles A. Harris	b. 1855	d. 1947
1922–1928	,,	Sir William L. Alderdyce		
1928–1932	,,	Sir John Middleton		
1932–1936	,,	Sir David Murray Anderson		
1936–1946	,,	Sir Humphrey Thomas Walwyn		
1946–1949	,,	Sir Gordon A. MacDonald		

(Newfoundland became the 10th Province of the Dominion of Canada in 1949)

NORTHWEST TERRITORIES

1870–1872	Lieutenant-Governor	Adams G. Archibald	b. 1814	d. 1892
1872–1876	,,	Alexander Morris	b. 1826	d. 1889
1876–1881	,,	David Laird	b. 1833	d. 1914
1881–1888	,,	Edgar Dewdney	b. 1835	d. 1916
1888–1893	,,	Joseph Royal	b. 1837	d. 1902
1893–1898	,,	Charles Herbert Mackintosh	b. 1843	d. 1931
1898	,,	Malcolm Colin Cameron	b. 1832	d. 1898

(Left) Sir John Alexander Macdonald, first Prime Minister of Canada (1867–1872, 1878–1891).

(Right) Sir Robert Laird Borden, Prime Minister of Canada (1911–1920).

1898–1905	Lieutenant-Governor	Amédée Emmanuel Forget	b. 1847	d. 1923
1905–1918	Commissioner	Frederick White	b. 1847	d. 1918
1919–1931	,,	W. W. Cory	b. 1865	d. 1943
1931–1934	,,	H. H. Rowatt	b. 1861	d. 1938
1936–1946	,,	Charles Camsell	b. 1876	d. 1957

Canada (continued)

1947–1950	Commissioner	H. L. Keenlyside	b. 1898	
1950–1953	,,	H. A. Young	b. 1898	
1953–1963	,,	R. Gordon Robertson	b. 1917	
1963–	,,	B. G. Sivertz	b. 1905	

NOVA SCOTIA

(Ceded to Britain in 1713)

1710–1713	Governor	Samuel Vetch	b. 1668	d. 1732
1713–1715	,,	Francis Nicholson	b. 1655	d. 1728
1715–1717	,,	Samuel Vetch		
1753–1760	,,	Charles Lawrence	b. 1709	d. 1760
1760–1763	,,	Jonathan Belcher	b. 1710	d. 1776
1776–1778	,,	Mariot Arbuthnot	b. 1711	d. 1794
1778–1781	,,	Richard Hughes	b. 1729 ?	d. 1812
1781–1782	,,	Sir Andrew Snop Hamond	b. 1738	d. 1828
1783–1786	,,	Edmund Fanning	b. 1737	d. 1818
1786–1791	,,	John Parr	b. 1725	d. 1791
1792–1808	,,	John Wentworth	b. 1737	d. 1820
1808–1811	,,	Sir George Prevost	b. 1767	d. 1816
1811–1816	,,	Sir John Coape Sherbrooke	b. 1764	d. 1830
1816–1820	,,	George Ramsay, Earl of Dalhousie	b. 1770	d. 1838
1820–1828	,,	Sir James Kempt	b. 1764	d. 1854
1828–1834	,,	Sir Peregrine Maitland	b. 1777	d. 1854
1834–1840	,,	Sir Colin Campbell	b. 1776	d. 1847
1840–1846	,,	Viscount Falkland	b. 1803	d. 1884
1846–1852	,,	Sir John Harvey	b. 1778	d. 1852
1852–1858	,,	Sir John Gaspard Le Marchant	b. 1803	d. 1874
1858–1863	,,	Sir George Augustus Constantine Phipps, Earl of Mulgrave	b. 1819	d. 1890
1864–1865	,,	Sir Richard Graves MacDonnell	b. 1814	d. 1881
1865–1867	,,	Sir F. W. Williams	b. 1800	d. 1883

(Became a province of the Dominion of Canada in 1867)

1867	,,	Sir F. W. Williams	b. 1800	d. 1883
1867–1868	,,	Sir C. Hastings Doyle	b. 1804	d. 1883
1873	,,	Joseph Howe	b. 1804	d. 1873
1873–1883	,,	Sir A. G. Archibald	b. 1814	d. 1892
1883–1888	,,	Matthew Henry Richey	b. 1828	d. 1911
1888–1890	,,	A. W. McLelan	b. 1824	d. 1890
1890–1900	,,	Sir Malachy Bowes Daly	b. 1836	d. 1920
1900–1906	,,	Alfred Gilpin Jones	b. 1824	d. 1906
1906–1910	,,	D. C. Fraser	b. 1845	d. 1910
1910–1915	,,	J. D. McGregor	b. 1838	d. 1918
1915–1916	,,	David MacKeen	b. 1839	d. 1916
1916–1925	,,	MacCallum Grant	b. 1845	d. 1928
1925	,,	James Robson Douglas	b. 1876	d. 1934
1925–1930	,,	James Cranswick Tory	b. 1862	d. 1944
1930–1931	,,	Frank Stanfield	b. 1872	d. 1931
1931–1937	,,	Walter Harold Covert	b. 1865	d. 1941
1937–1940	,,	Robert Irwin	b. 1865	d. 1949
1940–1942	,,	Frederick Francis Mathers	b. 1871	d. 1947
1942–1947	,,	C. M. Kendall	b. 1864	d. 1949
1947–1952	,,	John Alexander Douglas McCurdy	b. 1886	d. 1961
1952–1958	,,	Alistair Fraser	b. 1886	d. 1964
1958–1963	,,	Edward Chester Plow	b. 1904	
1963–	,,	Henry Poole MacKeen	b. 1892	

ONTARIO

1867–1868	Lieutenant-Governor	Henry William Stisted	b. 1817	d. 1875
1868–1873	,,	William Pearce Howland	b. 1811	d. 1907
1873–1875	,,	John Willoughby Crawford	b. 1817	d. 1875
1875–1880	,,	Donald Alexander Macdonald	b. 1817	d. 1896
1880–1887	,,	John Beverley Robinson	b. 1821	d. 1896
1887–1892	,,	Alexander Campbell	b. 1822	d. 1892
1892–1897	,,	George Airey Kirkpatrick	b. 1841	d. 1899
1897–1903	,,	Oliver Mowat	b. 1820	d. 1903
1903–1908	,,	William Mortimer Clark	b. 1836	d. 1917
1908–1914	,,	John Morison Gibson	b. 1842	d. 1929
1914–1919	,,	John Strathearn Hendrie	b. 1857	d. 1923
1919–1921	,,	Lionel Herbert Clarke	b. 1859	d. 1921
1921–1927	,,	Henry Cockshutt	b. 1868	d. 1944
1927–1932	,,	William Donald Ross	b. 1869	d. 1947
1932–1937	,,	Herbert Alexander Bruce	b. 1868	
1937–1946	,,	Albert Matthews	b. 1873	d. 1949
1946–1952	,,	Ray Lawson	b. 1886	
1952–1957	,,	Louis Orville Breithaupt	b. 1890	
1957–1963	,,	John Keiller Mackay	b. 1888	
1963–	,,	William Earl Rowe	b. 1894	

PRINCE EDWARD ISLAND

1770–1774	Lieutenant-Governor	Walter Patterson		d. 1798
1786–1805	,,	Edmund Fanning	b. 1737	d. 1818
1805–1812	,,	Joseph Frederick Walsh DesBarres	b. 1722	d. 1824
1812–1824	,,	Charles Douglas Smith		
1824–1831	,,	John Ready	b. 1845	
1831–1835	,,	Sir Aretas William Young	b. 1778	d. 1835
1836–1837	,,	Sir John Harvey	b. 1778	d. 1852
1837–1841	,,	Sir Charles Augustus FitzRoy	b. 1796	d. 1858
1841–1847	,,	Sir Henry Vere Huntley	b. 1795	d. 1864
1847–1850	,,	Sir Donald Campbell	b. 1800	d. 1850
1851–1854	,,	Sir Alexander Bannerman	b. 1783	d. 1864
1854–1859	,,	Sir Dominick Daly	b. 1798	d. 1868
1859–1868	,,	George Dundas	b. 1819	d. 1880
1870–1873	,,	William Cleaver Francis Robinson	b. 1834	d. 1897
1874–1879	,,	Sir Robert Hodgson	b. 1798	d. 1880
1879–1884	,,	Thomas Heath Haviland	b. 1822	d. 1895
1884–1889	,,	Andrew Archibald MacDonald	b. 1829	d. 1912
1889–1894	,,	Jedediah Slason Carvell	b. 1832	d. 1894
1894–1899	,,	George William Howlan	b. 1835	d. 1901
1899–1904	,,	Peter A. MacIntyre		
1904–1910	,,	Donald A. MacKinnon		
1910–1915	,,	Benjamin Rogers	b. 1837	d. 1923
1915–1919	,,	Austin A. MacDonald		
1919–1924	,,	Murdoch McKinnon	b. 1865	d. 1944
1924–1930	,,	Frank R. Heartz		
1930–1934	,,	Charles Dalton		
1934–1939	,,	George D. DeBlois		
1939–1945	,,	Bradford W. LePage		
1945–1950	,,	Joseph A. Bernard		
1950–1958	,,	T. W. L. Prowse		
1958–1963	,,	F. W. Hyndman		
1963–	,,	Willibald J. MacDonald		

QUEBEC

1867–1873	Lieutenant-Governor	Sir Narcisse-F. Belleau		
1873–1876	,,	René-Edouard Caron	b. 1800	d. 1876
1876–1879	,,	Luc Letellier de Saint-Just		
1879–1884	,,	Théodore Robitaille		
1884–1887	,,	L.-F. Rodrigue Masson		
1887–1892	,,	Auguste-Réal Angers		
1892–1898	,,	Sir J.-Adolphe Chapleau		
1898–1908	,,	Sir Louis-Amable Jetté	b. 1836	d. 1920
1908–1911	,,	Sir Charles Alphonse Pantaléon Pelletier	b. 1837	d. 1911
1911–1915	,,	Sir François Langelier		
1915–1918	,,	Sir P.-Evariste Leblanc		
1918–1923	,,	Sir Charles Fitzpatrick	b. 1853	d. 1942
1923–1924	,,	Louis-Philippe Brodeur	b. 1862	d. 1924
1924–1929	,,	Narcisse Pérodeau		
1929	,,	Sir Lomer Gouin	b. 1861	d. 1929
1929–1934	,,	Henry George Carroll		
1934–1939	,,	Esioff-Leon Patenaude	b. 1875	
1939–1950	,,	Sir Joseph Eugène Fiset	b. 1874	d. 1951
1950–1958	,,	Gaspard Fauteux	b. 1898	
1958–1961	,,	Onésime Gagnon	b. 1888	
1961–1966	,,	Paul Comtois	b. 1895	
1966–	,,	Hugues Lapointe		

SASKATCHEWAN

1905–1910	Lieutenant-Governor	Amédée Emmanuel Forget	b. 1847	d. 1923
1910–1915	,,	George William Brown	b. 1860	d. 1919
1915–1921	,,	Richard Stuart Lake	b. 1860	d. 1950
1921–1931	,,	Henry William Newlands	b. 1862	d. 1954
1931–1936	,,	Hugh Edwin Munroe	b. 1878	d. 1947
1936–1945	,,	Archibald Peter McNab	b. 1864	d. 1945

William Lyon Mackenzie King, Prime Minister of Canada (1921–1926, 1926–1930, 1935–1948).

Lester Bowles Pearson, Prime Minister of Canada (1963–1968).

1945	Lieutenant-Governor	Thomas Miller	b. 1876	d. 1945
1945–1948	,,	Reginald John Marsden Parker	b. 1881	d. 1948
1948–1951	,,	John Michael Uhrich	b. 1877	d. 1951

1951–1958	Lieutenant-Governor	William John Patterson	b. 1886
1958–1963	,,	Frank L. Bastedo	b. 1886
1963–	,,	Robert Leith Hanbidge	b. 1891

VANCOUVER ISLAND

1849–1851	Governor	Richard Blanshard		
1851–1864	,,	Sir James Douglas	b. 1803	d. 1877
1864–1866	,,	Arthur Edward Kennedy		

(In 1866, Vancouver Island was united with British Columbia)

YUKON TERRITORY

1894–1897	Dominion Government Agent	Charles Constantine (North West Mounted Police Inspector)
1897	Land Agent and Gold Commissioner	Thomas Fawcett
1897–1898	Commissioner	John M. Walsh
1898	,,	William Ogilvie
1898	Gold Commissioner	Thomas Fawcett
1898	,,	Gordon Hunter
1898–1901	,,	Edmund C. Senkler
1901–1903	Commissioner	James Hamilton Ross
1903–1905	,,	Frederick Tennyson Congdon

Inspector John M. Walsh, one of the original North West Mounted Policemen, known as "Wahonkeza" to the Sioux Indians who respected him for his just dealings with them, later served as Commissioner of the Yukon Territory (1897–1898).

1905–1907	Commissioner	William Wallace Burns McInnes
1907	,,	Alexander Henderson
1907–1912	Gold Commissioner	F. X. Gosselin
1912–1913	Commissioner	George Black
1913–1916	Gold Commissioner	George Patton MacKenzie
1916–1918	Administrator	George Norris Williams

(Offices of Commissioner and Administrator abolished and powers vested in Gold Commissioner, 1918)

1918–1925	Gold Commissioner	George P. MacKenzie
1925–1928	,,	Percy Reid
1928–1932	,,	George Ian MacLean
1932–1947	Controller	George Allen Jeckell
1947–1948	,,	John Edward Gibben
1948–1950	Commissioner	John Edward Gibben
1950–1951	,,	Andrew Harold Gibson
1951–1952	,,	Frederick Fraser
1952–1955	,,	William George Brown

1955–1962	Commissioner	Frederick Howard Collins
1962–1966	,,	Gordon Robertson Cameron
1966–	,,	James Smith

Cappadocia

(Cappadocia, situated in eastern Anatolia, emerged as an independent kingdom in the 3rd century B.C., after being successively under the rule of Persia, Macedonia, and Syria)

c. 250 B.C.	King	Ariarathes IV		
190	,,	Ariarathes V		
	,,	Mithridates		
	,,	Ariarathes VI		
	,,	Ariarathes VII		
	,,	Ariarathes VIII		
?90– 63	,,	Ariobarzanes I	d.	63
63– 51	,,	Ariobarzanes II	d.	51
51– 42	,,	Ariobarzanes III	d.	42
B.C. 34–17 A.D.	,,	Archelaus	d.	17 A.D.

Ariarathes IV, King of Cappadocia (c. 250 B.C.).

(In 17 A.D. Cappadocia became a Roman province)

Carthage

(Carthage began as a Phoenician colony in what is now Tunisia *circa* 900 B.C., rose to rule a great empire and was ultimately destroyed by Rome)

c. 400 B.C.	Suffete (head of oligarchic council)	Mago		
c. 250	Soldier and Statesman	Hamilcar Barca		d. 228
c. 250	Leader of aristocratic faction	Hanno		
221– 183?	General and Chief Magistrate	Hannibal	b. 247	d. 183?
?– 221	General and Statesman	Hasdrubal		d. 229

(Carthage was conquered finally by Rome in 146 B.C. and its home territory became the Roman province of Africa)

Central African Republic

(French colony of Ubangi Shari (Oubangui-Chari), 1910–1958; an autonomous republic within the French Community 1958–1960; fully independent from 1960)

1957–1959	President	Barthelemy Boganda	d. 1959
1959–1966	,,	David Dacko, cousin of B. Boganda	b. 1930
1966–	Chief of State	Jean Bedel Bokassa	b. 1921

Central American Federation

Francisco Morazán, President of the Central American Federation (1830–1838).

(Costa Rica, Guatemala, Honduras, Nicaragua, and Salvador were united under Spanish rule, became independent in 1821, came under Mexican rule 1821–1823, regained independence as the Central American Federation 1823–1838)

1825–1829	President Manuel José Arce (deposed)	d. 1847
1830–1838	,, Francisco Morazán	b. 1799 d. 1842
	(Federation dissolved 1838)	

Ceylon

(The ancient chronicles of Ceylon trace the country's rulers back to the 6th century B.C. However, except for Devanampiya Tissa, who ruled from 250 to 210 B.C., the Kings of Ceylon prior to the mid-2nd century B.C. have not been authenticated)

B.C.

161– 137	King	Dutthagamani
137– 119	,,	Saddhatissa
119	,,	Thulatthana
119– 109	,,	Lanjatissa
109– 103	,,	Khallata Naga
103– 102	,,	Vattagamani
102– 89		(under rule of Tamils from South India)
89– 77	,,	Vattagamani (restored)
76– 62	,,	Mahaculi Mahatissa
62– 50	,,	Coronaga
50– 47	,,	Tissa
47	,,	Siva
47	,,	Vatuka
47	,,	Darubhatika Tissa
47	,,	Niliya
47– 42	Queen	Anula
41– 19	King	Kutakanna Tissa
19–A.D.9	,,	Bhatika Abhaya
9– 21	,,	Mahadathika Mahanaga
22– 31	,,	Amanda-gamani Abhaya
31– 34	,,	Kanirajanu Tissa
34– 35	,,	Culabhaya
35	Queen	Sivali
35– 44	King	Ilanaga
44– 52	,,	Candamukha Siva
52– 59	,,	Yasalalaka Tissa
59– 65	,,	Sabha
65– 109	,,	Vasabha
109– 112	,,	Vankanasika Tissa
112– 134	,,	Gajabahu I

Ceylon (continued)

134– 140	King	Mahallaka Naga
140– 164	,,	Bhatika Tissa
164– 192	,,	Kanittha Tissa
192– 194	,,	Khujjanaga
194– 195	,,	Kuncanaga
195– 214	,,	Sirinaga I
214– 236	,,	Voharika Tissa
236– 244	,,	Abhayanaga
244– 246	,,	Sirinaga II
246– 247	,,	Vijaya-kumara
247– 251	,,	Samghatissa I
251– 253	,,	Sirisamghabodhi
253– 266	,,	Gothabhaya
266– 276	,,	Jetthatissa I
276– 303	,,	Mahasena
303– 331	,,	Sirimeghavanna
331– 340	,,	Jetthatissa II

King Dutthagamani of Ceylon (161–137 B.C.) began construction of the giant Ruvanveliseya Dagoba at Anuradhapura.

King Devanampiya Tissa (250–210 B.C.) of Ceylon, erected the Thuparama Dagoba at Anuradhapura to commemorate his conversion to Buddhism.

King Kasyapa of Ceylon (A.D. 477–495), a usurper, lived in fear of reprisal in a palace atop the isolated Rock of Sigiriya.

340– 368	King	Buddhadasa
368– 410	,,	Upatissa I
410– 432	,,	Mahanama

432	King	Chattagahaka Jantu
432– 433	,,	Mittasena
433– 459		(under rule of Tamils from South India)
459– 477	,,	Dhatusena
477– 495	,,	Kasyapa I
495– 512	,,	Moggallana I
512– 520	,,	Kumara-Dhatusena
520– 521	,,	Kittisena
521	,,	Siva
522	,,	Upatissa II
522– 535	,,	Silakala
535	,,	Dathapabhuti
535– 555	,,	Moggallana II
555– 573	,,	Kittisirimegha
573– 575	,,	Mahanaga
575– 608	,,	Aggabodhi I
608– 618	,,	Aggabodhi II
618	,,	Samghatissa II
618– 623	,,	Moggallana III
623– 632	,,	Silameghavanna
632	,,	Aggabodhi III
632	,,	Jetthatissa III
633– 643	,,	Aggabodhi III (restored)
643– 650	,,	Dathopatissa I
650– 659	,,	Kassapa II
659	,,	Dappula I
659– 667	,,	Hatthadatha I
667– 683	,,	Aggabodhi IV
683– 684	,,	Datta
684	,,	Hatthadatha II
684– 718	,,	Manavamma
718– 724	,,	Aggabodhi V
724– 730	,,	Kassapa III
730– 733	,,	Mahinda I
733– 772	,,	Aggabodhi VI
772– 777	,,	Aggabodhi VII
777– 797	,,	Mahinda II
797– 801	,,	Udaya I
801– 804	,,	Mahinda III
804– 815	,,	Aggabodhi VIII
815– 831	,,	Dappula II
831– 833	,,	Aggabodhi IX
833– 853	,,	Sena I
853– 887	,,	Sena II
887– 898	,,	Udaya II
898– 914	,,	Kassapa IV
914– 923	,,	Kassapa V
923– 924	,,	Dappula III
924– 935	,,	Dappula IV
935– 938	,,	Udaya III
938– 946	,,	Sena III
946– 954	,,	Udaya IV
954– 956	,,	Sena IV
956– 972	,,	Mahinda IV
972– 982	,,	Sena V
982–1029	,,	Mahinda V
1029–1040	,,	Kassapa VI
1040–1042	,,	Mahalana-Kitti

1042–1043	King	Vikkama-Pandu
1043–1046	,,	Jagatipala
1046–1048	,,	Parakkama-Pandu
1048–1054	,,	Loka
1054–1055	,,	Kassapa VII
1055–1110	,,	Vijayabahu I
1110–1111	,,	Jayabahu I
1111–1132	,,	Vikramabahu I
1132–1153	,,	Gajabahu II

This colossal statue at Polonnaruva, Ceylon, is believed to be of King Parakramabahu I (A.D. 1153–1186). Under this king the ancient Buddhist culture of Ceylon reached its peak.

1153–1186	King	Parakramabahu I
1186–1187	,,	Vijayabahu II
1187–1196	,,	Nissamkamalla
1196	,,	Vikramabahu II
1196–1197	,,	Codaganga
1197–1200	Queen	Lilavati
1200–1202	King	Sahassamalla
1202–1208	Queen	Kalyanavati
1208	King	Dharmasoka
1209	,,	Anikanga
1209–1210	Queen	Lilavati (restored)
1210–1211	King	Lokesvara
1211–1212	Queen	Lilavati (restored)
1212–1215	King	Parakrama Pandu
1215–1232	,,	Magha
1232–1236	,,	Vijayabahu III
1236–1270	,,	Parakramabahu II
1270–1272	,,	Vijayabahu IV
1272–1284	,,	Bhuvanaikabahu I
1285–1286	Interregnum	
1287–1293	King	Parakramabahu III
1293–1302	,,	Bhuvanaikabahu II
1302–1326	,,	Parakramabahu IV
1326– ?	,,	Bhuvanaikabahu III

? –1341	King	Vijayabahu V		
1341–1351	,,	Bhuvanaikabahu IV		
1344–1357	,,	Parakramabahu V (joint sovereign with preceding)		
1357–1374	,,	Vikramabahu III		
1372–1408	,,	Bhuvanaikabahu V (began reign as co-sovereign)		
1408–1467	,,	Parakramabahu VI		
1467–1469	,,	Jayabahu II		
1470–1478	,,	Bhuvanaikabahu VI		
1478–1484	,,	Parakramabahu VII		
1484–1508	,,	Parakramabahu VIII		

(Invaded by the Portuguese, 1505; captured by the Dutch in 1656; captured from the Dutch by the English in 1795)

1798–1805	Governor	Frederick North	b. 1766	d. 1827
		(Constituted a British Crown Colony, 1802)		
1805–1812	,,	Sir Thomas Maitland	b. 1759	d. 1824
1812–1822	,,	Sir Robert Brownrigg	b. 1759	d. 1833
1822–1824	,,	Sir Edward Paget	b. 1775	d. 1849
1824–1831	,,	Sir Edward Barnes	b. 1776	d. 1838
1831–1837	,,	Sir Robert Wilmot Horton	b. 1784	d. 1841
1837–1841	,,	J. A. Stewart Mackenzie	b. 1776	d. 1845
1841–1847	,,	Sir Colin Campbell	b. 1792	d. 1863
1847–1850	,,	Lord Torrington	b. 1812	d. 1884
1850–1855	,,	Sir George Anderson	b. 1791	d. 1857
1855–1860	,,	Sir Henry Ward	b. 1797	d. 1860
1860–1865	,,	Sir Charles MacCarthy	b. 1820	d. 1864
1865–1872	,,	Sir Hercules Robinson (1st Baron Rosmead)	b. 1824	d. 1897
1872–1877	,,	Sir William Gregory	b. 1817	d. 1892
1877–1883	,,	Sir James Longden	b. 1827	d. 1891
1883–1890	,,	Sir Arthur Hamilton Gordon	b. 1829	d. 1912
1890–1895	,,	Sir Arthur Havelock	b. 1844	d. 1908
1895–1903	,,	Sir Joseph West Ridgeway	b. 1844	d. 1930
1903–1907	,,	Sir Henry Blake	b. 1840	d. 1918
1907–1913	,,	Sir Henry McCallum	b. 1852	d. 1919
1913–1916	,,	Sir Robert Chalmers	b. 1853	d. 1938
1916–1918	,,	Sir John Anderson	b. 1858	d. 1918
1918–1925	,,	Sir William Manning	b. 1863	d. 1932
1925–1927	,,	Sir Hugh Clifford	b. 1866	d. 1941
1927–1931	,,	Sir Herbert Stanley	b. 1872	d. 1955
1931–1933	,,	Sir Graeme Thomson	b. 1875	d. 1933
1933–1937	,,	Sir Reginald Edward Stubbs	b. 1876	d. 1947
1937–1944	,,	Sir Andrew Caldecott	b. 1884	d. 1951
		(Self-government within the British Commonwealth, 1948)		
1944–1949	,,	Sir Henry Monck-Mason Moore	b. 1887	
1949–1954	Governor-General	Viscount Soulbury	b. 1887	
1954–1962	,,	Sir Oliver Ernest Goonetilleke	b. 1892	
1962–	,,	William Gopallawa	b. 1897	

(Left) William Gopallawa, Governor-General of Ceylon (1962–   ).

(Right) Sirimavo Bandaranaike, Prime Minister of Ceylon (1960–1965).

STATESMEN

| 1960–1965 | Prime Minister | Sirimavo Bandaranaike | b. 1916 |
| 1965– | „ | Dudley Senanayake | |

Dudley Senanayake, Prime Minister (1965–   ), is the son and namesake of the first Prime Minister of independent Ceylon. The elder Senanayake was instrumental in gaining dominion status for his country.

Chad *(Fr. Tchad)*

(The former French Overseas Territory of Chad; became an independent republic in 1960)

| 1960– | President | François Tombalbaye | b. 1918 |

Chile

José Miguel Carrera, Dictator of Chile (1811–1813).

Bernardo O'Higgins, Dictator of Chile (1817–1823).

(Settled by Spaniards, 1540–1565; independence declared, 1810)

? –1541		Araucanian Indians		
1541–1554	Conqueror	Pedro de Valdivia	b. 1510	killed 1554
1557–1561	,,	García Hurtado de Mendoza (conquest resumed)		
1561–1609		Conquest continued apathetically		
1609–1778		Administered by Spanish governors as part of the Peruvian vice-royalty		
1778–1810		Under Charles III (Spain) Chile became captaincy general, autonomous of Peru		
1788–1795	Governor	Ambrosio O'Higgins, later Marquis of Orsono. An Irish immigrant, father of Bernardo O'Higgins.	b. 1720?	d. 1801
1796–1801	Viceroy	Marquis of Osorno Chile declared independence, 1810		
1811–1813	Dictator	José Miguel Carrera	b. 1785	killed 1821
1813–1814	,,	Bernardo O'Higgins	b. 1776	d. 1842
1814–1818		War		

In 1814, royalist armies entered from Peru and reconquered Chile, but they were finally defeated in a decisive battle by Gen. José de San Martín, with

Jorge Montt, President of Chile (1891–1896).

Arturo Alessandri Palma, President of Chile (1920–1925, 1932–1938).

Carlos Ibáñez del Campo, President of Chile (1927–1931, 1952–1958).

the help of Argentine troops. Offered the dictatorship of Chile as reward, San Martín instead proclaimed O'Higgins "Supreme Director."

1823–1826	President	Ramón Freire	b. 1787	d. 1851
1826–1828	,,	Manuel Blanco Encalada	b. 1790	d. 1876
1828–1831	,,	Francisco A. Pinto	b. 1785	d. 1858
1831–1841	,,	Joaquín Prieto	b. 1786	d. 1854
1841–1851	,,	Manuel Bulnes	b. 1799	d. 1866
1851–1861	,,	Manuel Montt	b. 1809	d. 1880
1861–1871	,,	José Joaquín Pérez	b. 1801	d. 1889
1871–1876	,,	Federico Errázuriz Zañartu	b. 1825	d. 1877
1876–1881	,,	Aníbal Pinto	b. 1825	d. 1884
1881–1886	,,	Domingo Santa María	b. 1825	d. 1889
1886–1891	,,	José Manuel Balmaceda	b. 1838	d. 1891
1891–1896	,,	Jorge Montt	b. 1847	d. 1922
1896–1901	,,	Federico Errázuriz Echaurren	b. 1850	d. 1901
1901–1906	,,	Germán Riesco	b. 1854	d. 1916
1906–1910	,,	Pedro Montt	b. 1848	d. 1910
1910–1915	,,	Ramón Barros Luco	b. 1835	d. 1919
1915–1920	,,	Juan Luis Sanfuentes	b. 1858	d. 1930

1920–1925	President	Arturo Alessandri Palma	b. 1868	d. 1951

A political and social reformer, known as the "Lion of Tarapaca," he was the first man from the lower classes to become President. His most important contribution was a new constitution (1925), under which the cabinet was answerable to the President, rather than Congress.

1925	President	Luis Altamirano		d. 1936
1925–1927	„	Emiliano Figueroa Larrain		
1927–1931	„	Carlos Ibáñez del Campo	b. 1877	d. 1960
1931–1932	„	Juan Estaban Montero	b. 1879	d. 1952
1932	„	Carlos Dávila Espinoza		d. 1957
1932–1938	„	Arturo Alessandri Palma		
1938–1942	„	Pedro Aguirre Cerda	b. 1879	d. 1946
1942–1946	„	Juan Antonio Ríos	b. 1888	d. 1946
1946–1952	„	Gabriel González Videla	b. 1898	
1952–1958	„	Carlos Ibáñez del Campo		

A reactionary, vehement nationalist, and great admirer of Argentina's dictator Juan Perón, Ibañez restored order to Chile during his second administration, but was not able to curb inflation and discontent. This almost resulted in Communist control of Chile, but it was averted by the appointment of the liberal nephew of Arturo Alessandri, Jorge, as President in 1958.

1958–1964	President	Jorge Alessandri Rodríguez	b. 1896
1964–	„	Eduardo Frei	b. 1911

China

(An Empire from the 23rd century B.C. until 1912; a Republic since 1912)

Imperial Dynasties

2205–1766 B.C.	Dynasty	Hsia
1766–1122 B.C.	„	Shang (or Yin)
1122– 255 B.C.	„	Chou (or Chow)
255– 206 B.C.	„	Ch'in (or Ts'in)
202 B.C.–9 A.D.	„	Han, Earlier
25–220 A.D.	„	Han, Later
220– 264	„	Wei
265– 317	„	Chin or Tsin (Western)
317– 419	„	Chin or Tsin (Eastern)
420– 479	„	Sung (Liu Sung)
479– 502	„	Ch'i (Tsi)
502– 557	„	Liang
557– 589	„	Ch'en (Chen)
589– 618	„	Sui
618– 907	„	T'ang (Tang)
618– 626	Emperor	Kao-tsu
627– 649	„	Tai-tsung, son of Kao-tsu
650– 683	„	Kao-tsung, son of Tai-tsung
684– 704	„	Wu-hou, consort of Tai-tsung
713– 755	„	Ming-huang
756– 762	„	Su-tsung, son of Ming-huang
763– 779	„	Tai-tsung
750– 804	„	To-tsung
907–1125	Dynasty	Liang

Tai-tsung, Emperor of China (A.D. 627–649) signs a proclamation forbidding the mistreatment of prisoners.

923– 936	Dynasty	T'ang		
936– 946	"	Chin		
947– 950	"	Han		
951 –960	"	Chou		
960–1127	"	Sung (all China)		
1127–1280	"	Sung (in South China)		
	(Mongol invasion of North China 1127–1280)			
1206–1280	Dynasty	Yüan (in North China)		
1260–1294	Emperor	Kublai Khan	b. 1216?	d. 1294
1280–1368	Dynasty	Yüan		
1368–1644	"	Ming		
1368–1398		Emperor Hung-wu	b. 1328	d. 1398
1403–1424		" Yung-lo	b. 1359	d. 1424
1426–1435		" Hsüan-te		
1488–1505		" Hung-hsi		
1522–1566		" Chia-ching		d. 1566
1573–1619		" Wan-li	b. 1563	d. 1620
1644–1912	Dynasty	Ch'ing or Ta Ch'ing (Manchu)		

Rulers of Ch'ing Dynasty

1644–1661	Emperor	Shih-tsu (Shun-chih)	b. 1638	d. 1661
1662–1722	,,	K'ang-hsi, son of Shih-tsu	b. 1654	d. 1722
1723–1735	,,	Yung-cheng, son of K'ang-hsi	b. 1678	d. 1735
1736–1796	,,	Ch'lien-lung, son of Yung-cheng	b. 1711	d. 1799
1796–1820	,,	Jen-tsung, Chia-ch'ing, son of Ch'lien-lung	b. 1760	d. 1820
1820–1850	,,	Hsüan-tsung, Tao-kuang, son of Jen-tsung, Chia-ch'ing	b. 1782	d. 1850
1851–1861	,,	Wen-tsung, Hsien-feng, son of Hsüan-tsung, Tao-kuang	b. 1831	d. 1861
1862–1875	,,	Ki-tsiang, T'ung-chi, son of Wen-tsung, Hsien-feng	b. 1856	d. 1875
1862–1873	Regent	Tsu-hsi, wife of Wen-tsung, Hsien-feng	b. 1835	d. 1908
1875–1889	Empress	Tsu-hsi		
1875–1908	Emperor	Tsai-tien, Kuang-hsü, cousin of Ki-tsiang, T'ung-chi	b. 1871	d. 1908
1898–1908	Empress	Tsu-hsi		
1908–1912	Emperor	P'u-yi, Hsüan-t'ung, nephew of Tsai-tien, Kuang-hsü (Emperor of Manchukuo in 1934) abdicated 1912	b. 1906	d. 1967

REPUBLIC

1912–1913	Provisional President	Yüan-Shih-k'ai	b. 1859	d. 1916
1913–1916	President	Yüan-Shih-k'ai		
1916–1917	,,	Li-Yüan-hung	b. 1864	d. 1928
1917–1925	Head of Government in Canton	Sun Yat-sen	b. 1867	d. 1925
1917–1918	President	Feng Kuo-chang		
1918–1922	,,	Su Shi-chang		
1922–1923	,,	Li-Yüan-hung		
1923–1924	Provisional President	Ts'ao K'un	b. 1862	d. 1938
1924–1926	President	Tuan Ch'i-jui	b. 1864	d. 1936

Yüan-Shih-k'ai, President of China (1912–1916).

Sun Yat-sen, President of Canton Government (1917–1925).

1927–1931	President (in Nanking)	Chiang Kai-shek	b. 1886	
1932–1943	President	Lin Sen	b. 1867?	d. 1943
1939–1945	Prime Minister	H. H. Kung (Kung Hsiang-hse)	b. 1880	d. 1967

TAIWAN (FORMOSA)

1949–	Head of Government	Chiang Kai-shek

CHINESE PEOPLE'S REPUBLIC

1949–	Chairman	Mao Tse-tung	b. 1893

China (continued)

1949–	Prime Minister and Foreign Secretary	Chou En-lai	b. 1898?
1959–	President	Liu Shao-chi	b. 1898?

Chiang Kai-shek,
President of China
(Taiwan) (1949–   ).

Chou En-lai, Prime Minister
of Chinese People's Republic
(1949–   ).

Mao Tse-tung, Chairman of
Chinese People's Republic
(1949–   ).

Colombia

Francisco de Paula
Santander, President of
New Granada (1832–1836).

? –1536	Tipa (Chief)	Nemenquene, chief of Chibcha Indians at Bogota	
1499–1536		Discovery and partial conquest by Spain	
1536–1541	Conqueror	Gonzalo Jimenez de Quesada	b. 1500? d. 1579

The greatest of the conquerors, he subdued the mighty Chibcha Indian nation, assuring the conquest. In 1538, he founded Santa Fé (now Bogotá) and, reminded of his native land, he named Colombia "New Granada."

1542–1549		Spain continued conquest and colonization.
1549–1717		King of Spain made New Granada an *audiencia.*

The state was to be governed by presidents who would also have authority as captains general. Outstanding as presidents during this period were Andrés Vinero de Leiva, Francisco Briceño and Lope Armendariz.

1717–1810		Colombia became the Vice-royalty of New Granada.

The Vice-royalty encompassed what is now Venezuela, Panama, and Ecuador. Outstanding viceroys were José de Ezpeleta, Archbishop Antonio Caballero y Góngora, José Solis and Manuel Guirior.

? –1810	Viceroy	Antonio de Amar
1810–1821	President	Simón Bolívar

Revolution for independence, headed by Bolívar (see Venezuela), broke out in 1810. At the end of a series of fierce battles, Colombia overcame the Spanish and declared itself the Republic of Greater Colombia in 1819. Bolívar was proclaimed President in 1821.

1821		Became Republic of Greater Colombia		
1821–1828	Vice-President	Francisco de Paula Santander	b. 1792	d. 1840

A commander of the warriors of the plains during the revolution, Santander helped Bolívar win the decisive battle at Boyacá and was named Vice-President. He administered the country capably during the President's frequent absences, but, believing in constitutional government, in 1828 he revolted against Bolívar and was suspended from office. Accused of attempting to assassinate Bolívar, Santander was banished. After Bolívar's death in 1830, Greater Colombia dissolved, and Santander was recalled to serve as the first President of Colombia, renamed New Granada.

1831		Republic of New Granada organized		
1832–1836	President	Francisco de Paula Santander		
1836–1840	,,	José Ignacio de Marquez		
1840–1844	,,	Pedro Alcantara Herron		
1844–1849	,,	Tomás Cipriano de Mosquera	b. 1798	d. 1878
1849–1853	,,	José Hilario Lopez		
1853–1857	,,	José Maria Obando		
1857–1861	,,	Mariano Ospina Rodríguez		
	(Adopted name of United States of Colombia in 1863)			
1861–1863	Dictator	Tomás Cipriano de Mosquera	b. 1798	d. 1878
1863	President	Froilán Largacha		
1863–1864	,,	Tomás Cipriano de Mosquera		
1864	President (acting)	Juan Agustín Uricoechea		
1864–1866	President	Manuel Murillo Toro		
1866	President (acting)	José María Rojas Garrido		
1866–1867	President	Tomás Cipriano de Mosquera		
1867–1868	President (acting)	Santos Acosta		
1868–1870	President	Santos Gutiérrez		
1868–1869	President (acting)	Salvador Camacho Roldán		
1869–1870	,,	Santiago Pérez	b. 1830	d. 1900
1870–1872	President	Eustorgio Salgar		
1872–1874	,,	Manuel Murillo Toro		
1874–1876	,,	Santiago Pérez		
1876–1878	,,	Aquileo Parra		
1878–1880	,,	Julián Trujillo	b. 1829	d. 1884
1880–1882	,,	Rafael Núñez	b. 1825	d. 1894
1882	,,	Francisco Javier Zaldúa		d. 1882
1882	President (acting)	Climacho Calderón		
1882–1884	President	José Eusebio Otálora		
1884	President (acting)	Ezequiel Hurtado		
1884–1886	President	Rafael Núñez		
	(Became Republic of Colombia in 1885)			
1886	President (acting)	José María Campo Serrano		
1887	President	Eliseo Payán		
1887–1888	,,	Rafael Núñez		
1888–1892	,,	Carlos Holguín		
1892–1896	,,	Miguel Antonio Caro	b. 1843	d. 1909
1896	,,	Guillermo Quintero Calderón		
1896–1898	,,	Miguel Antonio Caro		
1898	President (acting)	José Manuel Marroquín	b. 1827	d. 1908
1898–1900	President	Manuel Antonio Sanclemente		
1900–1904	,,	José Manuel Marroquín		
1904–1908	,,	Rafael Reyes	b. 1850 ?	d. 1921
1908	,,	Euclides de Angulo		
1908–1909	,,	Rafael Reyes		
1909	President (acting)	Jorge Holguín		
1909–1910	President	Ramón González Valencia		
1910–1914	,,	Carlos E. Restrepo	b. 1867	d. 1937

Colombia (continued)

1914–1918	President	José Vicente Concha	
1918–1921	„	Marco Fidel Suárez	
1921–1922	President (acting)	Jorge Holguín	
1922–1926	President	Pedro Nel Ospina	
1926–1930	„	Miguel Abadía Méndez	b. 1867 d. 1947

Guillermo-León Valencia, President of Colombia (1962–1966).

1930–1934	President	Enrique Olaya Herrera	
1934–1938	„	Alfonso López	b. 1886 d. 1959
1938–1942	„	Eduardo Santos	b. 1888
1942–1945	„	Alfonso López	
1945–1946	„	Alberto Lleras Camargo	b. 1906
1946–1950	„	Mariano Ospina Pérez	b. 1891
1950–1953	„	Laureano Gómez	b. 1889
1951–1953	President (acting)	Roberto Urdaneta Arbeláez	b. 1890
1953–1957	Dictator	Gustavo Rojas Pinilla	b. 1900
1957–1958	President (acting)	Gabriel Paris	
		(Military Junta, 1957–1958)	
1958–1962	President	Alberto Lleras Camargo	
1960	President (acting)	Dario Echandía	
1962–1966	President	Guillermo-León Valencia	b. 1897
1966–	„	Carlos Lleras Restrepo	b. 1909
			b. 1908

Congo

Joseph Kasavubu, President of the Congo Republic (1960–1965) proclaims his country's independence. Seated in the middle is King Baudouin of Belgium.

(State of Congo founded 1885; Belgian colony, 1908–1960; an independent state from 1960. Known as Democratic Republic of Congo)

1960–1965	President	Joseph Kasavubu	b. 1913
1965–	President	Joseph Désiré Mobutu	b. 1930
1960–1961	Prime Minister	Patrice Lumumba	d. 1961
1961–1962	„	Antoine Gizenga	

Cyrille Adoulla, Prime Minister of the Congo Republic (1962–1963).

Moise Tshombe, Prime Minister of the Congo Republic (1964–1965).

1962–1963	Prime Minister	Cyrille Adoulla	
1964–1965	,,	Moise Tshombe	b. 1919
1965	,,	Evariste Kimba	
1965–	,,	Leonard Mulamba	b. 1928

Congo *(Brazzaville)*

(Former French colony of Moyen-Congo; member state of French Community, 1958–1960; fully independent from 1960. Known as Republic of Congo)

1960–1963	President	Fulbert Youlou	b. 1917
1963–	,,	Alphonse Massamba-Débat	b. 1921
1966–	Prime Minister	Ambroise Noumazalay	b. 1933

Costa Rica

(Independent republic since 1821; part of the Confederation of Central America 1824–1838)

1847–1849	President	José María Castro ("Founder of the Republic")	b. 1818	d. 1893
1859	,,	Juan Mora		
1859–1863	,,	José Montealegre		
1863–1866	,,	J. Jiménez		
1866–1868	,,	José María Castro		
1868–1871	Governor	J. Jiménez		
1871	President	Vicente Quadra		
1871–1876	,,	Tomás Guardia	b. 1832	d. 1882
1876	,,	Aniceto Esquivel		
1876	,,	Vicente Herrera		
1877–1882	Dictator	Tomás Guardia		
1882–1885	President	Próspero Fernández	b. 1834	d. 1885
1885–1890	,,	Bernardo Soto		

1890	President	J. J. Rodríguez		
1893–1902	,,	Rafael Iglesias		
1902–1906	,,	Ascensión Esquivel		
1906–1910	,,	Cleto González Víquez		
1910–1914	,,	Ricardo Jiménez Oreamuno	b. 1859	d. 1945
1914–1917	,,	Alfredo González Flores		
1917–1919	,,	Federico Tinoco Granados		
1919–1920	President (provisional)	Francisco Aguilar Barquero		
1920–1924	President	Julio Acosta	b. 1872	d. 1954
1924–1928	,,	Ricardo Jiménez Oreamuno		
1928–1932	,,	Cleto González Víquez		
1932–1936	,,	Ricardo Jiménez Oreamuno		
1936–1940	,,	León Cortés Castro	b. 1882	d. 1946
1940–1944	,,	Rafael Angel Calderón Guardia	b. 1900	
1944–1948	,,	Teodoro Picado Michalski		
1948–1949	,,	José Figueres Ferrer		
1949–1953	,,	Otilia Ulate		
1953–1958	,,	José Figueres Ferrer		
1958–1962	,,	Mario Echandi Jiménez		
1962–1966	,,	Francisco J. Orlich Bolmarich		
1966–	,,	José Joaquin Trejos		

Croatia, see Yugoslavia

Cuba

Osvaldo Dorticos Torrado, President of Cuba (1959–   ).

(Under Spanish rule from 1492 to 1898, except for British occupancy 1762–63)

SPANISH GOVERNORS

1834–1838	Governor	Miguel de Tacón	b. 1777	d. 1855
1838–1840	,,	Joaquín Ezpeleta y Enrille		
1840–1841	,,	Pedro Téllez de Girón		
1841–1843	,,	Gerónimo Valdés y Sierra		
1843	Governor (provisional)	Francisco Javier de Ulloa		
1843–1848	Governor	Leopoldo O'Donnell, Count of Lucena	b. 1809	d. 1867
1848–1850	,,	Federico Roncalí, Count of Alcoy		
1850–1852	,,	José Gutiérrez de la Concha		

1852–1853	Governor	Valentín Cañedo Miranda		
1853–1854	,,	Juan de la Pezuela		
1854–1859	,,	José Gutiérrez de la Concha		
1859–1862	,,	Francisco Serrano y Domínguez,		
		Duque de la Torre	b. 1810	d. 1885
1862–1866	,,	Domingo Dulce y Garay		
1866	,,	Francisco Lersundi		
1866–1867	,,	Joaquín del Manzano y Manzano		
1867	,,	Blas Villate y de la Hera,		
		Count of Balmaseda	b. 1825	d. 1882
1867–1869	,,	Francisco Lersundi		
1869	,,	Domingo Dulce y Garay		
1869	Governor (provisional)	Filipe Ginovés del Espinar		
1869–1870	Governor	Antonio Caballero y Fernández de Rodas		
1870–1872	,,	Blas Villate y de la Hera, Count of Balmaseda		
1872–1873	,,	Francisco Ceballos y Vargas		
1873	,,	Cándido Pieltain y Jove-Huelgo		
1873–1874	,,	Joaquín Jovellar y Soler		
1874–1875	,,	José Gutiérrez de la Concha		
1875	Governor (provisional)	Buenaventura Carbó		
1875–1876	Governor	Blas Villate y de la Hera, Count of Balmaseda		
1876–1878	,,	Joaquín Jovellar y Soler		
1876–1879	,,	Arsenio Martínez de Campos		
1879	Governor (provisional)	Cayetano Figueroa y Garahondo		
1879–1881	Governor	Ramón Blanco y Erenas		
1881–1883	,,	Luis Prendergast y Gordon		
1883	Governor (provisional)	Tomás de Reyna y Renya		
1883–1884	Governor	Ignacio María del Castillo		
1884–1886	,,	Ramón Fajardo y Izquierdo		
1886–1887	,,	Emilio Calleja e Isasi		
1887–1889	,,	Sabás Marín y González		
1889–1890	,,	Manuel Salamanca y Negrete		
1890	Governor (provisional)	José Sánchez Gómez		
1890	Governor	José Chinchilla y Díez de Oñate		
1890–1892	,,	Camilo Polavieja y del Castillo		
1892–1893	,,	Alejandro Rodríguez Arias		
1893	Governor (provisional)	José Arderius y García		
1893–1895	Governor	Emilio Calleja e Isasi		
1895–1896	,,	Arsenio Martínez de Campos		
1896	,,	Sabás Marín y González		
1896–1897	,,	Valeriano Weyler y Nicolau		
1897–1898	,,	Ramón Blanco y Erenas		
1898	,,	Adolfo Jimenez Castellanos		

First American Intervention

1899	Military Governor	John Rutter Brookè	b. 1838	d. 1926
1899–1902	,,	Leonard Wood	b. 1860	d. 1927

William Howard Taft, Governor of Cuba during the Second American Intervention (1906), later served as 27th President of the United States.

Cuban Republic

| 1902–1906 | President | Tomás Estrada Palma | b. 1835 | d. 1908 |

Second American Intervention

| 1906 | Governor (provisional) | William Howard Taft | b. 1857 | d. 1930 |
| 1906–1909 | „ | Charles Edward Magoon | b. 1861 | d. 1920 |

Fidel Castro Ruz, Prime Minister of Cuba (1959–).

Cuban Republic Restored

1909–1913	President	José Miguel Gómez	b. 1858	d. 1921
1913–1921	„	Mario Garciá Menocal	b. 1866	d. 1941
1921–1925	„	Alfredo Zayas y Alfonso	b. 1861	d. 1934
1925–1933	„	Gerardo Machado y Morales	b. 1871	d. 1939
1933	President (provisional)	Carlos Manuel de Céspedes y Quesada, son of Carlos Manuel de Céspedes (provisional junta, 1933)	b. 1871	d. 1939
1933–1934	President (provisional)	Ramón Grau San Martín		
1934–1935	„	Carlos Mendieta	b. 1873	d. 1960
1935–1936	„	José A. Barnet y Vinageras		
1936	President	Miguel Mariano Gómez y Arias, son of José Miguel Gómez		
1936–1940	„	Federico Laredo Bru	b. 1875	d. 1946
1940–1944	„	Fulgencio Batista y Zaldívar	b. 1901	
1944–	„	Ramón Grau San Martín		
1948–1952	„	Carlos Prío Socarrás		
1952–1959	„	Fulgencio Batista y Zaldívar		
1959	President (provisional)	Manuel Urrutia Lleo		
1959–	President	Osvaldo Dorticos Torrado		
1959–	Prime Minister	Fidel Castro Ruz	b. 1927	

Cyprus

Archbishop Makarios III (born Michael Christedoulos Mouskos), although a prelate of the Greek Orthodox Church, led resistance to British rule and became the first President of Cyprus in 1959.

(Under Turkish rule until annexed to Britain, 1914–1925; a British crown colony, 1925–1960; an independent sovereign republic from 1960)

1959–	President	Archbishop Makarios III	b. 1913
1960–	Vice-President	Dr. Fazil Kutchuk	

Cyrenaica, see Libya

Czechoslovakia

BOHEMIA (Ger. Böhmen)

PŘEMYSLID DYNASTY

871– 894	Count	Borivoj I		
894– 895	,,	Spithnjew I, son of Borivoj		
895– 912	Duke	Spithnjew I		
912– 926	,,	Vratislav I, son of Borivoj		
926– 928	Regent	Drahomire, von Stoder, widow of Vratislav I		
928– 935	Duke	Wenceslaus (Wenzel) the Holy, son of Vratislav I	b. 908	murdered 935
935– 967	,,	Boleslaus (Boleslav) I, brother of Wenceslaus the Holy		d. 967
967– 999	,,	Boleslaus (Boleslav) II, son of Boleslaus I		d. 999
999–1003	,,	Boleslaus (Boleslav), III son of Boleslaus II		d. 1037
1003–1035	,,	Vladivoj of Poland		
1035–1055	,,	Bretislav I		
1055–1061	,,	Spithnjew II, son of Bretislav I		
1061–1092	Duke	Vratislav II, son of Bretislav I		
1092–1100	,,	Bretislav II		
1100–1107	,,	Borivoj II		
1107–1109	,,	Swartopluk (Internal conflicts 1100–1140)		
1109–1125	,,	Ladislas I		
1125–1140	,,	Sobjislaw		
1140–1158	,,	Ladislas II		
1158–1173	King	Ladislas II (Internal conflicts 1173–1197)		
1197–1230	,,	Ottokar I, son of Ladislas II		d. 1230
1230–1253	,,	Wenceslaus (Wenzel) I, son of Ottokar I	b. 1205	d. 1253
1253–1278	,,	Ottokar II, son of Wenceslaus I	b. 1230 ?	killed 1278
1278–1305	,,	Wenceslaus (Wenzel) II, son of Ottokar II	b. 1271	d. 1305
1305–1306	,,	Wenceslaus (Wenzel) III, son of Wenceslaus II	b. 1289	d. 1306
1306–1307	,,	Rudolph, son of Albert, King of the Romans		d. 1307
1307–1310	,,	Henry, Duke of Carinthia		d. 1335

LUXEMBURG DYNASTY

1310–1346	,,	John the Blind, brother-in-law of Wenceslaus III	b. 1296	killed 1346
1346–1378	,,	Charles, son of John the Blind (See Holy Roman Empire)	b. 1316	d. 1378
1378–1419	,,	Wenceslaus (Wenzel) IV, (Holy Roman Emperor), son of Charles	b. 1361	d. 1419
		(Hussite Wars 1419–1436)		

| 1419–1437 | King | Sigismund of Hungary, brother of Wenceslaus IV | b. 1368 | d. 1437 |

HABSBURG (AND OTHER) DYNASTIES

1437–1439	„	Albert of Austria, son-in-law of Sigismund of Hungary	b. 1397	d. 1439
1440–1457	„	Ladislas Posthumus, son of Albert	b. 1440	d. 1457
1458–1471	„	George of Podebrad	b. 1420	d. 1471
1469	Rival king	Matthias of Hungary		
1471–1516	King	Ladislas II, (Vladislav), nephew of Ladislas posthumus	b. 1456	d. 1516
1516–1526	„	Louis, son of Vladislav	b. 1506	killed 1526
1526–1564	„	Ferdinand I of Austria, son-in-law of Louis	b. 1503	d. 1564
		(Bohemia was united with Austria under Habsburgs 1526–1918)		
1619–1620	„	Frederick V of the Palatinate	b. 1596	d. 1632
		(Part of Czechoslovakia since 1918)		

Tomáš Garrigue Masaryk, President of Czechoslovakia (1918–1935).

Frederick V of the Palatinate, the "Winter King" (1619–1620), was the last ruler of independent Bohemia.

Klement Gottwald, President of Czechoslovakia (1948–1953).

REPUBLIC
(Republic founded in 1918)

| 1918–1935 | President | Tomáš Garrigue Masaryk | b. 1850 | d. 1937 |

A strong critic of Austrian policies, Masaryk escaped from Austria at the beginning of the First World War and became president of the revolutionary Czechoslovak National Council, which was recognized in 1918 as the de facto government of the new state.

1935–1938	President	Eduard Beneš	b. 1884	d. 1948
1938	„	Jan Syrovy	b. 1885	
1938–1939	„	Emil Hácha	b. 1872	d. 1945
		(Annexed by Germany, 1939)		
1939–1945	President (in London)	Eduard Beneš		
1945–1948	President	Eduard Beneš		
		(Communist regime established 1948)		
1948–1953	„	Klement Gottwald	b. 1896	d. 1953
1953–1957	„	Antonín Zapotocky	b. 1884	d. 1957

| 1957–1968 | President | Antonín Novotny | b. 1904 |
| 1968– | ,, | Ludvik Svoboda | b. 1895 |

Protectorate of Bohemia and Moravia

| 1939–1943 | German Protector | Konstantin von Neurath | b. 1873 d. 1956 |
| 1939–1945 | President | Emil Hácha | |

Josef Tiso, President of the puppet state of Slovakia (1939–1945).

Slovakia

| 1939–1945 | President | Josef Tiso | b. 1887 hanged 1947 |

STATESMEN

1918–1919	Premier	Karel Kramár	b. 1860 d. 1937
1919–1920	,,	Vlastimil Tusar	b. 1880 d. 1924
1920–1921	,,	Jan Cerny	b. 1874 d. 1959
1921–1922	,,	Eduard Beneš	
1922–1925	,,	Antonín Svehla	b. 1873 d. 1933
1925–1926	,,	Antonín Svehla	
1926	,,	Jan Cerny	
1926–1929	,,	Antonín Svehla	
1929–1932	,,	Frantisek Udrzal	b. 1866 d. 1938
1932–1934	,,	Jan Malypetr	b. 1873 d. 1947
1934–1935	,,	Jan Malypetr	
1935–1937	,,	Milan Hodza	b. 1878 d. 1944
1937–1938	,,	Milan Hodza	
1938	,,	Jan Syrovy	
1938–1939	,,	Rudolf Beran	b. 1887 d. 1954
1940–1942	,,*	Jan Srámek	b. 1870 d. 1956
1942–1945	,,*	Jan Srámek	
1945–1946	,,	Zdenek Fierlinger	b. 1891
1946–1948	,,	Klement Gottwald	
1948–1953	,,	Antonín Zápotocky	
1953–1954	,,	Viliam Siroky	b. 1902
1954–1960	,,	Viliam Siroky	
1960–1963	,,	Viliam Siroky	
1963–1968	,,	Jozef Lenárt	b. 1923
1968–	,,	Oldrich Cernik	b. 1921
1968–	First Secretary Communist Party	Alexander Dubcek	

* of Government in exile

Dahomey

(Under French administration, 1892–1958; an independent republic within the French
Community, 1958–1960; fully independent outside the Community from 1960)

1957–1959	Prime Minister	Sorou-Migan Apithy	b. 1913
1959–1961	,,	Hubert Maga	b. 1916
1961–1963	President	Hubert Maga	
1963–1964		(Army coup 1963) Provisional Military Government	
1964–1965	,,	Sorou-Migan Apithy (deposed)	
1965–1967	,,	Christophe Soglo (deposed)	b. 1909
1967–	Chairman of Revolutionary Committee	Major Kouandette	

Danzig, see Poland

Denmark (Dan. Danmark)

Christian IV, King of Denmark
(1588–1648).

c. 60 B.C.	King	Skiold (mythical character)
794–803	,,	Sigfred (or Sigurd) Snogoje
798 ?– 810	,,	Godfred
810– 812	,,	Hemming, nephew of Godfred
812– 813 ⎫ 819– 822 ⎬ 825– 826 ⎭	,,	Harold Klak, nephew of Godfred
827– 854	,,	Haarik (Eric) the Old, son of Godfred
803– 850	,,	Hardicanute (Canute I)

(No authenticated information is available for the period before 900)

900– 950	,,	Gorm the Old	
950– 985	,,	Harold Bluetooth, son of Gorm the Old	d. 988 ?
985–1014	,,	Sweyn I Forkbeard, son of Harold Bluetooth	d. 1014

A Viking, in his youth, Sweyn raided England in 982 and 994. On a
subsequent invasion he forced Ethelred the Unready to flee the country
and was declared King of England. He died suddenly at Gainsborough,
Lincolnshire, after landing there and capturing the town.

Christian V, King of
Denmark (1670–1699).

Christian VII, King of
Denmark (1766–1808).

Frederik VI, King of
Denmark (1808–1839).

1014–1018	King	Harold, son of Sweyn Forkbeard		
1019–1035	„	Canute the Great, son of Sweyn Forkbeard	b. 1000	d. 1035
1035–1042	„	Canute III, son of Canute the Great	b. 1018	d. 1042
1042–1047	„	Magnus the Good, son of King Olav the Holy of Norway	b. 1024	d. 1047
1047–1074	„	Sweyn II Estrithson, nephew of Canute the Great		
1074–1080	„	Harold Hen, son of Sweyn Estrithson		d. 1080
1080–1086	„	Canute IV the Holy, son of Sweyn Estrithson	b. 1040	killed 1086
1086–1095	„	Oluf I Hunger, son of Sweyn Estrithson		d. 1095
1095–1103	„	Eric I Evergood, son of Sweyn Estrithson		d. 1103
1104–1134	„	Niels, son of Sweyn Estrithson		d. 1134
1134–1137	„	Eric II Emune the Memorable, son of Eric Evergood		d. 1137
1137–1146	„	Eric III Lam		d. 1146
1146–1157	„	Sweyn III Grade, son of Eric Emune		d. 1157
1157	„	Knud III Magnussen, son of Magnus Nielsen		d. 1157
1157–1182	„	Valdemar I the Great, son of Knud Lavard	b. 1131	d. 1182
1182–1202	„	Canute VI, son of Valdemar I the Great	b. 1163	d. 1202
1202–1241	„	Valdemar II the Victorious, son of Valdemar I the Great	b. 1170	d. 1241
1241–1250	„	Eric IV Ploughpenny, son of Valdemar II the Victorious	b. 1216	d. 1250
1250–1252	„	Abel, son of Valdemar II the Victorious		d. 1252
1252–1259	„	Christopher I, son of Valdemar II the Victorious	b. 1219	d. 1259
1259–1286	„	Eric V Klipping, son of Christopher I	b. 1249	d. 1286
1286–1319	„	Eric VI Maendved, son of Eric Klipping	b. 1274	d. 1319
1320–1332	„	Christopher II, son of Eric Klipping	b. 1276	d. 1332
1340–1375	„	Valdemar IV Atterdag, son of Christopher II	b. 1320	d. 1375
1376–1387	„	Oluf II, grandson of Valdemar Atterdag	b. 1370	d. 1387
1387–1412	Queen	Margrete, daughter of Valdemar IV Atterdag	b. 1353	d. 1412

Known as "Semiramis of the North," Queen Margrete conquered Sweden and brought about the Union of Kalmar (1397), providing for perpetual union of the three crowns.

(Denmark, Norway and Sweden united under Queen Margrete July 12, 1397; Sweden left the Union in 1523, Norway in 1814)

1412–1439	King	Eric VII of Pomerania, grand-nephew of Margrete	b. 1382	d. 1459
1440–1448	„	Christopher III of Bavaria, nephew of Eric of Pomerania	b. 1416	d. 1448
1448–1481	„	Christian I, son of Count Diderik the Happy of Oldenborg and Delmenhorst	b. 1426	d. 1481
1481–1513	„	Hans, son of Christian I	b. 1455	d. 1513
1513–1523	„	Christian II, son of Hans	b. 1481	d. 1559
1523–1533	„	Frederik I, son of Christian I	b. 1471	d. 1533
1534–1559	„	Christian III, son of Frederik I	b. 1503	d. 1559
1559–1588	„	Frederik II, son of Christian III	b. 1534	d. 1588
1588–1648	„	Christian IV, son of Frederik II	b. 1577	d. 1648
1648–1670	„	Frederik III, son of Christian IV	b. 1609	d. 1670
1670–1699	„	Christian V, son of Frederik III	b. 1646	d. 1699
1699–1730	„	Frederik IV, son of Christian V	b. 1671	d. 1730
1730–1746	„	Christian VI, son of Frederik IV	b. 1699	d. 1746
1746–1766	„	Frederik V, son of Christian VI	b. 1723	d. 1766
1766–1808	„	Christian VII, son of Frederik V	b. 1749	d. 1808
1808–1839	„	Frederik VI, son of Christian VII	b. 1768	d. 1839
1839–1848	„	Christian VIII, cousin of Frederik VI	b. 1786	d. 1848
1848–1863	„	Frederik VII, son of Christian VIII	b. 1808	d. 1863

1863–1906	King	Christian IX, son of William, Duke of Schleswig-Holstein-Sönderberg-Glücksborg	b. 1818	d. 1906
1906–1912	,,	Frederik VIII, son of Christian IX	b. 1843	d. 1912
1912–1947	,,	Christian X, son of Frederik VIII	b. 1870	d. 1947
1947–	,,	Frederik IX, son of Christian X	b. 1899	

(Left) Christian IX, King of Denmark (1863–1906).

(Right) Frederik VII, King of Denmark (1848–1863).

Frederik IX, King of Denmark (1947–   ).

Jens Otto Krag, Prime Minister of Denmark (1962–1968).

STATESMEN

1643–1651	Steward of the Court	Corfitz Ulfeldt	b. 1606	d. 1664
1673–1676	Leading Minister	Peder Schumacher Griffenfeld	b. 1635	d. 1699
1746–1770	Master of the Royal Household	Adam Gottlob Moltke	b. 1710	d. 1792
1770–1772	Leading Minister	Johann Friedrich Von Struensee	b. 1737	d. 1772
1772–1784	,,	Ove Høegh-Guldberg	b. 1731	d. 1808

PRIME MINISTERS

1781–1784	Prime Minister	Joachim Godske Moltke	b. 1746	d. 1818
1813–1818	,,	Joachim Godske Moltke		
1848–1852	,,	Adam Vilhelm Moltke	b. 1785	d. 1864
1852–1853	,,	Christian Albrecht Bluhme	b. 1794	d. 1866
1853–1854	,,	Andreas Sandø Ørsted	b. 1778	d. 1860
1854–1856	,,	Peter Georg Bang	b. 1797	d. 1861
1856–1857	,,	Carl C. G. Andrae	b. 1812	d. 1893
1857–1863	,,	Carl Christian Hall	b. 1812	d. 1888
1863–1864	,,	Ditlev Gothard Monrad	b. 1811	d. 1887
1864–1865	,,	Christian Albrecht Bluhme	b. 1797	d. 1866

1865–1870	Prime Minister	Christian Emil Frijs	b. 1817	d. 1896
1870–1874	,,	Ludvig Henrik C. H. Holstein	b. 1815	d. 1892
1874–1875	,,	Christian Andreas Fonnesbech	b. 1817	d. 1880
1875–1894	,,	Jacob B. S. Estrup	b. 1825	d. 1913
1894–1897	,,	K. T. Tage O. Reedtz-Thott	b. 1839	d. 1923
1897–1900	,,	Hugo Egmont Hørring	b. 1842	d. 1909
1900–1901	,,	Hannibal Sehested	b. 1842	d. 1924
1901–1905	,,	Johan Henrik Deuntzer	b. 1845	d. 1918
1905–1908	,,	Jens Christian Christensen	b. 1856	d. 1930
1908–1909	,,	Niels T. Neergaard	b. 1854	d. 1936
1909	,,	Johan Ludvig Holstein	b. 1839	d. 1912
1909–1910	,,	Carl Theodor Zahle	b. 1866	d. 1946
1910–1913	,,	Klaus Berntsen	b. 1844	d. 1927
1913–1920	,,	Carl Theodor Zahle		
1920	,,	C. J. Otto Liebe	b. 1860	d. 1929
1920	,,	Michael Petersen Friis	b. 1857	d. 1944
1920–1924	,,	Niels T. Neergaard	b. 1854	d. 1936
1924–1926	,,	Thorvald A. M. Stauning	b. 1873	d. 1942
1926–1929	,,	Thomas Madsen-Mygdal	b. 1876	d. 1943
1929–1942	,,	Thorvald A. M. Stauning		
1942	,,	Vilhelm Buhl	b. 1881	d. 1954
1942–1945	,,	Erik Scavenius	b. 1877	d. 1962
1945	,,	Vilhelm Buhl		
1945–1947	,,	Knud Kristensen	b. 1880	d. 1962
1947–1950	,,	Hans Hedtoft	b. 1903	d. 1955
1950–1953	,,	Erik Eriksen	b. 1902	
1953–1955	,,	Hans Hedtoft		
1955–1960	,,	Hans Chr. Hansen	b. 1906	d. 1960
1960–1962	,,	Viggo Kampmann	b. 1910	
1962–1968	,,	Jens Otto Krag	b. 1914	
1968–	,,	Hilmer Baumsgaard		

Dominican Republic

(Became an independent state in 1821; Republic founded in 1844)

1844–1848	President	Pedro Santana	b. 1801	d. 1864
1848–1849	,,	Manuel Jiménez		
1849–1853	,,	Buenaventura Baez		
1853–1856	,,	Pedro Santana		
1856–1858	,,	Buenaventura Baez		
1858–1861	,,	Pedro Santana		
1861–1865	,,	Pedro A. Pimentel		
1865	,,	José Maria Cabral		
1865–1866	,,	Buenaventura Baez		
1866–1868	,,	José Maria Cabral		
1868–1874	,,	Buenaventura Baez		
1874–1876	,,	Ignacio Maria González		
1876	,,	Ulises Francisco Espaillat		
1876–1878	,,	Ignacio Maria González		
1878–1880	,,	Gregorio Luperón		
1880–1882	,,	Fernando Arturo de Meriño		
1882–1884	,,	Ulises Heureaux		
1884–1887	,,	Alejandro Woss y Gil		
1887–1899	,,	Ulises Heureaux		

Rafael Leonidas Trujillo,
President and Dictator of
the Dominican Republic
(1930–1961).

Joaquín Balaguer, President of the Dominican Republic (1961–1962, 1966–   ).

1899–1901	President	Horacio Vasquez		
1901–1903	„	Juan Isidro Jiménez		
1903–1904	„	Alejandro Woss y Gil		
1904–1905	„	Carlos Morales Lauguasco		
1905–1911	„	Ramón Cáceres		
1911–1912	„	Alfredo Victoria		
1912–1913	„	Adolfo A. Nouel		
1913–1914	„	José Bordas Valdés		
1914–1915	„	Ramón Báez		
1915–1916	„	Juan Isidro Jiménez		
1916	„	Francisco Henríquez y Carvajal		

(1916–1924 American Intervention and U.S. Military Government)

1924–1930	„	Horacio Vasquez		
1930–1961	President and Dictator	Rafael Leonidas Trujillo	b. 1891	assassinated 1961
1961–1962	President	Joaquín Balaguer	b. 1907	
1962–1963	„	Rafael F. Bonnelly		
1963	„	Juan Bosch		
1963	„	Emilio de los Santos		
1963–1965	„	Donald Reid Cabral		
1965–1966		Military junta		
1966–	„	Joaquín Balaguer		

Dutch East Indies, see Indonesia

Ecuador

Gabriel García Moreno, President of Ecuador (1861–1865, 1869–1875).

(Became independent in 1830)

1830–1835	President	Juan José Flores	b. 1800	d. 1864
1835–1839	„	Vicente Rocafuerte	b. 1783	d. 1847

1839–1845	President	Juan José Flores		
1845–1850	,,	Vicente Ramón Roca	b. 1790 ?	d. 1850
1851	,,	Diego Noboa		
1852–1856	,,	José María Urvina (or Urbina)	b. 1808	d. 1891
1856–1859	,,	Francisco Robles	b. 1811	d. 1893
1861–1865	,,	Gabriel García Moreno		
		son-in-law of Flores	b. 1821	assassinated 1875
1865–1867	,,	Gerónimo Carrión	b. 1812	d. 1873
1868–1869	,,	Javier Espinosa		
1869–1875	,,	Gabriel García Moreno		
1875–1876	,,	Antonio Borrero		
1876–1883	,,	Ignacio de Veintemilla	b. 1830	d. 1909
1883–1888	,,	José María Plácido Caamaño	b. 1838	d. 1901
1888–1892	,,	Antonio Flores		
1892–1895	,,	Luis Cordero		
1897–1901	,,	Eloy Alfaro	b. 1864	murdered 1912
1901–1905	,,	Leonidas Plaza Gutiérrez		
1905–1906	,,	Lizardo García		
1907–1911	,,	Eloy Alfaro		
1911	,,	Emilio Estrada		
1912–1916	,,	Leonidas Plaza Gutiérrez		
1916–1920	,,	Alfredo Baquerizo Moreno	b. 1859	d. 1951
1920–1924	,,	José Luis Tamayo		
1924–1925	,,	Gonzalo S. Córdoba		
		(provisional junta, 1925–1926)		
1926–1931	,,	Isidro Ayora		
1931	President (provisional)	Luis A. Larrea Alba		
1931–1932	,,	Alfredo Baquerizo Moreno		
		(period of revolution, 1932)		

Clemente Yerovi Indaburu, President of Ecuador (1966).

1932	President (provisional)	Alberto Guerrero Martínez	
1932–1933	President	Juan de Dios Martínez Mera	
1933–1934	President (provisional)	Abelardo Montalvo	
1934–1935	President	José María Velasco Ibarra	
1935	President (provisional)	Antonio Pons	
1935–1937	,,	Federico Páez	
1937–1938	,,	G. Alberto Enríquez	
1938	,,	Manuel María Borrero	
1938–1939	,,	Aurelio Mosquera Narvaez	d. 1939
1938–1939	President	Aurelio Mosquera Narvaez	
1940	,,	Andrés F. Cordova	
1940–1944	,,	Carlos Alberto Arroyo del Río	b. 1893
1944–1947	,,	José María Velasco Ibarra	
		(military coup, 1947)	

Ecuador (continued)

1948–1952	President	Galo Plaza Lasso	
1952–1956	,,	José María Velasco Ibarra	
1956–1960	,,	Camillo Ponce Enríquez	
1960–1961	,,	José María Velasco Ibarra	
1961–1963	,,	Carlos J. Arosemena	(Exiled)
	,,	(Military junta, 1963–1966)	
1966	,,	Clemente Yerovi Indaburu	b. 1904
1966–	,,	Otto Arosemena Gomez	b. 1925

Egypt

Cleopatra VII, Queen of Egypt (51–30 B.C.), had several predecessors of the same name who were consorts of their brothers, the Ptolemies.

B.C.

THE OLD KINGDOM

3400	King	Menes (united north and south kingdoms)

3400–2980	**1ST AND 2ND (THINITE) DYNASTIES**	
2980–2900	**3RD (MEMPHITE) DYNASTY**	
	,,	Zoser
	,,	Seris
about 2920	,,	Snefru (or Sneferu)

2900–2750	**4TH (MEMPHITE) DYNASTY**	
2900–2877	,,	Cheops (Khufu)
	,,	Dedefrê
	,,	Chephren (Khafrê)
2800	,,	Menkure (Mycerinus)

2750–2625	**5TH (MEMPHITE) DYNASTY**	
	,,	Weserkef (Userkaf)
	,,	Sahure, brother of Weserkef
	,,	Nefererkere, brother of Weserkef

2625–2475	**6TH (MEMPHITE) DYNASTY**	
	,,	Teti
	,,	Weserkere (Userkere)
2590–2570	,,	Pepi (Pheops) I Merire
2566–2476	,,	Pepi (Pheops) II Neferkere, son of Pepi I
	,,	Mereme II

2475–2445	**7TH AND 8TH (MEMPHITE) DYNASTIES**
	The Age of Misrule

THE MIDDLE KINGDOM

2445–2160	**9TH AND 10TH (HERACLEOPOLITAN) DYNASTIES**	
	,,	Kheti (Achthoës)

B.C.
2160–2000 | | **11TH (THEBAN) DYNASTY**

	King	Mentuhotep I
	"	Mentuhotep II
	"	Mentuhotep III
	"	Mentuhotep IV
	"	Mentuhotep V

12TH (THEBAN) DYNASTY

2000–1970	"	Amenemhet I
1970–1938	"	Sesostris I, son of Amenemhet I
1938–1903	"	Amenemhet II, son of Sesostris I
1903–1887	"	Sesostris II, son of Amenemhet II
1887–1849	"	Sesostris III, son of Sesostris II
1849–1801	"	Amenemhet III, son of Sesostris III
1801–1792	"	Amenemhet IV, son of Amenemhet III
1792–1788	Princess	Sebeknefrure

THE HYKSOS or "SHEPHERD KINGS"
1788–1580 | | **13TH TO 17TH DYNASTIES**

THE NEW KINGDOM
1580–1350 | | **18TH (DIOSPOLITE) DYNASTY**

1580–1557	King	Ahmosi I (Amasis)
1557–1540	"	Amenhotep I, son of Ahmosi I
1540–1505	"	Thotmes I (Tuthmosis), son of Amenhotep I
1505–1501	"	Thotmes II, son of Thotmes I
1501–1498	Queen	Hatsepsut, (co-ruler) daughter of Thotmes II
1501–1447	King	Thotmes III, (co-ruler) brother of Hatshepsut
1447–1420	"	Amenhotep II, son of Thotmes III
1420–1411	"	Thotmes IV, son of Amenhotep II
1411–1375	"	Amenhotep III, son of Thotmes IV
1375–1358	"	Amenhotep IV (Aknaton), son of Amenhotep III
1358–1357	"	Sakere, son-in-law of Amenhotep IV (Aknaton)
1357–1351	"	Tutankhamen, son-in-law of Sakere
1351–1350	Queen	Eje

1350–1215 | | **19TH (DIOSPOLITE) DYNASTY**
1350–1315	King	Horemheb
1315–1314	"	Rameses I
1313–1292	"	Seti, son of Rameses I
1292–1225	"	Rameses II, son of Seti I
1225–1215	"	Merneptah, son of Rameses II
1215–1212	"	Seti II
1215–1209	rival regent	Siptak

Seti I, King of Egypt, 19th Dynasty (1313–1292 B.C.).

B.C.

1198–1150		**20TH (DIOSPOLITE) DYNASTY**
1198	King	Setnacht
1198–1167	,,	Rameses III
1167–1161	,,	Rameses IV
1161–1142	,,	Rameses V–VIII
1142–1123	,,	Rameses IX
	,,	Rameses X
1118–1090	,,	Rameses XII

(The high priests of Ammon were in power from 1150–1090)

1090– 945		**21ST (TARITE) DYNASTY**
945– 745		**22ND (BUBASTITE) DYNASTY**
745– 718		**23RD (TANITE) DYNASTY**
718– 712		**24TH (SAITE) DYNASTY**
718– 712	,,	Bocchoris of Sais

712– 663		**25TH (ETHIOPIAN) DYNASTY**
712– 700	,,	Sabaka
700– 688	,,	Sabataka
688– 663	King	Taharka, nephew of Shabaka

663– 525		**26TH (SAITE) DYNASTY**
670– 663	,,	Cecho I (Assyrian vassal)
663– 603	,,	Psammetichus, son of Nech I
609– 593	,,	Nech II, son of Psammetichus
593– 588	,,	Psammetichus II, son of Nech II
569– 525	,,	Ahmosi II (Amasis II)
525	,,	Psammetichus III, son of Ahmosi II

523– 332		**EGYPT UNDER PERSIA**	
332– 323	Conqueror	Alexander III the Great	b. 356 d. 323

Ptolemy I Soter, King of Egypt (323–285).

GREEK EPOCH

B.C.   B.C.

323– 285	King	Ptolemy I, Soter	b. 367? d. 283
285– 247	,,	Ptolemy II, Philadelphus, son of Ptolemy I	b. 309 d. 247
247– 221	,,	Ptolemy III, Euergetes, son of Ptolemy II	b. 282? d. 221
221– 203	,,	Ptolemy IV, Philopator, son of Ptolemy III	b. 244? d. 203
203– 180	,,	Ptolemy V, Epiphanes, son of Ptolemy IV	b. 210? d. 180
180– 144	,,	Ptolemy VI, Philometor, son of Ptolemy V	b. 186? killed 144
144– 117	,,	Ptolemy VII, Euergetes II, son of Ptolemy V	b. 184? d. 117
117– 108	,,	Ptolemy VIII, Lathyrus, son of Ptolemy VII	d. 81

88– 80	King	Ptolemy VIII	
108– 89	„	Ptolemy IX, Alexander I, son of Ptolemy VII	killed 89
81– 80	Queen	Berenice, daughter of Ptolemy VIII	murdered 80
81	King	Ptolemy X, Alexander II, son of Ptolemy IX	b. 105? killed 80
81– 51	„	Ptolemy XI, Auletes, son of Ptolemy VIII	b. 95? d. 51
51– 30	Queen (joint ruler)	Cleopatra VII, daughter of Ptolemy XI	b. 69 suicide 30
51– 47	King	Ptolemy XII, son of Ptolemy XI	b. 61 drowned 47
47– 44	„	Ptolemy XIII, brother of Cleopatra VII	b. 58? murdered 44
44– 30	„	Ptolemy XIV, Cesarion, son of Cleopatra VII and Julius Caesar	b. 47 murdered 30

(Roman Province 30 B.C.—A.D. 640)

A.D.		(Arab Conquest A.D. 640)	
868– 884	„	Ahmed ibn-Tulun	b. 835 d. 884
868– 884		**TULUNID DYNASTY**	
935– 969		**IKHSHIDITES**	
969–1171		**FATIMIDITES DYNASTY (14 CALIPHS)**	
1171–1193	Sultan	Saladin	b. 1137 d. 1193
1171–1250		**AYYUBID DYNASTY**	
1260–1382		Bahri Mamelukes (24 sultans)	
1260–1277	Mameluke Sultan	Bibars I	b. 1233 d. 1277
1291–1341	„	Nasir	b. 1284 d. 1341
1382–1517	„	Burji Mamelukes (23 sultans)	
1382–1399		Baruk	
1501–1516		Kansuh-el-Ghury	

(The Egyptian Caliphate was extinguished by Ottoman Conquest 1517)

TURKISH RULE

1805–1849	Viceroy	Mohammed Ali	b. 1769 d. 1849
1849–1854	„	Abbas I, grandson of Mohammed Ali	b. 1813 assassinated 1854
1854–1863	„	Said Pasha, son of Mohammed Ali	b. 1822 d. 1863
1863–1879	Khedive	Ismail Pasha, grandson of Mohammed Ali	b. 1830 d. 1895
1879–1892	„	Mohammed Tewfik Pasha, son of Ismail Pasha	b. 1852 d. 1892
1892–1914	„	Abbas II Hilmi, son of Tewfik Pasha	b. 1874 d. 1944

(British protectorate established in 1914)

(Left) Abbas II Hilmi, Khedive of Egypt (1892–1914).

(Right) Earl Kitchener of Khartoum, Consul-General of Egypt (1911–1916).

Egypt (continued)

BRITISH RULE
(British occupation 1882–1922)

1879–1883	Consul General	Sir Edward Baldwin Malet	b. 1837	d. 1908
1883–1907	,,	Evelyn Baring, Earl of Cromer	b. 1841	d. 1917
1907–1911	,,	Sir John Eldon Gorst	b. 1861	d. 1911
1911–1916	,,	Horatio Herbert Kitchener, Earl Kitchener of Khartoum	b. 1850	d. 1916

Farouk, King of Egypt (1936–1952).

Hussein Kemal, Sultan of Egypt (1914–1917).

Mohammed Naguib, Dictator and President of Egypt (1952–1954).

1914–1916	High Commissioner	Sir Arthur Henry MacMahon	b. 1862	d. 1949
1916–1919	,,	Sir Francis Reginald Wingate	b. 1861	d. 1953
1919–1925	,,	Edmund Henry Hynman, Viscount Allenby	b. 1861	d. 1936
1925–1929	,,	George Ambrose Lloyd, Baron Lloyd of Dolobran	b. 1879	d. 1941
1929–1933	,,	Sir Percy Loraine	b. 1880	
1934–1936	,,	Sir Miles Wedderburn Lampson	b. 1880	
1914–1917	Sultan	Hussein Kemal, son of Ismail Pasha	b. 1853	d. 1917
1917–1922	,,	Ahmed Fuad Pasha, brother of Hussein Kemal	b. 1868	d. 1936
1922–1936	King	Ahmed Fuad (Fuad I)		
1936–1952	,,	Farouk, son of Fuad I	b. 1920	d. 1965
1952–1953	,,	Ahmed II, son of Farouk	b. 1950	
1952–1953	Dictator	Mohammed Naguib	b. 1901	
1953–1954	President	Mohammed Naguib		
1956–1958	,,	Gamal Abdel Nasser	b. 1918	

STATESMEN

1924	Prime Minister	Saad Zaghlul Pasha	b. 1852	d. 1927
1928	,,	Mustafa el-Nahas Pasha	b. 1879	d. 1965
1930	,,	Mustafa el-Nahas Pasha		
1936–1937	,,	Mustafa el-Nahas Pasha		
1942–1944	,,	Mustafa el-Nahas Pasha		
1950–1952	,,	Mustafa el-Nahas Pasha		
1952–1956	,,	Gamal Abdel Nasser		

(In 1958, Egypt and Syria united to form the United Arab Republic; in 1961 when Syria seceded, Egypt retained the name United Arab Republic)

UNITED ARAB REPUBLIC

1958–	President	Gamal Abdel Nasser

El Salvador, see Salvador

England, see Great Britain

*Gamal Abdel Nasser,
President of Egypt
(1956–1958); President
of the United Arab
Republic (1958–   ).*

Epirus

(Epirus corresponded roughly to modern Albania and northwestern Greece)

c. 500 B.C.	King	Admetus		
	,,	Arymbas		
c. 400	,,	Alcetas I		
	,,	Neoptolemus	*Pyrrhus*	
	,,	Arybbas	*(295–272 B.C.).*	
–326	,,	Alexander I		d. 326
	,,	Neoptolemus II		
	,,	Alcetas II		
	,,	Aeacides		
295–272	,,	Pyrrhus	b. 318	d. 272
272–	,,	Alexander II		
	,,	Ptolemy		
	,,	Pyrrhus III		

(Epirus was conquered by Rome in 167 B.C. and remained under Rome and its Byzantine successor states until occupied by the Albanians in the 14th century A.D.)

Estonia

(Formerly a Province of the Russian Empire; an independent republic, 1918–1940; under German occupation, 1941–1944; a Soviet republic from 1944)

1921–1924	Chief of State	Konstantin Päts	b. 1874
1927–1928	,,	Jaan Tonisson	b. 1868

Estonia (continued)

1928–1929	Chief of State	August Rei	
1929–1931	„	Otto Strandmann	b. 1875
1931–1933	„	Konstantin Päts	
1932	„	Karl Einbund (resigned)	
1934–1938	Dictator	Konstantin Päts	
1938–1940	Chief of State	Konstantin Päts	
		(Occupied by Soviet Union in 1940)	

Ethiopia *(Abyssinia)*

Waizero (Zauditu),
Empress of Ethiopia
(1916–1930).

(Divided into semi-independent parts until 1855)

1855–1868	King (Negus)	Theodore (Kasa)	b. 1818 ? suicide 1868
		(Internal struggles 1868–1872)	
1871–1889	Negus negusti	John II (Kassai)	b. 1832 killed 1889
1889–1911	Emperor	Menelik II, son of King of Shoa	b. 1844 d. 1913
1911–1916	„	Lij Yasu, grandson of Menelik II	b. 1896 d. 1935
1916–1930	Empress	Waizero (Zauditu),	
		daughter of Menelik II	b. 1876 d. 1930

Menelik II, Emperor of
Ethiopia (1889–1911).

Haile Selassie, Emperor of
Ethiopia (1930–   ).

1916–1930	Co-ruler	Ras Tafari, son of Ras Makonnen	b. 1891
1930–1936	Emperor	Haile Selassie (Ras Tafari)	b. 1892
		(Italian occupation 1936–1941)	
1941–	„	Haile Selassie	

Finland *(Fin. Suomi)*

(No authenticated information is available for the period before 1284)
(Ruled by Sweden until 1808)

1284–1291	Duke	Bengt, son of Birger Jarl of Sweden
1302–1318	„	Waldemar Magnusson,
		son of Magnus Ladulås, King of Sweden

Finland (continued)

1322–1326	Duke	Matts Kettilmundsson		
1340–1348	,,	Dan Niklinsson		
1353–1357	,,	Bengt Algotsson		d. 1360
1357–1359	,,	Erik Magnusson (Erik XII of Sweden)	b. 1339	d. 1359
1371–1386	Lagman	Bo Jonsson Grip		
1440–1448	,,	Karl Knutsson Bonde (in Finland)	b. 1409	d. 1470
1465–1467	,,	Karl Knutsson Bonde		
1457–1481	,,	Erik Axelsson Tott (in Viborg)		
1495–1496	,,	Knut Posse (in Viborg)		d. 1500
1497–1501	,,	Sten Sture the Elder, son of sister of Charles VIII	b. 1440 ?	d. 1503
1499–1511	,,	Erik Turesson Bielke (in Viborg)		
1520–1522	Junker	Thomas Wolf		
1556–1563	Duke	Johan		d. 1592
1561–1566	Governor	Gustav Fincke		d. 1566
1566–1568	,,	Ivar Mansson Stiernkors		d. 1573
1568–1571	,,	Hans Larsson Björnram		d. 1571
1571–1576	,,	Henrik Klasson Horn		d. 1595
1576–1587	,,	Klas Åkesson Tott		d. 1592
1587–1590	,,	Axel Stensson Leijonhufvud		d. 1619
1591–1597	,,	Klas Eriksson Fleming		d. 1597
1597–1599	,,	Arvid Stålarm		d. 1620
1623–1631	Governor-General	Nils Bielke		d. 1639
1613–1633	,,	Gabriel Bengtsson Oxenstierna		d. 1656
1637–1640	,,	Per Brahe	b. 1602	d. 1680
1648–1654	,,	Per Brahe		
1657–1659	,,	Gustav Evertsson Horn		d. 1666
1664–1669	,,	Herman Fleming		d. 1673
1710–1712	,,	Karl Nieroth		d. 1712

(During the 18th century, Finland was invaded and partially annexed by Russia. In 1808, the entire country became an autonomous Grand Duchy united with the Russian Crown)

1808–1809	Governor-General	Göran Magnus Sprengtporten		d. 1819
1809–1810	,,	Mikael Barclay de Tolly		d. 1818
1810–1823	,,	Fabian Steinheil		d. 1831
1823–1831	,,	Arsenii Zakrevski		d. 1865
1831–1855	,,	Prince Alexander Menshikov	b. 1787	d. 1869
1833–1847	,,	Alexander A. Thesleff		d. 1847
1848–1854	,,	Platon Rokassovski		d. 1869
1854–1855	,,	Fredrik Wilhelm Berg	b. 1794	d. 1874
1854–1861	,,	Fredrik Wilhelm Berg		
1861–1866	,,	Platon Rokassovski		

(Left) Per Brahe, Governor-General of Finland (1637–1640, 1648–1654).

(Right) Carl Gustaf Emil von Mannerheim, President of Finland (1944–1946).

1866–1881	Governor-General	Nikolai Adlerberg	b. 1819	d. 1892
1881–1897	„	Feodor Heiden	b. 1821	d. 1900
1897–1898	„	Stepan Gontscharov		d. 1912
1898–1904	„	Nikolaj Bobrikoff	b. 1839	assassinated 1904

When in accordance with Nicholas II's policy of Russification, the governor, General Bobrikoff, began to rule dictatorially, the Finns replied vigorously. Their "national strike" forced the government to restore the power of the Finnish Diet, and freedom of speech.

1904–1905	Governor-General	Ivan M. Obolenski		d. 1910
1905–1908	„	Nikolaj N. Gerard		d. 1929
1908–1909	„	Vladimir K. Boeckmann		d. 1923
1909–1917	„	Frans A. Seyn		d. 1918
1917	„	Mikael Stahovich		d. 1923
1917	„	Nikolai Nekrasov	b. 1879	
1811–1834	Minister Secretary	Robert Rehbinder	b. 1777	d. 1841
1834–1841	„	Robert Rehbinder		
1841–1842	„	Alexander Armfelt	b. 1794	d. 1876
1876–1881	„	Karl Knut Emil Stiernwall-Wallen	b. 1806	d. 1890
1881–1888	„	Theodor Bruun	b. 1822	d. 1888
1888–1891	„	Johan Casimir Ehrnrooth	b. 1833	d. 1913
1891–1898	„	Waldemar Karl von Daehn	b. 1838	d. 1900
1898–1899	„	Victor Procopé	b. 1839	d. 1906
1899–1904	„	Vyacheslav von Pleve	b. 1846	d. 1904
1904–1905	„	Constantin Linder	b. 1836	d. 1908
1906–1913	„	Karl Fredrik August Langhoff	b. 1856	d. 1929
1913–1917	„	Vladimir Markov	b. 1859	d. 1919
1917	„	Carl Enckell	b. 1876	
1822–1826	Prime Minister	Carl Erik Mannerheim	b. 1759	d. 1857
1826–1828	„	Samuel Fredrik von Born	b. 1782	d. 1850
1828–1833	„	Anders Henrik Falck	b. 1772	d. 1851
1833–1841	„	Gustaf Hjärne	b. 1763	d. 1845
1841–1858	„	Lars Gabriel von Haartman	b. 1789	d. 1859
1858–1882	„	Johan Mauritz Nordenstam	b. 1802	d. 1882
1882–1885	„	Edvard af Forselles	b. 1817	d. 1891
1885–1891	„	Werner von Troil	b. 1833	d. 1900
1891–1900	„	Sten Carl Tudeer	b. 1840	d. 1905
1900–1905	„	Constantin Linder	b. 1836	d. 1908
1905	„	Emil Streng	b. 1838	d. 1911
1905–1908	„	Leo Mechelin	b. 1839	d. 1914
1908–1909	„	Edvard Hjelt	b. 1855	d. 1921
1909	„	August Hjelt	b. 1862	d. 1919
1909	„	Andrej Virenius		
1909–1913	„	Vladimir Markov	b. 1859	d. 1919
1913–1917	„	Michael Borovitinov	b. 1874	
1917	„	Andrej Virenius		
1917	„	Oskari Tokoi	b. 1873	
1917	„	Emil Nestor Setälä	b. 1864	d. 1955

(Finland has been an independent republic since 1918)

1918	Regent	Pehr Evind Svinhufvud	b. 1861	d. 1944
1918	Head of Red Government	Kullervo Manner	b. 1880	
1918	"King"	Frederick Charles of Hesse (monarchy not established)	b. 1868	d. 1940
1918–1919	Regent	Carl Gustaf Emil von Mannerheim	b. 1867	d. 1951
1919–1925	President	Kaarlo Juho Ståhlberg	b. 1865	d. 1952
1925–1931	„	Lauri Kristian Relander	b. 1883	d. 1942

Finland (continued)

1931–1937	President	Pehr Evind Svinhufvud		
1937–1940	„	Kyösti Kallio	b. 1873	d. 1940
1940–1944	„	Risto Heikki Ryti	b. 1889	d. 1956
1944–1946	„	Carl Gustaf Emil von Mannerheim		

Mannerheim, the "Liberator of Finland" served with distinction in the Russian army but after the Russian Revolution went to Finland and defeated the "Red Guards". He commanded the Finnish army against the Russians in 1939 and again after 1941.

1946–1956	President	Juho Kusti Paasikivi	b. 1870	d. 1956
1956–	„	Urho Kaleva Kekkonen	b. 1900	

1918	Prime Minister	Juho Kusti Paasikivi		
1918–1919	„	Lauri Johannes Ingman	b. 1868	d. 1934
1919	„	Kaarlo Castren	b. 1860	
1919–1920	„	Juho Heikki Vennola	b. 1872	d. 1938
1920–1921	„	Rafeal Erich	b. 1879	d. 1946
1921–1922	„	Juho Heikki Vennola		
1922	„	Aimo Kaarlo Cajander	b. 1879	
1922–1924	„	Kyösti Kallio		
1924	„	Aimo Kaarlo Cajander		
1924–1925	„	Lauri Johannes Ingman		
1925	„	Antti Agaton Tulenheimo	b. 1879	d. 1952
1925–1926	„	Kyösti Kallio		
1926–1927	„	Väinö Alfred Tanner	b. 1881	
1927–1928	„	Juho Emil Sunila	b. 1875	
1928–1929	„	Oskari Mantere	b. 1874	d. 1942
1929–1930	„	Kyösti Kallio		

(Left) Urho Kekkonen, President of Finland (1956–).

(Right) Reino Lehto, Prime Minister of Finland (1963–1964).

1930–1931	Prime Minister	Pehr Evind Svinhufvud		
1931–1932	„	Juho Emil Sunila		d. 1936
1932–1936	„	Toivo Mikael Kivimäki	b. 1886	
1936–1937	„	Kyösti Kallio		
1937–1939	„	Aimo Kaarlo Cajander		
1939–1940	„	Risto Heikki Ryti		
1941–1943	„	Johan Wilhelm Rangell	b. 1894	
1943–1944	„	Edwin Linkomies	b. 1894	
1944	„	Antti Hackzell	b. 1881	d. 1944
1944	„	Urho Castren	b. 1886	
1944–1946	„	Juho Kusti Paasikivi		
1946–1948	„	Mauno Pekkala	b. 1890	d. 1952
1948–1950	„	Karl-August Fagerholm	b. 1901	
1950–1953	„	Urho Kaleva Kekkonen		
1953–1954	„	Sakari Tuomioja	b. 1911	d. 1964
1954	„	Ralf Törngren	b. 1900	d. 1961

1954–1956	Prime Minister	Urho Kaleva Kekkonen	
1956–1957	,,	K.-A. Fagerholm	
1957	,,	V. J. Sukselainen	b. 1906
1957–1958	,,	Rainer von Fieandt	b. 1890
1958	,,	Reino Kuuskoski	b. 1907
1958–1959	,,	K.-A. Fagerholm	
1959–1961	,,	V. J. Sukselainen	
1961–1962	,,	Martti Miettunen	b. 1907
1962–1963	,,	Ahti Karjalainen	b. 1923
1963–1964	,,	Reino Lehto	b. 1898
1964–1966	,,	Johannes Virolainen	b. 1914
1966–	,,	Rafael Paasio	

France

English versions of the names of rulers of
French-speaking states are:

Baldwin–Baudouin   Odo–Eudes
Francis–François   Peter–Pierre
Henry–Henri   Philip–Philippe
Hugh–Hugues   Rudolph–Rodolphe
John–Jean   Stephen–Etienne
James–Jacques   Theobald–Thibaut
          William–Guillaume

*This Merovingian chair in the Louvre in Paris
is believed to have served as the throne of the
Frankish King Dagobert I (628–639).*

GAUL
(Roman province from 2nd century B.C. to A.D. 476)

462– 486	Independent Roman governor Syagrius	b. 430? d. 496

MEROVINGIAN DYNASTY
(First Frankish Dynasty)
(No authentic information is available for the period before the Merovingians emerged)

420– 428	King	Pharamond	
428– 448	,,	Clodio or Clodion	
448– 458	,,	Merovech or Mérovée	d. 456
458– 481	,,	Childeric I, son of Merovech	b. 437? d. 481
481– 511	,,	Clovis I, son of Childeric I	b. 456? d. 511

Clovis married a Christian princess and was converted by her, beating the
Germans, as he believed, with God's help. He overthrew Syagrius, and
made his court at Paris. He attempted to unite the whole Frankish race
in one kingdom.

511– 534	King	Thierry I of Austrasia, son of Clovis	d. 534
511– 524	,,	Clodomir of Neustria, son of Clovis	d. 524
511– 558	Co-regent	Childebert I of Neustria, son of Clovis	d. 558
511– 558	King of Soissons	Clothaire I of Neustria, son of Clovis	d. 561
534– 548	King	Theodebert of Austrasia, son of Thierry	d. 548

France (continued)

548– 555	King	Theobald of Austrasia, son of Theodebert		d. 555
558– 561	,,	Clothaire I		
561– 567	,,	Charibert, son of Clothaire I		d. 567
561– 593	,,	Gontram of Burgundy, son of Clothaire I		d. 593
561– 575	,,	Sigebert I of Austrasia, son of Clothaire I	b. 535	assassinated 575
561– 584	,,	Chilperic I of Neustria, son of Clothaire I		d. 584
575– 596	,,	Childebert II of Austrasia, son of Sigebert of Austrasia	b. 570	d. 596

MEROVINGIAN DYNASTY

Pharamond, King of the
Franks (420–428).

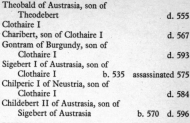

Clodio, King of the
Franks (428–448).

Merovech, King of the
Franks (448–458).

Childeric I, King of the
Franks (458–481).

Clovis I, King of the
Franks (481–511).

Childebert I, Co-ruler of
the Franks (511–558).

Clothaire I, King of the
Franks (511–561).

Charibert, King of the
Franks (561–567).

Chilperic I, King of the
Franks (561–584).

Clothaire III, King of the Franks (657–671).

Childeric II, King of the Franks (663–673).

Thierry III, King of the Franks (673–691?).

Clovis III, King of the Franks (691–695).

Childebert III, King of the Franks (695–711).

Dagobert III, King of the Franks (711–715).

Clothaire IV, King of the Franks (717–719).

Chilperic II, King of the Franks (715–720).

Thierry IV, King of the Franks (720–737).

575– 596	Regent	Brunhilde, consort of Sigebert of Austrasia	murdered 613
584– 628	King	Clothaire II of Neustria, son of Chilperic of Neustria	d. 628
584– 597	Regent	Fredegund, consort of Chilperic I of Neustria	d. 597
596– 612	King	Theodebert II of Austrasia, son of Childebert II of Austrasia	d. 612
596– 613	,,	Thierry II of Burgundy, son of Childebert of Austrasia	d. 613
613	,,	Sigebert II of Burgundy, son of Thierry of Burgundy	d. 613
613– 628	King (whole kingdom)	Clothaire II of Austrasia and Burgundy	
628– 639	,, ,,	Dagobert I, son of Clothaire of Austrasia and Burgundy	d. 639
639– 656	King	Sigebert III of Austrasia, son of Dagobert I	d. 656

638– 657	King	Clovis II of Neustria and Burgundy, son of Dagobert I	b. 632 d. 657
657– 671	„	Clothaire III of Neustria and Burgundy, son of Clovis of Neustria and Burgundy	d. 671
663– 673	„	Childeric II of Austrasia, son of Clovis II of Neustria and Burgundy	b. 653? d. 673
673– 678	„	Dagobert II of Austrasia, son of Sigebert III of Austrasia	d. 678
673– 691?	„	Thierry III of Neustria and Burgundy, son of Clovis II of Neustria and Burgundy	d. 691
678– 691	„	Thierry III of Austrasia	
691– 695	„	Clovis III of Neustria, son of Thierry III	b. 682 d. 695
695– 711	„	Childebert III, son of Thierry III	d. 711
711– 715	„	Dagobert III of Neustria, son of Childebert III	d. 715
715– 720	„	Chilperic II, son of Childeric II of Austrasia	d. 720
717– 719	„	Clothaire IV of Neustria	d. 719
720– 737	„	Thierry IV, son of Dagobert III (Interregnum 737–742)	d. 737
742– 751	„	Childeric III, son of Chilperic II	

Odo, Count of Paris (866–886) repels the Northmen.

CAROLINGIAN DYNASTY
(Second Frankish Dynasty)

628– 639	Mayor of the Palace	Pepin I the Elder	d. 640?
687– 714	„	Pepin II, son of Pepin the Elder	d. 714
714– 741	„	Charles Martel, son of Pepin II	b. 689? d. 741

When in 732 the Arabs attacked Tours, the holy town of Gaul, Charles Martel won a great victory over them, thereby ending the last great Arab invasion of Europe.

741– 747	Mayor of the Palace	Carloman of Austrasia, son of Charles Martel		d. 754
741– 751	,,	Pepin the Short, son of Charles Martel	b. 714?	d. 768
751– 768	King	Pepin the Short (Pepin III)		
768– 771	,,	Carloman, son of Pepin III		d. 771
768– 814	Joint ruler	Charlemagne, son of Pepin III (Holy Roman Emperor, 800–814)	b. 742	d. 814
814– 840	,,	Louis I the Pious, son of Charlemagne (Civil War 838–840)	b. 778	d. 840
840– 843	,,	Lothair, Louis and Charles the Bald, sons of Louis I		
843– 877	King	Charles I the Bald	b. 823	d. 877
877– 879	,,	Louis II, son of Charles I the Bald	b. 846	d. 879
879– 882	,,	Louis III, son of Louis II	b. 863	d. 882
879– 884	Co-regent	Carloman, brother of Louis III		d. 884
885– 887	King	Charles II the Fat, son of Louis (see Germany)	b. 839	d. 891
888– 898	,,	Odo, Count of Paris		d. 898
893– 922	,,	Charles III the Simple, posthumous son of Louis II	b. 879	d. 929
922– 923	Rival King	Robert, brother of Odo, Count of Paris		killed 923
923– 936	King	Rudolf (see Burgundy), son-in-law of Robert		d. 937
936– 954	,,	Louis IV, son of Charles the Simple	b. 921?	d. 954
954– 986	,,	Lothair, son of Louis IV	b. 941	d. 986
986– 987	,,	Louis V, son of Lothair	b. 967?	d. 987

Frankish Dukes of the House of Capet

861– 866	Duke	Robert the Strong, son-in-law of Louis the Pious		killed 866
866– 886	,,	Hugh the Abbot, brother of Robert the Strong		
866– 886	,,	Odo, Count of Paris, son of Robert the Strong		
889– 923	,,	Robert II, brother of Odo, Count of Paris	b. 865?	killed 923
923– 936	,,	Rudolf, brother-in-law of Robert II		d. 936
923– 956	,,	Hugh the Great, son of Robert, Count of Paris		d. 956
956– 987	,,	Hugh Capet, son of Hugh the Great (Duchy of Francia united with France)	b. 938?	d. 996

KINGDOM OF FRANCE: HOUSE OF CAPET

987– 996	King	Hugh Capet		
996–1031	,,	Robert II, son of Hugh Capet	b. 970?	d. 1031
1031–1060	,,	Henry I, son of Robert II	b. 1008	d. 1060
1060–1108	,,	Philip I, son of Henry I	b. 1052	d. 1108
1108–1137	,,	Louis VI, son of Philip I	b. 1081	d. 1137
1137–1180	,,	Louis VII, son of Louis VI	b. 1120	d. 1180
1180–1223	,,	Philip II, son of Louis VII	b. 1165	d. 1223
1223–1226	,,	Louis VIII, son of Philip II	b. 1187	d. 1226
1226–1270	,,	Louis IX (St. Louis), son of Louis VIII	b. 1214	d. 1270

France (continued)

1270–1285	King	Philip III the Bold, son of Louis IX	b. 1245	d. 1285
1285–1314	„	Philip IV the Fair, son of Philip III	b. 1268	d. 1314
1314–1316	„	Louis X, son of Philip IV	b. 1289	d. 1316
1316	„	John I, posthumous son of Louis X	b. 1316	d. 1316
1316–1322	„	Philip V the Tall, son of Philip IV	b. 1294	d. 1322
1322–1328	„	Charles IV the Fair, son of Philip IV	b. 1294	d. 1328

Charlemagne, King of the Franks (768–814) and Holy Roman Emperor (800–814).

Louis IX, King of France (1226–1270).

Charles IX, King of France (1560–1574).

Louis XIV, King of France (1643–1715).

HOUSE OF VALOIS

1328–1350	King	Philip VI, nephew of Philip IV	b. 1293	d. 1350
1350–1364	„	John II the Good, son of Philip VI	b. 1319	
1364–1380	„	Charles V the Wise, son of John II	b. 1337	d. 1380
1380–1422	„	Charles VI the Foolish, son of Charles V	b. 1368	d. 1422
1422–1461	„	Charles VII, son of Charles VI	b. 1403	d. 1461
1461–1483	„	Louis XI, son of Charles VII	b. 1423	d. 1483
1483–1498	„	Charles VIII, son of Louis XI	b. 1470	d. 1498
1498–1515	„	Louis XII, brother-in-law of Charles VIII	b. 1462	d. 1515
1515–1547	„	Francis I, second son of Louis XII	b. 1494	d. 1547
1547–1559	„	Henry II, son of Francis I	b. 1519	d. 1559
1559–1560	„	Francis II, son of Henry II	b. 1544	d. 1560
1560–1563	Regent	Catharine de' Medici, consort of Henry II	b. 1519	d. 1589
1560–1574	King	Charles IX, son of Henry II	b. 1550	d. 1574
1574–1589	„	Henry III, son of Henry II	b. 1551	assassinated 1589

HOUSE OF BOURBON

1589–1610	„	Henry IV, son-in-law of Henry II	b. 1553	assassinated 1610
1610–1617	Regent	Marie de' Medici, consort of Henry IV	b. 1573	d. 1642
1610–1643	King	Louis XIII, son of Henry IV	b. 1601	d. 1643
1643–1651	Regent	Anne of Austria, consort of Louis XIII	b. 1601	d. 1666
1643–1715	King	Louis XIV, son of Louis XIII	b. 1638	d. 1715
1715–1723	Regent	Philip of Orleans, nephew of Louis XIV	b. 1674	d. 1723
1715–1774	King	Louis XV, great-grandson of Louis XIV	b. 1710	d. 1774
1774–1792	„	Louis XVI, grandson of Louis XV	b. 1754	guillotined 1793
1793–1795	nominal King	Louis XVII, son of Louis XVI	b. 1785	d. 1795 ?

THE FIRST REPUBLIC
(National Convention, 1792; Directory, 1795; Consulate, 1799)

1799–1804	First consul	Napoleon Bonaparte	b. 1769	d. 1821

THE FIRST EMPIRE

1804–1814	Emperor	Napoleon I abdicated 1814	
1815	„	Napoleon I	

THE RESTORATION

1814–1824	King	Louis XVIII, brother of Louis XVI	b. 1755	d. 1824
1824–1830	„	Charles X, brother of Louis XVIII abdicated 1830	b. 1757	d. 1836
1830–1848	„	Louis-Philippe abdicated 1848	b. 1773	d. 1850

THE SECOND REPUBLIC

1848–1852	President	Charles Louis Napoleon Bonaparte, nephew of Napoleon I	b. 1808	d. 1873

THE SECOND EMPIRE

1852–1871	Emperor	Napoleon III (Charles Louis Napoleon)

(The Committee of Public Defence governed from 1870–1871)

THE THIRD REPUBLIC

1871–1873	President	Louis Adolphe Thiers	b. 1797	d. 1877
1873–1879	,,	Marie Edme Patrice Maurice de MacMahon	b. 1808	d. 1893
1879–1887	,,	François Paul Jules Grévy	b. 1807	d. 1891
1887–1894	,,	Marie-François Sadi-Carnot	b. 1837	d. 1894
1894–1895	,,	Jean Paul Pierre Casimir-Périer	b. 1847	d. 1907
1895–1899	,,	François Félix Faure	b. 1841	d. 1899
1899–1906	,,	Émile Loubet	b. 1838	d. 1929
1906–1913	,,	Clément Armand Fallières	b. 1841	d. 1931
1913–1920	,,	Raymond Poincaré	b. 1860	d. 1934
1920	,,	Paul Deschanel	b. 1856	d. 1922
1920–1924	,,	Alexandre Millerand	b. 1859	d. 1943
1924–1931	,,	Gaston Doumergue	b. 1863	d. 1937
1931–1932	,,	Paul Doumer	b. 1857	assassinated 1932
1932–1940	,,	Albert Lebrun	b. 1871	d. 1950

Napoleon III and his son the Prince Imperial pose at Fontainebleau in 1860 with the members of the Imperial family and court.

VICHY GOVERNMENT

1940–1944	Chief of State	Henri Philippe Pétain	b. 1856	d. 1951
1942–1944	Premier	Pierre Laval	b. 1883	executed 1945

PROVISIONAL GOVERNMENT

1944–1946	Head of State	Charles André Joseph Marie de Gaulle	b. 1890	
1946	President	Felix Gouin	b. 1884	
1946	President (provisional)	Georges Augustin Bidault	b. 1899	
1946	,,	Léon Blum	b. 1872	d. 1950

THE FOURTH REPUBLIC

1947–1954	President	Vincent Auriol	b. 1884	d. 1966
1954–1959	,,	René Coty	b. 1882	d. 1962

THE FIFTH REPUBLIC

1959–1969	President	Charles A. J. M. de Gaulle		

De Gaulle symbolized and led French resistance to Germany during the Second World War, and afterwards, as President of the Fifth Republic, provided his country with firm and efficient government.

STATESMEN

1624–1642	First Minister	Richelieu, Duc de (Armand Jean du Plessis)	b. 1585	d. 1642
1643–1661	,,	Jules Mazarin	b. 1602	d. 1661
1666–1691	Minister of War	Francois Michel Le Tellier, Marquis de Louvois	b. 1641	d. 1691
1665–1683	Treasurer	Jean Baptiste Colbert	b. 1619	d. 1683
1726–1743	First Minister	André Hercule de Fleury	b. 1653	d. 1743
1758–1761	Foreign Secretary	Étienne François de Choiseul	b. 1719	d. 1785
1766–1770	Minister of War	Étienne François de Choiseul		
1774–1776	Minister of Finance	Anne Robert Jacques Turgot	b. 1727	d. 1781
1776–1781	,,	Jacques Necker	b. 1732	d. 1804
1783–1787	,,	Charles Alexandre de Calonne	b. 1734	d. 1802
1788–1790	,,	Jacques Necker		
1793–1794	Dictator	Maximilien Robespierre	b. 1758	guillotined 1794
1797–1807	Foreign Secretary	Charles Maurice de Talleyrand-Périgord	b. 1754	d. 1838
1814–1815	Prime Minister	Charles Maurice de Talleyrand-Périgord		
1830–1834	Minister of War	Nicolas Jean de Dieu Soult	b. 1769	d. 1851
1840–1848	Premier	François Pierre Guillaume Guizot	b. 1787	d. 1874
1880–1881	,,	Jules Ferry	b. 1832	d. 1893
1881–1882	,,	Léon Gambetta	b. 1838	d. 1882
1883–1885	,,	Jules Ferry		
1906–1909	,,	Georges Clemenceau	b. 1841	d. 1929
1909–1911	,,	Aristide Briand	b. 1862	d. 1932
1912–1913	,,	Raymond Poincaré	b. 1860	d. 1934
1913–	,,	Aristide Briand		
1915–1917	Coalition head	Aristide Briand		
1917–1920	Premier	Georges Clemenceau		
1921–1922	Coalition head	Aristide Briand		
1922–1924	Premier	Raymond Poincaré		
1924–1925	,,	Edouard Herriot	b. 1872	d. 1957
1925–1926	,,	Aristide Briand		
1926–1929	,,	Raymond Poincaré		
1929	,,	Aristide Briand		
1930	,,	Camille Chautemps	b. 1885	d. 1963
1931–1932	,,	Pierre Laval	b. 1883	d. 1945
1932	,,	Aristide Briand		
1932	,,	Edouard Herriot		
1933	,,	Edouard Daladier	b. 1884	
1933–1934	,,	Camille Chautemps		
1934 (11 days)	,,	Edouard Daladier		
1936–1937	,,	Léon Blum	b. 1872	d. 1950
1937–1938	,,	Camille Chautemps		
1938–1940	,,	Edouard Daladier		
1940	,,	Paul Reynaud	b. 1878	d. 1966
1946–1947	,,	Léon Blum		
1947	,,	Paul Ramadier	b. 1888	
1947–1948	,,	Robert Schuman	b. 1886	
1948	,,	André Désiré Paul Marie	b. 1897	
1948	,,	Robert Schuman		

Pierre Mendès-France,
Premier of France
(1954–1955).

Charles de Gaulle,
President of France
(1959–1969).

Georges Pompidou,
Premier of France
(1962–1968).

1948–1949	Premier	Henri Queuille	b. 1884
1949–1950	,,	Georges Augustin Bidault	b. 1899
1950	,,	Henri Queuille	
1950–1951	,,	René Pleven	b. 1901
1951 (for 3 days)	,,	Henri Queuille	
1951–1952	,,	René Pleven	
1952	,,	Edgar Faure	b. 1908
1952–1953	,,	Antoine Pinay	b. 1891
1953	,,	René Joël Simon Mayer	b. 1895
1953–1954	,,	Joseph Laniel	b. 1889
1954–1955	,,	Pierre Mendès-France	b. 1907
1955–1956	,,	Edgar Faure	
1956–1957	,,	Guy Mollet	b. 1905
1957	,,	Maurice Jean-Marie Bourgès-Maunoury	b. 1914
1957–1958	,,	Félix Gaillard	b. 1919
1958	,,	Pierre Pflimlin	b. 1907
1958–1959	,,	Charles André Joseph Marie de Gaulle	
1959–1962	,,	Michel Jean-Pierre Debré	b. 1912
1962–1968	,,	Georges Jean Raymond Pompidou	b. 1911
1968–	,,	Maurice Couve de Murville	b. 1907

BRITTANY (Fr. Bretagne)

(In the 10th century Brittany threw off Frankish rule and maintained its identity until
the marriages of the Duchess Anne first to Charles VIII of France and then to
Louis XII led to its union with France)

987– 992	Duke	Conan I		d. 992
992–1008	,,	Geoffroi I		d. 1008
1008–1040	,,	Alain V		d. 1040
1040–1066	,,	Conan II		d. 1066
1066–1084	,,	Hoel V		d. 1084
1084–1112	,,	Alain VI		d. 1112
1112–1148	,,	Conan III	b. 1089	d. 1148
1148–1156	,,	Eudes		d. 1156
1156–1171	,,	Conan IV		d. 1171
1171–1186	,,	Geoffroi II	b. 1158	d. 1186
1196–1203	,,	Arthur I	b. 1187	d. 1203
1213–1237	,,	Pierre I		d. 1250
1237–1286	,,	Jean I	b. 1217	d. 1286
1286–1305	,,	Jean II	b. 1239	d. 1305
1305–1312	,,	Arthur II	b. 1262	d. 1312
1312–1341	,,	Jean III	b. 1276	d. 1341
1341–1364	,,	Charles		
1364–1399	,,	Jean IV		

1399–1442	Duke	Jean V		
1442–1450	,,	François I	b. 1414	d. 1450
1450–1457	,,	Pierre II		
1457–1458	,,	Arthur III	b. 1393	d. 1458
1458–1488	,,	François II		
1488–1514	Duchess	Anne	b. 1477	d. 1514

BURGUNDY (KINGDOM)
(Burgundian Kingdom established in Gaul by Gundicar)

413– 436	King	Gundicar		killed 436
436– 473?	,,	Gunderic		d. 473?
473– 516	,,	Gundobad, son of Gunderic		d. 516
516– 523	,,	Sigismund, son of Gundobad		d. 524
523– 532	,,	Gundimar, brother of Sigismund		killed 532

(Burgundy incorporated in the Kingdom of the Franks in 532; in 840 it again became an independent Kingdom)

840– 855	Emperor	Louis I	b. 795?	d. 855
855– 863	King	Charles, son of Louis I	b. 823	d. 877
863– 875	,,	Louis II, son of Louis I	b. 806?	d. 876
		(see Germany)		
875– 877	,,	Charles the Bald, son of Louis I	b. 823	d. 877
		(see France)		
877– 879	,,	Louis II the Stammerer, son of Charles the Bald	b. 846	d. 879

Charles the Bold, Duke of Burgundy (1467–1477) and his Council at Malines in 1474.

PROVENCE (LOWER BURGUNDY)

879– 887	King	Boso of Vienne, brother-in-law of Charles the Bald	d. 887
887– 924	,,	Louis, son of Boso of Vienne	d. 928
924– 933	,,	Hugh of Arles (King of Italy)	d. 947

UPPER (TRANSJURANE) BURGUNDY

888– 911	,,	Rudolf I, son of Conrad, Count of Auxerre	d. 911
911– 937	,,	Rudolf II, son of Rudolf I	d. 937
		(of Upper and Lower Burgundy)	

BURGUNDY

937– 993	,,	Conrad, son of Rudolf II	
993–1032	,,	Rudolf III, son of Conrad	d. 1032
		(Burgundy united with Germany 1034)	
1034–1039	Emperor	Conrad II (King of Germany)	b. 990? d. 1039

BURGUNDY (DUCHY)

956– 965	Duke	Otto, brother of Hugh Capet		
965–1002	„	Henry, brother of Otto		d. 1002
1002–1017	„	Robert II (see France), son of Hugh Capet		
1017–1031	„	Henry (see France), son of Robert II		
1031–1075	„	Robert, son of King Robert of France		d. 1075
1075–1078	„	Hugh I, grandson of Robert	b. 1040 ?	d. 1093
1078–1102	„	Odo (Eudes) I, brother of Hugh I		
1102–1142	„	Hugh II, nephew of Hugh I		
1162–1193	„	Hugh III, grandson of Hugh II	b. 1150 ?	d. 1193
1193–1218	„	Odo (Eudes) III, son of Hugh III		

John the Fearless, Duke of Burgundy (1404–1419) shown here with his consort, Margaret of Bavaria, was an ally of England in the Hundred Years' War.

1218–1272	Duke	Hugh IV, grandson of Hugh III	b. 1212	d. 1272
1272–1309	„	Robert II		
1305–1315	„	Hugh V, grandson of Hugh IV		
1315–1350	„	Odo (Eudes) IV, son of Robert II		
1350–1361	„	Philippe de Rouvres	b. 1345	d. 1361
		(Burgundy returned to the French crown in 1361)		
1363–1404	„	Philip the Bold, son of John the Good, King of France	b. 1342	d. 1404
1404–1419	„	John the Fearless, son of Philip the Bold	b. 1371	murdered 1419
1419–1467	„	Philip II the Good, son of John the Fearless	b. 1396	d. 1467
1467–1477	„	Charles the Bold, son of Philip II the Good	b. 1433	killed 1477
1477–1482	Duchess	Mary (wife of Maximilian of Austria), daughter of Charles the Bold	b. 1457	d. 1482
1482–1506	Duke	Philip the Fair (King of Spain), son of Mary of Burgundy	b. 1478	d. 1506
1506–1529	„	Charles V (Holy Roman Emperor), son of Philip the Fair	b. 1500	d. 1558
		(The Duchy was incorporated in France in 1529)		

CHAMPAGNE

(Champagne emerged as one of the most powerful vassal states of France in the Middle Ages)

864– 866	Count	Robert	d. 866
1004–1037	„	Eudes	d. 1037
1037–1047	„	Etienne	d. 1047
1047–1089	„	Thibaut I	d. 1089
1089–1125	„	Hugues I	d. 1125
1148–1152	„	Thibaut II	d. 1152

1152–1181	Count	Henri I		d. 1181
1181–1197	,,	Henri II	b. 1150	d. 1197
1197–1201	,,	Thibaut III		d. 1201
1201–1253	,,	Thibaut IV	b. 1201	d. 1253
1253–1270	,,	Henri III		d. 1274
1274–1304	Countess	Jeanne I	b. 1270	d. 1304
1304–1316	Count	Louis	b. 1289	d. 1316

(From the mid-13th century the Counts of Champagne were also Kings of Navarre. Jeanne I of Champagne, as Queen Juana of Navarre, married Philip IV of France. Their son, Louis X, inherited Champagne from his mother, and it subsequently was annexed to France)

LORRAINE (Ger. Lothringen)

(The Duchy of Lorraine emerged in the 10th century A.D. as a fief of the Holy Roman Empire)

1312–1328	Duke	Frédéric IV	
1328–1346	,,	Rodolphe	
1346–1391	,,	Jean	
1391–1431	,,	Charles I	
1431–1480	,,	René I	
1480–1508	,,	René II	
1508–1544	,,	Antoine	
1544–1545	,,	François	
1545–1608	,,	Charles II	
1608–1624	,,	Henri	
1624–1625	,,	François II	d. 1632
1625–1634	,,	Charles III	d. 1675
		(occupied by France)	
1659–1669	Duke	Nicolas François	d. 1670
		(re-occupied by France)	

Philip the Good, Duke of Burgundy (1419–1467) founded the Order of the Golden Fleece to commemorate his marriage to Isabella of Portugal.

(Left) Antoine, Duke of Lorraine (1508–1544).

(Right) Charles III, Duke of Lorraine (1625–1634)

1697–1729	Duke	Leopold	
1729–1735	,,	François Etienne	d. 1765

(François Etienne exchanged the throne of Lorraine for that of Tuscany in 1735, Lorraine then being given to Stanislaus I, the deposed King of Poland)

1735–1766   King   Stanislaus   b. 1677   d. 1766
(Lorraine was not raised to the rank of a kingdom, yet Stanislaus retained the title of
King, under the protection of his son-in-law, Louis XV of France. On the death of
Stanislaus, Lorraine became part of France)

NORMANDY
(Established by the North Men under Rollo)

911– 927 Viking Leader Rollo   b. 860?   d. 931?
After invading northwest France, Rollo seized Rouen and the land surround-
ing it and Charles the Simple granted him part of Neustria. Rollo then
embraced Christianity and became ruler of Normandy.

927– 942	Duke	William I Longsword, son of Rollo	assassinated 942
942– 996	,,	Richard I the Fearless, son of William Longsword	d. 996
996–1027	,,	Richard II the Good, son of Richard I	d. 1027
1027–1028	,,	Richard III	
1028–1035	,,	Robert the Devil, son of Richard II the Good	d. 1035
1035–1087	,,	William I the Conqueror, son of Robert the Devil	b. 1027 d. 1087
1087–1106	,,	Robert II, son of William the Conqueror	b. 1056 d. 1134
1106–1135	,,	Henry I, son of William the Conqueror	b. 1068 d. 1135
1135–1167	Duchess	Matilda, daughter of Henry I	b. 1102 d. 1167
1135–1151	Duke	Stephen of Blois, nephew of Henry I	b. 1094? d. 1154
1151–1189	,,	Henry II Plantagenet, grandson of Henry I	b. 1133 d. 1189
1189–1199	,,	Richard I Coeur de Lion, son of Henry II	b. 1157 d. 1199
1199–1204	,,	John Lackland, son of Henry II	b. 1167? d. 1216

(Normandy was incorporated in France in 1204)

Gabon

(One of the earliest French settlements on the African coast; elected to remain an
autonomous republic within the French Community, 1958; fully independent from 1960)

1960–1967	President	Léon M'ba	b. 1902 d. 1967
1967–	,,	Albert-Bernard Bongo	b. 1936

Gambia

*King George V of England (1910–
1936) reigned over the British
Empire at its greatest extent.
Gambia was one small part of his
realm.*

(Created a British colony, 1843; became an independent state within the Commonwealth,
1965)

1965–1966	Governor-General	Sir John Warburton Paul	b. 1916
1965–	Prime Minister	Sir Dauda Kairaba Jawara	b. 1924

Georgia, see Russia

Germany *(Ger. Deutschland)*

*William I, Emperor of Germany
(1871–1888).*

English versions of the names of rulers
of German-speaking states are:

Albert–Adalbert, Albrecht	Henry–Heinrich
Charles–Karl	Joseph–Josef
Ernest–Ernst	John–Johann
Eugene–Eugen	Louis–Ludwig
Francis–Franz	Maurice–Moritz
Frederick–Friedrich	Philip–Philipp
George–Georg	William–Wilhelm

EMPERORS
(Hohenzollern Dynasty)

1871–1888	Emperor	William I (of Prussia)	b. 1797	d. 1888
1888	„	Frederick III, son of William I	b. 1831	d. 1888
1888–1918	„	William II, son of Frederick III abdicated 1918	b. 1859	d. 1941

REPUBLIC

1919–1925	President	Friedrich Ebert	b. 1871	d. 1925
1925–1933	„	Paul von Hindenburg	b. 1847	d. 1934

NATIONAL SOCIALIST REGIME

1934	„	Paul von Hindenburg		
1934–1945	Leader	Adolf Hitler	b. 1889	d. 1945

Adolf Hitler's regime proved disastrous for Germany. When he committed
suicide in April 1945, Germany's cities were in ruins, millions of soldiers,
civilians and concentration camp inmates dead, and the entire country
was occupied by British, French, American and Russian troops.

(Allied occupation 1945–1949)

FEDERAL REPUBLIC

1949–1959	President	Theodor Heuss	b. 1884	d. 1959
1959–	„	Heinrich Lübke	b. 1894	
1949–1963	Federal Chancellor	Konrad Adenauer	b. 1876	d. 1967
1963–1966	„	Ludwig Erhard	b. 1897	
1966–	„	Kurt G. Kiesinger	b. 1904	

*(Left) Frederick III of Prussia,
Emperor of Germany (1888).*

*(Right) William II, Emperor
of Germany (1888–1918).*

Paul von Hindenburg,
President of Germany
(1925–1934).

Adolf Hitler, Führer
(Leader) of Germany
(1934–1945).

STATESMEN

1807–1808	First Minister	Karl von Stein	b. 1757	d. 1831
1813–1815	(Prussia)	Karl von Stein		
1862–1871	Prime Minister (Prussia)	Otto Eduard Leopold, Prince von Bismarck	b. 1815	d. 1898
1871–1890	Chancellor	Otto Eduard Leopold, Prince von Bismarck		

Bismarck aimed to free the German states from foreign control and unite them under the crown of Prussia. This he did, at the expense of Austria and France, restoring the German Empire under a Hohenzollern king, with himself as chancellor.

(Left) Otto von Bismarck, Chancellor of Germany (1871–1890); (Middle) Konrad Adenauer, Chancellor of West Germany (1949–1963); (Right) Ludwig Erhard, Chancellor of West Germany (1963–1966).

1890–1894	Chancellor	Count Georg Leo von Caprivi	b. 1831	d. 1899
1894–1900	,,	Prince Chlodwig Karl Viktor Hohenlohe-Schillingsfürst	b. 1819	d. 1901
1900–1909	,,	Prince Bernhard von Bülow	b. 1849	d. 1929
1909–1917	,,	Theobald von Bethmann-Hollweg	b. 1856	d. 1921
1917	,,	Georg Michaelis	b. 1857	d. 1936
1917–1918	,,	Count Georg von Hertling	b. 1843	d. 1919
1918	,,	Maximilian (Prince Max of Baden)	b. 1867	d. 1929
1918–1919	,,	Friedrich Ebert	b. 1871	d. 1925
1919	Prime Minister	Philipp Scheidemann	b. 1865	d. 1939
1919–1920	,,	Gustav Adolf Bauer	b. 1870	d. 1944
1920	Chancellor	Hermann Müller	b. 1876	d. 1931
1920–1921	,,	Konstantin Fehrenbach	b. 1852	d. 1926
1921–1922	,,	Karl Joseph Wirth	b. 1879	d. 1956
1922–1923	,,	Wilhelm Cuno	b. 1876	d. 1933
1923	,,	Gustav Stresemann	b. 1878	d. 1929
1923–1925	,,	Wilhelm Marx	b. 1863	d. 1946
1925–1926	,,	Hans Luther	b. 1879	d. 1962
1926–1928	,,	Wilhelm Marx		
1928–1930	,,	Hermann Müller		
1930–1932	,,	Heinrich Brüning	b. 1885	

1932	Chancellor	Franz von Papen	b. 1879	
1932–1933	„	Kurt von Schleicher	b. 1882	d. 1934
1933–1945	„	Adolf Hitler		
1945	„	Karl Dönitz	b. 1891	

DEMOCRATIC REPUBLIC (East Germany)
(Not officially recognized by the Western Powers)

1949–1960	Chairman, Council of State	Wilhelm Pieck		d. 1960
1960–	„	Walter Ulbricht	b. 1893	
1960–	Prime Minister	Otto Grotewohl	b. 1894	
1964–	„	Willi Stoph	b. 1914	

Walter Ulbricht, Chairman of the Council of State, German Democratic Republic (1960–   ).

BADEN

Karl Friedrich, Margrave, Elector and Grand Duke of Baden (1738–1811).

Leopold I, Grand Duke of Baden (1830–1852).

(Baden developed from several petty states, formerly part of Swabia)
HOUSE OF BADEN-DURLACH

1533–1552	Margrave	Ernst (abdicated)	b. 1482	d. 1553
1552–1577	„	Karl II	b. 1529	d. 1577
1577–1604	„	Ernst Friedrich	b. 1560	d. 1604
1604–1622	„	Georg Friedrich (abdicated)	b. 1573	d. 1638
1622–1659	„	Friedrich V	b. 1594	d. 1659
1659–1677	„	Friedrich VI	b. 1617	d. 1677
1677–1688	„	Friedrich VII	b. 1647	d. 1709
1688–1697		(French intervention)		
1697–1709	„	Friedrich VII (restored)		
1709–1738	„	Karl III Wilhelm	b. 1679	d. 1738
1738–1803	„	Karl Friedrich	b. 1728	d. 1811
1803–1806	Elector	Karl Friedrich		
1806–1811	Grand Duke	Karl Friedrich		
1811–1818	„	Karl Ludwig Friedrich		
1818–1830	„	Ludwig I	b. 1763	d. 1830
1830–1852	„	Leopold I	b. 1790	d. 1852
1852–1907	„	Friedrich I	b. 1826	d. 1907
1907–1918	„	Friedrich II	b. 1857	d. 1928

(The monarchy was abolished in 1918 and Baden became part of the German Republic)

Friedrich I, Grand Duke of Baden (1852–1907).

Friedrich II, Grand Duke of Baden (1907–1918).

(Right) Maximilian I Joseph, King of Bavaria (1806–1825).

(Left)
Charles Albert, Elector of Bavaria
(1726–1745).

BAVARIA (Ger. Bayern)

912– 937	Duke	Arnulf the Bad		
938– 947	,,	Berchtold, brother of Arnulf		d. 947
947– 955	,,	Henry I, brother of Otto the Great		d. 955
955– 978	,,	Henry II, son of Henry I	b. 915	d. 995
982– 985	,,	Henry III, son of Henry I		
985– 995	,,	Henry II		
995–1002	,,	Henry IV, son of Henry II, Emperor 1002-1024	b. 973	d. 1024
1002–1026	,,	Henry V of Lützelburg (Luxemburg)		d. 1026
1026–1042	,,	Henry VI (Emperor Henry III)		
1042–1047	,,	Henry VII		
1049–1053	,,	Konrad I		
1053–1056	,,	Henry VIII (Emperor Henry IV)		d. 1106
1056	,,	Konrad II		
1056–1061	Duchess	Agnes		

Guelph (or Welf) dynasty

1061–1070	Duke	Otto of Nordheim		d. 1083
1070–1101	,,	Guelph I, son-in-law of Henry IV, Emperor		
1101–1120	,,	Guelph II, son of Guelph I		
1120–1126	,,	Henry IX, brother of Guelph II		d. 1126
1126–1139	,,	Henry X the Proud, son of Henry IX	b. 1108 ?	d. 1139
1139–1141	,,	Leopold IV of Austria		d. 1141
1143–1156	,,	Henry XI, brother of Leopold of Austria		
1156–1180	,,	Henry XII the Lion, son of Henry X	deposed 1180 b. 1129	d. 1195

House of Wittelsbach

1180–1183	,,	Otto I	b. 1120 ?	d. 1183
1183–1231	,,	Ludwig I, son of Otto I	b. 1174	assassinated 1231
1231–1253	,,	Otto II the Illustrious, son of Ludwig I		d. 1253
1253–1294	,,	Ludwig II the Stern, son of Otto II	b. 1229	d. 1294
1294–1317	,,	Rudolph, son of Ludwig II	b. 1274	
1314–1347	Co-ruler	Emperor Ludwig III, brother of Rudolph	b. 1283 ?	d. 1347

(Country divided 1329 into Bavaria and the Palatinate; Bavaria divided after 1347 into several parts)

1375–1397	Duke	John of Munich, grandson of Emperor Ludwig	abdicated 1397	d. 1413?
1397–1438	,,	Ernst, son of John of Munich		d. 1438
1438–1460	,,	Albert III the Pious, son of Ernst		d. 1460
1460–1467	,,	Sigismund, son of Albert III	abdicated 1467	d. 1501
1460–1508	,,	Albert IV, brother of Sigismund		d. 1508
1508–1550	,,	William IV, son of Albert IV		d. 1550
1550–1579	,,	Albert V, son of William IV		d. 1579
1579–1597	,,	William V the Pious, son of Albert V		d. 1626
1597–1623	,,	Maximilian I, son of William V	b. 1573	d. 1651

(The Duchy became an Electorate in 1623)

1623–1651	Elector	Maximilian I (The Great)		
1651–1679	,,	Ferdinand Maria, son of Maximilian	b. 1636	d. 1679
1679–1706	,,	Maximilian II Emanuel, son of Ferdinand Maria	b. 1662	d. 1726

(Deposed after Blenheim, reinstated by Treaty of Utrecht)

1714–1726	,,	Maximilian II Emanuel		
1726–1745	,,	Charles Albert, son of Maximilian II Emanuel	b. 1697	d. 1745

(Holy Roman Emperor, 1742–1745)

1745–1777	,,	Maximilian III Joseph, son of Charles Albert	b. 1727	d. 1777
1777–1799	,,	Charles Theodore of the Palatinate, son of John Christian Joseph	b. 1724	d. 1799
1799–1805	,,	Maximilian IV Joseph	b. 1756	d. 1825
1806–1825	King	Maximilian I Joseph		
1825–1848	,,	Ludwig I, son of Elector Maximilian	b. 1786 abdicated 1848	d. 1868
1848–1864	,,	Maximilian II Joseph, son of Ludwig I	b. 1811	d. 1864
1864–1886	,,	Ludwig II, son of Maximilian II	b. 1845	d. 1886
1886–1913	,,	Otto III, brother of Ludwig II deposed 1913	b. 1848	d. 1916
1886–1912	Regent	Luitpold, brother of Maximilian II	b. 1821	d. 1912
1912–1913	,,	Ludwig III, son of Prince Regent Luitpold	b. 1845	d. 1921
1913–1918	King	Ludwig III	abdicated 1918	

(Left) Maximilian II Joseph, King of Bavaria (1848–1864).

(Right) Ludwig II, King of Bavaria (1864–1886).

BRANDENBURG
Ascanian dynasty

1134–1170	Margrave	Albert I the Bear	b. 1100?	d. 1170
1170–1184	,,	Otto I, son of Albert the Bear	b. 1130?	d. 1184
1184–1205	,,	Otto II, son of Otto I		
1205–1220	,,	Albert II, brother of Otto II	b. 1174?	d. 1220
1220–1266	,,	John I, son of Albert II		d. 1266
1220–1267	,,	Otto III, son of Albert II (ruled jointly with John I)		d. 1267
1266–1309	,,	Otto IV, son of John I		
1309–1319	,,	Waldemar the Great, nephew of Otto IV	b. 1281?	d. 1319
1319–1320	,,	Henry the Child, cousin of Waldemar		d. 1320

Wittelsbach dynasty

1322–1351	Margrave	Louis V, son of Emperor Louis III	b. 1315	d. 1361
1351–1365	Elector	Louis the Roman, brother of Louis V	b. 1330	d. 1365
1365–1373	„	Otto, brother of Louis	b. 1341	d. 1379
1373–1378	Emperor	Charles IV	b. 1316	d. 1378
1378–1417	„	Sigismund of Hungary, son of Charles IV	b. 1368	d. 1437

Hohenzollern dynasty

1417–1440	Elector	Frederick of Nuremberg	b. 1371	d. 1440
1440–1470	„	Frederick II, son of Frederick of Nuremberg	b. 1413	d. 1471
1470–1486	„	Albert III, brother of Frederick II	b. 1414	d. 1486
1486–1499	„	John Cicero, son of Albert III	b. 1455	d. 1499
1499–1535	„	Joachim I, son of John Cicero	b. 1484	d. 1535
1535–1571	„	Joachim II, son of Joachim I	b. 1513	d. 1571
1571–1598	„	John George, son of Joachim II	b. 1525	d. 1598
1598–1608	„	Joachim Frederick, son of John George	b. 1546	d. 1608
1608–1619	„	John Sigismund, son of Joachim Frederick	b. 1572	d. 1619
1619–1640	„	George William, son of John Sigismund	b. 1597	d. 1640
1640–1688	„	Frederick William, the "Great Elector," son of George William	b. 1620	d. 1688

After taking over a devastated country, Frederick William created a strong, standing army, rebuilt the war-damaged cities, including his capital, Berlin, founded the Prussian navy and even established colonies in West Africa.

(Left) John Sigismund, Elector of Brandenburg (1608–1619).

(Right) Frederick William, the "Great Elector" of Brandenburg (1640–1688).

1688–1701	Elector	Frederick III, son of Frederick William (see Prussia)	b. 1657	d. 1713

BRUNSWICK (Ger. Braunschweig)

(Wolfenbüttel Line)

(Brunswick appeared as a separate state in the 16th century)

1568–1589	Duke	Julius
1589–1613	„	Heinrich Julius
1613–1634	„	Friedrich Ulrich
1635–1666	„	August II
1666–1704	„	Rudolf August
1685–1714	„	Anton Ulrich (co-ruler)
1714–1731	„	August Wilhelm
1731–1735	„	Ludwig Rudolf
1735	„	Ferdinand Albrecht

Wilhelm, Duke of Brunswick (1831–1884).

Ernest August, Duke of Brunswick (1913–1918), with his consort Victoria Louise.

Friedrich Ulrich, Duke of Brunswick (1613–1634).

1735–1780	Duke	Karl		b. 1713	d. 1780
1780–1806	,,	Karl Wilhelm Ferdinand		b. 1735	d. 1806

(In 1806, taken by the French and in 1807 annexed to the Kingdom of Westphalia; in 1813, duchy restored)

1813–1815	Duke	Friedrich Wilhelm		b. 1771	d. 1815
1815–1830	,,	Karl II (deposed)		b. 1804	d. 1873
1831–1884	,,	Wilhelm		b. 1806	d. 1884

(The Dukes of Brunswick became extinct in the direct line in 1884 and the country was governed by Prussian regents until 1913)

1913–1918	Duke	Ernest August		b. 1887	d. 1953

(In 1918, Brunswick became part of the German Republic)

CLEVES (Ger. Kleve)

? –1448	Duke	Adolf I		d. 1448
1448–1481	,,	Johann I		
1481–1521	,,	Johann II		
1521–1539	,,	Johann III		
1539–1592	,,	Wilhelm		
1592–1609	,,	Johann Wilhelm		

(The Dukes of Cleves became extinct in 1609 and the Duchy was, after a long struggle, annexed to Brandenburg)

HANOVER (Ger. Hannover)

(Electorate of Hanover created in 1692 from the Duchy of Brunswick-Lüneburg)

1692–1698	Elector	Ernest Augustus		b. 1629	d. 1698
1698–1727	,,	George I		b. 1660	d. 1727

(George I succeeded to the throne of Great Britain in 1714)

1727–1760	Elector	George II		b. 1683	d. 1760
1760–1807	,,	George III		b. 1738	d. 1820
1807–1813		(Hanover annexed to Westphalia by Napoleon)			
1813–1815	,,	George III (restored)			

(1815 Hanover raised to a kingdom by the Congress of Vienna)

1815–1820	King	George III	

1820–1830	King	George IV	b. 1762	d. 1830
1830–1837	,,	William (William IV of England)	b. 1765	d. 1837

(Since women were barred from the throne of Hanover, the personal union with Great Britain ended with the death of William IV)

1837–1851	King	Ernest Augustus (son of George III)	b. 1771	d. 1851
1851–1866	,,	George V	b. 1819	d. 1878

(Hanover annexed by Prussia 1866)

(Left) George III, Elector (1760–1807, 1813–1815) and King (1815–1820) of Hanover; (Middle) Ernest Augustus, King of Hanover (1837–1851); (Right) George V, King of Hanover (1851–1866).

HESSE (Ger. Hessen)

(Hesse emerged as a fief of the Holy Roman Empire in the 13th century)

1247–1308	Landgrave	Heinrich I	b. 1244	d. 1308
1308–1328	,,	Otto	b. 1273	d. 1328
1328–1376	,,	Heinrich II	b. 1297	d. 1376
1377–1413	,,	Hermann I	b. 1340	d. 1413
1413–1458	,,	Ludwig I	b. 1402	d. 1458
1458–1471	,,	Ludwig II	b. 1438	d. 1471
1458–1483	,,	Henrich III	b. 1440	d. 1483
1471–1493	,,	Wilhelm I (abd.)	b. 1466	d. 1515
1493–1509	,,	Wilhelm II	b. 1468	d. 1509
1509–1567	,,	Philipp	b. 1504	d. 1567

(After the death of Philipp, Hesse was divided into several successor states, of which the chief were Hesse-Cassel and Hesse-Darmstadt)

HESSE-CASSEL (Ger. Hessen-Kassel)

1567–1592	Landgrave	Wilhelm IV	b. 1532	d. 1592
1592–1627	,,	Moritz (abd.)	b. 1572	d. 1632
1627–1637	,,	Wilhelm V	b. 1602	d. 1637
1637–1663	,,	Wilhelm VI	b. 1629	d. 1663
1663–1670	,,	Wilhelm VII	b. 1651	d. 1670
1670–1730	,,	Karl	b. 1654	d. 1730
1730–1751	,,	Friedrich I	b. 1676	d. 1751
1751–1760	,,	Wilhelm VIII	b. 1682	d. 1760
1760–1785	,,	Friedrich II	b. 1720	d. 1785
1785–1803	,,	Wilhelm IX	b. 1743	d. 1821

(The Landgrave of Hesse-Cassel assumed the title of Elector in 1803, Wilhelm IX becoming the Elector Wilhelm I)

1803–1807	Elector	Wilhelm I		
1807–1815		(Hesse-Cassel annexed to Kingdom of Westphalia)		
1815–1821	Elector	Wilhelm I (restored)		
1821–1847	,,	Wilhelm II	b. 1777	d. 1847
1847–1866	,,	Friedrich Wilhelm	b. 1802	d. 1875

(Hesse-Cassel annexed to Prussia in 1866)

(Left) Wilhelm II, Elector of Hesse-Cassel (1821–1847); (middle) Friedrich Wilhelm, Elector of Hesse-Cassel (1847–1866); (Right) Ludwig I, Grand Duke of Hesse-Darmstadt (1806–1830).

HESSE-DARMSTADT (Ger. Hessen-Darmstadt)

1567–1596	Landgrave	Georg I	b. 1547	d. 1596
1596–1626	,,	Ludwig V	b. 1577	d. 1626
1626–1661	,,	Georg II	b. 1605	d. 1661
1661–1678	,,	Ludwig VI	b. 1630	d. 1678
1678	,,	Ludwig VII	b. 1658	d. 1678
1678–1739	,,	Ernst Ludwig	b. 1667	d. 1739
1739–1768	,,	Ludwig VIII	b. 1691	d. 1768
1768–1790	,,	Ludwig IX	b. 1719	d. 1790

(In the course of the Napoleonic upheavals, Hesse-Darmstadt was raised to the rank of Grand Duchy)

1806–1830	Grand Duke	Ludwig I	b. 1753	d. 1830
1830–1848	,,	Ludwig II	b. 1777	d. 1848
1848–1877	,,	Ludwig III	b. 1806	d. 1877
1877–1892	,,	Ludwig IV	b. 1837	d. 1892
1892–1918	,,	Ernst Ludwig	b. 1868	

(In 1871 Hesse-Darmstadt entered the German Empire. In 1918 the Grand Duke was expelled and the country became part of the new German Republic)

PALATINATE (Ger. Pfalz)

1294–1319	Count Palatine	Rudolph of Bavaria		
1319–1327	,,	Adolph the Simple, son of Rudolph	b. 1300	d. 1327
1327–1353	,,	Rudolph II, son of Rudolph I	b. 1306	d. 1353
1353–1390	,,	Rupert I, son of Rudolph I	b. 1309	d. 1390
1390–1398	,,	Rupert II, son of Adolph the Simple	b. 1335	d. 1398
1398–1410	,,	Rupert III, son of Rupert II	b. 1352	d. 1410
		(see Emperors of the Holy Roman Empire, 1400)		
1410–1435	,,	Ludwig III, son of Rupert III		
1435–1449	,,	Ludwig IV, son of Ludwig III	b. 1424	d. 1449
1449–1476	,,	Frederick I the Victorious, son of Ludwig III	b. 1425	d. 1476
1476–1508	,,	Philip, son of Ludwig IV	b. 1448	d. 1508
1508–1544	,,	Ludwig V, son of Philip	b. 1478	d. 1544
1544–1556	,,	Frederick II the Wise, son of Philip	b. 1482	d. 1556
1556–1559	,,	Otto, grandson of Philip	b. 1502	d. 1559
1559–1576	Elector	Frederick III the Pious	b. 1515	d. 1576
1576–1583	,,	Ludwig VI, son of Frederick III	b. 1539	d. 1583
1583–1592	Guardian of Frederick IV John Casimir, son of Frederick III		b. 1543	d. 1592
1592–1610	Elector	Frederick IV the Upright, son of Ludwig VI	b. 1574	d. 1610

1610–1623	"The Winter King"	Frederick V, son of Frederick IV	b. 1596	d. 1632
		(see Czechoslovakia)		
		(Palatinate united with Bavaria 1623–1648)		
1648–1680	Elector	Charles Ludwig, son of Frederick V	b. 1617	d. 1680
1680–1685	,,	Charles, son of Charles Ludwig	b. 1651	d. 1685
1685–1690	,,	Philip William	b. 1615	d. 1690
1690–1716	,,	John William, son of Philip William	b. 1658	d. 1716
1716–1742	,,	Charles Philip, son of Philip William	b. 1661	d. 1742
1742–1799	,,	Charles Theodore (see Bavaria)	b. 1724	d. 1799

Charles Theodore was a patron of art and literature. A dispute with his heir, Charles of Zweibrücken, resulted in the War of the Bavarian Succession. War was declared and peace concluded without any actual battles taking place.

PRUSSIA (Ger. Preussen)
(Hohenzollern Dynasty)

1701–1713	King	Frederick I, (Frederick III of Brandenburg)	b. 1657	d. 1713
1713–1740	,,	Frederick William I, son of Frederick I	b. 1688	d. 1740
1740–1786	,,	Frederick II the Great, son of Frederick William I	b. 1712	d. 1786

Frederick the Great enlarged the boundaries of Prussia and developed its resources. He had a taste for music and French literature, and corresponded with Voltaire, whom he invited to live at his court. He built the palace of Sans Souci at Potsdam.

1786–1797	King	Frederick William II, nephew of Frederick II	b. 1744	d. 1797
1797–1840	,,	Frederick William III, son of Frederick William II	b. 1770	d. 1840
1840–1861	,,	Frederick William IV, son of Frederick William III	b. 1795	d. 1888
1861–1871	,,	William I, son of Frederick William IV	b. 1797	d. 1861

SAXONY (Ger. Sachsen)
(Wettin Dynasty)

1381–1423	Duke	Frederick I the Warlike, son of Frederick of Meissen	b. 1369	d. 1428
1423–1428	Elector	Frederick I the Warlike		
1428–1464	,,	Frederick II the Gentle, son of Frederick I	b. 1411?	d. 1464
1464–1486	,,	Ernest, son of Frederick II	b. 1441	d. 1486
1464–1500	Joint ruler	Albert III, son of Frederick II	b. 1443	d. 1500
		(Ernest and Albert divided Saxony in 1485)		
1486–1525	Elector	Frederick III the Wise, son of Ernest	b. 1463	d. 1525
1525–1532	,,	John the Constant, son of Ernest	b. 1469	d. 1532
1532–1547	,,	John Frederick the Magnanimous, son of John	b. 1503	d. 1554
1500–1539	Duke	George the Bearded, son of Albert	b. 1471	d. 1539
1539–1541	,,	Henry the Pious, son of Albert	b. 1473	d. 1541
1541–1547	,,	Maurice, son of Henry	b. 1521	d. 1553
1547–1553	Elector	Maurice, son of Henry		
1553–1586	,,	Augustus I, brother of Maurice	b. 1526	d. 1586
1586–1591	,,	Christian I, son of Augustus I	b. 1560	d. 1591
1591–1611	,,	Christian II, son of Christian I	b. 1583	d. 1611
1611–1656	,,	John George I, son of Christian I	b. 1585	d. 1656

1656–1680	Elector	John George II, son of John George I	b. 1613	d. 1680
1680–1691	„	John George III, son of John George II	b. 1647	d. 1691
1691–1694	„	John George IV, son of John George III	b. 1668	d. 1694
1694–1733	„	Frederick Augustus I, son of John George III (King of Poland from 1697)	b. 1670	d. 1733
1733–1763	„	Frederick Augustus II, son of Frederick Augustus I	b. 1696	d. 1763
1763	„	Frederick Christian, son of Frederick Augustus II	b. 1722	d. 1763
1763–1806	„	Frederick Augustus III, son of Frederick Christian	b. 1750	d. 1827

(Left) Frederick II the Great, King of Prussia (1740–1786).

(Right) Frederick Augustus II, Elector of Saxony (1733–1763).

1806–1827	King	Frederick Augustus I the Just		

Frederick Augustus I refused the Polish crown in 1791. Firstly an enemy of France and then an ally of Napoleon, he was deprived by the Congress of Vienna of half his kingdom.

1827–1836	King	Anthony, brother of Frederick Augustus I	b. 1755	d. 1836
1836–1854	„	Frederick Augustus II, nephew of Frederick Augustus I	b. 1797	d. 1854
1854–1873	„	John, brother of Frederick Augustus II	b. 1801	d. 1873
1873–1902	„	Albert, son of John	b. 1828	d. 1902
1902–1904	„	George, son of John	b. 1832	d. 1904
1904–1918	„	Frederick Augustus III, son of George abdicated 1918	b. 1865	d. 1932

SWABIA (Ger. Schwaben)

(Swabia was one of the principal states of the early Holy Roman Empire, corresponding roughly to Baden and Wurttemberg and adjacent territories.)

916– 926	Duke	Burchard I		d. 926
926– 948	„	Hermann I		d. 948
948– 957	„	Ludolf	b. 931	d. 957
957– 973	„	Burchard II		d. 973
973– 982	„	Otto I		d. 982
982– 997	„	Conrad I		d. 997
997–1004	„	Hermann II		d. 1004
1004–1012	„	Hermann III		d. 1012
1012–1015	„	Ernst I	b. 970	d. 1015
1015–1030	„	Ernst II	b. 1007	d. 1030
1030–1039	„	Hermann IV		d. 1039
1039–1045	„	Heinrich	b. 1017	d. 1056
1045–1047	„	Otto II		d. 1047
1047–1057	„	Otto III		d. 1057

1057–1080	Duke	Rudolf		d. 1080
1080–1105	,,	Friedrich I		d. 1105
1105–1147	,,	Friedrich II	b. 1090	d. 1147
1147–1152	,,	Friedrich III	b. 1122	d. 1190

(Friedrich III assumed the throne of Germany in 1152 and was crowned Emperor in 1155.
He is known to history as the Emperor Friedrich I Barbarossa)

1152–1167	Duke	Friedrich IV	b. 1144	d. 1167
1167–1191	,,	Friedrich V		d. 1191
1191–1196	,,	Conrad III	b. 1167	d. 1196
1196–1208	,,	Philipp	b. 1176	d. 1208
1208–1219	,,	Friedrich VI	b. 1194	d. 1250
1219–1235	,,	Heinrich II (abdicated)	b. 1212	d. 1242
1235–1254	,,	Conrad IV	b. 1228	d. 1254
1254–1268	,,	Conrad V	b. 1252	d. 1268

(The Duchy of Swabia broke up into many smaller successor states after 1268)

WESTPHALIA (Ger. Westfalen)

(The kingdom of Westphalia existed 1807–1814)

1807–1813	King	Jerome, brother of Napoleon abdicated 1813 b. 1784	d. 1860

Jerome Bonaparte's first wife was American but the French council of
state annulled this marriage. He settled in Florence after Napoleon's
abdication and after returning to France in 1847 was created marshal of
France by Louis Napoleon.

WURTTEMBERG (Ger. Wuerttemberg)

1083–1105	Count	Conrad I		
1110–	,,	Conrad II		
1134–1158	,,	Ludwig I		
1166–1181	,,	Ludwig II		
1201–1228	,,	Ludwig III		
1236–1241	,,	Eberhard I		
1241–1265	,,	Ulrich I		d. 1265
1265–1279	,,	Ulrich II		d. 1279
1279–1325	,,	Eberhard II	b. 1265	d. 1325
1325–1344	,,	Ulrich III	b. 1295	d. 1344
1344–1392	,,	Eberhard III	b. 1315	d. 1392
1344–1366	,,	Ulrich IV		d. 1366
1392–1417	,,	Eberhard IV		d. 1417
1417–1419	,,	Eberhard V	b. 1388	d. 1419
1419–1450	,,	Ludwig I	b. 1412	d. 1450
1450–1457	,,	Ludwig II	b. 1439	d. 1457
1457–1480	,,	Ulrich V	b. 1413	d. 1480

Wilhelm I, King of Wurttemberg (1816–1864).

Wilhelm II, King of Wurttemberg (1891–1918).

1480–1495	Count	Eberhard VI	b. 1445	d. 1496
1495–1496	Duke	Eberhard I		

(Count Eberhard VI assumed the title of Duke in 1495 as Eberhard I)

1496–1498	Duke	Eberhard II	b. 1447	d. 1504
1498–1519	,,	Heinrich	b. 1448	d. 1519
1498–1519	,,	Ulrich VI	b. 1487	d. 1550

(Interregnum)

1534–1550	,,	Ulrich VI (restored)		
1550–1568	,,	Christopher	b. 1515	d. 1568
1568–1593	,,	Ludwig III	b. 1554	d. 1593
1593–1608	,,	Friedrich I	b. 1557	d. 1608
1608–1628	,,	Johann Friedrich	b. 1585	d. 1628
1628–1674	,,	Eberhard III	b. 1614	d. 1674
1674–1677	,,	Wilhelm Ludwig	b. 1647	d. 1677
1677–1733	,,	Eberhard IV	b. 1676	d. 1733
1733–1737	,,	Karl Alexander	b. 1684	d. 1737
1737–1793	,,	Karl Eugen	b. 1728	d. 1793
1793–1795	,,	Ludwig Eugen	b. 1731	d. 1795
1795–1797	,,	Friedrich Eugen	b. 1732	d. 1797
1797–1802	,,	Friedrich II	b. 1754	d. 1816
1802–1806	Elector	Friedrich		

(In 1802 Duke Friedrich II assumed the title of Elector, and in 1806 that of King)

1806–1816	King	Friedrich		
1816–1864	,,	Wilhelm I	b. 1781	d. 1864
1864–1891	,,	Karl I	b. 1823	d. 1891
1891–1918	,,	Wilhelm II	b. 1848	d. 1921

(Wurttemberg had joined the German Empire in 1871. It remained a Kingdom within the Empire until 1918 when the monarchy was overthrown and the country became part of the German Republic)

Ghana

Kwame Nkrumah, President of Ghana (1960–1966), led his country to independence and was later ousted by a coup d'état.

(British colony of the Gold Coast established 1875; an independent state and member of the British Commonwealth, from 1957)

1957–1960	Prime Minister	Kwame Nkrumah	
1960–1966	President	(deposed)	b. 1909
1966–	Chairman of Liberation Council	Lt.-Gen. A. J. Ankrah	b. 1917

Gold Coast, see Ghana

Golden Horde, see Mongolia

Great Britain

St. Edward's Crown, used at the coronation of Queen Elizabeth II, is a replica made in 1660 of the crown used for six centuries at the coronation of British monarchs and destroyed during the Commonwealth period.

ENGLAND

(Anciently invaded by successive migrations of Celtic races; under the Romans from A.D. 43 to A.D. 410; divided into petty kingdoms during the period before Egbert)

Saxon Rulers of England

828– 839	King of Wessex	Egbert	d. 839
839– 858	,,	Ethelwulf, son of Egbert	d. 858
858– 860	,,	Ethelbald, son of Ethelwulf	
860– 866	,,	Ethelbert, son of Ethelwulf	
866– 871	King of Wessex and Kent	Ethelred I, son of Ethelwulf	d. 871
871– 899	King of Wessex and Overlord of England	Alfred the Great, son of Ethelwulf	b. 849 d. 899

Alfred the Great was sent to Rome at the age of five and confirmed by Leo IV. He began his battles with the Danes during the reign of his brother Ethelred, and in the succeeding years saved England and Western Europe from Scandinavian domination. By 896, the Danes realized he had beaten them. During the last years of his reign, Alfred made his famous series of translations to repair the intellectual vacuum caused by the Danish invasions.

Ethelbert, King of Wessex (860–866).

Alfred the Great, King of Wessex (871–899).

Ethelred II the Unready, King of England (978–1016).

899– 924	King of Angles and Saxons	Edward the Elder, son of Alfred	d. 924

(Note: Only the Danish invasions of the 9th century succeeded in converting the West Saxon overlordship into the Kingdom of all England)

924– 940	,,	Athelstan, son of Edward	b. 895? d. 940?
940– 946	King of England	Edmund I, brother of Athelstan	b. 922 d. 946
946– 955	,,	Edred, brother of Athelstan	d. 955
955– 958	,,	Edwy, son of Edmund I	b. 940 d. 958
959– 975	,,	Edgar, brother of Edwy	b. 944 d. 975
975– 978	,,	Edward the Martyr, son of Edgar	d. 978
978–1016	,,	Ethelred II the Unready, brother of Edward	b. 968 d. 1016
1016	,,	Edmund II Ironside, son of Ethelred II	b. 993? d. 1016

The body of Harold II (1066), last Saxon king of England, is brought before the Norman invader, William the Conqueror (thereafter William I of England) as depicted by Ford Madox Brown.

Danish Rulers of England

1016–1035 King of England Canute, son of Sweyn Forkbeard b. 1000 d. 1035

Son of Sweyn Forkbeard, King of Denmark, Canute took part in his father's conquest of Wessex at the age of 17 or 18. The first Danish king to coin money, he brought order to England, and as King of Denmark, defeated the combined fleets of Norway and Sweden.

1035–1040 King Harold I Harefoot, son of Canute d. 1040
1040–1042 „ Hardicanute, son of Canute b. 1019? d. 1042

Saxon Rulers Restored

1042–1066 „ Edward the Confessor, son of Ethelred II b. 1004? d. 1066
1066 „ Harold II, brother-in-law of Edward b. 1022? killed 1066

House of Normandy

1066–1087 „ William I the Conqueror b. 1027 d. 1087

William the Conqueror had three strong claims to the throne of England: his cousin, Edward the Confessor, probably promised the succession to him; his wife, Matilda, was a descendant of King Alfred; and his rival, Harold, had earlier promised to support his claim.

1087–1100 King William Rufus, son of William the Conqueror b. 1059 killed 1100
1100–1135 „ Henry I Beauclerc, son of William the Conqueror b. 1068 d. 1135

House of Blois

1135–1154 „ Stephen, nephew of Henry I b. 1094? d. 1154

House of Anjou (later called Plantagenet)

1154–1189 „ Henry II, grandson of Henry I b. 1133 d. 1189

Henry II, King of England (1154–1189) hears the plea of the Patriarch of Jerusalem to save the Holy Sepulchre.

(Left) Henry III, King of England (1216–1272); (Middle) Edward III, King of England (1327–1377); (Right) Richard II, King of England (1377–1399).

1189–1199	King	Richard I Coeur de Lion, son of Henry II	b. 1157	killed 1199
1199–1216	,,	John Lackland, son of Henry II	b. 1167	d. 1216
1216–1272	,,	Henry III, son of John	b. 1207	d. 1272
1272–1307	,,	Edward I Longshanks, son of Henry III	b. 1239	d. 1307
1307–1327	,,	Edward II, son of Edward I	b. 1284	murdered 1327
1327–1377	,,	Edward III, son of Edward II	b. 1312	d. 1377
1377–1399	,,	Richard II, grandson of Edward III	b. 1367	murdered 1400

House of Lancaster

| 1399–1413 | ,, | Henry IV Bolingbroke,
grandson of Edward III | b. 1367 | d. 1413 |
| 1413–1422 | ,, | Henry V, son of Henry IV | b. 1387 | d. 1422 |

Henry V is famous for the victory he won over the French at Agincourt— when 5,000 French nobles were killed as against the loss of 113 English.

| 1422–1461 | King | Henry VI, son of Henry V | b. 1421 | murdered 1471 |
| 1470–1471 | ,, | Henry VI (restored) | | |

House of York

| 1461–1470 | ,, | Edward IV, great-great-grandson of
Edward III | b. 1442 | d. 1483 |
| 1471–1483 | ,, | Edward IV (restored) | | |

Edward IV was a tyrannical despot, yet he had a remarkable ability to win popularity with ordinary citizens through his pleasant manners and fondness for the good things of life. He was a personal friend of William Caxton.

1483	King	Edward V, son of Edward IV b. 1470 murdered 1483
1483–1485	,,	Richard III,
		brother of Edward IV b. 1452 killed 1485

(Left) Henry IV, King of England (1399–1413); (Middle) Edward IV, King of England (1461–1483); (Right) Henry VII, King of England (1485–1509).

House of Tudor

1485–1509	King	Henry VII,
		son-in-law of Edward IV b. 1457 d. 1509
1509–1547	,,	Henry VIII, son of Henry VII b. 1491 d. 1547

Though many of his actions were inspired by selfish motives, Henry VIII performed vitally important services for his country. Although quite ruthless in dealing with his many wives and political opponents, during his reign religious civil war was prevented, national unity strengthened, the navy developed, and the powers of Parliament extended.

1547–1553	King	Edward VI, son of Henry VIII b. 1537 d. 1553
1553	Queen (for 9 days)	Jane (Lady Jane Grey) b. 1537 beheaded 1554
1553–1558	Queen	Mary I, daughter of Henry VIII b. 1516 d. 1558
1558–1603	,,	Elizabeth I, daughter of Henry VIII b. 1533 d. 1603

(Right) Mary I, Queen of England (1553–1558).

(Far right) Elizabeth I, Queen of England (1558–1603).

House of Stuart

1603–1625	King	James I, son of Mary, Queen of Scots b. 1566 d. 1625
1625–1649	,,	Charles I, son of James I b. 1600 beheaded 1649
		(Commonwealth 1649–1660)
1653–1658	Lord Protector	Oliver Cromwell b. 1599 d. 1658
1658–1659	,,	Richard Cromwell,
		son of Oliver Cromwell b. 1626 d. 1712

(Left) Charles I, King of England (1625–1649); (Middle) Oliver Cromwell, Lord Protector of England (1653–1658); (Right) James II, King of England (1685–1688).

(Left) Mary II, Queen of England (1689–1702); (Middle) George I, King of England (1714–1727); (Right) Victoria, Queen of England (1837–1901), with her consort, Prince Albert.

With the execution of Charles I, Oliver Cromwell thought the monarchy had been abolished forever. Yet three years after Cromwell's death, Charles's son, whom Cromwell had defeated at Worcester, was King of England, and Cromwell's body was disinterred from honorable burial in Westminster Abbey and hung on the gallows.

House of Stuart

1660–1685	King	Charles II, son of Charles I	b. 1630	d. 1685
1685–1688	„	James II, son of Charles I abdicated 1688	b. 1633	d. 1701

Houses of Orange and Stuart
(Revolution 1688)

1689–1702	Joint Rulers	{ William III of Orange	b. 1650	d. 1702
		{ Mary II, daughter of James II	b. 1662	d. 1694

House of Stuart

1702–1714	Queen	Anne, sister of Mary	b. 1665	d. 1714

House of Hanover or Brunswick

1714–1727	King	George I, great-grandson of James I	b. 1660	d. 1727
1727–1760	„	George II, son of George I	b. 1683	d. 1760
1760–1820	„	George III, grandson of George II	b. 1738	d. 1820

George III has gone down in history as the English king who lost the American colonies. Yet most people in England probably supported his American policies. At the age of 50 he became violently insane and had to be restrained in a straightjacket.

1820–1830	King	George IV, son of George III	b. 1762	d. 1830
1830–1837	,,	William IV, son of George III	b. 1765	d. 1837
1837–1901	Queen	Victoria, grand-daughter of George III	b. 1819	d. 1901

Victoria ruled Britain strongly while her country was at the peak of its imperial power. The early death of her husband, the Prince Consort, was a blow from which she never recovered.

House of Saxe-Coburg-Gotha

| 1901–1910 | King | Edward VII, son of Victoria | b. 1841 | d. 1910 |

House of Windsor (from 1917)

1910–1936	,,	George V, son of Edward VII	b. 1865	d. 1936
1936	,,	Edward VIII, son of George V abdicated 1936	b. 1894 d 1972	
1936–1952	,,	George VI, brother of Edward VIII	b. 1895	d. 1952
1952–	Queen	Elizabeth II, daughter of George VI	b. 1926	

Elizabeth II, Queen of England (1952–   ) with her consort, Prince Philip.

STATESMEN

1216–1219	Regent	William Marshall, Earl of Pembroke	b. 1146?	d. 1219
1377–1408	Earl Marshal	Henry Percy, Earl of Northumberland	b. 1342	d. 1408
1454–1460	Protector	Richard Plantagenet, Duke of York	b. 1411	killed 1460
1515–1529	Lord Chancellor	Thomas Cardinal Wolsey	b. 1475?	d. 1530
1529–1532	,,	Sir Thomas More	b. 1478	d. 1535
1533–1553	Archbishop of Canterbury	Thomas Cranmer	b. 1489	burned at stake 1556

Thomas Cranmer was responsible for placing the Bible in every English church, and was chief composer of the Thirty-nine Articles. At the stake he held out his right hand to be burned first—the hand that had signed recantations admitting papal supremacy.

1533–1540	Chief Minister	Thomas Cromwell, Earl of Essex	b. 1485?	beheaded 1540
1547–1550	Protector	Edward Seymour, Duke of Somerset	b. 1506?	beheaded 1552
1572–1598	Lord High Treasurer	William Cecil, Baron Burghley	b. 1520	d. 1598
1623–1628	Chief Minister	George Villiers, Duke of Buckingham	b. 1592	assassinated 1628
1628–1640	Chief Adviser	Thomas Wentworth, Earl of Strafford	b. 1593	beheaded 1641

(Left) Thomas Wolsey, Lord Chancellor of England (1515–1529); (Middle) Sir Thomas More, Lord Chancellor of England (1529–1532); (Right) William Cecil, Baron Burghley, Lord High Treasurer of England (1572–1598).

1702–1710	Lord High Treasurer	Sidney Godolphin, Earl of Godolphin	b. 1645	d. 1712
1710–1714	Head of ministry	Robert Harley, Earl of Oxford	b. 1661	d. 1724
1714	Lord High Treasurer	Charles Talbot, Duke of Shrewsbury	b. 1660	d. 1718
1714–1715	Prime Minister	Charles Montagu, Earl of Halifax	b. 1661	d. 1715
1715	First Lord of Treasury	Charles Howard, Earl of Carlisle	b. 1674	d. 1738
1715–1717	Prime Minister	Robert Walpole, Earl of Orford	b. 1676	d. 1745
1717–1718	First Lord of Treasury	James Stanhope, Earl Stanhope	b. 1673	d. 1721
1718–1721	,,	Charles Spencer, Earl of Sunderland	b. 1674	d. 1722
1721–1742	Prime Minister	Robert Walpole, Earl of Orford (Whig)		
1742–1743	First Lord of Treasury	Spencer Compton, Earl of Wilmington (Whig)	b. 1673?	d. 1743
1743–1754	Prime Minister	Henry Pelham (Whig)	b. 1695?	d. 1754
1754–1756	,,	Thomas Pelham-Holles, Duke of Newcastle, brother of Henry Pelham (Whig)	b. 1693	d. 1768

George Villiers, Duke of Buckingham, Chief Minister of James I and Charles I of England (1623–1628), shown with his family.

1756–1757	Prime Minister	William Cavendish, Duke of Devonshire (Whig)	b. 1720	d. 1764
1757–1762	,,	Thomas Pelham-Holles, Duke of Newcastle (Whig)		
1762–1763	,,	John Stuart, Earl of Bute (Tory)	b. 1713	d. 1792
1763–1765	,,	George Grenville (Whig)	b. 1712	d. 1770
1765–1766	,,	Charles Watson-Wentworth, Marquess of Rockingham (Coalition)	b. 1730	d. 1782

1766–1768	Privy Seal	William Pitt, Earl of Chatham (Whig)	b. 1708	d. 1778
1768–1770	First Minister	Augustus Henry Fitzroy, Duke of Grafton (Whig)	b. 1735	d. 1811
1770–1782	Prime Minister	Frederick North, Earl of Guildford (Tory)	b. 1732	d. 1792
1782	,,	Charles Watson-Wentworth, Marquess of Rockingham (Whig)		
1782–1783	,,	William Petty, Earl of Shelburne (Whig)	b. 1737	d. 1805
1783	,,	William Henry Cavendish Bentinck, Duke of Portland (Coalition)	b. 1738	d. 1809
1783–1801	,,	William Pitt the Younger (Tory)	b. 1759	d. 1806

Considered by many to be England's greatest Prime Minister, the Younger Pitt was responsible for the First (1793), Second (1798) and Third (1805) Coalitions against Napoleon. Already in poor health, news of the capitulation at Ulm and defeat at Austerlitz killed him.

1801–1804	Prime Minister	Henry Addington, Viscount Sidmouth (Tory)	b. 1757	d. 1844
1804–1806	,,	William Pitt (Tory)		
1806–1807	,,	William Wyndham Grenville, Lord Grenville, son of George Grenville (Whig)	b. 1759	d. 1834
1807–1809	,,	William Bentinck, Duke of Portland (Tory)		
1809–1812	,,	Spencer Perceval (Tory) b. 1762 assassinated 1812		
1812–1827	,,	Robert Banks Jenkinson, Earl of Liverpool (Tory)	b. 1770	d. 1828
1827	,,	George Canning (Tory)	b. 1770	d. 1827
1827–1828	,,	Frederick John Robinson, Viscount Goderich (Tory)	b. 1782	d. 1859
1828–1830	,,	Arthur Wellesley, Duke of Wellington (Tory)	b. 1769	d. 1852
1830–1834	,,	Charles Grey, Earl Grey (Whig)	b. 1764	d. 1845
1834	,,	William Lamb, Viscount Melbourne (Whig)	b. 1779	d. 1848
1834–1835	,,	Sir Robert Peel (Tory)	b. 1788	d. 1850
1835–1841	,,	William Lamb, Viscount Melbourne (Whig)		
1841–1846	,,	Sir Robert Peel (Tory)		
1846–1852	,,	John Russell, Earl Russell (Whig)	b. 1792	d. 1878
1852	,,	Edward George Geoffrey Smith Stanley, Earl of Derby (Tory)	b. 1799	d. 1869
1852–1855	,,	George Hamilton Gordon, Earl of Aberdeen (Peelite)	b. 1784	d. 1860
1855–1858	,,	Henry John Temple, Viscount Palmerston (Liberal)	b. 1784	d. 1865
1858	,,	Edward Stanley, Earl of Derby (Conservative)		
1858–1865	,,	Henry John Temple, Viscount Palmerston (Liberal)		
1865–1866	,,	John Russell, Earl Russell (Liberal)		
1866–1868	,,	Edward Stanley, Earl of Derby (Conservative)		
1868	,,	Benjamin Disraeli, Earl of Beaconsfield	b. 1804	d. 1881

Lord Beaconsfield's maiden speech as a member of Parliament was a failure—he was laughed down—yet he went on to become Prime Minister and the intimate friend and adviser of Queen Victoria. His greatest service to Britain was his acquisition of control of the Suez Canal. After his death the Queen visited his grave to lay a wreath on it—an unprecedented act.

1868–1874	Prime Minister	William Ewart Gladstone (Liberal) b. 1809 d. 1898	
1874–1880	„	Benjamin Disraeli (Conservative)	
1880–1885	„	William Ewart Gladstone (Liberal)	

Gladstone was for 60 years a member of Parliament and for many of those years he worked 16 hours a day. As Chancellor of the Exchequer, he aimed to abolish income-tax completely and he succeeded in reducing it to three-pence in the pound. He was, perhaps, the greatest orator of the nineteenth century.

1885–1886	Prime Minister	Robert Arthur Talbot Gascoyne-Cecil, Marquess of Salisbury (Conservative)	b. 1830	d. 1903
1886	„	William Ewart Gladstone (Liberal)		
1886–1892	„	Robert Arthur Talbot Gascoyne-Cecil, Marquess of Salisbury (Conservative)		
1892–1894	„	William Ewart Gladstone (Liberal)		
1894–1895	„	Archibald Philip Primrose, Earl of Rosebery (Liberal)	b. 1847	d. 1929
1895–1902	„	Robert Arthur Talbot Gascoyne-Cecil, Marquess of Salisbury (Conservative)		
1895–1903	Colonial Secretary	Joseph Chamberlain	b. 1836	d. 1914
1902–1905	Prime Minister	Arthur James Balfour (Conservative)	b. 1848	d. 1930
1905–1908	„	Sir Henry Campbell-Bannerman (Liberal)	b. 1836	d. 1908
1908–1915	„	Herbert Henry Asquith, Earl of Oxford and Asquith (Liberal)	b. 1852	d. 1928
1915–1916	„	Herbert Henry Asquith (Coalition)		
1916–1922	„	David Lloyd George, Earl of Dwyfor (Coalition)	b. 1863	d. 1945

In the First World War, Lloyd George occupied the position of semi-dictator of England from 1916 until victory in 1918. His desire for a conciliatory policy towards Germany put him in opposition to Clemenceau but press-led criticism at home made it impossible for him to successfully oppose French policy.

1922–1923	Prime Minister	Andrew Bonar Law (Conservative)	b. 1858	d. 1923
1923–1924	„	Stanley Baldwin, Earl Baldwin of Bewdley (Conservative)	b. 1867	d. 1947
1924	„	James Ramsay MacDonald (Labour)	b. 1866	d. 1937
1924–1929	„	Stanley Baldwin (Conservative)		
1929–1931	„	James Ramsay MacDonald (Labour)		
1931–1935	„	James Ramsay MacDonald (Coalition)		
1935–1937	„	Stanley Baldwin (Coalition)		
1937–1940	„	Arthur Neville Chamberlain (Coalition)	b. 1869	d. 1940
1940–1945	„	Winston Leonard Spencer Churchill (Coalition) (Conservative)	b. 1874	d. 1965
1945–1951	„	Clement Richard Attlee (Labour)	b. 1883	d. 1967
1951–1955	„	Sir Winston Churchill (Conservative)		

Sir Winston Churchill was a great writer as well as a great statesman. His books on the Second World War are magnificently written accounts of those historical events in which he played a major part.

1955–1957	Prime Minister	Anthony Eden, Earl of Avon (Conservative)	b. 1897
1957–1963	„	Harold Macmillan (Conservative)	b. 1894
1963–1964	„	Sir Alec Douglas-Home (Conservative)	b. 1903
1964–	„	James Harold Wilson (Labour)	b. 1916

BRITISH PRIME MINISTERS

(Left) William Pitt the Elder (1766–1768); (Middle) Lord North (1770–1782); (Right) William Pitt the Younger (1783–1801, 1804–1806).

(Left) Lord Palmerston (1855–1858); (Middle) William Gladstone (1868–1874, 1880–1885, 1886); (Right) Herbert Asquith (1908–1916).

(Left) James Ramsay MacDonald (1924, 1929–1935); (Middle) Sir Winston Churchill (1940–1945, 1951–1955); (Right) Sir Alec Douglas-Home (1963–1964).

SCOTLAND

(No authenticated information is available for the period before Kenneth MacAlpine united Picts and Scots)

846– 858?	King	Kenneth I MacAlpine	d. 858?
943– 954	„	Malcolm I MacDonald	d. 954
971– 995	„	Kenneth II, son of Malcolm I	assassinated 995
997–1005	„	Kenneth III, nephew of Kenneth II	
1005–1034	„	Malcolm II Mackenneth, son of Kenneth II	d. 1034
1034–1040	„	Duncan I, grandson of Malcolm II	killed 1040

(Scots, Picts, Angles and Britons united in Kingdom of Scotland, 1034)

1040–1057	King	Macbeth		killed 1057

Macbeth was immortalized by Shakespeare. In the play, he was incited by his wife to murder Duncan by treachery. In real life, he, too, slew Duncan and seized the kingdom, but was himself defeated and slain by Malcolm III, Duncan's son.

1057–1093	King	Malcolm III MacDuncan, son of Duncan I		killed 1093
1093–1094	,,	Duncan II, son of Malcolm III		d. 1094
1094–1097	,,	Donald Bane, brother of Malcolm III		
1097–1107	,,	Edgar, son of Malcolm III		d. 1107
1107–1124	,,	Alexander I, son of Malcolm III	b. 1078?	d. 1124
1124–1153	,,	David I, son of Malcolm III	b. 1084	d. 1153
1153–1165	,,	Malcolm IV the Maiden, grandson of David I	b. 1141	d. 1165
1165–1214	,,	William the Lion, brother of Malcolm IV	b. 1143	d. 1214
1214–1249	,,	Alexander II, son of William the Lion	b. 1198	d. 1249

James I, King of Scotland (1406–1437).

James II, King of Scotland (1437–1460).

James IV, King of Scotland (1488–1513).

Mary, Queen of Scotland (1542–1567).

1249–1286	King	Alexander III, son of Alexander II	b. 1241	d. 1286
1286–1290	(Queen)	Margaret ("The Maid of Norway"), granddaughter of Alexander III	b. 1282?	d. 1290
		(Interregnum, 1290–1292)		
1292–1296	King	John de Baliol or Balliol abdicated 1296	b. 1249	d. 1315
		(Scotland a dependency of England 1296–1306)		
1306–1329	,,	Robert I the Bruce	b. 1274	d. 1329
1329–1371	,,	David II, son of Robert I the Bruce	b. 1324	d. 1371

House of Stuart

1371–1390	King	Robert II, nephew of David II	b. 1316	d. 1390
1390–1406	,,	Robert III, son of Robert II	b. 1340?	d. 1406
1406–1437	,,	James I, son of Robert III	b. 1394	assassinated 1437
1437–1460	,,	James II, son of James I	b. 1430	killed 1460
1460–1488	,,	James III, son of James II	b. 1451	assassinated 1488
1488–1513	,,	James IV, son of James III	b. 1473	killed 1513
1513–1542	,,	James V, son of James IV	b. 1512	d. 1542
1542–1567	Queen	Mary Stuart, daughter of James V	b. 1542	beheaded 1587

Mary Queen of Scots succeeded her father when 6 days old. She married her Catholic cousin, Lord Darnley, and gave him the title of King. Mary probably connived at Darnley's murder and afterwards married the Earl of Bothwell. A prisoner of Elizabeth for nearly 20 years, she was accused of plotting Elizabeth's assassination, and beheaded.

1554–1560	Regent	Mary of Guise, consort of James V and mother of Mary Stuart	b. 1515	d. 1560
1567–1625	King	James VI, son of Mary Stuart and Henry, Lord Darnley	b. 1566	d. 1625

(Scottish Crown united with the Crown of England, 1603)

(See England, House of Stuart)

WALES

Owen Glendower, descendant of the native Welsh princes, led the Welsh in rebellion against Henry IV of England. Proclaimed Prince by his people in 1400, he ruled in Wales until 1415, when English rule was restored.

(Wales was subdued by Agricola after 78 A.D.; no authenticated information is available for the period before Rhodri)

Welsh Sovereign Princes

844– 878	Prince	Rhodri the Great (Rhodri Mawr)
878– 916	,,	Anarawd, son of Rhodri
916– 942	,,	Idwal the Bald, son of Anarawd
942– 950	"King of all the Welsh"	Hywel Dda the Good
950– 979	Prince	Iago ap Idwal (or Ieuaf)
979– 985	,,	Hywel ap Ieuaf the Bad, nephew of Iago
985– 986	,,	Cadwallon, brother of Hywel
986– 999	,,	Maredudd ab Owain ap Hywel Dda
999–1005	,,	Cynan ap Hywel, son of Hywel

1005–1023	Prince	Llewelyn ab Seisyll		
1023–1039	,,	Iago ap Idwal, son of Idwal ap Meurig		
1039–1063	,,	Gruffydd ap Llywelyn ap Seisyll		
1063–1075	,,	Bleddyn ap Cynfyn, brother of Gruffydd		
1075–1081	,,	Trahaearn ap Caradog, cousin of Bleddyn		
1081–1137	King of North Wales	Gruffyd ap Cynan ab Iago		
1137–1170	Prince	Owain Gwynedd, son of Gruffydd ap Cynan (Civil War, 1170–1175)		d. 1170
1175–1194	,,	Dafydd ab Owain Gwynedd		d. 1203
1175–1194	,,	Rhodri ab Owain		
1194–1240	,,	Llywelyn Fawr the Great, son-in-law of King John	b. 1173	d. 1240
1240–1246	,,	Dafydd ap Llywelyn		
1246–1282	,,	Llywelyn ab Gruffydd ap Llywelyn, grandson of Llywelyn the Great		killed 1282

Llywelyn allied himself with Simon de Montfort and was later recognized as overlord of Wales. He was attacked by Edward I for refusing to do him homage and forced through hunger to submit. The last champion of Welsh liberty, he was killed in a skirmish.

(Conquered by England, 1277–1283)

1400–1415	Prince	Owen Glendower	b. 1359?	d. 1416?

English Princes of Wales
Created 1301

1301	,,	Edward of Carnarvon (Edward II)	b. 1284	murdered 1327

Edward II was born at Carnarvon Castle, but the story that Edward I presented his new-born son to the people of Wales as their future native prince is untrue. An unsatisfactory monarch, frivolous and incompetent, Edward suffered defeat at the hands of Robert Bruce at Bannockburn. His wife, Isabella of France, deposed him—and had him put to death.

1343	Prince	Edward the Black Prince, son of Edward III	b. 1330	d. 1376

Edward II, King of England (1307–1327) was the first English Prince of Wales.

Edward the Black Prince, son of King Edward III of England, was made Prince of Wales in 1343.

1377	Prince	Richard of Bordeaux (Richard II), son of the Black Prince	b. 1367	murdered 1400
1399	,,	Henry of Monmouth (Henry V), son of Henry IV	b. 1387	d. 1422
1454	,,	Edward of Westminster, son of Henry VI	b. 1453	killed 1471
1471	,,	Edward of Westminster (Edward V), son of Edward IV	b. 1470	murdered 1483
1483	,,	Edward of Middleham, son of Richard III		d. 1484
1489	,,	Arthur Tudor, son of Henry VII	b. 1487	d. 1502

(Right) Unlike his half-sisters Mary I and Anne, James Francis Edward Stuart, Prince of Wales ("The Old Pretender") was barred from the English throne after their father, James I, was deposed.

(Left) King George IV of England (1820–1830), seen here as Prince of Wales, became Prince Regent in 1811 after George III went mad.

(Right) The present Prince of Wales, Prince Charles, takes part in a polo match in Jamaica with his father Prince Philip, Duke of Edinburgh. Prince Charles is scheduled to be invested with his title during the summer of 1969, just before his 21st birthday.

| 1503 | Prince | Henry Tudor (Henry VIII), son of Henry VII | b. 1491 | d. 1547 |

(Wales was united with England, 1536–1547)

1610	,,	Henry Stuart, son of James I	b. 1594	d. 1612
1616	,,	Charles Stuart (Charles I), son of James I	b. 1600	beheaded 1649
1638?	,,	Charles Stuart (Charles II), son of Charles I	b. 1630	d. 1685
1688	,,	James Francis Edward Stuart, son of James II ("The Old Pretender") (attainted 1702)	b. 1688	d. 1766

"The Old Pretender" was one Prince of Wales who did not afterwards become King. Louis XIV of France proclaimed him his father's successor, but James' attempts to regain the throne were unsuccessful. He married the King of Poland's granddaughter, and the Pope gave him a palace in Rome.

1714	Prince	George Augustus (George II), son of George I	b. 1683	d. 1760
1727	,,	Frederick Louis, son of George II	b. 1707	d. 1751
1751	,,	George William Frederick (George III), grandson of George II	b. 1738	d. 1820
1762	,,	George Augustus Frederick (George IV), son of George III	b. 1762	d. 1830
1841	,,	Albert Edward (Edward VII), son of Queen Victoria	b. 1841	d. 1910
1901	,,	George (George V), son of Edward VII	b. 1865	d. 1936
1911	,,	Edward Albert Christian George Andrew Patrick David (Edward VIII—Duke of Windsor), son of George V	b. 1894	d. 1972
1958	,,	Charles Philip Arthur George, son of Elizabeth II	b. 1948	

Greece

Otto I, King of Greece
(1832–1862).

George I, King of Greece
(1863–1913).

Note: It is impossible to provide accurate lists of the rulers of all the provinces and republics of Ancient Greece. These are listed on the following pages: Athens, Sparta and Syracuse.

(Greece was ruled by Rome from 146 B.C. to A.D. 395; it became part of the Eastern Empire and was conquered by the Turks in 1460; achieved independence from Turkey 1821–1827)

MODERN GREECE

| 1828–1831 | President | Giovanni Capo d'Istria | b. 1776 | assassinated 1831 |
| 1831–1832 | ,, | Agostino Capo d'Istria, brother of Giovanni Capo d'Istria | b. 1778 | d. 1857 |

1832–1862	King	Otto I, son of Ludwig I of Bavaria	deposed 1862	b. 1815	d. 1867

(Interregnum 1862–1863)

1863–1913	King	George I, son of Christian IX of Denmark		b. 1845	assassinated 1913

Son of King Christian IX of Denmark, George I served in the Danish navy. After Otto I was deposed, George was elected King of the Hellenes by the Greek National Assembly in 1863. His wife, Grand Duchess Olga, was a niece of the Tsar of Russia.

1913–1917	,,	Constantine I, son of George I	abdicated 1917	b. 1868	d. 1923
1917–1920	,,	Alexander, son of Constantine I		b. 1893	d. 1920
1920–1922	,,	Constantine I			
1922–1924	,,	George II, son of Constantine I	abdicated 1924	b. 1890	d. 1947

(A republic, 1924–1935)

1924–1926	President	Pavlos Konduriotis		b. 1857	d. 1935
1926	,,	Theodoros Pangalos		b. 1878	d. 1952
1926–1929	President (provisional)	Pavlos Konduriotis			
1929–1935	,,	Alexandros Zaimis		b. 1856	d. 1936
1935	Regent	Georgios Kondylis		b. 1879	d. 1936
1935–1941	King	George II			

(German occupation 1941–1944)

1946–1947	,,	George II			
1944–1946	Administrator	Archbishop Damaskinos		b. 1889	d. 1949
1947–1964	King	Paul I, son of Constantine I		b. 1901	d. 1964
1964–	,,	Constantine II, son of Paul I		b. 1941	

(exiled 1967)

Paul I, King of Greece (1947–1964).

Constantine II, King of Greece (1964–   ).

STATESMEN

1910–1915	Prime Minister	Eleutherios Venizelos	b. 1864	d. 1936
1917–1920	,,	Eleutherios Venizelos		
1924	,,	Eleutherios Venizelos		
1928–1932	,,	Eleutherios Venizelos		
1933	,,	Eleutherios Venizelos		

Venizelos strongly supported the Allied cause in the First World War but was opposed by the King, who was pro-German. After King Constantine was forced to abdicate, Venizelos brought Greece into the war. In 1935 he was condemned to death but received an amnesty on George II's return.

Panayiotis Pipinelis, Prime Minister of Greece (1963).

George Papandreou, Prime Minister of Greece (1963, 1964–1965).

1936–1941	Prime Minister	Ioannis Metaxas	b. 1871	d. 1941
1944–1945	,,	George Papandreou	b. 1888	
1945	,,	Nicolas Plastiras	b. 1883	d. 1953
1945	,,	Petros Voulgaris	b. 1883	d. 1957
1945	,,	Archbishop Damaskinos		
1945	,,	Panaghiotis Canellopoulos	b. 1902	
1945–1946	,,	Themistoclis Sophoulis	b. 1862	d. 1949
1946	,,	Panaghiotis Poulitsas	b. 1881	
1946	,,	Constantine Tsaldaris	b. 1885	
1946–1947	,,	Constantine Tsaldaris		
1947	,,	Demetrios Maximos	b. 1873	d. 1955
1947	,,	Constantine Tsaldaris		
1947–1948	,,	Themistocles Sophoulis		
1948–1949	,,	Themistocles Sophoulis		
1949	,,	Themistocles Sophoulis		
1949–1950	,,	Alexander Diomides	b. 1875	d. 1950
1950	,,	John Theotokis	b. 1880	d. 1963
1950	,,	Sophocles Venizelos	b. 1894	d. 1964
1950	,,	Nicolas Plastiras		
1950–1951	,,	Sophocles Venizelos		
1951–1952	,,	Nicholas Plastiras		
1952	,,	Demetrios Kioussopoulos	b. 1892	
1952–1955	,,	Alexander Papagos	b. 1883	d. 1955
1955–1958	,,	Constantine Caramanlis	b. 1907	
1958	,,	Constantine Georgacopoulos	b. 1890	
1958–1961	,,	Constantine Caramanlis		
1961	,,	Constantine Dovas	b. 1898	
1961–1963	,,	Constantine Caramanlis		
1963	,,	Panayiotis Pipinelis	b. 1899	
1963	,,	Stylianos Mavromihalis	b. 1900	
1963	,,	George Papandreou		
1963–1964	,,	John Paraskevopoulos	b. 1900	
1964–1965	,,	George Papandreou		
1965	,,	George Athanassiadis-Novas	b. 1893	
1965	,,	Elias Tsirimokos	b. 1907	d. 1968
1965–1966	,,	Stephanos Stephanopoulos	b. 1899	
1966–1967	,,	Ioannis Paraskevopoulos		
1967	,,	Panayiotis Kanellopoulos	b. 1902	
1967	,,	Constantine Kollias		
1967–	,,	George Papadepoulous		

*Stephanos Stephanopoulos,
Prime Minister of Greece
(1965–1966).*

*Coin of Athens c. 450 B.C.
showing Athene, Patroness
of the city.*

ATHENS

(Came into existence under a monarchy; monarchy replaced by hereditary nobility,
1000–683 B.C.)

B.C.			B.C.
c. 621	Lawgiver	Draco	
c. 594–570	Archon	Solon	b. 638? d. 559?
560–527	Tyrant	Pisistratus	d. 527
527–511	,,	Hippias, son of Pisistratus	banished 511
527–514	,,	Hipparchus, son of Pisistratus	assassinated 514
509–506	"Founder of democracy"	Cleisthenes	
493–c. 470	General	Themistocles b. 527?	banished 470 d. 460?
		(Persians defeated at Marathon, 490 B.C.)	
c. 470	,,	Miltiades	b. 540? d. 489?
489–488	Chief archon	Aristeides the Just, son of Lysimachus	b. 530? d. 468?
480–479	Strategos	Aristeides the Just	
		(Athens sacked by Xerxes, 480)	
470–460	Leader	Cimon, son of Miltiades	b. 507? d. 449
c. 460–429	,,	Pericles, son of Xanthippus	b. 495? d. 429
		(Peloponnesian War 431–404)	
411–410	Government of Four Hundred		
		(Oligarchy of "Thirty Tyrants," 404)	
404	General	Theramenes	poisoned 404
404–403	,,	Critias	killed 403
403	,,	Thrasybulus	killed 389
		(War with Philip of Macedon, 338)	
334–323	Regent	Antipater	b. 398? d. 319
317–307	Governor	Demetrius Phalereus	b. 345? d. 283
306–300	King	Demetrius 1 Poliorcetes	b. 337? d. 283
295	Dictator	Lachares	
295–288	King	Demetrius 1 Poliorcetes	

(Chremonidean War, 266–263; subdued by Romans, 146; joined Mithridates, 88;
stormed by Sulla, 86 B.C.)

SPARTA (Laconia)

(Conquered by Dorians in about 1100 B.C.; Sparta's constitution provided for two hereditary kings)

B.C.			
9th cent.	"Lawgiver"	Lycurgus	
	King	Aristodemus	
		(First Messenian War, c. 725 B.C.)	
	,,	{ Eurysthenes	
		{ Procles	

	King	{ Agis { Soüs	
		{ Echestratus	
	,,	{ Eurypon	
		{ Labotas	
	,,	{ Prytanis	
		{ Doryssus	
	,,	{ [Eunomus]	
		{ Agesilaus	
	,,	{ Polydectes	
		{ Archelaus	
	,,	{ Charilaus	
		{ Teleclus, son of Archelaus	
	,,	{ Nicander	
		{ Alcamenes, son of Teleclus	
	,,	{ Theopompus	

Coin of Laconia c. 200 B.C., showing Zeus and wreathed amphora. Sparta was the chief city of Laconia.

(Second Messenian War, c. 625 B.C.)

	,,	Polydorus	
	,,	{ Eurycrates { Zeuxidamus	
	,,	{ Anaxander { Anaxidamus	
	,,	{ Eurycratides { Archidamus I	
	,,	{ Leon { Agesicles	
	,,	{ Anaxandrides { Ariston	

(Victory over Argos, c. 545 B.C.)

c. 519–491	,,	{ Cleomenes I { Demaratus	suicide c. 488

(War with Athens, 505 B.C.)

490?–480	,,	{ Leonidas I { Leotychides	killed 480 B.C.

(Rebellion of Messenian Helots, 466 B.C.)

480	,,	Pleistarchus	
458	,,	{ Pleistoanax { Archidamus II	
431–422	General	Brasidas	killed 422

(Peloponnesian War, 431–404 B.C.)

c. 426–399	King	{ Pausanias { Agis II	
c. 400–360	,,	{ Agesipolis I { Agesilaus II	d. 360?
380–371	,,	Cleombrotus I	killed 371
371	,,	Agesipolis II	
370–309	,,	{ Cleomenes II { Archidamus III	

(Defeated by Philip of Macedon, 344 B.C.)

338–331	,,	Agis III	killed 331
330	,,	Eudamidas I	
309	,,	{ Areus I { Archidamus IV	
265	,,	{ Acrotatus { Eudamidas II	
264	,,	Areus II	
244–?241	,,	Agis IV	

285–236	King	{Leonidas II Eurydamidas	
242–240	,,	Cleombrotus II	
235–219	,,	{Cleomenes III, son of Leonidas Archidamus V	suicide 221

(Captured by Antigonus Doson of Macedon, 221 B.C.)

219	King	{Agesipolis III Lycurgus	
210	,,	Machanidas	
207–192	Tyrant	Nabis	assassinated 192

(Conquered by Rome, 146 B.C.)

SYRACUSE

Hieron II, Tyrant of Syracuse (270?–215).

Hieronymus, Tyrant of Syracuse (215 B.C.).

(Founded by Corinthian settlers in about 733 B.C.; no authenticated information is available for the period before 485 B.C.)

B.C.   B.C.

485– 478	Tyrant	Gelon (or Gelo)	d. 478
478– 467	,,	Hieron I, brother of Gelon	d. 467
466	,,	Thrasybulus, brother of Gelon	

(Became a democratic commonwealth in 466)

406– 367	,,	Dionysius the Elder	b. 430? d. 367

Dionysius the Elder is reputed to have had a great terror of attacks on his life and to have taken the most elaborate protective precautions. Yet he subdued the other Sicilian cities, warred against Carthage, and extended his territory.

367– 356	Tyrant	Dionysius II the Younger, son of Dionysius the Elder	
355– 354	,,	Dion	b. 408? assassinated 354
347– 344	,,	Dionysius II	
343– 337	,,	Timoleon	d. 337?

(Oligarchy, 337–316)

316– 289	,,	Agathocles	b. 361 d. 289
288– 279	,,	Hicetas	
270?–215	,,	Hieron II, relative of Archimedes	b. 308? d. 215
215	,,	Hieronymus, grandson of Hieron II	assassinated 215

(Conquered by Rome in 212 B.C.)

Guatemala

Rafael Carrera, Dictator of Guatemala (1838–1865).

(Republic of Guatemala established in 1839)

1838–1865	Dictator	Rafael Carrera	b. 1814	d. 1865
1865–1871	President	Vicente Cerna		
1871–1873	President (provisional)	Miguel García Granados		
1873–1885	President	Justo Rufino Barrios	b. 1837?	killed 1885
1885–1892	,,	Manuel Lisandro Barillas		
1892–1898	,,	José María Reyna Barrios, nephew of		
		J. R. Barrios	b. 1853	assassinated 1898
1898–1920	Dictator	Manuel Estrada Cabrera	b. 1857	d. 1924
1920–1921	President	Carlos Herrera		
1921–1926	,,	José María Orellana	b. 1872	d. 1926
1926–1930	,,	Lázaro Chacón	b. 1873	d. 1931
1931	President (provisional)	José María Reyna Andrade		
1931–1944	Dictator	Jorge Ubico Castañeda	b. 1878	d. 1946
1944	President (provisional)	Federico Ponce Vaides		

(revolutionary junta, 1944–1945)

1945–1951	President	Juan José Arevalo	
1951–1954	,,	Jacobo Arbenz Guzman	
1954–1957	,,	Carlos Castillo Armas	
1958–1963	,,	Miguel Ydigoras Fuentes	b. 1895
1963–1966	,,	Enrique Peralta Azurdia	
1966–	,,	Julio Cesar Mendez Montenegro	b. 1915

Justo Rufino Barrios,
President of Guatemala
(1873–1885).

Miguel García Granados,
President (Provisional) of
Guatemala (1871–1873).

Guinea

Ahmed Sékou Touré, President
of Guinea (1958–   ).

(Separated from Senegal and administered by France as a separate colony, 1891–1958; became an independent republic, 1958)

1958–	President	Ahmed Sékou Touré	b. 1922

Guyana

(Former colony of British Guiana, became independent in 1966)

1966–	Governor-General	Sir David Rose	b. 1922
1966–	Prime Minister	Lindon Forbes Sampson Burnham	b. 1923

Haiti

Jean Pierre Boyer, President of southern Haiti (1818–1843).

(Ruled by France, 1697–1792)

1794–1802	General-in-Chief	Pierre Dominique Toussaint l'Ouverture	b. 1743 d. 1803

(Independence proclaimed 1803)

1803	Governor	Jean Jacques Dessalines	b. 1758 assassinated 1806
1804–1806	Emperor	Jacques I (Dessalines)	
1808–1810	President (of northern Haiti)	Henri Christophe	b. 1767 committed suicide 1820
1811–1820	Emperor	Henri Christophe (Henri I)	
1808–1818	President (of southern Haiti)	Alexandre Sabès Pétion	b. 1770 d. 1818
1818–1843	"	Jean Pierre Boyer	b. 1776 d. 1850
1845–1846	"	Louis Pierrot	
1846–1847	"	Jean Baptiste Riche	
1847–1849	"	Faustin Elie Soulouque	b. 1785 d. 1867
1849–1858	Emperor	Faustin I (Soulouque)	

Nord Alexis, President of Haiti (1902–1908).

Henri Christophe, President of northern Haiti (1808–1810), Emperor of Haiti (1811–1820).

Dumarsais Estimé, President of Haiti (1946–1950).

Paul Magloire, President of Haiti (1951–1956).

François Duvalier, President of Haiti (1957–   ).

1859–1867	President	Nicholas Fabre Geffrard	b. 1806 d. 1879
1867–1868	"	Salnave	shot 1870

1870–1874	President	Nissage Saget		
1874–1876	"	Michel Domingue		
1876–1879	"	Boisrond Canal		
1879–1888	"	Louis Etienne Félicité Saloman	b. 1820	d. 1888
1889–1896	"	Florvil Hippolyte		
1896–1902	"	Tiresias Simon Sam		
1902	Provisional President	Boisrond Canal		
1902–1908	President	Nord Alexis		
1908–1911	"	Antoine Simon		
1911–1913	"	Simon Cincinnatus Leconte		
1913	"	Tancred Auguste		
1913–1914	"	Michel Oreste		
1914	"	Oreste Zamor		
1914	"	Davilmar Theodore		
1915	"	Vilbrun Guillaume Sam		massacred 1915
		(Ruled by U.S.A. 1915–1934)		
1915–1922	"	Philippe Sudre Dartiguenave		
		(under American supervision)		
1922–1930	President	Louis Borno	b. 1865	d. 1942
1930–1941	"	Sténio Joseph Vincent	b. 1874	d. 1959
1941–1946	"	Elie Lescot	b. 1883	
1946–1950	"	Dumarsais Estimé		
1951–1956	"	Paul Magloire		
1957–	"	François Duvalier	b. 1907	

Hittite Empire

OLD KINGDOM

B.C.

1740–1710	King	Tudhaliyas I
1710–1680	"	Pu-sarrumas, son of Tudhaliyas I
1680–1650	"	Labarnas I, son of Pu-sarrumas
1650–1620	"	Labarnas II (=Hattusilis I), son of Labarnas I
1620–1590	"	Mursilis I, adopted son of Labarnas II
1590–1560	"	Hantilis I, son-in-law of Mursilis I
1560–1550	"	Zidantas I, son-in-law (?) of Hantilis I
1550–1530	"	Ammunas, son of Zidantas I
1530–1525	"	Huzziyas I
1525–1500	"	Telipinus, brother-in-law of Huzziyas I
1500–1490	"	Alluwamnas, son (?) of Telipinus
1490–1480	"	Hantilis II (?)
1480–1470	"	Zidantas I (?)
1470–1460	"	Huzziyas II (?)

EMPIRE

1460–1440	"	Tudhaliyas II
1440–1420	"	Arnuwandas I, son of Tudhaliyas II
1420–1400	"	Hattusilis II, brother of Arnuwandas I
1400–1385	"	Tudhaliyas III, son of Hattusilis II
1385–1375	"	Arnuwandas II, son of Tudhaliyas III
1375–1335	"	Suppiluliumas, brother of Arnuwandas II
1335–1334	"	Arnuwandus III, son of Suppiluliumas
1334–1306	"	Mursilis II, brother of Arnuwandas III

1306–1282	King	Muwatallis, son of Mursilis II
1282–1275	„	Urhi-Teshub, son of Muwatallis
1275–1250	„	Hattusilis III, uncle of Urhi-Teshub
1250–1220	„	Tudhaliyas IV, son of Hattusilis III
1220–1190	„	Arnuwandas IV, son of Tudhaliyas IV
	„	Suppiluliumas II (?), brother (?) of Arnuwandas IV

(The Hittite Empire fell in about 1190 B.C. under attack of the Thracians, Phrygians and Armenians)

Holland, see Netherlands

Holy Roman Empire

Otto III, Holy Roman Emperor (983–1002).

(The Holy Roman Empire was a revival of the Roman Empire of the West)

A.D.
FRANKISH (CAROLINGIAN) DYNASTY

| 800– 814 | Emperor of the West | Charlemagne, son of Pepin the Short | b. 742 | d. 814 |

Originally King of the Franks, Charlemagne became Emperor of the Romans, and built an empire consisting of Gaul, Italy, and large areas of Germany and Spain. After being crowned in Rome on Christmas Day, 800, he enacted laws, patronized letters and established schools.

814– 840	Emperor of the West	Louis I the Pious, son of Charlemagne	b. 778	d. 840
840– 855	Emperor	Lothair I, son of Louis I	b. 795?	d. 855
855– 875	„	Louis II, son of Lothair I	b. 825	d. 875
875– 877	„	Charles II the Bald, son of Louis I	b. 823	d. 877

(No Emperor from 877 to 881)

881– 887	Emperor	Charles II the Fat, son of Louis II	b. 832	d. 888
887– 899	”	Arnulf of Carinthia, son of Carloman of Bavaria	b. 850?	d. 899
899– 911	Emperor (not crowned)	Louis III the Child, son of Arnulf of Carinthia	b. 893	d. 911
911– 918	”	Conrad I, of Franconia		d. 918

SAXON DYNASTY

919– 936	”	Henry I the Fowler	b. 876	d. 936
936– 973	Emperor	Otto I the Great, son of Henry I	b. 912	d. 973
973– 983	”	Otto II, son of Otto I	b. 954	d. 983
983–1002	”	Otto III, son of Otto II	b. 980	d. 1002
1002–1024	”	Henry II the Saint, great-grandson of Otto I the Great	b. 973	d. 1024

FRANCONIAN (SALIAN) DYNASTY

1024–1039	”	Conrad II, descendant of Otto the Great	b. 990	d. 1039
1039–1056	”	Henry III the Black, son of Conrad II	b. 1017	d. 1056
1056–1106	”	Henry IV, son of Henry III	b. 1050	d. 1106
1106–1125	”	Henry V, son of Henry IV	b. 1081	d. 1125
1125–1137	”	Lothair II of Saxony	b. 1070	d. 1137

HOHENSTAUFEN DYNASTY

1138–1152	Emperor (not crowned)	Conrad III, grandson of Henry IV	b. 1093	d. 1152
1152–1190	Emperor	Frederick I (Barbarossa), nephew of Conrad III	b. 1123	d. 1190

Frederick "Redbeard" extended the Holy Roman Empire to Poland, Hungary, Burgundy and Denmark and ruled it with an iron hand. On his way to join the third crusade against Saladin and the Moslems he was drowned in Cilicia.

Frederick I (Barbarossa), Holy Roman Emperor (1152–1190).

1190–1197	Emperor	Henry VI, son of Frederick I (Barbarossa)	b. 1165	d. 1197
1198–1208	Emperor (not crowned)	Philip of Swabia, brother of Henry VI	b. 1177	d. 1208
1198–1215	Emperor (rival)	Otto IV (of Brunswick), son of Henry the Lion	b. 1182	d. 1218
1215–1250	Emperor	Frederick II, son of Henry VI	b. 1194	d. 1250
1250–1254	Emperor (not crowned)	Conrad IV, son of Frederick II	b. 1228	d. 1254
1256–1271	King of the Romans	Richard, Earl of Cornwall, son of King John	b. 1209	d. 1272

(The Great Interregnum 1254–1273)

RULERS OF VARIOUS HOUSES

1273–1291	Emperor (not crowned)	Rudolf I of Habsburg, son of Albert IV	b. 1218	d. 1291

1292–1298	Emperor (not crowned)	Adolf of Nassau, son of Walfram II	b. 1255	killed 1298
1298–1308	,,	Albert I of Austria, son of Rudolf I	b. 1250	murdered 1308
1308–1313	Emperor	Henry VII of Luxemburg	b. 1269	d. 1313
1314–1325	Rival King	Frederick III of Austria, son of Albert I	b. 1286	d. 1330
1314–1347	Emperor	Ludwig IV of Bavaria	b. 1287	d. 1347
1347–1378	,,	Charles IV of Luxemburg, son of John of Luxemburg	b. 1316	d. 1378
1378–1400	,,	Wenceslaus of Bohemia, son of Charles IV	b. 1361	d. 1419
1400–1410	Emperor (not crowned)	Rupert of the Palatinate	b. 1352	d. 1410
1410–1411	Emperor	Jossus of Moravia, nephew of Charles IV		
1411–1437	,,	Sigismund of Hungary, brother of Wenceslaus	b. 1368	d. 1437

Emperor Frederick II (1215–1250) and his consort, Constance of Aragon.

Emperor Charles V (1519–1556).

Emperor Leopold I (1658–1705).

Maximilian I, Holy Roman Emperor (1493–1519), through marriage, war, and treaty, laid the groundwork for the vast realm inherited by his grandson and successor, Charles V.

HOUSE OF HABSBURG

1438–1439	Emperor (not crowned)	Albert II of Habsburg	b. 1397	d. 1439
1440–1493	Emperor	Frederick III, great-great-grandson of Albert I	b. 1415	d. 1493

1493–1519	Emperor	Maximilian I, son of Frederick III	b. 1459	d. 1519
1519–1556	"	Charles V, grandson of Maximilian I	b. 1500	d. 1558
1556–1564	"	Ferdinand I, brother of Charles V abdicated 1555	b. 1503	d. 1564
1564–1576	"	Maximilian II, son of Ferdinand I	b. 1527	d. 1576
1576–1612	"	Rudolf II, son of Maximilian II	b. 1552	d. 1612
1612–1619	"	Matthias, son of Maximilian II	b. 1557	d. 1619
1619–1637	"	Ferdinand II, nephew of Maximilian II	b. 1578	d. 1637
1637–1658	"	Ferdinand III, son of Ferdinand II	b. 1608	d. 1658
1658–1705	"	Leopold I, son of Ferdinand III	b. 1640	d. 1705
1705–1711	"	Joseph I, son of Leopold I	b. 1678	d. 1711
1711–1740 (Interregnum)	"	Charles VI, son of Leopold I	b. 1685	d. 1740
1742–1745	Emperor	Charles VII, son of Maximilian Emanuel, Elector of Bavaria	b. 1697	d. 1745

HOUSE OF HABSBURG-LORRAINE

1745–1765	"	Francis I, son of Leopold, Duke of Lorraine and Consort of Maria Theresa	b. 1708	d. 1765
1765–1790	"	Joseph II, son of Francis I and Maria Theresa	b. 1741	d. 1790
1790–1792	"	Leopold II, brother of Joseph II	b. 1747	d. 1792
1792–1806	"	Francis II, son of Leopold II abdicated 1806	b. 1768	d. 1835

(Emperor of Austria from 1804 to 1835)

(The Holy Roman Empire was formally abolished under Napoleon's pressure in 1806)

Emperor Charles VI (1711–1740).

Archduchess Maria Theresa (1740–1780) was the mother of Queen Marie Antoinette of France.

Francis II (1792–1806) was the last Holy Roman Emperor and the first Emperor of Austria.

Honduras

Coat-of-arms of the Republic of Honduras as depicted on a coin.

(Proclaimed an independent sovereign state in 1838)

1864–1872	President	José M. Medina		
1872–1874	„	Celio Arias		
1874–1875	„	Marco Aurelio Soto	b. 1846	d. 1908
1875–1876	„	Ponciano Leiva		
1877–1883	„	Marco Aurelio Soto		
1883–1891	„	Luis Bográn		
1891–1894	„	Ponciano Leiva		
1894–1900	„	Policarpo Bonilla	b. 1858	d. 1926
1900–1903	„	Terencio Sierra		
1903–1907	„	Manuel Bonilla	b. 1849	d. 1913
1907–1911	„	Miguel R. Dávila		d. 1927
1911–1912	President (provisional)	Francisco Bertrand		d. 1927
1912–1913	President	Manuel Bonilla		
1913–1919	„	Francisco Bertrand		
1919–1924	„	Rafael López Gutiérrez (Civil War, 1924)		d. 1924
1924–1925	President (provisional)	Vicente Tosta		d. 1928
1925–1929	President	Miguel Paz Baraona		d. 1931
1929–1933	„	Vicente Mejía Colindres		
1932–1948	„	Tiburcio Carías Andino	b. 1876	
1949–1953	„	Juan Manuel Galvez		
1954–1956	Chief of State	Julio Lozano Diaz		d. 1957
1957–1963	President	José Ramón Villeda Morales		
1963–	Chief of State	Oswaldo López Arellano	b. 1921	

Spain ruled Honduras from the early 16th century until 1821, when the country became independent as part of the Central American Federation; was under the rule of Mexico until 1824 when the Federation was re-established; became fully independent in 1838. The lempira, a currency unit, is named for an Indian chief who resisted the first Spaniards.

Hong Kong

Coin of the Crown Colony of Hong Kong struck during the reign of King Edward VII of England (1901–1910).

(Ceded to Britain by China in 1842)

1843–1844	Governor	Sir Henry Pottinger	b. 1789	d. 1856
1844–1848	„	Sir John Francis Davis		

1848–1854	Governor	Sir Samuel George Bonham		
1854–1859	,,	Sir John Bowring	b. 1792	d. 1872
1859–1866	,,	Sir Hercules George Robert Robinson, Baron Rosmead	b. 1824	d. 1897
1866–1872	,,	Sir Richard Graves MacDonnell		
1872–1877	,,	Sir Arthur Edward Kennedy		
1877–1883	,,	Sir John Pope Hennessy		
1883–1887	,,	Sir George Ferguson Bowen	b. 1821	d. 1899
1887–1891	,,	Sir George William Des Voeux	b. 1834	d. 1909
1891–1898	,,	Sir William Robinson	b. 1836	d. 1912
1898–1904	,,	Sir Henry Arthur Blake	b. 1840	d. 1918
1904–1907	,,	Sir Matthew Nathan	b. 1862	d. 1939
1907–1912	,,	Sir Frederick John Dealtry Lugard, Baron Lugard	b. 1858	d. 1945

An energetic colonial administrator, Lord Lugard did much to abolish slave trading and build up the British dominions during his long service as a commissioner and governor.

(Left) Sir David Clive Crosbie-Trench, Governor of Hong Kong (1964–   ).

(Right) Queen Elizabeth II of England, as ruler of Hong Kong appears on a stamp of the Crown Colony.

1912–1919	Governor	Sir Francis Henry May	b. 1860	d. 1922
1919–1925	,,	Sir Reginald Edward Stubbs	b. 1876	d. 1947
1925–1930	,,	Sir Cecil Clementi	b. 1875	d. 1947
1930–1935	,,	Sir William Peel	b. 1875	d. 1945
1935–1937	,,	Sir Andrew Caldecott	b. 1884	d. 1951
1937–1941	,,	Sir Geoffry Alexander Stafford Northcote	b. 1881	d. 1948
1941–1947	,,	Sir Mark Aitchison Young	b. 1886	
1947–1958	,,	Sir Alexander William George Herder Grantham	b. 1899	
1958–1964	,,	Sir Robert Brown Black	b. 1906	
1964–	,,	Sir David Clive Crosbie-Trench	b. 1915	

Hungary *(Hun. Magyar Nepkoztarsasag)*

Stephen I, King of Hungary (997–1038), is the patron saint of his country.

(No authenticated information is available for the period before arrival of the Magyars (Hunagars) under Arpád)

875– 907		Arpád		d. 907
		(Arpád Dynasty ruled Hungary until 1301)		
972– 997	Duke	Geza		
997–1038	King	Stephen I (St. Stephen), son of Geza	b. 975?	d. 1038

Stephen I was known as "the Apostle of Hungary." He was crowned King with a crown sent by Pope Sylvester III, and his title of "Apostolic King" was used by all subsequent Hungarian sovereigns. He suppressed paganism, encouraged trade, and became the patron saint of Hungary, being canonized in 1087.

1038–1041	King	Peter Orseolo, son-in-law of Stephen I	b. 1011?	d. 1050?
1041–1044	,,	Aba Samuel, brother-in-law of Stephen I		
1044–1046	,,	Peter Orseolo		
1046–1060	,,	Andrew I, cousin of Peter Orseolo		d. 1060
1060–1063	,,	Bela I, brother of Andrew I		
1063–1074	,,	Salomon, son of Andrew I		
1074–1077	,,	Geza I, son of Bela I		
1077–1095	,,	Ladislaus I, (St. Laszlo), son of Bela I	b. 1040	d. 1095
1095–1116	,,	Salomon, nephew of Ladislaus I	b. 1070	d. 1116
1116–1131	,,	Stephen II, son of Salomon abdicated 1131	b. 1100	d. 1131
1131–1141	,,	Bela II, grandson of Bela I		
1141–1161	,,	Geza II, son of Bela II		
1161–1162	,,	Stephen III, son of Geza II		
1162–1163	,,	Ladislaus II, son of Bela II	b. 1134	d. 1163
1163–1165	,,	Stephen IV, son of Bela II		d. 1166
1165–1172	,,	Stephen III		
1173–1196	,,	Bela III, grandson of Bela II		d. 1196
1196–1204	,,	Emeric, son of Bela III		
1204–1205	,,	Ladislaus III, son of Emeric	b. 1179	d. 1205
1205–1235	,,	Andrew II, son of Emeric	b. 1175	d. 1235
1235–1270	,,	Bela IV, son of Andrew II	b. 1206	d. 1270
1270–1272	,,	Stephen V, son of Bela IV	b. 1239	d. 1272
1272–1290	,,	Ladislaus IV	b. 1262	murdered 1290
1290–1301	,,	Andrew III, grandson of Andrew II		d. 1301
		(End of Arpád Dynasty)		
1301–1305	,,	Wenceslaus of Bohemia	b. 1289	d. 1306
1305–1307	,,	Otho of Bavaria	abdicated 1309	d. 1312
1308–1342	,,	Charles I, grand-nephew of Ladislaus IV	b. 1288	d. 1342
1342–1382	,,	Louis the Great, son of Charles I	b. 1326	d. 1382
		(see Poland)		
1382–1387	Queen	Mary, daughter of Louis the Great	b. 1370	d. 1395
1387–1437	King	Sigismund, husband of Mary	b. 1368	d. 1437
		(see Bohemia)		
1437–1439	,,	Albert, son-in-law of Sigismund	b. 1397	d. 1439

Ladislaus I, King of Hungary (1077–1095), depicted on a 16th-century coin.

Gabriel Bethlen, Prince of Transylvania (1613–1629).

Hungary (continued)

1439–1440	Queen	Elizabeth, wife of Albert		d. 1443
1440–1444	King	Ladislaus of Poland, grandson of Mary	b. 1423?	d. 1444
1444–1457	,,	Ladislaus V, son of Albert	b. 1440	d. 1457
		(see Bohemia)		
1458–1490	,,	Matthias Corvinus	b. 1440	d. 1490
1490–1516	,,	Ladislaus of Bohemia, nephew of Ladislaus V	b. 1456	d. 1516
1516–1526	,,	Louis II, son of Vladislav II of Bohemia	b. 1506	d. 1526
		(Hungary was divided after 1526 between Turkey and Austria)		
		(see Holy Roman Empire)		

VOIVODES OF TRANSYLVANIA

1526–1540	Prince (Governor)	John Zapolya	b. 1487	d. 1540
1540–1571	,,	John Sigismund, son of John Zapolya	b. 1540	d. 1571
1571–1572	,,	Gaspar Békesy		
1571–1576	,,	Stephen Bathory (King of Poland)	b. 1533	d. 1586
1576–1581	,,	Christopher,		
		brother of Stephen Bathory	b. 1530	d. 1581
1581–1598	,,	Sigismund, son of Christopher	b. 1572	d. 1613
1599–1600	,,	Andrew, cousin of Sigismund	b. 1562	
1600–1602	,,	Michael the Brave		
1602–1603	,,	Moyses Szekely		
1602–1605	,,	Rudolph II (Emperor)		
1605–1606	,,	Stephen Bocskai	b. 1557	d. 1606

Stephen Bocskai freed Transylvania from Habsburg oppression. With Turkish help, he overran northern Hungary, and at the Treaty of Vienna obtained political autonomy and religious liberty for Hungarian Protestants. He is said to have been poisoned.

1607–1608	Prince (Governor)	Sigismund Rakoczi	b. 1544	d. 1608
1608–1613	,,	Gabriel Bathory,		
		son of Stephen Bathory	b. 1589	murdered 1613
1613–1629	,,	Gabriel Bethlen	b. 1580	
1630	,,	Stephen Bethlen		
1630–1648	,,	George Rakoczi, son of Sigismund	b. 1591	d. 1648
1648–1660	,,	George II, son of George Rakoczi	b. 1621	killed 1660
1658–1660	,,	Achatius Bocskai		
1661–1662	,,	Johann Kemeny		
1682–1699	,,	Emerich Tököli		
1662–1690	Governor (Turkish)	Michael Apafi	b. 1632	d. 1690
1690–1699	,,	Michael II Apafi, son of Michael		
		Apafi abdicated 1699	b. 1680	d. 1713
		(To Habsburg Hungary, 1699)		
1704–1711	Prince	Francis Rakoczi	b. 1676	d. 1735

Francis Rakoczi, Prince of Transylvania (1704–1711).

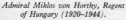

Admiral Miklos von Horthy, Regent of Hungary (1920–1944).

Lajos Kossuth, Governor of Hungary (1848–1849) was also President of a short-lived Hungarian Republic in 1849.

(Hungary under Austria 1711–1918)

(Republic proclaimed 1919)

1919	President	Mihaly Karolyi	b. 1875	d. 1955
1919	Head of Bolshevik Government	Bela Kun	b. 1886	d. 1939

(Kingless monarchy established 1919)

1919	Regent	Joseph of Austria	b. 1872	
1920–1944	Regent	Admiral Miklos von Horthy of Nagybanya	b. 1868	d. 1957

Admiral Horthy served with distinction in the Austro-Hungarian navy during the First World War and towards its end was appointed naval commander-in-chief. After the war he fought the Bolsheviks and became Regent of Hungary.

1944–1945	Regent	Ferenc Szalasi	b. 1897	d. 1946
1944–1945	Regent (opposition government)	Bela Miklos	b. 1890	d. 1948

(Republic proclaimed in 1946)

1946–1948	President	Zoltan Tildy	b. 1889	
1948–1950	,,	Arpad Szakasits	b. 1888	

(Communist regime established in 1949)

1950–1952	,,	Sandoe Ronai	b. 1892	
1952–1967	,,	Istvan Dobi	b. 1898	
1967–	,,	Pal Losonczy	b. 1919	

STATESMEN

1848–1849	Governor	Lajos Kossuth	b. 1802	d. 1884
1849	Commander-in-Chief of the Army	Arthur Gorgei	b. 1818	d. 1916
1867–1871	Prime Minister	Count Gyula Andrassy	b. 1823	d. 1890
1875–1890	,,	Koloman Tisza	b. 1830	d. 1902
1903–1905	,,	Istvan Tisza	b. 1861	d. 1918
1913–1917	,,	Istvan Tisza		
1892–1894	,,	Alexander Wekerle	b. 1848	d. 1921
1906–1910	,,	Alexander Wekerle		
1917–1918	,,	Alexander Wekerle		
1918–1919	,,	Mihaly Karolyi		
1919–1920	,,	Karoly Huszar	b. 1882	
1920–1921	,,	Pal Teleki	b. 1879	d. 1941
1921–1931	,,	Count Istvan Bethlen	b. 1874	
1932–1936	,,	Gyula Gombos	b. 1886	d. 1936
1936–1938	,,	Kalman Daranyi	b. 1886	d. 1939
1938–1939	,,	Bela Imredy	b. 1891	d. 1946
1939–1941	,,	Pal Teleki		
1942–1944	,,	Miklos Kallay	b. 1887	
1945–1946	,,	Zoltan Tildy	b. 1889	
1946–1947	,,	Ferenc Nagy	b. 1903	
1948–1952	,,	Istvan Dobi	b. 1898	
1952–1953	,,	Matyas Rakosi	b. 1892	
1953–1955	,,	Imre Nagy	b. 1895	executed 1958
1956–1958	Council President	Janos Kadar	b. 1912	
1958–1961	,,	Ferenc Münnich	b. 1886	d. 1967
1961–1965	,,	Janos Kadar		
1965–1967	,,	Gyula Kallai		
1967–	,,	Jeno Fock		

(Left) Istvan Dobi, President
of Hungary (1952–1967).

(Right) Gyula Kallai,
Council President of
Hungary (1965–1967).

Iceland *(Ice. Island)*

(Ruled by Denmark from 1380; recognized by Denmark as an independent, sovereign
state in 1918)

1918–1944	King	Christian X of Denmark	b. 1870	d. 1947

King Christian was responsible for the Act of Union between Denmark and
Iceland. This made Iceland independent, but for its personal connection
with Denmark through a single sovereign.

1941–1944	Regent	Sveinn Björnsson	b. 1881	d. 1952

(An independent Republic since 1944)

1944–1952	President	Sveinn Björnsson		
1952–1968	,,	Asgeir Asgeirsson	b. 1894	
1968	,,	Kristian Eldjarn	b. 1917	

STATESMEN

1918–1922	Prime Minister	Jon Magnusson	b. 1859	d. 1926
1922–1924	,,	Sigurdur Eggerz	b. 1875	d. 1945
1924–1926	,,	Jon Magnusson		
1926–1927	,,	Jon Thorlaksson	b. 1877	d. 1935
1927–1932	,,	Tryggvi Thorhallsson	b. 1889	d. 1935
1932–1934	,,	Asgeir Asgeirsson		
1934–1942	,,	Hermann Jonasson	b. 1896	
1942	,,	Olafur Thors	b. 1892	d. 1964
1942–1944	,,	Björn Thordarson	b. 1879	d. 1963
1944–1947	,,	Olafur Thors		
1947–1949	,,	Stefan Joh. Stefansson	b. 1894	
1949–1950	,,	Olafur Thors		
1950–1953	,,	Steingrimur Steinthorsson	b. 1893	
1953–1956	,,	Olafur Thors		
1956–1958	,,	Hermann Jonasson		
1958–1959	,,	Emil Jonsson	b. 1902	
1959–1963	,,	Olafur Thors		
1963–	,,	Bjarni Benediktsson	b. 1908	

Asgeir Asgeirsson,
President of Iceland
(1952–1968).

Bjarni Benediktsson,
Prime Minister of Iceland
(1963–   ).

The Mogul Emperor Jahangir (1605–1627) dispenses justice in his court at Delhi.

India

(Before the Mogul conquest, the history of India was largely that of many separate states)

B.C.

320– 298	Emperor	Chandra Gupta Maurya	d. 286 B.C. ?
259– 232	„	Asoka, grandson of Chandra Gupta	b. 273 d. 232 B.C.

MOGUL EMPERORS

1526–1530	Emperor	Baber (Babar or Babur)	b. 1483 d. 1530
1530–1556	„	Humayun, son of Baber	b. 1507 d. 1556

(Interregnum from 1544–1555 when Sher Shah ruled)

1556–1605   „   Jalaluddin Mohammed Akbar, (Akbar the Great), son of Humayun   b. 1542   d. 1605

After assuming the reins of government at the age of 18, Akbar the Great won the empire back from the Hindus, conquering the Punjab, Gujarat, Bengal, Kashmir and Sind. An able administrator, he was tolerant towards the many Indian religious faiths and he established schools for Hindus, Muslims and Parsees. He became known as "the Guardian of Mankind."

1605–1627	Emperor	Jahangir, son of Jalaluddin Mohammed Akbar	b. 1569 d. 1627
1628–1658	„	Shah Jahan, son of Jahangir deposed 1658	b. 1592 d. 1666
1658–1707	„	Aurangzeb, son of Shah Jahan	b. 1618 d. 1707

(Persian conquests from 1738)

1837–1857   Emperor (nominal)   Bahadur Shah II   deposed 1857   b. 1768 ? d. 1862

(Indian Mutiny, 1857–1858)

EUROPEAN GOVERNORS

1505–1509	Portuguese Viceroy	Francisco de Almeida	b. 1450 ? d. 1510
1509–1515	„	Alfonso d'Albuquerque	b. 1453 d. 1515
1742–1754	French Governor-General	Joseph François Dupleix	b. 1697 d. 1763

English Governors-General:

| 1758–1760 | Governor-General | Robert Clive, Baron Clive of Plassey | b. 1725 | d. 1774 |
| 1765–1767 | „ | Robert Clive, Baron Clive of Plassey | | |

Robert Clive founded the empire of British India, avenged the atrocity of the Black Hole of Calcutta, and defeated the Nawab of Bengal, Suraj-ud Dowlah. Yet when he finally returned to England he met a storm of calumny and was accused of abusing his powers. As a result of this accusation he first took to opium and then committed suicide.

| 1772–1785 | Governor-General | Warren Hastings | b. 1732 | d. 1818 |
| 1786–1793 | „ | Charles Cornwallis, Marquis Cornwallis | b. 1738 | d. 1805 |

Robert Clive, Governor-General of British India (1758–1760, 1765–1767).

James Ramsay, Marquis of Dalhousie, Governor-General of British India (1848–1856).

1793–1798	Governor-General	John Shore, Baron Teignmouth	b. 1751	d. 1834
1797–1805	„	Richard Colley Wellesley, Marquis Wellesley	b. 1760	d. 1842
1804–1805	„	Charles Cornwallis, Marquis Cornwallis		
1807–1813	„	Sir Gilbert Elliot-Murray-Kynynmound, Earl of Minto	b. 1751	d. 1814
1813–1823	„	Francis Rawdon-Hastings, Marquis of Hastings	b. 1754	d. 1826
1823–1828	„	William Pitt Amherst, Earl Amherst	b. 1773	d. 1857
1828–1835	„	Lord William Cavendish Bentinck	b. 1774	d. 1839
1836–1842	„	George Eden, Earl of Auckland	b. 1784	d. 1849
1842–1844	„	Edward Law, Earl of Ellenborough	b. 1790	d. 1871
1844–1848	„	Sir Henry Hardinge, Viscount Hardinge of Lahore	b. 1785	d. 1856
1848–1856	„	James Andrew Broun Ramsay, Earl and Marquis of Dalhousie	b. 1812	d. 1860
1856–1858	„	Charles John Canning, Earl Canning	b. 1812	d. 1862

(Government transferred from East India Company to British Government in 1858)

VICEROYS

1858–1862	Viceroy	Charles John Canning, Earl Canning		
1862–1863	„	James Bruce, Earl of Elgin	b. 1811	d. 1863
1864–1869	„	John Laird Mair, Baron Lawrence	b. 1811	d. 1879
1869–1872	„	Richard Southwell Bourke, Earl of Mayo	b. 1822	murdered 1872
1872–1876	„	Thomas George Baring, Earl of Northbrook	b. 1826	d. 1904
1876–1880	„	Edward Robert Bulwer Lytton, Earl of Lytton	b. 1831	d. 1891
		(Indian Empire proclaimed in 1877)		

India (continued)

1880–1884	Viceroy	George Frederick Samuel Robinson, Marquis of Ripon	b. 1827	d. 1909
1884–1888	„	Frederick Temple Hamilton-Temple-Blackwood, Marquis of Dufferin and Ava	b. 1826	d. 1902
1888–1894	„	Henry Charles Keith Petty-Fitzmaurice, Marquis of Lansdowne	b. 1845	d. 1927
1894–1899	„	Victor Alexander Bruce, Earl of Elgin	b. 1849	d. 1917
1899–1905	„	George Nathaniel Curzon, Marquis of Kedleston	b. 1859	d. 1925

Lord Curzon was made Under-Secretary of State for India in 1891. Appointed Viceroy at 39, he stabilized the financial relations of the Indian government and provinces and he reduced the salt tax. He resigned over a dispute with Lord Kitchener, the army commander-in-chief. In 1923, as Foreign Secretary, he induced the Russians to suspend anti-British propaganda.

| 1905–1910 | Viceroy | Gilbert John Elliot-Murray-Kynynmound, Earl of Minto | b. 1845 | d. 1914 |

Lord Hardinge, Viceroy of India (1910–1916) rides in state atop an elephant.

1910–1916	Viceroy	Charles Hardinge, Baron Hardinge of Penshurst	b. 1858	d. 1944
1916–1921	„	Frederick John Napier Thesiger, Viscount Chelmsford	b. 1868	d. 1933
1921–1926	„	Rufus Daniel Isaacs, Marquis of Reading	b. 1860	d. 1935
1926–1931	„	Edward Frederick Lindley Wood, Earl of Halifax	b. 1881	d. 1959
1931–1936	„	Freeman Freeman-Thomas, Marquis of Willingdon	b. 1866	d. 1941
1936–1943	„	Victor Alexander John Hope, Earl of Hopetoun and Marquis of Linlithgow	b. 1887	d. 1951
1943–1947	„	Archibald Percival Wavell, Earl Wavell (Dominion established in 1947)	b. 1883	d. 1950

1947–1948	Viceroy	Louis Francis Albert Victor Nicholas Mountbatten, Earl Mountbatten of Burma	b. 1900
1948–1950	,,	Chakravarti Rajagopalachari	b. 1879

REPUBLIC

1950–1962	President	Rajendra Prasad	b. 1884 d. 1963
1962–1967	,,	Sarvepalli Radhakrishnan	b. 1888
1967–	,,	Zakir Hussain	b. 1897
1947–1964	Prime Minister	Pandit Jawaharlal Nehru	b. 1889 d. 1964

Pandit Nehru studied science and law at Harrow and Cambridge. As a Congress Party leader he was frequently imprisoned. He played a leading part in the final negotiations for India's independence, and his country made important social and industrial advances during his premiership.

1964–1966	Prime Minister	Lal Bahadur Shastri	b. 1904 d. 1966
1966–	,,	Indira Gandhi, daughter of Jawaharlal Nehru	b. 1917

(Left) Sarvepalli Radhakrishnan, President of India (1962–1967);
(Right) Pandit Jawaharlal Nehru, Prime Minister of India (1947–1964).

(Left) Lal Bahadur Shastri, Prime Minister of India (1964–1966);
(Right) Indira Gandhi, Prime Minister of India (1966–   ).

NATIONAL LEADERS

Gopal Krishna Gokhale	b. 1866 d. 1915
Bal Gangadhar Tilak	b. 1856 d. 1920
Subhas Chandra Bose	b. 1897 d. 1945
Mohandas Karamchand Gandhi	b. 1869 assassinated 1948

Gandhi tried to bring about the co-operation of all Indians during the difficult situation that developed after the granting of independence to India. But on his way to a prayer meeting the great moral teacher of non-violence was assassinated by a fanatic.

Bal Gangadhar Tilak was one of the chief leaders of the movement for "swaraj" (independence from British rule).

Mohandas Karamchand Gandhi guided India toward independence through the non-violent disciplines of "satyagraha," literally, "holding on to truth."

Indo-China, see Cambodia, Laos, Vietnam

Indonesia

(As the Dutch East Indies, Indonesia was governed by the Netherlands 1610–1945)

DUTCH EAST INDIES

1610–1614	Governor-General	Pieter Both
1614–1615	,,	Gerrit Reijnst
1615–1619	,,	Laurens Real
1619–1623	,,	Jan Pietersz. Coen
1623–1627	,,	Pieter Carpentier
1627–1629	,,	Jan Pietersz. Coen
1629–1632	,,	Jacques Specx
1632–1636	,,	Hendrik Brouwer
1636–1645	,,	Antonie van Diemen
1645–1650	,,	Cornelis van der Lijn
1650–1653	,,	Carel Reiniersz
1653–1678	,,	Joan Maetsuyker
1678–1681	,,	Rijklof van Goens
1681–1684	,,	Cornelis Janszoon Speelman
1684–1694	,,	Johannes Camphuys
1691–1704	,,	Willem van Outhoorn
1704–1709	,,	Joan van Hoorn
1709–1713	,,	Abraham van Riebeeck
1713–1718	,,	Christoffel van Swol
1718–1725	,,	Hendrik Zwaardecroon
1725–1729	,,	Mattheus de Haan
1729–1732	,,	Diedrik Durven
1732–1735	,,	Dirk van Cloon
1735–1737	,,	Abraham Patras
1737–1741	,,	Adriaan Valckenier

Coat-of-arms of the Republic of Indonesia.

Indonesia (continued)

1714–1743	Governor-General	Joannes Thedens
1743–1750	"	Gustaaf Willem baron van Imhoff
1750–1761	"	Jacob Mossel
1761–1775	"	Petrus Albertus van des Parra
1775–1777	"	Jeremias van Riemsdijk
1777–1780	"	Reinier de Klerk
1780–1796	"	Willem Arnold Alting
1796–1801	"	Pieter Gerardus van Overstraten
1801–1804	"	Johannes Siberg
1804–1808	"	Albertus Henricus Wiese
1808–1811	"	Herman Willem Daendels
1811	"	Jan Willem Janssens
1811	English Governor	Sir Gilbert Elliot-Murray-Kynynmound, 1st Earl of Minto b. 1751 d. 1814

During the Napoleonic Wars the British occupied the Dutch East Indies. The Earl of Minto, then Governor of British India, served simultaneously as Governor of the East Indies.

Johan Paul graaf van Limburg Stirum, Governor-General of the Dutch East Indies (1916–1921), presides over a council meeting.

1811–1816	English Governor	Sir Thomas Stamford Raffles b. 1781 d. 1836
1816	"	John Fendall
1819–1826	Governor-General	Godert Alexander Gerard Philip baron van der Capellen
1826–1830	"	Hendrik Merkus baron de Kok
1830–1833	"	Johannes graaf van der Bosch
1833–1836	Governor-General (acting)	Jean Chrétien Baud
1836–1840	Governor-General	Dominique Jacques de Eerens
1840–1841	Governor-General (acting)	Carel Sirardus Willem van Hogendorp
1841–1843	"	Pieter Merkus
1843–1844	Governor-General	Pieter Merkus
1844–1845	Governor-General (acting)	Joan Cornelis Reijnst
1845–1851	Governor-General	Jan Jacob Rochussen
1851–1856	"	Albertus Jacob Duymaer van Twist
1856–1861	"	Charles Ferdinand Pahud
1861	Governor-General (acting)	Arij Prins
1861–1866	Governor-General	Ludolf Anne Jan Wilt baron Sloet van der Beele
1866	Governor-General (acting)	Arij Prins

1866–1872	Governor-General	Pieter Mijer
1872–1875	,,	James Loudon
1875–1881	,,	Johan Willem van Lansberge
1881–1884	,,	Frederiks' Jacob
1884–1888	,,	Otto van Rees
1888–1893	,,	Cornelis Pijnacker Hordijk
1893–1899	,,	Carel Herman Aart
1899–1904	,,	Willem Rooseboom
1904–1909	,,	Joannes Benedictus van Heutsz
1909–1916	,,	Alexander Willem Frederik Idenburg
1916–1921	,,	Johan Paul graaf van Limburg Stirum
1921–1926	,,	Dirk Fock
1926–1931	,,	Andries Cornelis Dirk de Graeff
1931–1936	,,	Bonifacius Cornelis de Jonge
1936–1945	,,	Alidius Warmoldus Lambertus Tjarda van Starkenborgh Stachouwer

(Civil War, 1945–1949)

REPUBLIC OF INDONESIA

1950–1967	President	Mohammad Achmad Sukarno (or Soekarno)	b. 1901
1966–1967	Chairman of the Presidium	General Raden Suharto	b. 1921
1967–	President	,, ,, ,,	

Mohammad Achmad Sukarno, President of Indonesia (1950–1967), at right, greets President Nkrumah of Ghana, while Prime Minister Nehru of India looks on.

Iran, see Persia

Iraq Also see Assyria, Babylonia

(Known to the Greeks and Romans as Mesopotamia, Iraq corresponds to ancient Assyria and Babylonia; under Turkish rule until 1919; British Mandate, 1919–1921)

1921–1933	King	Faisal I, son of Husein ibn-Ali of Hejaz	b. 1885	d. 1933
1933–1939	,,	Ghazi, son of Faisal I	b. 1912	d. 1939
1939–1958	,,	Faisal II, son of Ghazi	b. 1935	assassinated 1958
1939–1953	Regent	Abdullah, uncle of Faisal II		assassinated 1958
		(A military republic since 1958)		
1963–1966	President	Abdul Salam Mohammed Aref	b. 1921	d. 1966

| 1966–1968 | President | Abdul Razhman Arif | b. 1916 |
| 1968– | ,, | Ahmad Hassan al-Bakr | b. 1912 |

Tahir Yahia, Prime Minister of Iraq (1963–1964).

Abdul Salam Mohammed Aref, President of Iraq (1963–1966).

Faisal I, King of Iraq (1921–1933) collaborated with T. E. Lawrence in the Arab revolt against Turkish domination in 1916.

STATESMEN

1938–1940	Prime Minister	Nuri al-Said (Nuri es-Sa'id)	b. 1888	assassinated 1958
1941–1944	″	Nuri al-Said		
1946–1948	″	Nuri al-Said		
1954–1958	″	Nuri al-Said		
1958–1963	″	Abdul Karim Kassem	b. 1914	assassinated 1963
1963–1964	″	Tahir Yahia	b. 1913	
1964–1965	″	Abdal Arif Razzak		
1965–1966	″	Abdul Rahman al Bazzaz		
1966–	″	Naji Talib		

Ireland (Irish: Eire)

James Butler, first Duke of Ormonde, served as Lord Lieutenant of Ireland three times during the period 1644–1685.

[Conn Céd-cathach founded the Middle Kingdom (Meath) and began the High Kingship of Tara in A.D. 200]

377– 405	High King	Niall of the Nine Hostages	d. 405
		(Owen (Eoghan) and Conall founded the Kingdom of Aileach in 400)	
– 432	″	Loeguire, son of Niall	
		(St. Patrick began his mission in Ireland in 432)	
		(Norse invasions, 795–1014)	
900– 908	King of Cashel	Cormac MacCullenan	
– 919	High King	Niall Glundubh	d. 919
–1002	King	Malachy II	
1002–1014	″	Brian Boru	b. 926 killed 1014
		(Interregnum, 1022–1072)	
1014–1064	King of Munster	Donnchad, son of Brian	
1064–1086	″ ″	Turlough (Toirdelbach) nephew of Donnchad	b. 1009 d. 1086
1086–1119	″ ″	Muirchertach O'Brien, son of Turlough (Toirdelbach)	d. 1119

(Before the Anglo-Norman invasions began in the 12th century, Ireland was a loose organization of four or five kings, under an elective overlord)

1119–1153	High King	Turlough (Toirdelbach) More O'Connor	d. 1153
1134–1171	King of Leinster	Dermot MacMurrough	b. 1110? d. 1171
1153–1166	King	Muirchertach MacLochlainn	
1166–1175	High King	Roderic *or* Rory O'Connor, son of Turlough (Toirdelbach)	b. 1116? d. 1198

(Last native King of Ireland; the Pope granted Ireland to King Henry II of England in 1172)

1177	Dominus Hiberniae	John, son of Henry II	b. 1167? d. 1216
1235	Ruler of Connaught	Richard de Burgo	
1376–1417	King of Leinster	Art MacMurrough	
1477–1513	„ „	Gerald Fitzgerald, Earl of Kildare	d. 1513
1487	King	Edward VI (Lambert Simnel)	b. 1477? d. 1525

Lambert Simnel was an English imposter to the throne groomed to impersonate the son of the Duke of Clarence. He was taken to Ireland and crowned King Edward VI in the cathedral in Dublin. Pardoned for his role in the plot, he became royal falconer.

1513–1534	Deputy Governor	Gerald Fitzgerald, Earl of Kildare	b. 1487 d. 1534
1541	King of Ireland	Henry VIII of England	b. 1491 d. 1547
1547–1553	„	Edward VI, son of Henry VIII	b. 1537 d. 1553

(Plantation of Leix and Offaly, 1556; Plantation of Munster, 1586; Tyrone War 1594–1603; foundation of British Colony in Ulster. 1608–1610)

1599	Lord Lieutenant of Ireland	Robert Devereux, 2nd Earl of Essex	b. 1566 d. 1601
1632–1638	Lord Deputy	Sir Thomas Wentworth, Earl of Strafford	b. 1593 beheaded 1641
1640	Lord Lieutenant	Sir Thomas Wentworth, Earl of Strafford	
1644–1649	„	James Butler, Earl, Marquis and Duke of Ormonde	b. 1610 d. 1688
1649–1650	„	Oliver Cromwell	b. 1599 d. 1658
1653–1658	Lord Protector	Oliver Cromwell	
1660–1685	King	Charles II	b. 1630 d. 1685

(Left) Henry VIII of England, King of Ireland (1541); (Middle) Edward VI, son of Henry VIII, King of Ireland (1547–1553); (Right) Robert Devereux, Lord Lieutenant of Ireland (1599).

1661–1669	Lord Lieutenant	James Butler, Earl, Marquis and Duke of Ormonde	
1670–1672	„	John Berkeley, Baron Berkeley	d. 1678
1672–1677	„	Arthur Capel, Earl of Essex	b. 1631 d. 1683
1677–1685	„	James Butler, Earl, Marquis and Duke of Ormonde	
1687–1691	Lord Deputy	Richard Talbot, Earl of Tyrconnell	b. 1630 d. 1691
1703–1705	Lord Lieutenant	James Butler, Earl, Marquis and Duke of Ormonde	b. 1665 d. 1745
1710–1711	„	James Butler, Earl, Marquis and Duke of Ormonde	
1713	„	Charles Talbot, Earl and Duke of Shrewsbury	b. 1660 d. 1718
1722–1730	„	John Carteret, Earl Granville	b. 1690 d. 1763

Charles II, King of England and Ireland (1660–1685) poses at left with his brother James and sister Mary. Known as the "Merry Monarch," his accession to the throne began the Restoration, a brilliant period in literature and art. Before he died, Charles was converted to Roman Catholicism.

1767–1774	Lord Lieutenant	George Townshend, Viscount and Marquis Townshend	b. 1724	d. 1807
1795	,,	William Wentworth, Earl Fitzwilliam	b. 1748	d. 1833
1795–1798	,,	Sir John Jeffreys Pratt, Earl and Marquis of Camden	b. 1759	d. 1840
1798–1801	,,	Charles Cornwallis, Marquis Cornwallis (Rebellion 1798)	b. 1738	d. 1805
		(United with England in 1801)		
1801–1806	,,	Earl of Hardwicke	b. 1757	d. 1834
1806–1807	,,	Duke of Bedford	b. 1792	d. 1839
1807–1813	,,	Duke of Richmond	b. 1764	d. 1819
1813–1817	,,	Earl Whitworth	b. 1752	d. 1825
1817–1821	,,	Earl Talbot	b. 1777	d. 1849
1821–1828	,,	Marquis of Wellesley	b. 1760	d. 1842
1828–1829	,,	Marquis of Anglesey	b. 1768	d. 1854
1829–1830	,,	Duke of Northumberland	b. 1785	d. 1847
1830–1833	,,	Marquis of Anglesey		
1833–1834	,,	Marquis of Wellesley		
1834–1835	,,	Earl of Haddington	b. 1780	d. 1858
1835–1839	,,	Marquis of Normanby	b. 1797	d. 1863
1839–1841	,,	Viscount Ebrington (afterwards Earl Fortescue)	b. 1783	d. 1861
1841–1844	,,	Earl de Grey	b. 1781	d. 1859
1844–1846	,,	Lord Heytesbury	b. 1779	d. 1860
1846–1847	,,	Earl of Bessborough	b. 1781	d. 1847
1847–1852	,,	Earl of Clarendon	b. 1800	d. 1870
1852–1853	,,	Earl of Eglinton	b. 1812	d. 1861
1853–1855	,,	Earl of St. Germans	b. 1798	d. 1877
1855–1858	,,	Earl of Carlisle	b. 1802	d. 1864
1858–1859	,,	Earl of Eglinton		
1859–1864	,,	Earl of Carlisle		
1864–1866	,,	Lord Wodehouse (afterwards Earl of Kimberley)	b. 1826	d. 1902
1866–1868	,,	Marquis of Abercorn	b. 1811	d. 1885
1868–1874	,,	Earl Spencer	b. 1835	d. 1910

Richard Talbot, Earl of Tyrconnell, Lord Deputy of Ireland (1687–1691).

George Townshend, Lord Lieutenant of Ireland (1767–1774), in a portrait by Sir Joshua Reynolds.

1874–1876	Lord Lieutenant	Duke of Abercorn		
1876–1880	,,	Duke of Marlborough	b. 1822	d. 1883
1880–1882	,,	Earl Cowper	b. 1834	d. 1905
1882–1885	,,	Earl Spencer	b. 1835	d. 1910
1885–1886	,,	Earl of Carnarvon	b. 1831	d. 1890
1886	,,	Earl of Aberdeen	b. 1847	d. 1934
1886–1889	,,	Marquis of Londonderry	b. 1852	d. 1915
1889–1892	,,	Earl of Zetland	b. 1844	d. 1929
1892–1895	,,	Lord Houghton	b. 1858	d. 1945
1895–1902	,,	Earl Cadogan	b. 1840	d. 1915
1902–1905	,,	Earl of Dudley	b. 1867	d. 1932
1905–1915	,,	Earl of Aberdeen	b. 1847	d. 1934
1915–1918	,,	Baron Wimborne	b. 1873	d. 1939
1918–1921	,,	Viscount French	b. 1852	d. 1925
1921–1922	,,	Viscount Fitzallen of Derwent	b. 1855	d. 1947
1875–1891	Nationalist leader	Charles Stewart Parnell	b. 1846	d. 1891
1916–1921	,,	Eamon de Valera	b. 1882	

Born in New York of a Spanish father and an Irish mother, De Valera was sentenced in 1916 by the British to life imprisonment for his part in the Easter week rebellion. He was amnestied in 1917, rearrested in 1918 and escaped from prison in 1919. Subsequently he became president of the League of Nations Assembly as well as Premier and President of the Irish Republic.

IRISH FREE STATE

1922	President	Arthur Griffith	b. 1872 d. 1922
1922	Head of Provisional Government	Michael Collins	b. 1890 killed 1922
1922–1932	President of Executive Council	William Thomas Cosgrave	b. 1880
1932–1937	,,	Eamon de Valera	

Eamon de Valera, President of the Republic of Ireland (1959–).

Seán Lemass, Taoiseach (Prime Minister) of the Republic of Ireland (1959–1966).

Charles Stewart Parnell, Nationalist leader of Ireland (1875–1891).

Michael Collins, Head of the Provisional Government of the Irish Free State (1922).

1921–1927	Governor-General of Free State	Timothy Michael Healy	b. 1855	d. 1931
1928–1932	Governor-General	James McNeill	b. 1869	d. 1938
1932–1937	,,	Donal Buckley	b. 1866	

REPUBLIC OF IRELAND

1938–1945	President	Douglas Hyde	b. 1860	
1945–1959	,,	Seán Thomas O'Kelly (O Ceallaigh)	b. 1883	d. 1966
1959–	,,	Eamon de Valera		

1937–1948	Prime Minister	Eamon de Valera		
1948–1951	,,	John Aloysius Costello	b. 1891	
1951–1954	,,	Eamon de Valera		
1954–1957	,,	John A. Costello		
1957–1959	,,	Eamon de Valera		
1959–1966	Taoiseach (Prime Minister)	Seán F. Lemass	b. 1899	
1966–	,,	John Lynch	b. 1917	

Lord Wakehurst, Governor of Northern Ireland (1952–1964).

NORTHERN IRELAND

(Separate government established in 1920)

1922–1945	Governor	James Albert Edward Hamilton, Duke of Abercorn	b. 1869	d. 1953
1945–1952	,,	William Spencer Leveson Gower, Earl Granville	b. 1880	d. 1953
1952–1964	,,	John De Vere Loder, Baron Wakehurst	b. 1895	
1964–	,,	Lord Erskine of Rerrick	b. 1893	
1921–1940	Prime Minister	James Craig, Viscount Craigavon	b. 1871	d. 1940

Viscount Craigavon resigned the position of financial secretary to the British Admiralty in 1920 to become the first Prime Minister of Northern Ireland—a post he held until his death. He was a firm opponent of Home Rule.

1940–1943	Prime Minister	John Miller Andrews	b. 1871	d. 1956
1943–1963	,,	Basil Stanlake Brooke, Viscount Brookeborough	b. 1888	d. 1963
1963–	,,	Terence Marne O'Neill	b. 1914	

Israel and Judah

Detail of Michelangelo's sculpture of David, King of Israel and Judah (1011–971 B.C.). This statue in Florence, Italy, is a full-size replica.

PERIOD OF UNITED MONARCHY

B.C.

1050–1011	King	Saul	killed 1011 B.C.
1011– 971	,,	David	d. 971 B.C. ?
971– 931	,,	Solomon, son of David	d. 931 B.C. ?

PERIOD OF DIVIDED MONARCHY
Northern Kingdom of Israel

B.C.			B.C.
931–910	King	Jeroboam I	d. 910 ?
910–909	,,	Nadab, son of Jeroboam I	assassinated 909
909–886	,,	Baasha	d. 886 ?
886–885	,,	Elah, son of Baasha,	assassinated 885
885–884	,,	Zimri	
885–880	,,	Tibni	
885–874	,,	Omri	d. 874 ?
874–853	,,	Ahab, son of Omri	d. 853 ?
853–852	,,	Ahaziah, son of Ahab	d. 852 ?
852–841	,,	Jehoram, brother of Ahaziah	d. 841 ?
841–814	,,	Jehu ben-Nimshi	d. 814 ?
814–798	,,	Jehoahaz, son of Jehu	d. 798 ?
798–782	,,	Joash, son of Jehoahaz	d. 782 ?
793–792	Co-regent	Jeroboam	d. 753 ?
782–753	King	Jeroboam II, son of Joash	
753–752	,,	Zachariah, son of Jeroboam II	assassinated 752
752	,,	Shallum	killed 752
752–742	,,	Menahem	d. 742 ?

742–740	King	Pekahiah, son of Menahem	assassinated 741
740–732	,,	Pekah	killed 732
732–723	,,	Hoshea	d. 723 ?
		(End of Kingdom of Israel)	

Southern Kingdom of Judah

B.C.			B.C.
931–913	,,	Rehoboam, son of Solomon	
913–911	,,	Abijah (or Abijam), son of Rehoboam	
911–870	,,	Asa, son of Abijah	d. 870 ?
873–872	Co-regent	Jehoshaphat	
870–848	King	Jehoshaphat, son of Asa	d. 848 ?
848–841	,,	Jehoram, son of Jehoshaphat	d. 841 ?
843–842	,,	Ahaziah, son of Jehoram	killed 842 ?
842–837	Queen	Athaliah, mother of Ahaziah	killed 837
835–791	King	Joash, son of Ahaziah	assassinated 791
791	,,	Amaziah, son of Joash	assassinated 791
791–740	,,	Uzziah, son of Amaziah	
750–	Co-regent	Jotham, son of Uzziah	d. 732 ?
740–732	King	Jotham	
740–732	,,	Ahaz, son of Jotham	d. 716 ?
744–743	Co-regent	Ahaz	
732–716	,,	Ahaz	
716–687	King	Hezekiah, son of Ahaz (Co-regent 729)	b. 740 ? d. 687 ?
696–695	Co-regent	Manasseh, son of Hezekiah	d. 642 ?
687–642	King	Manasseh	
642–640	,,	Amon, son of Manasseh	assassinated 640
640–609	,,	Josiah, son of Amon	b. 638 ? d. 608 ?
609	,,	Jehoahaz, son of Josiah	
609–597	,,	Jehoiakim, son of Josiah	d. 597 ?
597	,,	Jehoiachin (Coniah), son of Jehoiakim	b. 615 ? d. 560 ?
597–587	,,	Zedekiah (Mattaniah), son of Josiah	
		(Zedekiah was the last King of Judah)	

Solomon, King of Israel and Judah (971–931 B.C.) and the Queen of Sheba are depicted in this 15th-century painting by Konrad Witz.

(Jews conquered by Babylonians; thereafter they were under foreign rule until the revolt of the Maccabees against the successors of Alexander the Great of Macedonia)

MACCABEES

B.C.			B.C.	
168–167		Mattathias	d. 166?	
166–161		Judas Maccabaeus, son of Mattathias	d. 160	
161–143	High Priest	Jonathan, son of Mattathias		
143–135	,,	Simon, son of Mattathias		
135–105	,,	John Hyrcanus, son of Simon		
104–103	King	Judah (Aristobulus I), son of John Hyrcanus	b. 140?	d. 103
103– 76	,,	Alexander Jannaeus, son of John Hyrcanus		
76– 67	,,	Alexandra, wife of Alexander Jannaeus		d. 67
67– 63	,,	Hyrcanus II, son of Alexandra		d. 30
67– 63	Rival King	Aristobulus II		d. 48

(Maccabean state came under Roman rule)

TETRARCHS

63– 40	Ethnarch	Hyrcanus II		
40– 37	Rival King	Antigonus II, son of Aristobulus II	b. 80?	d. 37

"Herod's Feast" by Donatello portrays the presentation of John the Baptist's head to Herod Antipas, Ethnarch of Judah (4 B.C.–A.D. 38). In a plot to kill John, Herod was tricked by Salome, who demanded John's head as a reward for her dancing.

41– 4	Ethnarch	Herod the Great	b. 73?	d. 4
4 B.C.–6 A.D.	,,	Herod Archelaus, son of Herod the Great		d. 18 A.D. ?
4 B.C.–38 A.D.	,,	Herod Antipas, son of Herod the Great		d. 40 A.D. ?
4 B.C.–34 A.D.	,,	Philip, son of Herod the Great		d. 34 A.D.
40– 44	,,	Herod Agrippa I, grandson of Herod the Great	b. 10? B.C.	d. 44 A.D.

(Palestine governed by proconsuls from A.D. 44; Jerusalem destroyed A.D. 70; Persian dominion, 614–629; Arab dominion, 636–1099; Crusaders established Kingdom of Jerusalem)

KINGS OF JERUSALEM

1099–1100	Protector of the Holy Sepulchre	Godfrey of Bouillon	b. 1060	d. 1100
1100–1118	King	Baldwin I, brother of Godfrey of Bouillon	b. 1058	d. 1118
1118–1131	,,	Baldwin II, nephew of Baldwin I		d. 1131
1131–1143	,,	Fulk of Anjou, son-in-law of Baldwin II	b. 1092	d. 1143
1143–1162	,,	Baldwin III, son of Fulk of Anjou	b. 1130	d. 1162
1162–1174	,,	Amalric I, brother of Baldwin III	b. 1135	d. 1174
1174–1185	,,	Baldwin IV, son of Amalric I	b. 1161	d. 1185
1185–1186	,,	Baldwin V, nephew of Baldwin IV	b. 1178	d. 1186
1186–1192	,,	Guy of Lusignan (Saladin captured Jerusalem 1187) (Third Crusade 1189–1192)	b. 1140	d. 1194
1190–1192	Rival Regent	Conrad of Montferrat, son-in-law of Amalric	assassinated 1192	
1192–1197	King	Henry of Champagne		
1197–1205	,,	Amalric II of Cyprus, brother of Guy of Lusignan	b. 1144	d. 1205
1205–1229	,,	John of Brienne	b. 1148	d. 1237
1229–1244	,,	Frederick II (German Emperor), son-in-law of John of Brienne	b. 1148	d. 1250

(Jerusalem conquered by the Sultan of Egypt, 1244; Palestine under Turkish rule, 1518–1918; conquered by Britain, 1917–18; League of Nations mandate, 1923; divided into Israel and Jordan, 1948)

MODERN ISRAEL

David Ben-Gurion, first Prime Minister of modern Israel (1948–1953) reads the Declaration of Independence under a portrait of Theodor Herzl, leader of the Zionist movement.

1948–1952	President	Chaim Weizmann	b. 1874	d. 1952
1952–1963	,,	Itzhak Ben-Zvi	b. 1884	d. 1963
1963–	,,	Zalman Shazar	b. 1889	

1948–1953	Prime Minister	David Ben-Gurion	b. 1886	
1953–1955	,,	Moshe Sharett	b. 1894	
1955–1963	,,	David Ben-Gurion		
1963–	,,	Levi Eshkol	b. 1895	

Levi Eshkol, Prime Minister of
Israel (1963–   ).

Moshe Sharett, Prime Minister of
Israel (1953–1955).

Zalman Shazar, President of Israel (1963–   ).

Italy

Vittorio Emanuele II, King of Sardinia, was the first king of a united
Italy (1861–1878).

(Romulus Augustulus, last emperor of the West, was deposed by Odoacer in 476)

SCIRIANS

476– 493   King   Odoacer   b. 434? murdered 493

OSTROGOTHS

493– 526	„	Theodoric the Great, son of Theodemir	b. 454?	d. 526

Theodoric was for 10 years a youthful hostage at the Byzantine Court at Constantinople. After succeeding his chieftain father he became the most powerful Gothic King, invading and conquering Italy and murdering Odoacer with his own hand. He appears in the Nibelungenlied as "Dietrich von Bern."

526– 534	King	Athalaric, grandson of Theodoric	b. 516	d. 534
534– 536	„	Theodat		assassinated 536
536– 540	„	Vitiges, brother-in-law of Athalaric		
540	„	Theodebald (Hildibald)		assassinated 540
540– 541	„	Eraric		
541– 552	„	Totila, nephew of Theodebald		killed 552
552– 553	„	Teias		

(Italy under Byzantine Empire, 553–568)

LOMBARDS

568– 573	„	Alboin	d. 573
573– 575	„	Cleph	

(Interregnum, 575–584)

584– 590	„	Autharis, husband of Theodelinda, son of Cleph	d. 590
590	Queen	Theodelinda, wife of Autharis	
590– 615	King	Agilulf, Theodelinda's consort	
615– 625	„	Adaloald, son of Agilulf	
625– 636	„	Arioald, son-in-law of Agilulf	
636– 652	„	Rotharis, son-in-law of Agilulf	d. 652
652– 661	„	Aribert I	
662– 671	„	Grimoald, son-in-law of Aribert	
671– 674	„	Garibald, son of Grimoald	
674– 688	„	Bertharit, son of Aribert	
688– 700	„	Cunibert, son of Bertharit	
701– 712	„	Aribert II	
712– 744	„	Liutpand (Luitprand)	b. 690? d. 744
744– 749	„	Rachis of Friuli	
749– 756	„	Aistulf, brother of Rachis of Friuli	d. 756
756– 774	„	Desiderius	deposed 774

CAROLINGIAN DYNASTY

774– 814	„	Charlemagne, son-in-law of Desiderius	b. 742	d. 814
814– 818	„	Bernard, grandson of Charlemagne		
818– 855	„	Lothair I, grandson of Charlemagne	b. 796?	d. 855
		(see Germany and France)		
855– 875	„	Louis II, son of Louis I	b. 804?	d. 876
875– 877	„	Charles the Bald, son of Louis I	b. 823	d. 877
		(see France)		
877– 880	„	Carloman, nephew of Lothair I	d. 828	d. 880
		(see Germany)		
880– 887	„	Charles the Fat, brother of Carloman	b. 839	d. 888

OTHER KINGS

888– 894	„	Guy of Spoleto	d. 894
894– 898	„	Lambert, son of Guy of Spoleto	
899– 905	„	Louis III of Burgundy, grandson of Louis II	b. 880 d. 928?
888– 923	King (rival)	Berengarius of Friuli, great-grandson of Charlemagne	d. 924
923– 933	King	Rudolph II of Burgundy, son of Rudolph I	d. 937

Italy (continued)

933– 947	King	Hugh of Arles		d. 947
		(see Burgundy)		
947– 950	,,	Lothair II, son of Hugh of Arles		d. 950
950– 961	,,	Berengarius II of Ivrea, grandson of		
		Berengarius of Friuli		d. 966
961– 973	,,	Otto the Great, son of Henry I the Fowler	b. 912	d. 973
		(see Germany)		

(Italy was subject to the Holy Roman Empire, 961–1254)

(Italy divided into many small states until reunification in 1861)

English versions of the names of rulers of Italian-speaking states are:

Alexander–Alessandro	Henry–Enrico	Maximilian–Massimiliano
Caesar–Cesare	Humbert–Umberto	Peter–Pier, Piero, Pietro
Charles–Carlo	Joanna–Giovanna	Philip–Filippo
Conrad–Corrado	John–Giovanni	Roger–Ruggiero
Francis–Francesco	Joseph-Giuseppe	Victor–Vittorio
Frederick–Federigo	Louis–Lodovico, Luigi	

KINGDOM OF ITALY

1861–1878	King	Vittorio Emanuele II		
1878–1900	,,	Umberto I, son of Vittorio		
		Emanuele II	b. 1844	assassinated 1900
1900–1946	,,	Vittorio Emanuele III, son of Umberto I	b. 1869	d. 1947

Vittorio Emanuele III was King of Italy for nearly half a century. Although he became "Emperor of Ethiopia" in 1936 and "King of Albania" in 1939 his real power and authority declined under the Fascist regime.

1946	King	Umberto II, son of Vittorio		
		Emanuele III	b. 1904	
		(Republic declared in 1946)		

HEADS OF STATE

1945–1948	President (provisional)	Enrico de Nicola	b. 1877	
1948–1955	President	Luigi Einaudi	b. 1874	d. 1961
1955–1962	,,	Giovanni Gronchi	b. 1887	
1962–1964	,,	Antonio Segni	b. 1895	
1964–	,,	Giuseppe Saragat	b. 1898	

Antonio Segni,
President of Italy
(1962–1964).

Umberto I, King of Italy
(1878–1900).

Giuseppe Saragat,
President of Italy
(1964–   ).

STATESMEN

1852–1859	Premier	Count Camillo Cavour	b. 1810	d. 1861
1860–1861	,,	Count Camillo Cavour		

Hero of the Risorgimento, Cavour devoted himself to the liberation and unification of Italy. This he accomplished through the extraordinary diplomatic skill with which he conducted his difficult relations with Prince Louis Napoleon, Vittorio Emmanuele and Garibaldi.

1876–1879	Premier	Agostino Depretis	b. 1813	d. 1887
1881–1887	,,	Agostino Depretis		
1878	,,	Benedetto Cairoli	b. 1825	d. 1889
1879–1881	,,	Benedetto Cairoli		
1887–1891	,,	Francesco Crispi	b. 1819	d. 1901
1892–1893	,,	Giovanni Giolitti	b. 1842	d. 1928
1893–1896	,,	Francesco Crispi		
1903–1905	,,	Giovanni Giolitti		
1906–1909	,,	Giovanni Giolitti		
1911–1914	,,	Giovanni Giolitti		
1920–1921	,,	Giovanni Giolitti		
1922–1943	Dictator	Benito Mussolini	b. 1883	murdered 1945
1944–1945	Premier	Ivanoe Bonomi	b. 1873	
1945	,,	Ferruccio Parri	b. 1890	
1945–1953	,,	Alcide De Gasperi	b. 1881	d. 1954

Vittorio Emmanuele III, King of Italy (1900–1946).

Founder of the Fascist Movement, Benito Mussolini became Dictator of Italy (1922–1943). In 1945, toward the end of World War II, he was put to death by Italian partisans.

(Left) Aldo Moro, Premier of Italy (1963–   ).

(Right) Alcide De Gaspari, Premier of Italy (1945–1953).

Italy (continued)

1953–1954	Premier	Giuseppe Pella	b. 1902
1954	,,	Amintore Fanfani	b. 1908
1954–1955	,,	Mario Scelba	b. 1901
1955–1957	,,	Antonio Segni	b. 1895
1957–1958	,,	Adone Zoli	b. 1887
1958–1959	,,	Amintore Fanfani	
1959–1960	,,	Antonio Segni	
1960	,,	Fernando Tambroni	b. 1901
1960–1963	,,	Amintore Fanfani	
1963	,,	Giovanni Leone	b. 1908
1963–1968	,,	Aldo Moro	b. 1916
		(resigned but remained head of interim government)	

APULIA and CALABRIA

1057–1059	Count	Robert Guiscard, brother of Roger Guiscard	b. 1015? d. 1085
1059–1085	Duke	Robert Guiscard (see Sicily)	
1085–1111	,,	Roger Bursa, son of Robert Guiscard	
1111–1127	,,	Guillaume, son of Roger Bursa	
		(Apulia was united with Sicily in 1127)	

GENOA

(The city-state of Genoa developed into a maritime power of the first rank by the 13th century A.D. Ruled at first by consuls of the republic, then by doges from 1339)

| 1339–1363 | Doge | Simone Boccanera | b. 1300? d. 1363 |
| 1528–1560 | Dictator (Censor) | Andrea Doria | b. 1466 d. 1560 |

(Fell to French 1797, becoming the Ligurian Republic; in 1815 annexed to Kingdom of Sardinia)

(Left) Galeazzo Maria Sforza, Duke of Milan (1466–1476); (Middle) Giovanni Galeazzo Sforza, Duke of Milan (1476–1481); (Right) Lodovico (il Moro) Sforza, Duke of Milan (1481–1499).

MILAN

House of Visconti

1277–1295	Duke	Ottone V	b. 1207? d. 1295
1295–1302	,,	Matteo, grandnephew of Ottone V	b. 1255 d. 1322
1311–1322	,,	Matteo	
1322–1328	,,	Galeazzo I, son of Matteo	b. 1277? d. 1328
1328–1339	,,	Azzo, son of Galeazzo I	b. 1302 d. 1339
1339–1349	,,	Lucchino, son of Matteo	b. 1287? murdered 1349
1349–1354	,,	Giovanni, brother of Lucchino	b. 1290? d. 1354
1354–1355	,,	Matteo II, nephew of Giovanni	assassinated 1355
1355–1378	,,	Galeazzo II, nephew of Giovanni	b. 1320 d. 1378
1354–1385	,,	Bernabo, nephew of Giovanni	murdered 1385
1378–1402	,,	Giovanni Galeazzo, son of Galeazzo II	b. 1351 d. 1402

Giovanni Galeazzo became ruler of central and northern Italy, and tried to see Milan recognized as a duchy of the Holy Roman Empire. He bought

Pisa and founded the Milan Cathedral. A patron of art and literature, he died of the plague.

1402–1412	Duke	Gianmaria, son of Giovanni Galeazzo	b. 1389	assassinated 1412
1412–1447	,,	Filippo Maria, son of Giovanni Galeazzo (Ambrosian Republic 1447–1450)	b. 1392	d. 1447

House of Sforza

1450–1466	,,	Francesco Sforza, son-in-law of Filippo Maria	b. 1401	d. 1466
1466–1476	,,	Galeazzo Maria, son of Francesco Sforza	b. 1444	assassinated 1476
1476–1481	,,	Giovanni Galeazzo, son of Galeazzo Maria	b. 1469	d. 1494
1481–1499	,,	Lodovico (il Moro), son of Francesco Sforza (Milan under France, 1499–1512)	b. 1451	d. 1508
1512–1515	Duke	Massimiliano, son of Lodovico il Moro (Milan under France, 1515–1522)	b. 1491	d. 1530
1522–1535	,,	Francesco II, son of Lodovico il Moro	b. 1492	d. 1535

(Milan was under Spain, 1535–1714; Austria, 1714–1797; France, 1797–1814; Austria, 1814–1859; united with Sardinia, 1859)

Ercole II, Duke of Modena (1534–1559).

MODENA

House of Este

1452–1471	Duke	Borso d'Este	b. 1413	d. 1471
1471–1505	,,	Ercole I, brother of Borso d'Este	b. 1431	d. 1505
1505–1534	,,	Alfonso I, son of Ercole I	b. 1486	d. 1534
1534–1559	,,	Ercole II, sòn of Alfonso I	b. 1508	d. 1559
1559–1597	,,	Alfonso II, son of Ercole II	b. 1533	d. 1597
1597–1628	,,	Cesare, grandson of Alfonso I	b. 1533	d. 1628
1628–1629	,,	Alfonso III, son of Cesare		d. 1644
1629–1658	,,	Francesco I, brother of Alfonso III	b. 1610	d. 1658
1658–1662	,,	Alfonso IV, son of Francesco I	b. 1634	d. 1662

Alfonso IV was father of the Catholic princess Mary Beatrice, who became the second wife of King James II of England. She bore him seven children, among them James Francis Edward, "The Old Pretender."

1662–1694	,,	Francesco II, son of Alfonso IV	b. 1660	d. 1694
1694–1737	,,	Raynold Rinaldo	b. 1655	d. 1737
1737–1745	,,	Francesco III, son of Raynold Rinaldo	b. 1698	d. 1780
1748–1780	,,	Francesco III		
1780–1796	,,	Ercole III Rinaldo, son of Francesco III (under France 1796–1814)	b. 1727	d. 1803
1814–1846	,,	Francesco IV, son of Ercole III Rinaldo	b. 1779	d. 1846
1846–1859	,,	Francesco V, son of Francesco IV	b. 1819	d. 1875

(Modena was incorporated in the Kingdom of Italy in 1860)

NAPLES

(The Kingdom of Naples was united with Sicily, 1130–1282, 1435–1458, 1503–1713, 1720–1806, 1815–1860)

House of Anjou

1266–1285	King	Charles I, brother of Louis IX	b. 1226	d. 1285
1285–1309	,,	Charles II, son of Charles I	b. 1246	d. 1309
1309–1343	,,	Robert the Good, son of Charles II		d. 1343
1343–1381	Queen	Joanna I, granddaughter of Robert the Good	b. 1327?	murdered 1382
1381–1386	King	Charles III of Durazzo, great-grandson of Charles II	b. 1345	d. 1386
1386–1414	,,	Ladislas, son of Charles III of Durazzo	b. 1379?	d. 1414
1414–1435	Queen	Joanna II, sister of Ladislas	b. 1371	d. 1435
1435–1442	Titular King	René I, son of Louis of Anjou	b. 1409	d. 1480

House of Aragon

1435–1458	King	Alfonso I, son of Ferdinand I of Aragon	b. 1385	d. 1458
1458–1494	,,	Ferdinand (Ferrante) I, son of Alfonso I	b. 1423	d. 1494
1494–1495	,,	Alfonso II, son of Ferrante I abdicated 1495	b. 1448	d. 1495
1495–1496	,,	Ferrante II, son of Alfonso II	b. 1469	d. 1496
1496–1501	,,	Federigo, uncle of Ferrante II	b. 1452	d. 1504

(Naples was united with France, 1501–1503; Spain, 1503–1707; Austria, 1707–1734; Spain, 1734–1759; part of the Kingdom of the Two Sicilies, 1759–1860)

Bourbon Dynasty

1735–1759	King	Carlo III, son of Philip V of Spain abdicated 1759	b. 1716	d. 1788
1759–1806	,,	Ferrante IV, son of Carlo III	b. 1751	d. 1825
1806–1808	,,	Joseph Bonaparte abdicated 1808	b. 1768	d. 1844
1808–1815	,,	Joachim I Napoleon (Murat)	b. 1767	shot 1815
1815–1816	,,	Ferrante IV		

(Left) Ferrante IV, King of Naples (1759–1806); (Middle) Joseph Bonaparte, King of Naples (1806–1808); (Right) Joachim Murat, King of Naples (1808–1815).

(Left) Ferrante I, King of the Two Sicilies (1816–1825) was also Ferrante IV of Naples (see above); (Middle) Francesco I, King of the Two Sicilies (1825–1830); (Right) Ferrante II, King of the Two Sicilies (1830–1859).

Kingdom of the Two Sicilies

1816–1825	King	Ferrante I (Ferrante IV of Naples)		
1825–1830	„	Francesco I, son of Ferrante I	b. 1777	d. 1830
1830–1859	„	Ferrante II, son of Francesco I	b. 1810	d. 1859
1859–1860	„	Francesco II, son of Ferrante II	b. 1846	d. 1894
1860	Dictator	Giuseppe Garibaldi	b. 1807	d. 1882

Garibaldi organized the expedition of "the thousand heroes"—the famous Redshirts—and invaded Sicily, landing under the protection of British naval vessels. Four months later, he expelled Francesco II from Naples, thus defeating the Kingdom of the Two Sicilies.

(Naples was incorporated in the Kingdom of Italy in 1860)

Francesco II, King of the Two Sicilies (1859–1860).

Giuseppe Garibaldi, Dictator (1860) who overthrew the Kingdom of the Two Sicilies.

(Above left) Alessandro, Duke of Parma (1586–1592); (Below left) Odoardo, Duke of Parma (1622–1646); (Above right) Carlo I, Duke of Parma (1731–1735) depicted on a Spanish coin as Charles III of Spain.

PARMA

Farnese Dynasty

1545–1547	Duke	Pier Luigi, son of Alessandro Farnese (Pope Paul III)	b. 1503	assassinated 1547
1547–1586	„	Ottavio, son of Pier Luigi	b. 1520	d. 1586

1586–1592	Duke	Alessandro, son of Ottavio	b. 1545	d. 1592
1592–1622	„	Ranuccio I, son of Alessandro	b. 1569	d. 1622
1622–1646	„	Odoardo, son of Ranuccio I	b. 1612	d. 1646
1646–1694	„	Ranuccio II, son of Odoardo	b. 1630	d. 1694
1694–1727	„	Francesco, son of Ranuccio II	b. 1678	d. 1727
1727–1731	„	Antonio, brother of Francesco	b. 1679	d. 1731

Bourbon Dynasty

1731–1735	„	Carlo I (Charles III, King of Spain)	b. 1716	d. 1788
		(Parma was under Austrian rule, 1735–1748)		
1748–1765	„	Philip I, son of Philip V, King of Spain	b. 1720	d. 1765
1765–1802	„	Ferdinand (Ferrante) I, son of Philip I		d. 1802
1803–1807	„	Carlo II (Charles Louis), son of Louis I, King of Etruria	b. 1799	d. 1883

Empress Marie Louise of France, Duchess of Parma (1815–1847).

(Parma was in the possession of France, 1802–1815)
1815–1847 French Empress Marie Louise, second wife of Napoleon I   b. 1791   d. 1847
1847–1849   Duke   Carlo II, abdicated 1849
1849–1854   „   Carlo III, son of Carlo II   b. 1823   assassinated 1854
1854–1859   „   Roberto I, son of Carlo III   b. 1848   d. 1907
1854–1859 Duchess-regent Louise Marie, mother of Roberto   b. 1819   d. 1864
(Parma was incorporated in the Kingdom of Italy in 1860)

(Left) Vittorio Emanuele I, King
of Sardinia (1802–1821).

(Right) Carlo Felice, King of
Sardinia (1821–1831).

(Left) Carlo Alberto, King of
Sardinia (1831–1849).

(Right) Vittorio Emanuele II,
King of Sardinia (1849–1861).

SARDINIA

(Acquired by the Dukes of Savoy in 1720)
1720–1730	King	Vittorio Amedeo abdicated 1730		

(Vittorio Amedeo II, of Savoy)

1730–1773	„	Carlo Emanuele I, son of Vittorio Amedeo	b. 1701	d. 1773
1773–1796	„	Vittorio Amedeo II, son of Carlo Emanuele I	b. 1726	d. 1796
1796–1802	„	Carlo Emanuele II, son of Vittorio Amedeo III abdicated 1802	b. 1751	d. 1819
1805–1814	Viceroy	Eugene de Beauharnais, stepson of Napoleon	b. 1781	d. 1824
1802–1821	King	Vittorio Emanuele I, son of Vittorio Amedeo III abdicated 1821	b. 1759	d. 1824
1821–1831	„	Carlo Felice, son of Vittorio Amedeo III	b. 1756	d. 1831
1831–1849	„	Carlo Alberto, son of Carlo Emanuele abdicated 1849	b. 1798	d. 1849
1849–1861	„	Vittorio Emanuele II, son of Carlo Alberto	b. 1820	d. 1878

(Sardinia was incorporated in the Kingdom of Italy in 1861)

SAVOY

(Given to Umberto in 1048 by Conrad, Emperor of Germany)
1048–1050	Count	Umberto I (Umberto Biancamano)	b. 970?	d. 1050?
1050–1056	„	Amedeo I, son of Umberto		d. 1056

1056–1060	Count	Oddone, son of Umberto		d. 1060
1060–1080	,,	Amedeo II, son of Oddone		d. 1080
1080–1103	,,	Umberto II, son of Amedeo II		d. 1103
1103–1149	,,	Amedeo III, son of Umberto II		d. 1149
1149–1189	,,	Umberto III, son of Amedeo III		d. 1189
1189–1222	,,	Tommaso I		d. 1222
1233–1253	,,	Amedeo IV, son of Tommaso I		d. 1253
1253–1263	,,	Boniface, son of Amedeo IV		d. 1263
1263–1268	,,	Pietro II, brother of Amedeo IV		d. 1268
1268–1285	,,	Filippo I, brother of Amedeo IV	b. 1207	d. 1285
1285–1323	,,	Amedeo V, brother of Filippo I	b. 1249	d. 1323
1323–1329	,,	Eduardo, son of Amedeo V		d. 1329
1329–1343	,,	Aimone, son of Amedeo V		d. 1343
1343–1383	,,	Amedeo VI, son of Aimone	b. 1334	d. 1383
1383–1391	,,	Amedeo VII, son of Amedeo VI	b. 1360	d. 1391
1391–1416	,,	Amedeo VIII, son of Amedeo VII	b. 1383	d. 1451
1416–1434	Duke	Amedeo VIII		

Amedeo VIII of Savoy became the last antipope, Felix V. After forming a monastic order on the Lake of Geneva, he was chosen pope by the Council of Basel, excommunicated by Pope Eugenius IV, and made a cardinal.

1434–1465	Duke	Louis, son of Amedeo VIII		d. 1465
1465–1471	,,	Amedeo IX, son of Louis	b. 1435	d. 1472
1472–1482	,,	Philibert I, son of Amedeo IX	b. 1464	d. 1482
1482–1489	,,	Carlo I, son of Philibert I	b. 1468	d. 1490
1489–1496	,,	Carlo II, son of Carlo I		d. 1496
1496–1497	,,	Filippo II, son of Louis		d. 1497
1497–1504	,,	Philibert II, son of Filippo II		d. 1504
1504–1553	,,	Carlo III, brother of Philibert II		d. 1553
1553–1580	,,	Emanuele Philibert, son of Carlo III	b. 1528	d. 1580

Carlo I, Duke of Savoy (1482–1489).

Carlo II, Duke of Savoy (1489–1496).

Carlo Emanuele I, Duke of Savoy (1580–1630).

Vittorio Amedeo I, Duke of Savoy (1630–1637).

1580–1630	Duke	Carlo Emanuele I, son of Emanuele Philibert	b. 1562	d. 1630
1630–1637	,,	Vittorio Amedeo I, son of Carlo Emanuele	b. 1587	d. 1637

1637–1638	Duke	Francesco, son of Vittorio Amedeo I		d. 1638
1638–1675	„	Carlo Emanuele II, son of Vittorio Amedeo I	b. 1634	d. 1675
1675–1713	„	Vittorio Amedeo II, son of Carlo Emanuele II (see Sardinia)	b. 1666	d. 1732

SICILY

Norman Rulers

1072–1101	Count	Roger I, brother of Robert Guiscard	b. 1031	d. 1101
1101–1105	„	Simon, son of Roger I		
1105–1130	„	Roger II, son of Roger I	b. 1093	d. 1154
1130–1154	King	Roger II		
1154–1166	„	Guillaume I the Bad, son of Roger II		d. 1166
1166–1189	„	Guillaume II the Good, son of Guillaume I		d. 1189
1189–1194	„	Tancred, grandson of Roger II		d. 1194

Hohenstaufen Dynasty

1194–1197	Emperor	Henry VI, son of Frederick I	b. 1165	d. 1197

Henry VI kept the crusader king Richard I a prisoner for two years, before ransoming him at a heavy price. Henry died as he was about to set off on a crusade of his own to the Holy Land.

1197–1250	Emperor	Frederick II, son of Henry VI	b. 1194	d. 1250

Frederick I Barbarossa, crowned Holy Roman Emperor at Rome in 1155, established the Hohenstaufen Dynasty in Sicily through the marriage of his son, Henry VI to Constance, heiress to the island throne. He was known as "Redbeard" (Barbarossa) to the Italians.

1250–1254	King	Conrad IV, son of Frederick II	b. 1228	d. 1254
1258–1266	„	Manfred, son of Frederick II	b. 1232?	killed 1266
1266–1268	„	Conradin, son of Conrad IV	b. 1252	beheaded 1268
1268–1282	„	Charles I of Anjou, son of Louis VIII (see Naples)	b. 1226	d. 1285

House of Aragon

1282–1285	„	Pedro III, son-in-law of Manfred (see Aragon)	b. 1236	d. 1285
1285–1295	„	James II, son of Pedro III	b. 1260?	d. 1327

1296–1337	King	Frederick II, son of Pedro III	b. 1272	d. 1337
1337–1342	,,	Pedro II, son of Frederick II		
1342–1355	,,	Louis, son of Pedro II		
1355–1377	,,	Frederick III, son of Pedro II	b. 1341	d. 1377
1377–1402	Queen	Maria, daughter of Frederick III		
1402–1409	King	Martin I, son-in-law of Frederick III		
1409–1410	,,	Martin II		
1410–1416	,,	Ferdinand I		
1416–1458	,,	Alphonso I		
		(King of Naples and Sicily, 1435–1458)		
1458–1479	,,	John		
1479–1516	,,	Ferdinand II		
		(Ferdinand of United Spain)		

(Sicily was under Spain, 1479–1707; Austria, 1707–1713; Savoy, 1713–1720; Austria, 1720–1734; Spain, 1734–1759; part of the Kingdom of the Two Sicilies, 1759–1860)

(Above) Lorenzo I the Magnificent, Ruler of Florence (1469–1491).

(Above right) Alessandro, Duke of Tuscany (1531–1537).

(Right) Cosimo the Elder (1434–1464) in a portrait by Pontormo.

TUSCANY

House of Medici of Florence

1434–1464	Ruler	Cosimo the Elder	b. 1389	d. 1464
1464–1469	,,	Piero, son of Cosimo	b. 1414	d. 1469
1469–1491	,,	Lorenzo I the Magnificent, son of Piero	b. 1449	d. 1492

Lorenzo the Magnificent was a tyrannical ruler but he made Florence rich and prosperous and was largely responsible for causing the Tuscan dialect to become the standard speech of all Italy. He was himself a distinguished writer and poet, and patron of the arts.

1492–1494	Ruler	Pietro, son of Lorenzo I	b. 1471	d. 1503
1494–1498	,,	Girolamo Savonarola	b. 1452	executed 1498
		(Medici banished from Florence)		
1498–1502		Period of disorder		
1502–1512	,,	Piero Soderini	b. 1448	d. 1552
		(Medici restored)		
1512–1514	,,	Giuliano	b. 1479	d. 1516
1513–1519	Duke	Lorenzo II, son of Pietro	b. 1492	d. 1519
1519–1523	,,	Giulio (Pope Clement VII)	b. *c.* 1475	d. *c.* 1534

1524–1527	Duke	Ippolito, grandson of Pietro	b. 1511	d. 1535
1531–1537	,,	Alessandro, son of Lorenzo	b. 1510	assassinated 1537
1537–1569	,,	Cosimo I, son of Giovanni	b. 1519	d. 1574
1569–1574	Grand Duke	Cosimo I		
1574–1587	,,	Francesco, son of Cosimo I	b. 1541	d. 1587
1587–1609	,,	Ferrante I, son of Cosimo I	b. 1549	d. 1609
1609–1621	,,	Cosimo II, son of Ferrante I	b. 1590	d. 1621
1621–1670	,,	Ferrante II, son of Cosimo II	b. 1610	d. 1670
1670–1723	,,	Cosimo III, son of Ferrante II	b. 1642	d. 1723
1723–1737	,,	Giovanni, son of Cosimo III	b. 1671	d. 1737

House of Lorraine

1737–1765	,,	Francis I (Franz Stefan)	b. 1708	d. 1765
		(Emperor of Holy Roman Empire, 1745)		
1765–1790	,,	Leopold I, son of Francis I	b. 1747	d. 1792
1790–1801	,,	Ferrante III, son of Leopold I	b. 1769	d. 1824
		(Tuscany was a French protectorate, 1801–1814)		

ETRURIA

(Napoleonic revival of Latin name for Tuscany)

1801–1803	King	Louis I of Parma (see Parma)	b. 1773	d. 1803
1803–1807	,,	Charles Louis, son of Louis I of Parma	b. 1799	d. 1883·
		(Etruria was a French department, 1807–1809)		

TUSCANY

1809–1814	Grand Duchess	Elisa Bonaparte, sister of Napoleon	b. 1777	d. 1820
		(Made Princess of Piombino and Lucca 1805)		

(House of Lorraine restored)

1814–1824	Grand Duke	Ferrante III (restored)		
1824–1859	King	Leopold II, son of Ferrante III		
		abdicated 1859	b. 1797	d. 1870
1859–1860	,,	Ferrante IV, son of Leopold II	b. 1835	d. 1908
		(Tuscany was incorporated in the Kingdom of Italy in 1861)		

Louis I of Parma, King of Etruria (1801–1803).

Elisa Bonaparte, Grand Duchess of Tuscany (1809–1814) shown on a coin of Lucca with her husband Felix Bacciocchi.

Charles Louis, King of Etruria (1803–1807) shown on a coin of Parma with the French Empress Marie Louise.

VENICE

(Venice emerged as an independent city state in A.D. 697, ruled by an elected duke or "doge," and acquired control over much of the eastern Mediterranean coast. The later doges are listed here)

1423–1457	Doge	Francesco Foscari	d. 1457
1457–1462	,,	Pasquale Malipiero	
1462–1471	,,	Cristoforo Moro	

The Palace of the Doges in Venice was built in the 14th and 15th centuries.

1471–1473	Doge	Nicolo Trono
1473–1474	,,	Nicolo Marcello
1474–1476	,,	Pietro Mocenigo
1476–1478	,,	Andrea Vendramin
1478–1485	,,	Giovanni Mocenigo
1485–1486	,,	Marco Barbarigo
1486–1501	,,	Agostino Barbarigo
1501–1521	,,	Leonardo Loredano
1521–1523	,,	Antonio Grimani
1523–1539	,,	Andrea Gritti
1539–1545	,,	Pietro Lando
1545–1553	,,	Francesco Donato
1553–1554	,,	Marcantonio Trevisano
1554–1556	,,	Francesco Venier
1556–1559	,,	Lorenzo Priuli
1559–1567	,,	Girolamo Priuli
1567–1570	,,	Pietro Loredano
1570–1577	,,	Alviso I Mocenigo
1577–1578	,,	Sebastiano Venier
1578–1585	,,	Nicolo da Ponte
1585–1595	,,	Pasquale Cicogna
1595–1606	,,	Marino Grimani
1607–1612	,,	Leonardo Donato
1612–1615	,,	Marcantonio Memo
1615–1618	,,	Giovanni Bembo
1618	,,	Nicolo Dona
1618–1623	,,	Antonio Priuli
1623–1625	,,	Francesco Centurioni
1625–1630	,,	Giovanni I Cornari
1630–1631	,,	Nicolo Centurioni
1631–1646	,,	Francesco Erizzo
1646–1655	,,	Francesco Molin
1655–1656	,,	Carlo Contarini
1656–1658	,,	Bertuccio Valier
1658–1659	,,	Giovanni Pesaro

b. 1436   d. 1523

Doge Francesco Donato (1545–1553) kneels before St. Mark, Patron of Venice, as shown on a gold ducat of the Venetian Republic.

Italy (continued)

1659–1675	Doge	Domenico Contarini	
1675–1676	,,	Nicolo Sagredo	
1676–1683	,,	Alviso Contarini	
1683–1688	,,	Marcantonio Giustiniani	
1688–1694	,,	Francesco Morosini	b. 1618 d. 1694
1694–1700	,,	Silvestro Valier	
1700–1709	,,	Alviso II Mocenigo	
1709–1722	,,	Giovanni II Cornari	
1722–1732	,,	Alviso III Mocenigo	
1733–1734	,,	Carlo Ruzzini	
1734–1741	,,	Alviso Pisani	
1741–1752	,,	Pietro Grimani	
1752–1762	,,	Francesco Loredano	
1762–1763	,,	Marco Foscarini	b. 1696 d. 1763
1763–1779	,,	Alviso IV Mocenigo	
1779–1789	,,	Paolo Renier	
1789–1797	,,	Lodovico Manin	

(Napoleon conquered Venice in 1797 and ceded it to Austria; it was ceded to the Napoleonic Kingdom of Italy in 1805, regained by Austria in 1814, and in 1866 fell to the new Kingdom of Italy under the House of Savoy)

Ivory Coast (Fr. *Côte d'Ivoire*)

Under the guidance of President Félix Houphouët-Boigny (1960–   ), the Ivory Coast has pursued a course of peaceful development while maintaining close ties with France, which formerly ruled it.

(French colony 1893–1958; an autonomous republic within the French Community, 1958–1960; fully independent outside the Community from 1960)

1960–	President Félix Houphouët-Boigny	b. 1905

Jamaica

Sir Alexander Bustamante, Prime Minister of Jamaica (1962–1967), with Lady Bustamante.

(Discovered by Christopher Columbus, 1494; under Spanish rule to 1655; under British rule, from 1670; an independent state and a member of the British Commonwealth, from 1962)

1962–	Governor-General	Sir Clifford Clarence Campbell	b. 1892
1962–1967	Prime Minister	Sir William Alexander Bustamante	b. 1884
1967	,,	Sir Donald Burns Sangster	b. 1911 d. 1967
1967–	,,	Hugh Lawson Shearer	

Sir Donald Sangster, Prime Minister of Jamaica, died shortly after taking office in 1967.

Sir Clifford Campbell, Governor-General of Jamaica (1962–) shakes hands with the Queen Mother as she arrives at Kingston airport.

Japan

Minamoto Yoritomo, Shogun of Japan (1185–1199).

(Legend says the Japanese state was founded in 660 B.C. Authenticated dates are not available for the periods prior to the 6th century A.D.)

592– 628	Empress	Suiko Tenno
592– 622	Regent	Prince Shotoku
628– ?	Emperor	Jomei
? – 645	Empress	Kogyoku
645– 661	Heads of State	} Nakatomi Kamatari Naka-no-oe
661– 671	Emperor	Tenchi
672– 686	,,	Temmu
686– 697	Empress	Jito
697– 703	Emperor	Mommu
703– 724?	Empress	Gemmyo
724– 749	Emperor	Shomu
749– 758	Empress	Koken (abdicated)
758– 764	Emperor	Junnin
764– 770	Empress	Shotoku (Koken restored, assumed new name)
770– 781	Emperor	Konin
781– 806	,,	Kammu

(Following the reign of Kammu power passed to noble families, notably the Fujiwaras, while emperors became mere figureheads)

1017–1067	Regent	Fujiwara Yorimichi
1068–1072	Emperor	Gosanjo
1072–1129	,,	Shirakawa
1129–1156	,,	Toba
1156–1158	,,	Goshirakawa
1160–1181	Regent	Taira Kiyomori
1180–1185	Emperor	Antoku
1185–1199	Shogun	Minamoto Yoritomo
1199–1203	,,	Minamoto Yorii
1203–1219	,,	Minamoto Sanetomo
1224–1242	Shogunal Regent	Hojo Yasutoki
1318–1339	Emperor	Godaigo
1338–1573		(Period of feudal disorder)

(Empire for more than 2,000 years; Shogunate, 1600–1867)

YEDO SHOGUNATE

1603–1605	Shogun	Iyeyasu Tokugawa	b. 1542	d. 1616
1605–1623	,,	Hidetada, son of Iyeyasu	b. 1579	d. 1633

*Emperor Meiji of Japan
(1867–1912) poses with
the Imperial family.*

1623–1651	Shogun	Iyemitsu, son of Hidetada	b. 1604	d. 1651
1651–1680	,,	Iyetsuna	b. 1641	d. 1680
1680–1709	,,	Tsunayoshi	b. 1646	d. 1709
1709–1712	,,	Iyenobu	b. 1662	d. 1712
1713–1716	,,	Iyetsugu	b. 1709	d. 1716
1716–1745	,,	Yoshimune	b. 1684	d. 1751
1754–1760	,,	Iyeshize	b. 1711	d. 1761
1760–1786	,,	Iyeharu	b. 1736	d. 1786
1787–1837	,,	Iyenari	b. 1773	d. 1841
1837–1853	,,	Iyeoshi, son of Iyenari	b. 1793	d. 1853
1853–1858	,,	Iyesada, brother of Iyeoshi	b. 1853	d. 1858
1858–1866	,,	Iyemochi	b. 1846	d. 1866
1866–1867	,,	Yoshinobu (Hitotsubashi)	b. 1837	d. 1913

(Shogunate, or rule by hereditary prime ministers comes to an end)

1847–1866	Emperor	Komei (originally Osahito)	b. 1831	d. 1866
1867–1912	,,	Meiji (Mutsuhito), son of Komei	b. 1852	d. 1912

Emperor Hirohito of Japan (1926–   ) portrayed with his Empress in coronation robes.

1912–1926	Emperor	Taisho (Yoshihito), son of Mutsuhito	b. 1879	d. 1926
1926–	,,	Hirohito, son of Yoshihito	b. 1901	

STATESMEN

1886–1901	Prime Minister	Hirobumi Ito	b. 1841	d. 1909
1913–1914	,,	Gombei Yamamoto	b. 1852	d. 1933
1923–1924	,,	Gombei Yamamoto		
1936–1937	,,	Koki Hirota	b. 1878	d. 1948
1937–1939	,,	Fumimaro Konoye	b. 1891	d. 1945
1940–1941	,,	Fumimaro Konoye		
1945	,,	Prince Higashikuni		
1945–1946	,,	Kijuro Shidehara	b. 1872	d. 1951
1946–1947	,,	Shigeru Yoshida	b. 1878	d. 1967
1947–1948	,,	Tetsu Katayama	b. 1887	
1948	,,	Hitoshi Ashida		
1948–1954	,,	Shigeru Yoshida		

(American occupation 1945–1952)

1945–1951	Allied C in C	Douglas MacArthur	b. 1878	d. 1964
1951–1952	,,	Matthew B. Ridgway	b. 1895	

(Japan became a sovereign power again in 1952)

1954–1956	Prime Minister	Ichiro Hatoyama		
1956–1957	,,	Tanzan Ishibashi		
1957–1960	,,	Nobusuke Kishi		
1960–1964	,,	Hayato Ikeda	b. 1899	
1964–	,,	Eisaku Sato	b. 1901	

Jordan

(Transjordanian Palestine previously under Turkish rule and British mandate; declared independent in 1923)

1921–1946 Amir Abdullah Ben Al-Hussein   b. 1882   assassinated 1951
          (Name changed to the Hashemite Kingdom of the Jordan in 1946)
1946–1951 King Abdullah Ben Al-Hussein
1951–1952 „   Talal Ben Abdullah   b. 1909   abdicated 1952
1952–   „   Hussein Ben Tala   b. 1935

Hussein, King of Jordan
(1952–   ).

Abdullah, Amir, and later King, of
Jordan (1921–1951).

Kenya

Joseph Murumbi, Vice-President
of Kenya (1964–   ).

(Formerly a British colony; became an independent state and a member of the British Commonwealth, 1963; a republic from 1964)

1964–   President and Prime Minister   Jomo Kenyatta   b. 1889?
1964–   Vice-President   Joseph Murumbi   b. 1911

Jomo Kenyatta, President and Prime Minister of Kenya (1964–   ).

Korea

Emperor Yi-hieung, last Korean ruler of the native Yi-Choson dynasty.

(The history of Korea can be traced back to A.D. 668 when the Silla Dynasty began)
(A Japanese province, 1910–1945; occupied and partitioned by U.S.A. and U.S.S.R. in 1945; both parts independent, 1948)

(The Yi- Choson-Dynasty ruled from 1392 until 1910)

1392–1408	King	T'aejo (Yi Song-gye)	b. 1335	d. 1408
		(Occupied by Japan in 1905)		
1905–1909	Japanese Protector	Hirobumi Ito	b. 1841	assassinated 1909

*President Syngman Rhee of Korea
(1948–1960) with General Doug-
las MacArthur after the re-taking
of Seoul in 1950.*

SOUTH KOREA

(Republic of Korea)

1948–1960	President	Syngman Rhee (Li Sung-man)	b. 1875	
1960	President (acting)	Yun Po-son		
1961	"	Pak Chong-hui (Chung Hee Park)		
1960–1961	Premier	John M. Chang (Chang Myun)	b. 1899	d. 1966
1961	"	Chang To-yong (Do Young Chang)	b. 1923	
1961–1962	"	Song Yo Chan	b. 1919	
1962–1963	"	Chul Kim		
1963	President	Pak Chung Hi	b. 1917	
1964–	Prime Minister	Chung Il-Kwon		

NORTH KOREA

(Democratic People's Republic of Korea)

1948–	President	Kim-du Bon	
1948–	Premier	Kim Il Sung	b. 1912

Kuwait

Shaikh Abdullah as-Salim as-Sabah, Amir of Kuwait (1950–1965).

(Special relationship with Britain 1899–1961; completely independent from 1961)
1950–1965	Amir	Shaikh Abdullah as-Salim as-Sabah	b. 1890
1965–	,,	Shaikh Sabah al-Salim al-Sabah, brother of Shaikh Abdullah	b. 1913
1963–	Prime Minister	Shaikh Sabah as-Salim as-Sabah	

Laos

Sri Savang Vatthana, King of Laos (1959–).

Souvanna Phouma, Prime Minister of Laos (1962–).

Laos (continued)

(French Protectorate 1893; became independent sovereign state within French Union, 1949)

1949–1959	King	Sisavang Vong	b. 1885 d. 1959
1959–	,,	Baromo Setha Khatya Sourya Vongsa Phra Maha Sri Savang Vatthana, son of Sisavang Vong	b. 1907
1962–	Prime Minister	Souvanna Phouma	

Latvia

(Formerly a Province of the Russian Empire; an independent state, 1918–1940; German occupation, 1941–1944; Soviet republic from 1944)

1918–1920	Chairman of Council	Jan Chakste	
1920–1922	President of Assembly	Jan Chakste	
1922–1925	President	Jan Chakste	
1925–1927	,,	Jan Chakste	d. 1927
1927–1929	,,	Gustav Zemgals	
1930–1933	,,	Albert Kviesis	
1933–1936	,,	Albert Kviesis	
1936–1940	,,	Karlis Ulmanis	

(In 1940 occupied by Russian troops and made a Soviet Republic)

Lebanon

Historic Mount Lebanon appears on a stamp of the Republic of the same name.

(Corresponds roughly to ancient Phoenicia; later under Macedonian, Roman, Byzantine and Ottoman rule)

(Part of Ottoman Empire in 1861)

1873–1883	Governor	Rustem Pasha	
1883–1892	,,	Wassa Pasha	d. 1892
1892–1902	,,	Naoum Pasha	

(French Mandate 1921–1941; became an independent state in 1941; evacuation of last foreign troops 1946)

1943–1952	President	Sheikh Bishara el Khoury	
1952–1958	,,	Camille Chamoun	
1958–1964	,,	Fuad Chehab	
1964–	,,	Charles Helou	b. 1913

Lesotho

(Formerly the British Protectorate of Basutoland, Lesotho became an independent monarchy in 1966)

1966–	King	Motlotlehi Moshoeshoe	b. 1938
1966–	Prime Minister	Chief Joseph Leabua Jonathan	b. 1914

Liberia

(Founded by the American Colonization Society, 1822; recognized as an independent
Negro Republic, 1847)

| 1943– | President | William Jacanarat Shadrach Tubman | b. 1895 |
| | Vice-President | William Richard Tolbert, Jr. | b. 1913 |

Libya

Idris I, King of Libya
(1951–   ).

(Former Turkish territories of Tripolitania and Cyrenaica; occupied by Italy 1911–1939;
incorporated in Italy 1939; an independent state from 1951)

| 1951– | King   Idris I | | b. 1890 |

Liechtenstein

Franz Josef II, Prince of Liechtenstein (1938–   ).

(Principality of Vaduz, formed 1342; constituted as Principality of Liechtenstein, 1719;
independent since 1866)

| 1938– | Prince   Franz Josef II | | b. 1906 |

Lithuania

Antanas Smetona, President of Lithuania (1919–1921, 1926–1940).

(Lithuania was an independent Grand Duchy until 1385, when it was united with Poland; from 1795 a Province of the Russian Empire; an independent republic, 1918–1940; under German occupation, 1941–1944; Soviet Republic since 1944)

1919–1921	Provisional President	Antanas Smetona	b. 1874	d. 1944
1922–1926	President	Antanas Stulgenskis		
1926	,,	V. Grinius (overthrown)		
1926–1940	,,	Antanas Smetona		

(In 1940 occupied by Russian troops and made a Soviet Republic)

Luxembourg

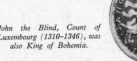

John the Blind, Count of Luxembourg (1310–1346), was also King of Bohemia.

(Luxembourg was a county until Wenceslaus I, 1st Duke of Luxembourg; then a duchy until 1815 when it became a Grand Duchy)

House of Ardennes

963– 998	Count	Sigefroi		
998–1026	,,	Henry I		
1026–1047	,,	Henry II		
1047–1059	,,	Giselbert		
1059–1086	,,	Conrad I		d. 1086
1086–1096	,,	Henry III		
1096–1129	,,	William		
1129–1136	,,	Conrad II		

House of Namur

1136–1196	,,	Henry IV the Blind		d. 1196
1196–1247	Countess	Ermesinde		d. 1247

House of Limbourg

1247–1281	Count	Henry V	b. 1217	d. 1281
1281–1288	,,	Henry VI		
1288–1310	,,	Henry VII	b. 1275?	d. 1313
		(German emperor 1308–1313)		
1310–1346	,,	John the Blind of Bohemia, son of Henry VII	b. 1296	d. 1346
1346–1353	,,	Charles I, son of John (emperor Charles IV)	b. 1316	d. 1378
1353–1383	Duke	Wenceslaus I, son of John the Blind (Became a Duchy in 1354)	b. 1337	d. 1383
1383–1388	,,	Wenceslaus II (Emperor), son of Charles	b. 1361	d. 1419

1388–1411	Duke	Jobst of Moravia		
1411–1412	„	Wenceslaus II		
1412–1415	„	Anton of Brabant and Elizabeth of Görlitz (pretenders)		
1415–1419	Duchess	Elizabeth (alone)		
1419–1425	Duke	Johann of Bavaria		
1425–1444	Duchess	Elizabeth (alone)		
		(Joined to Burgundy, 1444)		

House of Burgundy

1443–1467	Duke	Philip III the Good,		
		son of John the Fearless	b. 1396	d. 1467
1467–1477	„	Charles the Bold, son of Philip the Good	b. 1433	d. 1477
1477–1482	Duchess	Mary of Burgundy,		
		daughter of Charles the Bold	b. 1456	d. 1482
1482–1506	Duke	Philip I the Handsome, son of Mary	b. 1478	d. 1506
1506–1555	Emperor	Charles V, son of Philip I	b. 1500	d. 1558

Spanish Rule

1555–1598	King	Philip II, son of Charles V	b. 1527	d. 1598
1598–1621	Archduke	Albert	b. 1559	d. 1621
1621–1665	King	Philip IV, son of Philip III	b. 1605	d. 1665
1665–1684	„	Charles II, son of Philip IV	b. 1661	d. 1700

French Rule

| 1684–1697 | „ | Louis XIV, son of Louis XIII | b. 1638 | d. 1715 |

Spanish Rule

1697–1700	„	Charles II	b. 1661	d. 1700
1700–1711	„	Philip of Anjou,		
		grandson of Louis XIV	b. 1683	d. 1746
1711–1714	Elector	Maximilian II Emanuel of Bavaria	b. 1662	d. 1726

Austrian Rule

1714–1740	Emperor	Charles VI, son of Leopold I	b. 1685	d. 1740
1740–1780	Empress	Maria Theresa, daughter of Charles VI	b. 1717	d. 1780
1780–1790	Emperor	Joseph II, son of Maria Theresa	b. 1741	d. 1790
1790–1792	„	Leopold II, brother of Joseph II	b. 1747	d. 1792
1792–1795	„	Francis II	b. 1768	d. 1835

Charles the Bold, Duke of Burgundy (1467–1477).

French Rule

1795–1799		The Directory
1799–1814		Consulate and Empire
		(Grand Duchy created by Congress of Vienna 1814–1815)

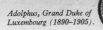

Adolphus, Grand Duke of Luxembourg (1890–1905).

William IV, Grand Duke of Luxembourg (1905–1912).

House of Orange
(Grand Duchy linked by personal union with the crown of Holland)

1815–1840	Grand Duke	William I, King of the Netherlands, son of William V, Prince of Orange	b. 1772	d. 1843

In 1806, William VI of Nassau lost his lands because he refused to join the Confederation of the Rhine. When he became King of the Netherlands (as William I) in 1815, he was granted the title of Grand Duke of Luxembourg.

1840–1849	Grand Duke	William II, son of William I	b. 1792	d. 1849
1849–1890	„	William III, son of William II	b. 1817	d. 1890

House of Nassau

1890–1905	„	Adolphus, Duke of Nassau	b. 1817	d. 1905
1905–1912	„	William IV, son of Adolphus	b. 1852	d. 1912
1912–1919	Grand Duchess	Marie-Adélaïde, daughter of William IV abdicated 1919	b. 1894	d. 1924
1919–1964	„	Charlotte, sister of Marie-Adélaïde	b. 1896	
1964–	Grand Duke	Jean, son of Charlotte	b. 1921	

Charlotte, Grand Duchess of Luxembourg (1919–1964).

Jean, Grand Duke of Luxembourg (1964–   ).

Lydia

King Croesus of Lydia (560–546 B.C.), the first ruler to mint gold and silver coins such as shown here, is recalled today in the expression "rich as Croesus."

B.C.		(Lydia was situated on the Aegean coast of Asia Minor)
c. 700	King	Gyges
617– 560	„	Alyattes
560– 546	„	Croesus

(Conquered by Cyrus the Great of Persia in 546 B.C. and thereafter was a dependency of Persia, Macedonia, Syria, and eventually became a province of Rome)

Macedonia

Coin of Zeus minted during reign of Philip II, King of Macedonia (359–335 B.C.).

B.C.			B.C.
729	King	Perdiccas I	
700	„	Philip I	
500	„	Amyntas I	
498– 454	„	Alexander I	d. 498
454– 413	„	Perdiccas II, son of Alexander I	d. 413?
413– 399	„	Archelaus, son of Perdiccas II	murdered 399
394– 370	„	Amyntas II, nephew of Perdiccas II	
369– 368	„	Alexander II	
368– 360	„	Perdiccas III, brother of Philip II	d. 359
360– 359	„	Amyntas III, grandson of Amyntas II	executed 336
359– 335	„	Philip II, brother of Perdiccas III	b. 382 assassinated 336
336– 323	„	Alexander III the Great, son of Philip II	b. 356 d. 323

At the age of 16, Alexander the Great quelled a rising of Macedonian hill tribes. Appointed captain-general of the Hellenes he crossed into Asia in

Perseus, King of Macedonia (179–168 B.C.).

Alexander III the Great, King of Macedonia (336–323 B.C.).

334 B.C. and within 12 years had destroyed the Persian Empire and conquered Syria, Phoenicia, Egypt, Persia, Bactria, Bokhara, and the Punjab. Alexander took the Macedonian army as far eastward as the Hyphasis (Beas) in India.

323	King	Philip III (Aridaeus), son of Philip II	murdered 317
323– 310	„	Alexander IV, son of Alexander the Great	murdered 310
316– 297	„	Cassander, son of Antipater	b. 350? d. 297
306– 301	„	Antigonus I	b. 382 d. 301

Antigonus Cyclops, one of Alexander the Great's generals, tried to make himself master of Asia. He briefly secured control of Asia Minor and Syria after a war with Seleucus, Lysimachus and Cassander. His invasion of Ptolemy's Egypt was unsuccessful, and subsequently, during a battle at the age of 81 with the armies of his three old enemies, Antigonus fell.

297– 294	King	Alexander V, son of Cassander	murdered 294

294– 283	King	Demetrius I Poliorcetes, son of Antigonus	b. 337?	d. 283
283– 273	,,	Antigonus II Gonatas, grandson of Antigonus I	b. 319?	
273	,,	Pyrrhus of Epirus	b. 318?	killed 272
272– 239	,,	Antigonus II Gonatus		
239– 232	,,	Demetrius II, son of Antigonus Gonatus		d. 230
232	,,	Philip		
229– 221	,,	Antigonus III Doson, nephew of Antigonus Gonatas		d. 221
220– 179	,,	Philip V, son of Demetrius II	b. 237	d. 179
179– 168	,,	Perseus, son of Philip V		d. 165?
		(a Roman province from 168 B.C.)		

Madagascar (Malagasy Republic)

(Discovered by the Portuguese in 1506, Madagascar remained independent under a native dynasty until annexed by France in the late 19th century. Most recent sovereigns are listed below)

1810–1828	King	Radama I	
1828–1861	Queen	Ranavalona I	
1861–1863	King	Radama II (assassinated)	d. 1863
1863–1868	Queen	Rasoaherina	
1868–1883	,,	Ranavalona II	
1883–1896	,,	Ranavalona III (deposed)	b. 1861 d. 1916
		(Monarchy abolished under French rule)	

MALAGASY REPUBLIC
(Madagascar became independent in 1960 as the Malagasy Republic)

1960–	President	Philibert Tsiranana	b. 1912

(Left) Hastings Kamuzu Banda, Prime Minister of Malawi (1964–1966) and President (1966–).

(Right) Philibert Tsiranana, President of the Malagasy Republic (1960–).

Malawi

(Formerly the British Protectorate of Nyasaland; became an independent state and member of the British Commonwealth, 1964)

1964–1966	Governor-General	Sir Glyn Smallwood Jones	b. 1908
1964–1966	Prime Minister	Hastings Kamuzu Banda	b. 1905
	(Republic proclaimed 1966)		
1966–	President	Hastings Kamuzu Banda	

Malaysia

Also see Singapore

Tunku Abdul Rahman,
Prime Minister of Malaysia
(1965–   ).

Prince Tuanku Syed, Paramount Ruler
of Malaysia (1963–1965).

(The Federation of Malaysia came into being in 1963, uniting the Federation of Malaya with the former British Possessions of Singapore, Sabah (British North Borneo) and Sarawak. Singapore seceded from the Federation in 1965)

1963–1965	Paramount Ruler	Prince Tuanku Syed, Raja of Perlis	b. 1920
1965–	,,	Ismail Nasiruddin Shah,	
		Sultan of Trengganu	b. 1907
1965–	Prime Minister	Tunku Abdul Rahman	b. 1903

Maldive Islands

(An independent elective Sultanate; under British protection from 1963)

1964–	Sultan	Al Amir Mohamed Farid Didi	b. 1901
	Prime Minister	Ibrahim Nasir	

Mali *Also see Senegal*

(Formerly the French Overseas Territory of Soudan; an autonomous republic within the French Community, 1958–1960; under name of the Sudanese Republic, became independent jointly with Senegal in 1960, as the Mali Federation; after withdrawal of Senegal from the Federation in the same year, the Sudanese Republic retained the name of Mali)

1960–	President	Modibo Keita	b. 1915

Malta

(Under Roman rule, 216 B.C.–A.D. 870; under Arabs, 870–1090; under Normans, 1090; under Knights of St. John, 1530–1798; under protection of Britain, 1802–1814; annexed to Britain, 1814–1964; an independent state within the British Commonwealth from 1964)

1964–	Governor-General	Sir Maurice Henry Dorman	b. 1912
1964–	Prime Minister	George Borg Olivier	b. 1911

Modibo Keita, President of Mali (1960–   ).

George Borg Olivier, Prime Minister of Malta (1964–   ).

Manchuria

Henry Pu-yi, at left, the last Emperor of China (1908–1912), was later made puppet ruler of Manchukuo by the Japanese, serving first as Chief Executive (1932–1934) and then as Emperor (1934–1945).

(Part of China until the fall of the Chinese Empire in 1911)

1911–1928	Military Governor	Chang Tso-lin	b. 1873	assassinated 1928
1928–1932	„	Chang Hsueh-liang, son of Chang Tso-lin	b. 1898	

(Manchuria occupied by Japan, 1930–1932)

MANCHUKUO

(The Japanese established a puppet state in Manchuria in 1932 under the name of Manchukuo)

1932–1934	Chief Executive	Henry Pu-yi (Hsüan T'ung) (See China)	b. 1906	d. 1967
1934–1945	Emperor	Kang Teh (Hsüan T'ung)		

(Part of China since 1945)

Mauretania, see Numidia

Mauritania

The French revived the ancient name of Mauretania (with a slight change of spelling) for the West African territory which is now the independent Republic of Mauritania. The modern state is not, however, co-extensive with ancient Mauretania, which lay in what is now Algeria and Morocco. The first President and Prime Minister, Moktar Ould Daddah, is shown here at the left.

(An autonomous republic within the French Community, 1958–1960; fully independent from 1960)

1960	Prime Minister	Moktar Ould Daddah	b. 1924
1961–	President and Prime Minister	Moktar Ould Daddah	

(The modern republic of Mauritania does not correspond territorially to the ancient North African Kingdom of the same name)

Mauritius

Coat-of-arms of Mauritius.

(Settled by the Dutch 1638; under the French 1721–1810; a British colony 1810–1968; became independent 1968)

1968–	Governor-General	Sir John Rennie
1968–	Prime Minister	Sir Seewoosagur Ramgoolam

Mesopotamia, see Assyria, Babylonia, Iraq

Mexico

Cuauhtémoc, Aztec Emperor (1520–1525).

(Prior to Spanish conquest of Mexico, many civilizations rose and declined there, including those of the Olmecs, Mayas and Toltecs. The Aztecs were descended from barbarian tribes who had conquered earlier people of a higher culture and assumed their ways)

AZTEC CIVILIZATION
c. 1200 A.D.-1524 A.D.

	King	Huitzilihuitl	sacrificed
		City-state of Tlatelolco (*Tlatelolca*)	
		Founded between 1325 and 1338	
1375–	,,	Cuacuauhpitzahuac	
–1428	,,	Tlacateotl	executed 1428
c. 1429–1440	,,	Nezahualcoyotl	
–1473	,,	Moquiuix	
		City-state of Tenochitlan (*Tenochca*)	
		Founded *c.* 1325	
1375–	*Huetlatoani* (Emperor)	Acamapícktli	
–1428	,,	Chimalpopoca	executed 1428
1428–1436	,,	Itzcoatl	b. 1360? d. 1440?
1440–1469	,,	Moteczuma Ilhuicamira (Montezuma I)	*c.* 1390–1464
1469–1481	,,	Axayacatl	d. 1477
1486–1502	,,	Ahuitzotl	
1502–1520	,,	Moteczuma Xocoyotzin (Montezuma II)	b. 1480 d. 1520

Montezuma II, grandson of Montezuma I, was a warlike, despotic and unpopular ruler. Cortés manipulated popular unrest to his own advantage, and was able to seize Montezuma II as a hostage. In a short-lived uprising, Montezuma II was killed, by the Spanish or the Aztecs, in June, 1520.

1520–1525	*Huetlatoani* (Emperor)	Cuauhtémoc	d. 1525

TEPANEC EMPIRE
1347–1427

–1427	*Huetlatoani* (Emperor)	Tezozomoc	d. 1427

TARASCAN CIVILIZATION
c. 1400–1522

c. 1370	King	Tariacuri	
	,,	Tzitzie Pandacuare	
–1522	,,	Tagoxoan Zincicha	

SPANISH CONQUEST AND COLONIZATION

1517	Discoverer	Francisco Fernandez de Córdoba	wounded by Indians d. 1518
1518	,,	Juan de Grijalva	d. 1527 ?
1519	,,	Hernán Cortés	b. 1485 d. 1547

Hernán Cortés served as Governor and Captain-General of Mexico during the period of Spanish Conquest.

Cortés, against odds of 350 to 1, conquered the Aztecs in less than two years, aided in part by those superstitious Aztecs who thought him a descendant of the god Quetzalcoatl. Subsequently, he expanded Spanish conquest throughout Mexico, but later, out of grace with Charles V, he died, neglected, in his native Spain.

1520		Colony organized by Cortés		
1522–1524	Governor, Capt.-General Hernán Cortés			
1524–1526		Government disintegrated in absence of Cortés		
1527–1528	„	Hernán Cortés		
1528–1530		Ruled by first *audencia*, composed of:		
		Beltrán Nuño de Guzmán, pres.		d. 1544
		Alonso Parada		
		Francisco Maldonado		
		Juan Ortíz de Matienzo		
		Diego Delgadillo		
1530		Cortés returned as captain-general		
1531		Second *audencia*, composed of:		
		Sebastian Ramírez de Fuenleal, bishop of Santo Domingo		
		Juan Salmerón		
		Francisco Ceynos		
		Vasco de Quiroga		
		Alonso Maldonado		
1535–1550	Viceroy	Antonio Mendoza	b. 1490?	d. 1552
1550–1564	„	Luis de Velasco		d. 1564
1590–1595 ⎫ 1607–1611 ⎭	„	Luis de Velasco	b. 1534	d. 1617
1673–1680	„	Fray Payo Enríque de Rivera		
1711–1716	„	Fernando de Alencastre Noroña y Silva		
1722–1734	„	Juan de Acuña	b. 1658	d. 1734
1746–1755	„	Juan Francisco de Güemes y Horcasitas, Count of Revillagigedo	b. 1682?	d. 1766
1766–1771	„	Carlos Francisco de Croix, Marqués de Crois	b. 1702	d. 1786
1771–1779	„	Antonio María Bucareli y Ursúas	b. 1717	d. 1779
1789–1794	„	Juan Vicente de Güemes Pacheco y Padillo, Count of Revillagigedo	b. 1740	d. 1799
1803–1808	„	José de Iturrigaray	b. 1742	d. 1814
	„	Pedro de Garibay		
	„	Archbishop Francisco Javier de Lizana		
1810–1813	„	Francisco Javier Venegas		
1813–1816	„	Félix María Calleja del Rey	b. 1750	d. 1828
1816–1821	„	Juan Ruiz de Apodeca	b. 1754	d. 1835

INDEPENDENT MEXICO

Agustín de Iturbide, Emperor of Mexico.

1822–1823	Emperor	Agustín de Iturbide	b. 1783	shot 1824

Proclaimed Emperor Agustín I in 1821 after establishing Mexican independence, Iturbide led a conservative instead of a liberal state. Forced into exile in 1823, and later executed, conservatives think of him as the father of Mexican independence.

(Republic established 1823–1824)

1824–1829	President	Guadalupe Victoria	b. 1789	d. 1843
1829	"	Vicente Guerrero	b. 1783?	shot 1831
1829	President (acting)	José María de Bocanegra		
1829–1832	President	Anastasio Bustamante	b. 1780	d. 1853
1832	President (acting)	Melchor Múzquiz		
1832–1833	President	Manuel Gómez Pedraza	b. 1788?	d. 1851
1833–1835	"	Antonio López de Santa Anna	b. 1795?	d. 1876

General Santa Anna was acclaimed a hero after many victories over the Spanish during Mexico's fight for independence. He was sent, because of this experience, to Texas to crush the revolution there, and was commander at the Battle of the Alamo and Goliad before his defeat by Sam Houston.

1835–1836	President	Miguel Barragán		
1836–1837	"	José Justo Corro		
1837–1841	"	Anastasio Bustamante		
1841	President (acting)	Javier Echeverría		
1841–1842	President	Antonio López de Santa Anna		
1842–1843	"	Nicolás Bravo	b. 1787?	d. 1854
1843	President (provisional)	Antonio López de Santa Anna		
1843–1844	President	Valentín Canalizo	b. 1797?	d. 1847?
1844	"	Antonio López de Santa Anna		
1844	President (acting)	José Joaquín Herrera	b. 1792	d. 1854
1844	"	Valentín Canalizo		
1844–1845	President	José Joaquín Herrera		
1846	"	Mariano Paredes y Arrillaga		
1846	"	Nicolás Bravo		
1846	President (acting)	José Mariano Salas		

(War with the United States, 1846–1848)

1846–1847	President (acting)	Valentín Gómes Farías		
1847	President	Antonio López de Santa Anna		
1847	"	Pedro María Anaya		
1847	"	Antonio López de Santa Anna		
1847	President (provisional)	Manuel de la Peña y Peña	b. 1789	d. 1850
1847–1848	President (acting)	Pedro María Anaya		
1848	President	Manuel de la Peña y Peña		
1848–1851	"	José Joaquín Herrera		
1851–1853	"	Mariano Arista	b. 1802	d. 1855
1853	President (acting)	Juan Bautista Ceballos		
1853	"	Manuel M. Lombardine		
1853–1855	Dictator	Antonio López de Santa Anna		
1855	President (acting)	Martín Carrera		
1855	"	Juan Álvarez	b. 1790?	d. 1867
1855–1857	President	Ignacio Comonfort	b. 1812	killed 1863
1857–1861	President (provisional)	Benito Pablo Juárez	b. 1806	d. 1872

An Indian, and Mexico's most revered political hero, Juárez was the first man to achieve a truly liberal government. He opposed the privileges of the clerics and military, and transferred political power from the rich few to the masses.

(French intervention, 1861–1867)

1864–1867	Emperor	Maximilian	b. 1832	executed 1867

Sent by Napoleon to be Emperor of Mexico because France was unable to collect from Juárez Mexico's unpaid debts, Maximilian of Austria was opposed by nationalist liberals and later deserted by Napoleon, who had been influenced by the United States. He was executed by Juárez after a short reign.

Benito Pablo Juárez, President of Mexico (1857–1861).

Maximilian, Emperor of Mexico (1864–1867).

1872–1876	President	Sebastián Lerdo de Tejada			
1876	President (provisional)	Porfirio Díaz		b. 1830	d. 1915
1876–1877	President (acting)	Juan N. Méndez			
1877	President (provisional)	Porfirio Díaz			
1877–1880	President	Porfirio Díaz			
1880–1884	,,	Manuel González		b. 1833	d. 1893
1884–1911	,,	Porfirio Díaz			
1911	President (provisional)	Francisco León De la Barra		b. 1863	d. 1939
1911–1931	President	Francisco Indalecio Madero		b. 1873	shot 1913
1913	President (provisional)	Pedro Lascurain			
1913–1914	,,	Victoriano Huerta		b. 1854	d. 1916
1914	,,	Francisco Carbajal			
1914	President	Venustiano Carranza	b. 1859	murdered 1920	
1914–1915	,,	Eulalio Martín Gutiérrez			
1915	President (provisional)	Roque González Garza			
1915	,,	Francisco Lagos Cházaro			
1915–1917	,,	Venustiano Carranza			
1917–1920	President	Venustiano Carranza			

In 1917 Carranza drew up the Constitution which is the basis of Mexican government today. It provided for freedom of worship, divided large land estates, declared the nation was owner of all natural resources, and confiscated all church property.

1920	President (provisional)	Adolfo de la Huerta			d. 1955
1920–1924	President	Alvaro Obregón	b. 1880	assassinated 1928	
1924–1928	,,	Plutarco Elías Calles		b. 1877	d. 1945
1928–1930	President (provisional)	Emilio Portes Gil			
1930–1932	President	Pascual Ortiz Rubio			
1932–1934	President (provisional)	Abelardo L. Rodríguez		b. 1889	
1934–1940	President	Lázaro Cárdenas		b. 1895	
1940–1946	,,	Manuel Ávila Camacho		b. 1897	d. 1955
1946–1952	,,	Miguel Alemán Valdés			
1952–1958	,,	Adolfo Ruiz Cortines			
1958–1964	,,	Adolfo López Mateos			
1964–	,,	Gustavo Diaz Ordaz		b. 1911	

NATIONAL LEADERS

1810–1815	Revolutionary leader	José María Morélos y Pavón	b. 1765	executed 1815
1810–1811	,,	Miguel Hidalgo y Castillo	b. 1753	executed 1811

(Left) José Maria Morélos y Pavón.

(Right) Miguel Hidalgo y Castillo and Francisco Indalecio Madero.

(Left) Venustiano Carranza.

(Right) Adolfo López Mateos.

Monaco

Rainier III, Prince of Monaco
(1949–   ), appears on a Mone-
gasque stamp with his consort
Princess Grace.

English versions of the names of rulers of French-speaking states are:

Baldwin–Baudouin	John–Jean	Philip–Philippe
Francis–François	James–Jacques	Rudolph–Rodolphe
Henry–Henri	Odo–Eudes	Stephen–Etienne
Hugh–Hugues	Peter–Pierre	Theobald–Thibaut
		William–Guillaume

c. 1100	Ruler	Otto Canella	b. 1070	d. 1143
	″	Grimaldo		
	″	Oberto		
	″	Grimaldo		
	″	Lanfranco		
1310	Seigneur of Cagnes	Rainier I Grimaldi	b. 1267	d. 1314
	Seigneur	Charles I		d. 1357
1407	″	Rainier II, son of Charles I	b. 1350	d. 1407
	″	{ Ambroise John I Antoine } sons of Rainier II		
1427–1454	Sole seigneur	John I	b. 1382	d. 1454
1454–1457	Seigneur	Catalan, son of John I		d. 1457
1457	Sovereign	Claudine, daughter of Catalan	b. 1451	d. 1514
1465	Seigneur	Lambert, husband of Claudine	b. 1420	d. 1494
1494–1505	″	John II, son of Claudine and Lambert		d. 1505
1505–1523	″	Lucien, brother of John		d. 1523
1523–1532	″	Augustin, brother of John		d. 1532
1532–1581	″	Honoré I, son of Lucien	b. 1522	d. 1581
1581–1589	″	Charles II, son of Honoré I	b. 1555	d. 1589
1589–1604	″	Hercules I, brother of Charles II	b. 1562	d. 1604
1604–1612	″	Honoré II, son of Hercules I	b. 1597	d. 1662

(Left) Charles II, Seigneur of Monaco (1581–1589); (Middle) Albert I, Prince of Monaco (1889–1922); (Right) Louis II, Prince of Monaco (1922–1949).

1612–1662	Prince	Honoré II		
1662–1701	,,	Louis I, grandson of Honoré II	b. 1642	d. 1701
1701–1731	,,	Antoine I, son of Louis I	b. 1661	d. 1731
1731	Princess	Louise-Hippolyte, daughter of Antoine I	b. 1697	d. 1731
1731–1733	Prince	James I, husband of Louise-Hippolyte	abdicated 1733	
1733–1795	,,	Honoré III, son of Louise-Hippolyte, and James I	b. 1720	d. 1795

(Monaco was annexed to France in 1793 and restored to the Grimaldis in 1814)

1795–1819	Prince	Honoré IV, son of Honoré III	b. 1758	d. 1819
1819–1841	,,	Honoré V, son of Honoré IV	b. 1778	d. 1841
1841–1856	,,	Florestan I, brother of Honoré V	b. 1785	d. 1856
1856–1889	,,	Charles III, son of Florestan I	b. 1818	d. 1889
1889–1922	,,	Albert I, son of Charles III	b. 1848	d. 1922
1922–1949	,,	Louis II, son of Albert I	b. 1870	d. 1949
1949–	,,	Rainier III, grandson of Louis II	b. 1923	

Prince Rainier III met and married the American actress, Grace Kelly. His grandfather, Albert I, was a keen oceanographer who equipped several yachts for deep-sea research work and opened an oceanographical museum in the town of Monaco in 1910. Rainier III shares this interest.

Coat-of-arms of Monaco.

Mongolia

Genghis Khan, founder of the Mongol Empire, came of a warrior family. A 17th-century Persian artist depicted the Great Khan's mother, Ho'elan, leading her troops into battle.

(As Outer Mongolia, Mongolia was tributary to China prior to 1924, when the Republic of
Mongolia was established, under Russian protection. Inner Mongolia remained under
Chinese rule)

? –1924	Khan	Bogdo Gegen Khan	

(In 1924 the Khan was deposed and the Republic declared)

1966–	Chairman of the presidium	Zhamsarangin Sambu
	Premier	Yumzhagin Tsedenbal

MONGOL EMPIRE

1206–1227 Khan Genghis Khan (Temujin)   b. 1162   d. 1227

Genghis Khan (Very Mighty Ruler) succeeded his father as chief of their
tribe at the age of 13. A military genius, he became Khan of all the Mongols,
and he invaded China, Korea, India, Persia and Russia. At his death, his
kingdom stretched from the Pacific to the Volga, and from Siberia to the
Persian Gulf.

1227–1232	Khan	Tului (Tule), son of Genghis Khan	
1227–1229	,,	Jagatai (Chagatai), son of Genghis Khan	d. 1242
1229–1241	,,	Ogadai, son of Genghis Khan	b. 1185 d. 1241
	,,	Juji (Juchi), son of Genghis Khan	
1241–1255	,,	Batu Khan, son of Juji (see Golden Horde)	d. 1255
1246–1248	,,	Kuyuk, son of Ogadai	d. 1248
1248	,,	Kaidu, grandson of Ogadai	d. 1301
1251–1259	,,	Mangu Khan, son of Tului	b. 1207? d. 1259
1259–1294	,,	Kublai Khan, son of Tului	b. 1216 d. 1294
1260–1265	,,	Hulagu, son of Tului (see China)	b. 1217 d. 1265

GOLDEN HORDE

(The Golden Horde was an offshoot of the Mongols who ruled briefly over Russia and
Eastern Europe. Their Empire fell to Tamerlane in 1395)

1223–1256	Khan	Batu Khan, grandson of Genghis Khan	d. 1256
1257–1267	,,	Birkai, brother of Batu Khan	d. 1267
1267–1280	,,	Mangu	
1290–1312	,,	Toktai	
1313–1340	,,	Uzbek	d. 1340
1340–1357	,,	Janibeg Khan, son of Uzbek	murdered 1357
1357	,,	Berdibek, son of Janibeg Khan	murdered 1370
1370–1381	,,	Mamai	
1381–1395	,,	Toktamish (of Eastern Kipchaks)	
1395–1405	,,	Timur Lenk (Tamerlane), descendant of Ghengis Khan	b. 1336? d. 1405

Montenegro, see Yugoslavia

Morocco

(Morocco corresponds in part to ancient Mauretania. Under Romans 1st to 5th centuries
A.D.; fell to the Vandals 5th century; to the Arabs in 682; under Almoravide dynasty
1061–1149; Almohade dynasty 1149–1269; Marinide dynasty 1269–1471; Wattasi
dynasty 1471–1548; Sa'adi (Sherifian) dynasty 1550–1668; Filali (Alaouite) dynasty from
1668). Recent rulers are as follows:

1822–1859	Sultan	Abd ur-Rahman II		b. 1778	d. 1859
1859–1873	,,	Mohammed XVII		b. 1803	d. 1873
1873–1894	,,	Al-Hasan			
1894–1908	,,	Abd-ul-Aziz IV (deposed)		b. 1881 (?)	d. 1943
1908–1912	,,	Mulai Hafid		b. 1875 (?)	d. 1937
1912–1927	,,	Mulai Yusef			

(A French Protectorate, 1912–1956; an independent sovereign state from 1956)

1927–1957	Sultan	Sidi Mohammed ben Yusef	b. 1911	d. 1961

(Title changed from Sultan to King)

1957–1961	King	Mohammed V (Sidi Mohammed ben Yusef)
1961–	,,	Hassan II, son of Mohammed V	b. 1930
1961–	Prime Minister	Hassan II

(King declared himself his own Prime Minister)

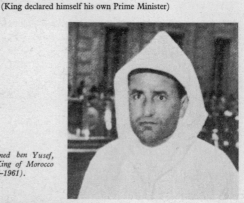

Sidi Mohammed ben Yusef, Sultan and King of Morocco (1927–1961).

Hassan II, King of Morocco (1961–), also assumed the post of Prime Minister of his country in the year of his accession to the throne. Earlier he had assisted his father in the negotiations at Paris which led to the independence of Morocco.

Moyen-Congo, see Congo (Brazzaville)

Muscat and Oman

(The Sultanate of Muscat and Oman was under Portuguese rule from 1508; fell under Persian influence after 1648. Now independent under British protection; present dynasty dates from 1741)

1932–	Sultan	Sir Said bin Taimur		b. 1910

Nauru

(Former United Nations Trust Territory, administered by Australia, New Zealand and the United Kingdom jointly; became independent in 1968)

1968–	Chairman of Council of State	Chief Hammer De Roburt

Nepal

Tribhubana, King of Nepal (1911–1955).

(Although a kingdom, Nepal was actually ruled from 1848–1951 by hereditary Prime Ministers, the Ranas, who kept the Kings in protective custody. In 1951 the King was restored to real power)

1911–1955	King	Tribhubana	b. 1906	d. 1955
1955–	„	Mahendra	b. 1920	
1965–	Prime Minister	Soorya Bahadur Thapa	b. 1928	

King Mahendra of Nepal (1955–   ) and his Queen pose with the late Dag Hammar-skjöld at the United Nations.

Netherlands (Holland)

(Inhabited in early times by the Batavi, Frisii and Saxons; split into many small, independent states after 843 A.D.; attached to Burgundy in the 15th century; ruled by the Habsburgs from 1477)

1482–1506	Count	Philip the Handsome, son of Maximilian I and Mary of Burgundy	b. 1478	d. 1506
1506–1555	„	Charles V, son of Philip the Handsome	b. 1500	d. 1558
1555–1581	„	Philip II, son of Charles V (Revolt against Spain, 1572–1609)	b. 1527	d. 1598

Queen Juliana of the Netherlands arrives with Prince Bernhard, her consort, for the opening of Parliament in The Hague.

Governors

1507–1530	Governor	Margaret of Savoy, daughter of Mary of Burgundy	b. 1480	d. 1530
1531–1555	,,	Mary of Hungary, daughter of Philip the Handsome	b. 1505	d. 1558
1555–1559	,,	Emmanuel Philibert of Savoy, nephew of Margaret	b. 1528	d. 1580
1559–1567	,,	Margaret of Parma, daughter of Charles V	b. 1522	d. 1586
1567–1573	,,	Fernando Alvarez de Toledo, Duke of Alba	b. 1508	d. 1582?
1573–1576	,,	Luis de Zuñiga y Requesens		d. 1576
1576–1578	,,	Don John of Austria, son of Charles V	b. 1547	d. 1578
1578–1592	,,	Alessandro Farnese, son of Margaret of Parma (see Parma)	b. 1545	killed 1592

DUTCH REPUBLIC

1579–1584	Stadholder	William I, the Silent, Prince of Orange	b. 1533	assassinated 1584

William the Silent became a page to the Emperor Charles V in 1548. He led the "War of Liberation" against the Spanish armies of the Duke of Alba, and after the provinces of Holland declared their independence of Spain he became hereditary stadholder.

1584–1625	Stadholder	Maurice, son of William, Prince of Orange	b. 1567	d. 1625
		(War with Spain, 1621–1648)		
1625–1647	,,	Frederick Henry, half-brother of Maurice	b. 1584	d. 1647
1647–1650	,,	William II, son of Frederick Henry	b. 1626	d. 1650
		(Stadholdership suspended, 1650–1672)		
1672–1702	,,	William III of Orange, son of William II	b. 1650	d. 1702

		(Succeeded to the English Throne, 1688)		
		(Republic, 1702–1747)		
1747–1751	Hereditary	William IV Friso, son of		
	Stadholder	John William Friso	b. 1711	d. 1751
	of all provinces			
1751–1795	Stadholder	William V, son of William IV Friso	b. 1748	d. 1806

BONAPARTES

(Batavian Republic established by France, 1795–1806)

1806–1810	King	Louis Bonaparte, nephew of		
		Napoleon abdicated 1810	b. 1778	d. 1846

(Holland incorporated in France, 1810–1813)

Louis Bonaparte, King of Holland (1806–1810).

William III of Orange, Stadholder of the Netherlands (1672–1702), ascended the English throne in 1688.

William II, King of the Netherlands (1840–1849).

William III, King of the Netherlands (1849–1890).

William I, King of the Netherlands (1815–1840).

Wilhelmina, Queen of the Netherlands (1890–1948).

KINGDOM OF THE NETHERLANDS
(Belgium annexed to Netherlands, 1815)

1815–1840	King	William I, son of William V		
		abdicated 1840	b. 1772	d. 1843
		(Belgian provinces seceded, 1830)		
1840–1849	,,	William II, son of William I	b. 1792	d. 1849
1849–1890	,,	William III, son of William II	b. 1817	d. 1890
1890–1948	Queen	Wilhelmina, daughter of		
		William III abdicated 1948	b. 1880	d. 1962
1948–	,,	Juliana, daughter of Wilhelmina	b. 1909	

Queen Juliana married a German Prince, Bernhard of Lippe-Biesterfeld, in 1937. This marriage caused controversy at the time and the marriages of Juliana's daughters to Spanish and German husbands nearly 30 years later were also strongly criticized, on religious and political grounds.

1940–1945	German High Commissioner	Artur von Seyss-Inquart	b. 1892	hanged 1946

STATESMEN

1572–1585	Grand Pensionary	Paulus Buys	b. 1531	d. 1594
1586–1619	,,	Johan van Olden Barnevelt	b. 1547	executed 1619

Van Olden Barnevelt fought for Holland's independence, but opposed the ambitions and warlike policies of Maurice of Nassau. He was illegally arrested, condemned to death as a traitor and executed—at the age of 71.

1621–1629	Grand Pensionary	Anthonis Duyck	b. 1560	d. 1629
1631–1636	,,	Adriaan Pauw	b. 1585	d. 1653
1636–1651	,,	Jacob Cats	b. 1577	d. 1660
1651–1653	,,	Adriaan Pauw		
1653–1672	,,	Johan de Witt	b. 1625	murdered 1672
1672–1689	,,	Gaspar Fagel	b. 1629	d. 1689
1689–1720	,,	Anthonie Heinsius	b. 1641	d. 1720
1720–1727	,,	Isaac van Hoornbeek	b. 1665	d. 1727
1727–1736	,,	Simon van Slingelandt	b. 1664	d. 1736
1736–1746	,,	Anthony van der Heim	b. 1693	d. 1746
1746–1749	,,	Jacob Gilles	b. 1691	d. 1765
1749–1772	,,	Pieter Steyn	b. 1706	d. 1772
1772–1787	,,	Pieter van Bleiswijk	b. 1724	d. 1790
1787–1795	,,	Laurens Pieter van de Spiegel	b. 1737	d. 1800
1945	Prime Minister	Pieter Sjoerd Gerbrandy	b. 1885	d. 1961
1945–1946	,,	Willem Schermerhorn	b. 1894	

(Above) Victor Gerard Marie Marijnen, Prime Minister of the Netherlands (1963–1965).

(Right) Juliana, Queen of the Netherlands (1948–   ).

Netherlands (continued)

1946–1948	Prime Minister	Louis Joseph Maria Beel	b. 1902
1948–1951	,,	Willem Drees	b. 1886
1951–1952	,,	Willem Drees	
1952–1956	,,	Willem Drees	
1956–1958	,,	Willem Drees	
1958–1959	,,	Louis Joseph Maria Beel	
1959–1963	,,	Jan Eduard de Quay	b. 1901
1963–1965	,,	Victor Gerard Marie Marijnen	b. 1917
1965–1967	,,	Joseph Maria Laurens Theo Cals	b. 1914
1967–	,,	Pieter de Jong	

New Zealand

(Prior to British settlement in 1840 New Zealand was under the rule of chieftains of the Maori race, the Polynesian inhabitants of the country)

1840–1842	Governor	William Hobson		d. 1842
1842–1843	Administrator	Willoughby Shortland		
1843–1845	Governor	Robert R. FitzRoy, natural descendant of King Charles II	b. 1805	d. 1865
1845–1853	,,	Sir George Grey	b. 1812	d. 1898
1854–1855	Administrator	Robert Henry Wynyard		
1855–1861	Governor	Thomas Gore Browne		
1861–1868	,,	Sir George Grey		
1868–1873	,,	Sir George Ferguson Bowen	b. 1821	d. 1899
1873	Administrator	Sir George Alfred Arney		
1873–1874	Governor	Sir James Fergusson	b. 1832	d. 1907
1874–1879	,,	The Marquess of Normanby	b. 1819	d. 1890
1879	Administrator	Sir James Prendergast		
1879–1880	Governor	Sir Hercules George Robert Robinson, Baron Rosmead	b. 1824	d. 1897
1880	Administrator	Sir James Prendergast		
1880–1882	Governor	Sir Arthur Charles Hamilton Gordon, Baron Stanmore	b. 1829	d. 1912

New Zealand became a British colony when the Maori chiefs signed the Treaty of Waitangi in 1840.

William Hobson, first Governor of New Zealand (1840–1842).

Sir Bernard Edward Fergusson, Governor-General of New Zealand (1962–1966).

1882–1883	Administrator	Sir James Prendergast		
1883–1889	Governor	Sir William Francis Drummond Jervois		
1889	Administrator	Sir James Prendergast		
1889–1892	Governor	William Hillier, Earl of Onslow	b. 1853	d. 1911
1892	Administrator	Sir James Prendergast		
1892–1897	Governor	The Earl of Glasgow	b. 1833	d. 1915
1897	Administrator	Sir James Prendergast		
1897–1904	Governor	Uchter John Mark, Earl of Ranfurly	b. 1856	d. 1933
1904–1910	,,	William Lee, Baron Plunket	b. 1864	d. 1920
1910	Administrator	Sir Robert Stout		
1910–1912	Governor	John Poynder Dickson-Poynder, Baron Islington		
1912–	Administrator	Sir Robert Stout		
1912–1917	Governor	Arthur William de Brito Savile Foljambe, Earl of Liverpool	b. 1870	d. 1941
1917–1920	Governor-General	Arthur William de Brito Savile Foljambe, Earl of Liverpool		
1920	Administrator	Sir Robert Stout		
1920–1924	Governor-General	John Rushworth, Viscount Jellicoe of Scapa	b. 1859	d. 1935
1924	Administrator	Sir Robert Stout		
1924–1930	Governor-General	Sir Charles Fergusson, son of Sir James Fergusson	b. 1865	d. 1951
1930	Administrator	Sir Michael Myers		
1930–1935	Governor-General	Sir Charles Bathurst, Viscount Bledisloe	b. 1867	
1935–1941	,,	George Vere Arundell Monckton-Arundell, Viscount Galway	b. 1882	d. 1943
1941–1946	,,	Cyril Louis Norton, Baron Newall	b. 1886	d. 1964
1946–1952	,,	Bernard Cyril, Baron Freyberg	b. 1890	
1952–1957	,,	Charles Willoughby Moke, Baron Norrie	b. 1893	
1957–1962	,,	Charles John Lyttelton, Viscount Cobham	b. 1909	
1962–1966	,,	Sir Bernard Edward Fergusson, son of Sir Charles Fergusson	b. 1911	
1966–	,,	Sir Arthur Porritt	b. 1900	

PRIME MINISTERS

1856	Prime Minister	Henry Sewell	b. 1807	d. 1879
1856	,,	Sir William Fox	b. 1812	d. 1893
1856–1861	,,	Edward William Stafford	b. 1819	d. 1901

1861–1862	Prime Minister	Sir William Fox		
1862–1863	,,	Alfred Domett	b. 1811	d. 1887
1863–1864	,,	Sir Frederick Whitaker	b. 1812	d. 1891
1864–1865	,,	Frederick Aloysius Weld	b. 1823	d. 1891
1865–1869	,,	Edward William Stafford		
1869–1872	,,	Sir William Fox		
1872	,,	Edward William Stafford		
1872–1873	,,	George Marsden Waterhouse	b. 1824	d. 1906
1873	,,	Sir William Fox		
1873–1875	,,	Sir Julius Vogel	b. 1835	d. 1899
1875–1876	,,	Daniel Pollen	b. 1813	d. 1896
1876	,,	Sir Julius Vogel		
1876–1877	,,	Sir Harry Albert Atkinson	b. 1831	d. 1892
1877–1879	,,	Sir George Grey	b. 1812	d. 1898
1879–1882	,,	Sir John Hall	b. 1824	d. 1906
1882–1883	,,	Frederick Whitaker		
1883–1884	,,	Sir Harry Albert Atkinson		
1884	,,	Robert Stout	b. 1844	d. 1930
1884	,,	Sir Harry Albert Atkinson		
1884–1887	,,	Sir Robert Stout		
1887–1891	,,	Sir Harry Albert Atkinson		
1891–1893	,,	John Ballance	b. 1839	d. 1893
1893–1906	,,	Richard John Seddon	b. 1845	d. 1906
1906	,,	William Hall-Jones	b. 1851	d. 1936
1906–1912	,,	Sir Joseph George Ward	b. 1856	d. 1930
1912	,,	Thomas Mackenzie	b. 1854	d. 1930
1912–1925	,,	William Ferguson Massey	b. 1856	d. 1925
1925	,,	Sir Francis Henry Dillon Bell	b. 1821	d. 1898
1925–1928	,,	Joseph Gordon Coates	b. 1878	d. 1943
1928–1930	,,	Sir Joseph George Ward	b. 1856	d. 1930
1930–1935	,,	George William Forbes	b. 1869	d. 1947
1935–1940	,,	Michael Joseph Savage	b. 1872	d. 1940
1940–1949	,,	Peter Fraser	b. 1884	d. 1950
1949–1957	,,	Sir Sidney George Holland	b. 1893	d. 1961
1957	,,	Keith Jacka Holyoake	b. 1904	
1957–1960	,,	Walter Nash	b. 1882	
1960–	,,	Keith Jacka Holyoake		

(Left) Richard John Seddon, Prime Minister of New Zealand (1893–1906).

(Right) William Ferguson Massey, Prime Minister of New Zealand (1912–1925).

(Left) Keith Jacka Holyoake, Prime Minister of New Zealand (1957, 1960–).

(Right) Walter Nash, Prime Minister of New Zealand (1957–1960).

Nicaragua

(Under Spain 1524–1821; briefly part of Mexican Empire of Iturbide before joining the Central American Confederation in 1825; independent since 1838)

1853–1854	President	Frutos Chamorro		
1855	"	José Maria Estrada		
1859–1867	"	Tomás Martínez	b. 1812	d. 1873
1867–1871	"	Fernando Guzmán		
1871–1875	"	Vicente Cuadra		
1875–1879	"	Pedro Joaquin Chamorro		
1879–1883	"	Joaquin Zavala		
1883–1887	"	Adan Cárdenas		
1887–1889	"	Evaristo Carazo		d. 1889
1889–1893	"	Roberto Sacasa		
1893–1909	"	José Santos Zelaya	b. 1853	d. 1919
1909–1910	President (provisional)	José Madriz		
1911	President	Juan J. Estrada		
1911–1916	"	Adolfo Díaz	b. 1874	
1917–1920	"	Emiliano Chamorro Vargas	b. 1871	
1921–1923	"	Diego Manuel Chamorro, nephew of Emiliano Chamorro Vargas		d. 1923
1923–1924	President (provisional)	Bartolome Martínez		
1925–1926	President	Carlos Solorzano		
1926	"	Emiliano Chamorro Vargas		
1926–1928	"	Adolfo Díaz		

Anastasio Somoza, President of Nicaragua (1937–1947, 1951–1956).

René Schick Gutiérrez, President of Nicaragua (1963–1966).

1929–1932	President	José María Moncada		d. 1945
1933–1936	,,	Juan Bautista Sacasa	b. 1874	d. 1946
1936	President (provisional)	Carlos Brenes Jarquin		
1937–1947	President	Anastasio Somoza	b. 1896	assassinated 1956
1947	,,	Leonardo Arguello		
1947	,,	Benjamin Lacayo-Sacasa		
1947–1950	,,	Victor M. Roman y Reyes		
1951–1956	,,	Anastasio Somoza		
1957–1963	,,	Luis A. Somoza Debayle, son of Anastasio Somoza	b. 1922	
1963–1966	,,	René Schick Gutiérrez	b. 1909	
1966–1967	,,	Lorenzo Guerrero	b. 1900	
1967–	,,	Anastasio Somoza Debayle		

Niger

(Former French Overseas Territory, Niger became independent in 1960)

1960–	President	Hamani Diori	b. 1916
	Prime Minister	Boubou Hama	

Nigeria

(Formerly a British colony; independent and a member of the British Commonwealth, 1960–1963; a Republic from 1963)

1960–1963	Governor-General	Nnamdi Azikiwe	
1963–1966	President	Nnamdi Azikiwe	b. 1904
	Prime Minister	Sir Abubakar Tafawa Balewa	
1966	Head of Military Council	Johnson Aguiyi-Ironsi	assassinated 1966 b. 1924
1966–	,,	Lt.-Col. Yokubu Gowon	assassinated 1966 b. 1935

Johnson Aguiyi-Ironsi served as Head of the Nigeria Military Council in 1966, following a coup d'état.

(In 1967, Nigeria's eastern region declared itself independent as the Democratic Republic of Biafra with Odumegwu Ojukwu as Chief of State)

Northern Ireland, see Ireland

Norway (Nor. Norge)

Olaf II Haraldson (St. Olaf), King of Norway (1016–1030).

872– 930   King   Harald Fairhair (Harald I)   b. 850? d. 933

After conquering and deposing other Norwegian earls, Harald compelled these rulers to leave Norway. They settled in the Orkneys, Hebrides, Shetlands and, most importantly, in Normandy, where their descendants became dukes, kings and crusaders.

930– 934	King	Erik Bloodaxe (Eric I), son of Harald	d. 954?
934– 961	,,	Haakon the Good (Haakon I), son of Harald	b. 914? killed 961
961– 970	,,	Harald Graypelt (Harald II) son of Erik	b. 930? killed 970
970– 995	Ruler	Earl Haakon	b. 937? d. 995
995–1000	King	Olaf Tryggvason (Olaf I)	b. 969 killed 1000
1000–1016	Rulers	Earls Erik and Svein, sons of Earl Haakon	Erik d. 1024?
1016–1030	King	Olaf II Haraldson (St. Olaf)	b. 995? killed 1030

Following his own conversion, St. Olaf attempted to forcibly convert the whole of Norway to Christianity. The various petty rulers reacted by appealing (successfully) for help to Canute the Great of Denmark. Olaf fled to Sweden, tried to reconquer Norway, was defeated and killed. He was canonized in 1164.

1030–1035	King	Canute the Great, son of Sweyn Forkbeard	b. 1000 d. 1035
1035–1047	,,	Magnus the Good (Magnus I), son of St. Olaf	d. 1047
1047–1066	,,	Harald Hardrade (Harald III) descendant of Harald I	b. 1015 d. 1066
1066–1093	,,	Olaf the Peaceful (Olaf III), son of Harald III	d. 1093
1093–1103	,,	Magnus Barefoot (Magnus II), son of Olaf III	b. 1073 d. 1103
1103–1122	,,	Eystein I, son of Magnus	b. 1089 d. 1122
1103–1130	,,	Sigurd the Crusader (Sigurd I), son of Magnus	b. 1089? d. 1130
1130–1135	,,	Magnus the Blind (Magnus III), son of Sigurd	b. 1115? killed 1139
1130–1136	Rival King	Harald Gilchrist (Harald IV) (Civil War 1134–1135)	b. 1103? killed 1136
1136–1161	Joint Kings	{ Inge I, son of Harald	killed 1161
		Sigurd II Mund, son of Harald	b. 1134 killed 1155
1142–1157	King	Eystein II, son of Harald	assassinated 1157
1161–1162	,,	Haakon (Haakon II), son of Sigurd	b. 1147 killed 1162
1163–1184	,,	Magnus (Magnus IV), son of Erling Skakke	b. 1156 killed 1184
1184–1202	,,	Sverre, ? son of Sigurd Mund	b. 1152? d. 1202
1202–1204	,,	Haakon Sverreson (Haakon III)	d. 1204
1204–1217	,,	Inge Baardson	

1217–1263	King	Haakon (Haakon IV), ? son of Haakon III	b. 1204	d. 1263
1263–1280	,,	Magnus the Lawmender (Magnus VI), son of Haakon	b. 1238	d. 1280
1280–1299	,,	Erik (Erik II), son of Magnus	b. 1268	d. 1299
1299–1319	,,	Haakon (Haakon V), son of Magnus	b. 1270	d. 1319
1319–1355	,,	Magnus (Magnus VII), grandson of Haakon	b. 1316	d. 1374
1355–1380	,,	Haakon (Haakon VI), son of Magnus	b. 1339	d. 1380

KINGS OF DENMARK AND NORWAY 1380–1814

1380–1387	,,	Olav (Olav IV), son of Haakon	b. 1370	d. 1387
1387–1412	Queen	Margaret, mother of Olav	b. 1353	d. 1412
1389–1442	King	Erik of Pomerania (Erik III), grandnephew of Margaret (Union of Kalmar, 1397)	b. 1382	d. 1459

(Left) Christian IV, King of Denmark and Norway (1588–1648).

(Right) Frederik III, King of Denmark and Norway (1648–1670).

1442–1448	King	Christopher III of Bavaria, nephew of Eric	b. 1418	d. 1448
1448–1481	,,	Christian I, son of Theodoric, Count of Oldenburg	b. 1426	d. 1481
1481–1513	,,	John I, son of Christian I	b. 1455	d. 1513
1513–1523	,,	Christian II, son of John of Saxony	b. 1481	d. 1559
1523–1533	,,	Frederik I, son of Christian I	b. 1471 ?	d. 1533
1534–1559	,,	Christian III, son of Frederik I	b. 1503	d. 1559
1559–1588	,,	Frederik II, son of Christian III	b. 1534	d. 1588
1588–1648	,,	Christian IV, son of Frederik II	b. 1577	d. 1648
1648–1670	,,	Frederik III, son of Christian IV	b. 1609	d. 1670
1670–1699	,,	Christian V, son of Frederik III	b. 1646	d. 1699
1699–1730	,,	Frederik IV, son of Christian V	b. 1671	d. 1730
1730–1746	,,	Christian VI, son of Frederik IV	b. 1699	d. 1746
1746–1766	,,	Frederik V, son of Christian VI	b. 1723	d. 1766
1766–1808	,,	Christian VII, son of Frederik V	b. 1749	d. 1808
1808–1814	,,	Frederik VI, son of Christian VII	b. 1768	d. 1839
1814	Danish governor	Christian Frederik		

KINGS OF SWEDEN AND NORWAY 1814–1905

1814–1818	King	Carl XIII, son of Adolphus Frederik	b. 1748	d. 1818

(Left) Frederik IV, King of Denmark and Norway (1699–1730).

(Right) Carl XIV Johan (Bernadotte), King of Sweden and Norway (1818–1844).

*Haakon VII, King of Norway (1905–
1957), and Crown Prince Harald.*

Olaf V, King of Norway (1957–   ).

1818–1844   King   Carl XIV Johan (Marshal Bernadotte)   b. 1763?   d. 1844
  Bernadotte was a French soldier who rose from the ranks to become one of
  Napoleon's marshals—though not one of his most trusted generals. Elected
  Crown Prince of Sweden, he fought for the Allies against Napoleon in 1813.

1844–1859	King	Oscar I, son of Carl Johan	b. 1799	d. 1859
1859–1872	,,	Carl XV, son of Oscar I	b. 1826	d. 1872
1872–1905	,,	Oscar II, son of Oscar I abdicated 1905	b. 1829	d. 1907
		(An independent Kingdom from 1905)		

KINGS OF NORWAY SINCE 1905

1905–1957	,,	Haakon VII, son of Frederik VIII of Denmark	b. 1872	d. 1957
		(German occupation, 1940–1945)		
1957–	,,	Olav V, son of Haakon VII	b. 1903	

STATESMEN

1814–1822	Head of government	J. C. Wedel Jarlsberg	b. 1779	d. 1840
		Jonas Collett	b. 1727	d. 1851
1822–1858	,,	J. C. Wedel Jarlsberg		
		Severin Lovenskiold	b. 1777	d. 1856
		Jorgen Herman Vogt	b. 1784	d. 1862
1858–1861	,,	Chr. Birch-Reichenwald	b. 1814	d. 1891
1861–1880	Prime Minister	Frederik Stang	b. 1808	d. 1884
1880–1884	,,	Chr. Aug. Selmer	b. 1816	d. 1889
1884	,,	Chr. Schweigaard	b. 1838	d. 1899
1884–1889	,,	Johan Sverdrup	b. 1816	d. 1892
1889–1891	,,	Emil Stang	b. 1834	d. 1912
1891–1893	,,	Johannes Steen	b. 1853	d. 1921
1893–1895	,,	Emil Stang		
1895–1898	,,	Georg Francis Hagerup	b. 1853	d. 1921
1898–1902	,,	Johannes Steen		
1902–1903	,,	Otto Blehr	b. 1847	d. 1927
1903–1905	,,	Georg Francis Hagerup		
1905–1907	,,	Christian Michelsen	b. 1857	d. 1925
1907–1908	,,	J. Lövland	b. 1857	d. 1925
1908–1910	,,	Gunnar Knudsen	b. 1848	d. 1928
1910–1912	,,	Wollert Konow	b. 1848	d. 1928

1912–1913	Prime Minister	Jens Bratlie		
1913–1920	,,	Gunnar Knudsen	b. 1856	d. 1939
1920–1921	,,	Otto B. Halvorsen	b. 1848	d. 1928
1921–1923	,,	Otto Blehr	b. 1872	d. 1923
1923	,,	Otto B. Halvorsen		
1923–1924	,,	Abraham Berge	b. 1851	d. 1936
1924–1926	,,	Johan Ludwig Mowinckel	b. 1870	d. 1943
1926–1928	,,	Ivar Lykke	b. 1872	d. 1949
1928	,,	Christopher Hornsrud	b. 1859	d. 1960

Johan Sverdrup, Prime Minister of Norway (1884–1889).

Christian Michelsen, Prime Minister of Norway (1905–1907).

Einar Gerhardsen, Prime Minister of Norway (1945–1951).

Trygve Lie, Secretary-General of the United Nations (1946–1953).

1928–1931	Prime Minister	Johan Ludwig Mowinckel		
1931–1932	,,	Peder Kilstad	b. 1878	d. 1932
1932–1933	,,	Jens Hundseid	b. 1883	d. 1965
1933–1935	,,	Johan Ludwig Mowinckel		
1935–1945	,,	Johan Nygaardsvold	b. 1879	d. 1952

1945–1951	Prime Minister	Einar Gerhardsen	b. 1897	
1951–1955	”	Oscar Torp	b. 1893	d. 1958
1955–1963	”	Einar Gerhardsen		
1963	”	John Lyng	b. 1905	
1963–1965	”	Einar Gerhardsen		
1965–	”	Per Borthen	b. 1913	
1946–1953	Secretary-General of the United Nations	Trygve Lie	b. 1896	

Numidia

The last of the royal line of ancient Numidia, Ptolemy, ruled over part of Mauretania, as had his father, Juba II. The Romans had annexed Numidia, giving Juba Mauretania as his realm and a daughter of Cleopatra and Antony as his Queen. Ptolemy (shown here) was thus a grandson of Antony.

(Numidia was a kingdom of North Africa corresponding roughly to modern Algeria)

c.	200 B.C.	King	Narva		
		”	Gala		
		”	Desalces		
		”	Capusa		
		”	Lacumaces		
201– 148		”	Masinissa	b. c. 238	d. 148
148– 118		”	Micipsa		d. 118
		”	Gulussa		
		”	Atherbal		
112– 104		”	Jugurtha (deposed)		d. 104
		”	Hiempsal I		
		”	Hierta		
		”	Hiempsal II		
?– 46		”	Juba I		d. 46
30– 25		”	Juba II		d. A.D. 19
		”	Ptolemy		d. A.D. 40

(Most of Numidia was annexed to Rome after 46 B.C. Juba II and Ptolemy actually ruled the adjacent territory of Mauretania)

(Left) Masinissa, King of Numidia (201–148 B.C.); (Right) Jugurtha, King of Numidia (112–104 B.C.).

(Left) Hiempsal II, King of Numidia (c. 60 B.C.); (Right) Juba I, King of Numidia (?–46 B.C.).

Nyasaland, see Malawi

Pakistan   *Also see India*

(Separated from India and established as a British Dominion in 1947)

| 1947–1948 | Governor-General | Mohammed Ali Jinnah | b. 1876 | d. 1948 |

A Moslem lawyer in India and president of the All-India Moslem League, Mohammed Ali Jinnah was the "Father of Pakistan".

1948–1951	Governor-General	Khwaja Nazimuddin	b. 1894	
1951–1955	,,	Ghulam Mohammed	b. 1895	d. 1956
1955–1958	,,	Iskander Mirza	b. 1899	
	and later President			
1958–	President	Mohammed Ayub Khan	b. 1907	

(Islamic Republic proclaimed in 1956)

1947–1951	Prime Minister	Liaquat Ali Khan	b. 1895	d. 1951
1951–1953	,,	Khwaja Nazimuddin		
1953–1955	,,	Mohammed Ali	b. 1909	d. 1963
1955–1956	,,	Chaudhri Mohammed Ali	b. 1905	
1956–1958	,,	H. S. Suhrawardy	b. 1893	d. 1963

Mohammed Ali Jinnah,
Governor-General of
Pakistan (1947–1948).

Mohammed Ayub Khan,
President of Pakistan
(1958–   ).

Palestine, see Israel, Jordan

Panama

Roberto F. Chiari, at the left,
President of Panama (1960–1964),
with a member of his cabinet at the
United Nations.

(A department of the United States of Colombia until 1903)

1904–1908	President	Manuel Amador Guerrero	b. 1833	d. 1909
1908–1910	,,	José Domingo de Obaldía		
1910	President (acting)	Carlos Antonio Mendoza		
1910–1912	,,	Pablo Arosemena		
1912–1916	President	Belisario Porras	b. 1856	d. 1942
1916–1918	,,	Ramón Váldez		

1918	President (acting)	Ciro Luis Urriola		
1918–1920	,,	Belisario Porras		
1920	President	Ernesto Lefevre		
1920–1924	,,	Belisario Porras		
1924–1928	,,	Rodolfo Chiari		
1928–1931	,,	Florencio Harmodio Arosemena	b. 1873	d. 1945
1931	President (provisional)	Harmodio Arias	b. 1886	
1931–1932	President	Ricardo J. Alfaro	b. 1882	
1932–1936	,,	Harmodio Arias		
1936–1939	,,	Juan Demóstenes Arosemena	b. 1879	d. 1939
1939–1940	President (acting)	Augusto Samuel Boyd	b. 1879	d. 1957
1940–1941	President	Arnulfo Arias	b. 1897	
1941–1945	,,	Ricardo Adolfo de la Guardia	b. 1899	
1945–1948	,,	Enrique Adolfo Jiménez		
1948–1949	,,	Domingo Díaz Arosemena		
1949–1951	,,	Arnulfo Arias		
1951–1952	,,	Alcibíades Arosemena		
1952–1955	,,	José Antonio Remon Cantesa	assassinated 1955	
1955–1956	,,	José Arias Espinosa		
1956–1960	,,	Ernesto de la Guardia		
1960–1964	,,	Roberto F. Chiari	b. 1905	
1964–1968	,,	Marco Aurelio Robles	b. 1905	
1968	,,	Arnulfo Arias		
1968–	President (Military Junta)	José Pinilla		

Papacy, see Popes

Paraguay

Coin of the Republic of Paraguay.

(Gained independence from Spain in 1811)

1811–1840	Dictator	José Gaspar Rodríguez Francia		d. 1840
1842–1862	,,	Carlos Antonio López, nephew of José Gaspar Rodríguez Francia	b. 1790	d. 1862
1862–1870	,,	Francisco Solano López, son of Carlos Antonio López	b. 1827	killed 1870
1870–1871	President	Cirilo Rivarola		d. 1871
1871–1874	,,	Salvador Jovellanos		
1874	,,	Juan Bautista Gil	assassinated 1874	
1877–1878	President (acting)	Higinio Uriarte		
1878–1880	President	Cándido Barreiro		d. 1880
1880–1885	,,	Bernardino Caballero	b. 1831	d. 1885
1886–1890	,,	Patricio Escobar		
1890–1894	,,	Juan González		
1894–1898	,,	Juan Bautista Egusquiza		
1898–1902	,,	Emilio Aceval		
1902	,,	Hector Carvallo		
1902–1904	,,	Juan B. Escurra		
1904–1905	President (provisional)	Juan Gaona		
1906	President	Cecilio Báez	b. 1862	d. 1941
1906–1908	,,	Benigno Ferreira		

1908–1910	President	Emiliano González Navero	b. 1861	d. 1938
1910–1911	,,	Manuel Gondra		
1911	President (provisional)	Albino Jara		
1911–1912	,,	Liberato Marcial Rojas		
1912	,,	Pedro Peña		
1912	,,	Emiliano González Navero		
1912–1916	President	Eduardo Schaerer		
1916–1919	,,	Manuel Franco		d. 1919
1919–1920	President (acting)	José Montero		
1920–1921	President	Manuel Gondra		
1921	President (acting)	Félix Paiva	b. 1877	
1921–1923	President (provisional)	Eusebio Ayala	b. 1875	d. 1942
1923–1924	,,	Eligio Ayala		
1924	,,	Luis Riart		
1924–1928	President	Eligio Ayala		
1928–1931	,,	José Patricio Guggiari	b. 1884	d. 1957
1931–1932	President (provisional)	Emiliano González Navero		
1932	President	José Patricio Guggiari		
1932–1936	,,	Eusebio Ayala		
1936–1937	President (provisional)	Rafael Franco		
1937–1938	,,	Félix Paiva		
1938–1939	,,	Félix Paiva		
1939–1940	President	José Félix Estigarribia	b. 1888	d. 1940
1940–1948	,,	Higinio Morínigo	b. 1887	
1948	President (provisional)	Juan Manuel Frutos		
1948–1949	President	J. Natalicio González		
1949	President (provisional)	Raimundo Rolón		
1949–1950	President	Felipe Molas López		
1950–1954	,,	Federico Chávez		
1954	,,	Tomas Romero Pereira		
1954–	,,	Alfredo Stroessner	b. 1912	

Pergamum (Pergamus)

Eumenes I of Pergamum.

Attalus I of Pergamum.

B.C.				B.C.
263– 241	Ruler	Eumenes I		d. 241
241– 197	King	Attalus I Soter, nephew of Eumenes I	b. 269	d. 197
197–158?	,,	Eumenes II, son of Attalus I		d. 158?
158?– 138	,,	Attalus II Philadelphus, son of Attalus I	b. 220	d. 138
138– 133	,,	Attalus III Philometor, nephew of Attalus II	b. 171	d. 133

(King Attalus III bequeathed the Kingdom to Rome in 133 B.C.)

Mohammed Riza Pahlevi, Shah of Persia
(Iran) (1941–   ).

Persia (Iran)

ACHAEMENID DYNASTY

B.C.   B.C.

Years	Title	Ruler	Notes
550– 529	King	Cyrus the Great, son of Cambyses (I)	b. 600? killed 529
529– 522	„	Cambyses II, son of Cyrus the Great	d. 522
522– 521	Usurper	Pseudo-Smerdis (Gaumata)	killed 521
521– 486	King	Darius I	b. 558? d. 486
486– 465	„	Xerxes I, son of Darius I	b. 519? murdered 465
464– 424	„	Artaxerxes I, son of Xerxes I	d. 424
424	„	Xerxes II, son of Artaxerxes I	murdered 424
423– 404	„	Darius II, son of Artaxerxes I	d. 404
404– 359	„	Artaxerxes II, son of Darius II	d. 359
359– 338	„	Artaxerxes III, son of Artaxerxes II	murdered 338
338– 336	„	Arses, son of Artaxerxes III	murdered 336
331– 328	„	Artaxerxes IV	
331– 323	Conqueror	Alexander the Great, son of Philip II of Macedon (Internal conflicts 323– 312)	b. 356 d. 323

SELEUCID DYNASTY 312– 250

Years	Title	Ruler	Notes
312– 281	Ruler	Seleucus I (see Syria)	b. 358? assassinated 280

(The Seleucid Empire dissolved c.250 B.C.)

ARSACID DYNASTY OF PARTHIAN KINGS

c.250– 248	King	Arsaces I
248– 214	„	Arsaces II Tiridates, brother of Arsaces I
214– 196	„	Arsaces III Artabanus, son of Arsaces II Tiridates
196– 181	„	Arsaces IV Priapatius
181– 174	„	Arsaces V Phraates, son of Arsaces IV Priapatius
174– 136	„	Arsaces IV Mithridates, son of Arsaces V Phraates
136– 127	„	Arsaces VII Phraates II, son of Arsaces VI Mithridates
127– 124	„	Arsaces VIII Artabanus II, uncle of Arsaces VII Phraates II
124– 87	„	Arsaces IX Mithridates II, son of Arsaces VIII Artabanus II

Persia (continued)

B.C.

87–	77	King	Arsaces X Mnasciras	
76–	69	,,	Arsaces XI Sanatroices	
69–	60	,,	Arsaces XII Phraates III	
60–	56	,,	Arsaces XIII Mithridates III, son of Arsaces XII Phraates III	
56–	37	,,	Arsaces XIV Orodes I, son of Arsaces XII Phraates III	
37 ?–	2	,,	Arsaces XV Phraates IV	murdered? 2
37–	27	Rival king	Tiridates II	
12–	9	,,	Mithridates IV	
			(Throne disputes 2 B.C.–A.D. 10)	

Phraates III (Arsaces XII).

A.D.

10 ?–	40	King	Artabanus II	A.D. d. 40
51–	91	,,	Vologesus I	
107–	130	,,	Arsaces XXVI Osroes	
130–	148	,,	Arsaces XXVII Bolagases II	
148–	190	,,	Arsaces XXVIII Bolagases III, son of Arsaces XXVII Bolagases II	
190–	208	,,	Arsaces XXIX Bolagases IV	
208–	222	,,	Arsaces XXX Bolagases V, son of Arsaces XXX Bolagases V	
222–	226	,,	Arsaces XXXI Artabanus IV, brother of Arsaces XXX Bolagases V	

Artabanus II.

Phraates II (Arsaces VII).

Mithridates II (Arsaces IX).

Orodes I (Arsaces XIV).

Yazdegerd III, King of Persia (A.D. 632–641), receives an Arab emissary. Not long afterward Persia fell to the Arabs and Islam.

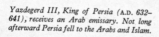

Hormisdas II, King of Persia (A.D. 301–309).

SASSANID DYNASTY

226– 241	King	Ardashir I (Artaxerxes), grandson of Sassan	
241– 272	,,	Sapor I, (Shapur) son of Ardashir (Artaxerxes)	
272– 273	,,	Hormisdas I (Hormuzd)	
273– 276	,,	Baranes I, (Bahram) son of Sapor I	
276– 292	,,	Baranes II, son of Baranes I	
292– 293	,,	Baranes III, son of Baranes II	
293– 303	,,	Narses (Narse)	
301– 309	,,	Hormisdas II, (Hormuzd) son of Narses	
309– 379	,,	Sapor II, (Shapur) son of Hormisdas II	
379– 383	,,	Ardashir II, brother of Sapor II	
383– 388	,,	Sapor III, (Shapur) son of Sapor II	
388– 399	,,	Baranes IV, (Bahram) son of Sapor II	
399– 420	,,	Yazdegerd I, grandson of Sapor II	
420– 440	,,	Baranes V, (Bahram) son of Yazdegerd I	
440– 457	,,	Yazdegerd II, son of Baranes V	
457– 458	,,	Hormisdas III, (Hormuzd) son of Yazdegerd II	
458– 484	,,	Peroz, (Firus) son of Yazdegerd II	
484– 488	,,	Balash, son of Yazdegerd II	
488– 531	,,	Kobad I, (Kavadh) son of Peroz	
531– 578	,,	Chosroes I, (Khustan) son of Kobad I	d. 579
578– 590	,,	Hormisdas IV, (Hormuzd) son of Chosroes I	assassinated 590
590– 628	,,	Chosroes II, son of Hormisdas IV	murdered 628
628	,,	Kobad II, son of Chosroes II	
628– 630	,,	Ardashir III, grandson of Chosroes II	b. 621 murdered 630
632– 641	,,	(Anarchy 630– 632) Yazdegerd III, grandson of Chosroes II	murdered 651

(Persia under the Caliphates, 641–1037; the Seljuks, 1037–1223; the Mongols, 1223–1499)

SAFAWID DYNASTY

1499–1524	Shah	Ismail I	b. 1486	d. 1524
1524–1576	,,	Tahmasp I, son of Ismail I	b. 1514	d. 1576
1576–1577	,,	Ismail II, son of Tahmasp I	b. 1551	d. 1577
1577–1586	,,	Mohammed, son of Tahmasp I		
1586–1628	,,	Abbas I (the Great), son of Shah Mohammed	b. 1557	d. 1628?
1628–1642	,,	Safi I, grandson of Abbas I (the Great)		
1642–1667	,,	Abbas II, son of Safi I	b. 1632	d. 1667
1668–1694	,,	Safi II Suleiman, grandson of Safi I		
1694–1725	,,	Husein, son of Safi II Suleiman	b. 1675?	d. 1729
1725–1732	,,	Tahmasp II, son of Husein	deposed 1732	d. 1739
1732–1736	,,	Abbas III, son of Tahmasp II		deposed 1736
1736–1747	,,	Nadir (Tahmasp Kuli Khan)	b. 1688	assassinated 1747
1747–1749	,,	Ali Mardan		d. 1753
1748–1796	Counter-regent	Ruch, grandson of Nadir		
1749–1760	Shah	Ismail III		

ZAND DYNASTY

1760–1779	Regent	Karim Khan	b. 1699?	d. 1779
1785–1795	Shah	Luft Ali Khan, son of Karim Khan		murdered 1795

KAJAR DYNASTY

1795–1797	,,	Agha Mohammed Khan	b. 1720	murdered 1797
1797–1834	,,	Fath Ali, nephew of Agha Mohammed Khan	b. 1762?	d. 1834
1834–1848	,,	Mohammed, grandson of Fath Ali		d. 1848
1848–1896	,,	Nasir-ad-Din, son of Mohammed	b. 1831	assassinated 1896
1896–1907	,,	Muzaffar-ad-Din, son of Nasir-ad-Din	b. 1853	d. 1907
1907–1909	,,	Mohammed Ali, son of Muzaffar-ad-Din	b. 1872	d. 1930
1909–1925	,,	Ahmed Mirza, son of Mohammed Ali	b. 1898	d. 1930

PAHLEVI DYNASTY

1923–1926	Dictator	Riza Pahlevi	b. 1878	d. 1944
1926–1941	Shah	Riza Pahlevi		
1941–	,,	Mohammed Riza Pahlevi, son of Riza Pahlevi	b. 1919	

Ahmed Mirza, Shah of Persia (1909–1925).

Muzaffar-ad-Din, Shah of Persia (1896–1907).

Riza Pahlevi, Dictator and Shah of Persia (1923–1941).

Peru

Francisco Pizarro discovered and explored Peru. In 1532 he launched the conquest of the Inca Empire, which he then governed for Spain until his assassination in 1541.

(Before Spanish conquest, Peru was the heart of a large empire ruled by the Inca race. The Inca emperors were overthrown and Peru was ruled by Spanish viceroys until the establishment of the republic in 1821)

1821–1822   Protector   José de San Martín   b. 1778 d. 1850

Upon liberating Chile, San Martín began the liberation of Peru. After numerous successes, he established himself as "protector" of Peru. In the meantime, Simón Bolívar (see Venezuela) landed at Guayaquil, and, as San Martín wanted no rivalry for power, the two generals agreed to meet. Details of the meeting are one of the best-kept secrets in history, and to this day no one knows why San Martín, a selfless, social-minded patriot, resigned and retired to Europe, leaving the total conquest of Peru to Bolívar. (Also see Chile.)

1823	President	José de la Riva Agüero	b. 1783 d. 1858
1823	„	José Bernardo Tagle	
1823–1827	Dictator	Simón Bolívar (see Venezuela)	b. 1783 d. 1830
1827–1829	President	José de la Mar	
1829–1833	„	Agustín Gamarra	b. 1785 killed 1841
1833–1834	President (acting)	Luis José de Orbegoso	

José de San Martín, Protector of Peru (1821–1822), is commemorated on a coin of Argentina.

Ramón Castilla, President of Peru (1845–1851, 1855–1862).

Simón Bolívar, liberator of much of South America, is also remembered as Dictator of Peru (1823–1827).

1834–1835	President	Manuel Salazar y Baquíjano		
1835–1836	"	Felipe Santiago Salaverry	b. 1806	shot 1836
1836–1839	"	Andrés Santa Cruz	b. 1792?	d. 1865
1839–1841	"	Agustín Gamarra		
1841–1845	President (acting)	Manuel Menéndez	b. 1790?	d. 1845?
1845–1851	President	Ramón Castilla	b. 1797	d. 1867
1851–1855	"	José Rufino Echenique		
1855–1862	"	Ramón Castilla		
1862–1863	"	Miguel de San Román		
1863–1865	President (acting)	Juan Antonio Pezet		
1865–1868	Dictator	Mariano Ignacio Prado	b. 1826	d. 1901
1868–1872	President	José Balta	b. 1816	murdered 1872
1872–1876	"	Manuel Pardo	b. 1834	assassinated 1878
1876–1879	"	Mariano Ignacio Prado		
1879–1881	"	Nicolás de Piérola	b. 1839	d. 1913
1881	President (acting)	Francisco García Calderón	b. 1832	d. 1905
1881–1883	President	Lizardo Montero		
1883–1885	"	Miguel Iglesias	b. 1822	d. 1901
1885–1886	"	Antonio Arenas		
1886–1890	"	Andrés Avelino Cáceres	b. 1836?	d. 1923
1890–1894	"	Remigio Morales Bermúdez	b. 1836	d. 1894
1894	"	Justiniano Borgoño		
1894–1895	"	Andrés Avelino Cáceres		
1895–1899	"	Nicolás de Piérola		
1899–1903	"	Eduardo López de Romaña		
1903–1904	"	Manuel Candamo	b. 1842	d. 1904
1904	"	Serapio Calderón		
1904–1908	"	José Pardo, son of Manuel Pardo	b. 1864	d. 1947
1908–1912	"	Augusto Bernadino Leguía	b. 1863	d. 1932

Although Leguía modernized and developed Peru during his administrations and promulgated the constitution of 1920, he was violently condemned for his compromises during the Tacna-Arica Controversy settlement. A ruthless dictator, he was overthrown and imprisoned in 1929, accused of misappropriating government funds.

1912–1914	President	Guillermo Enrique Billinghurst	b. 1851	d. 1915
1914	President (provisional)	Óscar Raimundo Benavides	b. 1876	d. 1945
1915–1919	President	José Pardo		
1919	President (provisional)	Augusto Bernadino Leguía		
1919–1924	President	Augusto Bernadino Leguía		
1924–1929	"	Augusto Bernadino Leguía (Junta, 1930–1931)		
1931	President (provisional)	Ricardo Leonicio Elías		
1931	"	Gustavo A. Jiménez		
1931	"	David Samamez Ocampo		
1931—1933	President	Luis M. Sánchez Cerro	b. 1889	assassinated 1933
1933–1939	"	Óscar Raimundo Benavides	b. 1876	d. 1945
1939–1945	"	Manuel Prado Ugarteche		
1945–1948	"	José Luis Bustamante y Rivero		
1948–1950	President (Military Junta)	Manuel A. Odría		
1950–1956	President (Constitutional)	Manuel A. Odría		
1956–1962	President	Manuel Prado Ugarteche		
1962	Statesman	Victor Raul Hoya de la Torre	b. 1895	

Founder of APRA (Peru's radical reform but anti-Communist party) and defender of Indian rights, de la Torre has been perhaps the most influential figure in Latin American politics in recent years. Championing the nationalist revolutionary cause, he has suffered years of exile and bitter

hatred. When in 1962 he won the Presidency by a narrow plurality, a
military junta invalidated the elections and seized power.

1962–1963	President (Military Junta)	Ricardo Pérez Godoy
1963–1968	President	Fernando Belaunde Terry
1968	,,	Juan Velasco Alvarado

*Manuel Prado Ugarteche,
President of Peru (1939–1945,
1956–1962).*

Philippines

*Frank Murphy, Governor (1933–
1934) and High Commissioner
(1935–1937) of the Philippines,
appears on a Filipino coin with
President Quezon.*

(Ruled by Spain from 1565 to 1897)

1898–1901	President	Emilio Aguinaldo	b. 1870 ?	d. 1964
		(Ruled by United States from 1898 to 1946)		
1900	U.S. Military Governor	Wesley Merritt	b. 1834	d. 1910
1901–1904	U.S. Civil Governor	William Howard Taft	b. 1857	d. 1930
1904–1906	,,	Luke Edward Wright	b. 1846	d. 1922
1906	,,	Henry Clay Ide	b. 1844	d. 1921
1906–1909	,,	James Francis Smith	b. 1859	d. 1928
1909–1913	,,	William Cameron Forbes	b. 1870	d. 1959
1913–1921	,,	Francis Burton Harrison	b. 1873	d. 1957
1921–1927	,,	Leonard Wood	b. 1860	d. 1927
1927–1929	,,	Henry Lewis Stimson	b. 1867	d. 1950
1929–1932	,,	Dwight Filley Davis	b. 1879	d. 1945
1932–1933	,,	Theodore Roosevelt, Jr., son of President Theodore Roosevelt	b. 1887	d. 1944
1933–1934	,,	Frank Murphy	b. 1890	d. 1949
1935–1937	U.S. High Commissioner	Frank Murphy		
1937–1939	,,	Paul Vories McNutt	b. 1891	d. 1955
1939–1942	,,	Francis Bowes Sayre, son-in-law of President Wilson	b. 1885	
		(Commonwealth Government inaugurated in 1935)		
1935–1944	President	Manuel Luis Quezon y Molina	b. 1878	d. 1944
		(Japanese occupation 1942–1945)		
1943–1945	,,	José P. Laurel		
1944–1946	,,	Sergio Osmeña	b. 1878	d. 1961
		(Republic inaugurated in 1946)		

Philippines (continued)

1946–1948	President	Manuel Roxas y Acuña	b. 1892	d. 1948
1948–1953	,,	Elpidio Quirino		
1954–1957	,,	Ramón Magsaysay		d. 1957
1957–1961	,,	Carlos P. García		
1961–1965	,,	Diosdado Macapagal		
1965–	,,	Ferdinand E. Marcos	b. 1917	

(Left) Emilio Aguinaldo, President of the Philippines (1898–1901); (Right) Manuel Luis Quezon, President of the Philippines (1935–1944).

(Left) Ramón Magsaysay, President of the Philippines (1954–1957); (Right) Ferdinand E. Marcos, President of the Philippines (1965–).

Poland

Boleslaus I, King of Poland
(992–1025).

Casimir III, King of Poland
(1333–1370).

Piast Dynasty

(No authenticated information is available for the period before the Kingdom of the
Piasts was founded)

962– 992	King	Mieszko I	b. 922	d. 992
992–1025	„	Boleslaus I, son of Mieszko I	b. 967	d. 1025
1025–1034	„	Mieszko II, son of Boleslaus I	b. 990	d. 1034
1034–1058	„	Casimir I, son of Mieszko II	b. 1016	d. 1058
1058–1079	„	Boleslaus II, son of Casimir I	b. 1039	d. 1081
1079–1102	„	Ladislaus I, son of Casimir I	b. 1043	d. 1102
1102–1138	„	Boleslaus III, son of Ladislaus I	b. 1085	d. 1138
1138–1146	„	Ladislaus II, son of Boleslaus III	b. 1105	d. 1159
1146–1173	„	Boleslaus IV, son of Boleslaus III	b. 1120	d. 1173
1173–1177	„	Mieszko III, son of Boleslaus III	b. 1126	d. 1202
1177–1194	„	Casimir II, son of Boleslaus III	b. 1138	d. 1197
1194–1227	„	Leszek the White, son of Casimir II	b. 1186	d. 1227
1232–1238	„	Henry I, son of Boleslaus of Silesia	b. 1163	d. 1238
1238–1241	„	Henry II, son of Henry I	b. 1191	d. 1241
1241–1243	„	Konrad I, son of Casimir II	b. 1181	d. 1247
1241–1279	„	Boleslaus V, the Chaste	b. 1226	d. 1279
1279–1288	„	Leszek the Black, son of Casimir I of Cuyavia	b. 1240	d. 1288
1288–1290	„	Henry IV Probus, son of Henry III of Silesia	b. 1257	d. 1290
1295–1296	„	Przemyslav II, son of Przemyslav I	b. 1257	d. 1296
1300–1305	„	Wenceslaus II of Bohemia, son of Ottokar of Bohemia	b. 1271	d. 1305
1306–1333	„	Ladislaus I, son of Casimir I of Cuyavia (King from 1320)	b. 1261	d. 1333
1333–1370	„	Casimir III, son of Ladislaus I	b. 1310	d. 1370

Casimir the Great was a born ruler. He gave his country good government
for nearly 40 years, befriended the peasants and codified the laws.

Sigismund III, King of Poland (1587–
1632).

Sigismund I, King of Poland
(1506–1548).

| 1370–1382 | King | Louis of Hungary, nephew of Casimir III | b. 1326 | d. 1382 |

(Civil Wars, 1382–1384)

House of Jagello

1384–1399	Queen	Hedwig, wife of Jagello, daughter of Louis of Hungary	b. 1374	d. 1399
1386–1434	King	Ladislaus II Jagello, consort of Hedwig	b. 1348	d. 1434
1434–1444	„	Ladislaus III, son of Ladislaus II Jagello	b. 1424	d. 1444
1447–1492	„	Casimir IV, son of Ladislaus II Jagello	b. 1427	d. 1492
1492–1501	„	John I, son of Casimir IV	b. 1459	d. 1501
1501–1506	„	Alexander, son of Casimir IV	b. 1461	d. 1506
1506–1548	„	Sigismund I, son of Casimir IV	b. 1467	d. 1548
1548–1572	„	Sigismund II, son of Sigismund I	b. 1520	d. 1572

Elective Kings

1573–1574	King	Henry III of Anjou	b. 1551	d. 1589
1576–1586	„	Stephen Batory, son-in-law of Sigismund I	b. 1533	d. 1586
1587–1632	„	Sigismund III, grandson of Sigismund I	b. 1566	d. 1632

Stephen Batory, King of Poland (1576–1586).

John III Sobieski, King of Poland (1674–1696).

Stanislaus Augustus Poniatowski, King of Poland (1764–1795).

1632–1648	King	Ladislaus IV, son of Sigismund III	b. 1595	d. 1648
1648–1668	„	John II Casimir, son of Sigismund III abdicated 1668	b. 1609	d. 1672
1669–1673	„	Michael Wiśniowiecki	b. 1640	d. 1673
1674–1696	„	John III Sobieski	b. 1629	d. 1696

With 20,000 Polish troops, John III Sobieski relieved the Turkish siege of Vienna in 1683, drove the Turks back to the Raab, and thereby freed Hungary. Sobieski himself led the decisive charge of Polish cavalry that brought victory. For this act, he was acclaimed the hero of Christendom.

1697–1704	King	Augustus II of Saxony, son of John George of Saxony	b. 1670	d. 1733
1704–1709	,,	Stanislaus Leszczynski	b. 1677	d. 1766
1709–1733	,,	Augustus II of Saxony		
1733–1763	,,	Augustus III, son of Augustus II	b. 1696	d. 1763
1764–1795	,,	Stanislaus Augustus Poniatowski		

abdicated 1795 b. 1732 d. 1798

(Partitioned by Russia, Austria and Prussia in 1772, 1793, and 1795)

(Central Poland created Grand Duchy of Warsaw by Napoleon with Frederick Augustus I of Saxony as ruler 1807–1814)

(Regained independence 1918)

Republic

1918–1922   Head of State   Joseph Pilsudski   b. 1867   d. 1935

Pilsudski organized a private Polish army and on the outbreak of war in 1914 fought with his army under the Austrians against the Russians. He refused to join the Central Powers and after they collapsed he went to Warsaw. From 1920, he was virtual dictator of Poland.

1922	President	Gabriel Narutowicz	b. 1865	d. 1922
1922–1926	,,	Stanislaw Wojciechowski	b. 1869	d. 1953
1926–1939	,,	Ignacy Moscicki	b. 1867	d. 1946

(German occupation 1939–1945)

Joseph Pilsudski, Head of Polish Government (1918–1922).

| 1939–1945 | London Government | Wladyslaw Raczkiewicz | b. 1885 | d. 1947 |
| 1945–1947 | Chairman of the National Council of the People | Boleslaw Bierut | b. 1892 | d. 1956 |

(Communist regime established in 1947)

1947–1952	President	Boleslaw Bierut		
1952–1964	Chairman of the Council of State	Aleksander Zawadzki	b. 1899	d. 1964
1964–1968	,,	Edward Ochab	b. 1906	
1968–	,,	Marion Spychalski	b. 1906	

STATESMEN

1923–1925	Premier	Wladyslaw Grabski	b. 1874	d. 1938
1935–1939	Vice-Premier	Nugeniusz Kwiatkowski	b. 1888	
1932–1939	Foreign Secretary	Józef Beck	b. 1894	d. 1944
1939–1943	Premier	Wladyslaw Sikorski	b. 1881	d. 1943
1947–1952	,,	Józef Cyrankiewicz	b. 1911	
1954–	,,	Józef Cyrankiewicz		
1956–	1st Secretary Polish United Workers' Party	Wladyslaw Gomulka	b. 1905	
1956–	Foreign Secretary	Adam Rapacki	b. 1909	

DANZIG

(The city of Danzig and its environs were detached from Germany after World War I and made a free city)

1920–1930 President of Senate Dr. Heinrich Sahm

Poland (continued)

1931–1933	President of Senate	Dr. E. Ziehm
1933–1934	„	Dr. Herman Rauschning
1934–1937	„	Arthur Greiser

(By 1938 Danzig was in the hands of the local Nazi Party and was virtually administered as a German possession. Formal German control took place after the outbreak of World War II. After the war the territory was assigned to Poland)

Aleksander Zawadzki, Chairman of the Polish Republic (1952–1964).

Józef Cyrankiewicz, Premier of Poland (1954–).

Adam Rapacki, Foreign Secretary of Poland (1956–).

Pontus

(Pontus corresponded to what is now northeastern Turkey)

B.C.				B.C.
486– 479	King	Artabazes		d. 479
479– ?	„	?		
? – 401	„	Rhodobates		
401– 363	„	Mithridates I		
363– 337	„	Ariobarzanes		
337– 302	„	Mithridates II		
302– 266	„	Mithridates III		
266– 214	„	Mithridates IV		
214– 157	„	Pharnaces		

Mithridates the Great.

157– 122	King	Mithridates V		d. 122
122– 63	„	Mithridates VI the Great	b. 132	d. 63

(Mithridates VI was defeated and deposed by the Romans, after which Pontus was
partitioned into states tributary to the Roman Empire)

Popes

The First Bishops of Rome

A.D.   A.D.

41?– 67?	Pope	St. Peter		d. 67?

Saint Peter was a disciple of John the Baptist and later of Jesus. He was
imprisoned by Herod Agrippa I but escaped and established the see of
Antioch. Tradition says that he went to Rome and died a martyr during
Nero's persecutions of the Christians.

67?– ?79	Pope	St. Linus		d. 79?
79?– ?91	„	St. Anacletus or Cletus		d. 91?
91–?100	„	St. Clement I (Clement of Rome)		d. 100?
100–?107	„	St. Evaristus		d. 107?
107–?116	„	St. Alexander I		d. 115
116–?125	„	St. Sixtus I		d. 125?
125–?136	„	St. Telesphorus		d. 136?
136–?140	„	St. Hyginus		d. 140?
140–?154	„	St. Pius I		d. 154?
154–?165	„	St. Anicetus		d. 165?
165– 174	„	St. Soterus		d. 174?
174– 189	„	St. Eleutherius		d. 189
189– 198	„	St. Victor I		d. 198?
198– 217	„	St. Zephyrinus		d. 217
217– 222	„	St. Calixtus or Callistus I		d. 222
222– 230	„	St. Urban I		d. 230
230– 235	„	St. Pontian		
235– 236	„	St. Anterus		d. 236
236– 250	„	St. Fabian		
251– 253	„	St. Cornelius		
251–?258	„	Novatianus (anti-pope *)		
253– 254	„	St. Lucius I		d. 254
254– 257	„	St. Stephen I		d. 257
257– 258	„	St. Sixtus II		d. 258
258– 268	„	St. Dionysius		d. 268
268– 274	„	St. Felix I		d. 274
274– 283	„	St. Eutychian		d. 283
282– 296	„	St. Caius		d. 296
296– 304	„	St. Marcellinus		d. 304
308– 309	„	St. Marcellus I		d. 309
309?	„	St. Eusebius		
310?–314	„	St. Miltiades or Melchiades		d. 314
314– 335	„	St. Sylvester I		d. 335
336	„	St. Mark		d. 336
337– 352	„	St. Julius I (Rusticus)		d. 352
352– 366	„	Liberius		d. 366
355– 365	„	Felix II (anti-pope)		d. 365
366– 367	„	Ursinus (anti-pope)		
366– 384	„	St. Damasus I	b. 304?	d. 384
384– 399	„	St. Siricius		d. 399
399– 401	„	St. Anastasius I		d. 401

St. Peter.

* Pope set up in opposition to the canonically elected Pope.

401– 417	Pope	St. Innocent I		d. 417
417– 418	„	St. Zosimus		d. 418
418– 419	„	Eulalius (anti-pope)		d. 423
418– 422	„	St. Boniface I		d. 422
422– 432	„	St. Celestine I		d. 432
432– 440	„	St. Sixtus III		d. 440

Popes

| 440– 461 | „ | St. Leo I the Great | b. 390? | d. 461 |

Saint Leo the Great was renowned for his zeal against heretics. He induced the Emperor to recognize the primacy of the bishop of Rome, persuaded Attila to spare the city and prevented Genseric from destroying Rome by making him moderate his troops' outrages.

461– 468	Pope	St. Hilary		d. 468
468– 483	„	St. Simplicius		d. 483
483– 492	„	St. Felix III (II)		d. 492
492– 496	„	St. Gelasius I		d. 496
496– 498	„	Anastasius II		d. 498
498– 514	„	St. Symmachus		d. 514
498– 505	„	Laurentius (anti-pope)		
514– 523	„	St. Hormisdas		d. 523
523– 526	„	St. John I	b. 470?	d. 526
526– 530	„	St. Felix IV (III)		d. 530
530– 532	„	Boniface II		d. 532
530	„	Dioscorus (anti-pope)		
532– 535	„	John II		d. 535
535– 536	„	St. Agapetus I		d. 536
536– 537	„	St. Silverius		d. 537
537?–555	„	Vigilius		d. 555
556– 561	„	Pelagius I		d. 561
561– 574	„	John III		d. 574
575– 579	„	Benedict I		d. 579
579– 590	„	Pelagius II		d. 590
590– 604	„	St. Gregory I the Great	b. 540?	d. 604

Saint Gregory I relinquished the office of praetor of Rome to become a monk. When, after seeing some fair-haired youths in the slave market, he was told that they were Angles, he said they should be Angels, and immediately resolved on the conversion of their nation.

604– 606	Pope	Sabinian	d. 606
607	„	Boniface III	d. 607
608– 615	„	St. Boniface IV	d. 615
615– 618	„	St. Deusdedit or Adeodatus I	d. 618
619– 625	„	Boniface V	d. 625
625– 638	„	Honorius I	d. 638
638– 640	„	Severinus	d. 640
640– 642	„	John IV	d. 642
642– 649	„	Theodore I	d. 649
649– 653	„	St. Martin I	d. 655
654– 657	„	St. Eugene I	d. 657
657– 672	„	St. Vitalian	d. 672
672– 676	„	Adeodatus II	d. 676
676– 678	„	Donus	d. 678
678– 681	„	St. Agatho	d. 681
682– 683	„	St. Leo II	d. 683
683– 685	„	St. Benedict II	d. 685
685– 686	„	John V	d. 686
686– 687	„	Conon	d. 687
687– 692	„	Paschal I	
687	„	Theodorus (anti-pope)	

St. Gregory I the Great (590–604).

Pope Honorius III (1216–1227) approving the Franciscan Order, by Giotto.

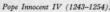

Pope Innocent IV (1243–1254).

687– 701	Pope	St. Sergius I	d. 701
701– 705	,,	John VI	d. 705
705– 707	,,	John VII	d. 707
708	,,	Sisinnius	d. 708
708– 715	,,	Constantine I	d. 715
715– 731	,,	St. Gregory II (Savelli)	d. 731
731– 741	,,	St. Gregory III	d. 741
741– 752	,,	St. Zachary	d. 752
752	,,	Stephen II	d. 752
752– 757	,,	St. Stephen III	d. 757
757– 767	,,	St. Paul I	d. 767
767– 768	,,	Constantine (II) (anti-pope)	d. 769
768	,,	Philippus	
768– 772	,,	Stephen IV	d. 772
772– 795	,,	Adrian I	d. 795
795– 816	,,	St. Leo III	d. 816
816– 817	,,	Stephen V	d. 817
817– 824	,,	St. Pascal I	d. 824
824– 827	,,	Eugene II	d. 827
827	,,	Valentine	d. 827
827– 844	,,	Gregory IV	d. 844
844	,,	John (anti-pope)	
844– 847	,,	Sergius II	d. 847
847– 855	,,	St. Leo IV	d. 855
855– 858	,,	Benedict III	d. 858
855	,,	Anastasius (anti-pope)	
858– 867	,,	St. Nicholas I the Great	d. 867
867– 872	,,	Adrian II	d. 872
872– 882	,,	John VIII	d. 882
882– 884	,,	Marinus I (sometimes misnamed Martin II)	d. 884
884– 885	,,	St. Adrian III	d. 885
885– 891	,,	Stephen VI	d. 891
891– 896	,,	Formosus	d. 896
896	,,	Boniface VI	d. 896
896– 897	,,	Stephen VII	d. 897
897	,,	Romanus	d. 897
897	,,	Theodore II	d. 897
898– 900	,,	John IX	d. 900
900– 903	,,	Benedict IV	d. 903
903	,,	Leo V	d. 903
903– 904	,,	Christopher	d. 904
904– 911	,,	Sergius III	d. 911

911– 913	Pope	Anastasius III		d. 913
913– 914	,,	Landus		d. 914
914– 928	,,	John X		d. 928
928	,,	Leo VI		d. 928
929– 931	,,	Stephen VIII		d. 931
931– 935	,,	John XI		d. 935
936– 939	,,	Leo VII		d. 939
939– 942	,,	Stephen IX		d. 942
942– 946	,,	Marinus II (sometimes misnamed Martin III)		d. 946
946– 955	,,	Agapetus II		d. 955
955– 964	,,	John XII	b. 937?	d. 964
964– 965	,,	Leo VIII		d. 965
964	,,	Benedict V (anti-pope)		d. 966
965– 972	,,	John XIII		d. 972
973– 974	,,	Benedict VI		d. 974
974– 983	,,	Benedict VII		d. 983
983– 984	,,	John XIV		d. 984
984– 985	,,	Boniface VII (anti-pope)		
985– 996	,,	John XV		d. 996
996– 999	,,	Gregory V, nephew of Emperor Otto III		d. 999
997– 998	,,	John XVI (anti-pope)		d. 1013
999–1003	,,	Sylvester II		d. 1003
1003	,,	John XVII		d. 1003
1003–1009	,,	John XVIII		d. 1009
1009–1012	,,	Sergius IV		d. 1012
1012–1024	,,	Benedict VIII		d. 1024
1012	,,	Gregory (anti-pope)		
1024–1032	,,	John XIX		d. 1032
1032–1044	,,	Benedict IX		d. 1056

Pope Benedict IX, "the Boy Pope," had three terms as Pope. He appears to
have been only 11 or 12 years old when first elected to the papal see. In his
third and last term, he was held to be anti-pope to Clement II.

1044–1045	Pope	Sylvester III (anti-pope)	d. 1045
1045	,,	Benedict IX	
1045–1046	,,	Gregory VI	d. 1048
1046–1047	,,	Clement II	d. 1047
1047–1048	,,	Benedict IX (anti-pope)	
1048	,,	Damasus II (Poppo)	d. 1048
1049–1054	,,	St. Leo IX	d. 1054
1055–1057	,,	Victor II	d. 1057
1057–1058	,,	Stephen X	d. 1058
1058–1059	,,	Benedict X (anti-pope)	
1058–1061	,,	Nicholas II	d. 1061
1061–1073	,,	Alexander II (di Badagio)	d. 1073
1061–1064	,,	Honorius II (anti-pope)	d. 1072
1073–1085	,,	St. Gregory VII (Hildebrand)	b. 1025? d. 1085
1080–1100	,,	Clement III (anti-pope)	b. 1030? d. 1100
1087	,,	Victor III	d. 1087
1088–1099	,,	Urban II	d. 1099
1099–1118	,,	Pascal II	d. 1118
1100	,,	Theodoric (anti-pope)	
1102	,,	Albertus (anti-pope)	
1105–1111	,,	Sylvester IV (anti-pope)	
1118–1119	,,	Gelasius II	d. 1119
1119–1124	,,	Calixtus or Callistus II	d. 1124
1118–1121	,,	Gregory VIII (anti-pope)	d. 1125
1124	,,	Celestine (anti-pope)	

1124–1130	Pope	Honorius II	d. 1130
1130–1143	,,	Innocent II	d. 1143
1130–1138	,,	Anacletus II (anti-pope)	d. 1138
1138	,,	Victor IV (anti-pope)	
1143–1144	,,	Celestine II	d. 1144
1144–1145	,,	Lucius II	d. 1145
1145–1153	,,	Eugene III	d. 1153
1153–1154	,,	Anastasius IV	d. 1154
1154–1159	,,	Adrian IV (Breakspear)	d. 1159

Adrian IV, born Nicholas Breakspear of Langley, Hertfordshire, was the only Englishman who ever attained the Papal dignity. He insisted on papal supremacy and gave Ireland to King Henry II.

(Left) The Anti-pope Clement VII (1378–1394); (Middle) Pope Pius II (1458–1464); (Right) Pope Alexander VI (1492–1503).

(Above) Pope Leo X (1513–1521), by Raphael.

(Above right) Pope Adrian VI (1522–1523).

(Right) Pope Gregory XIII (1572–1585).

1159–1181	Pope	Alexander III (Orlando)		d. 1181
1159–1164	,,	Victor V (anti-pope)		
1164–1168	,,	Pascal III (anti-pope)		d. 1168
1168–1178	,,	Calixtus or Callistus III (anti-pope)		
1178–1180	,,	Innocent III (anti-pope)		
1181–1185	,,	Lucius III		d. 1185
1185–1187	,,	Urban III		d. 1187
1187	,,	Gregory VIII (Morra)		d. 1187
1187–1191	,,	Clement III (Scolari)		d. 1191
1191–1198	,,	Celestine III (Bobone)	b. 1106?	d. 1198
1198–1216	,,	Innocent III (Conti)	b. 1160	d. 1216
1216–1227	,,	Honorius III (Savilli)		d. 1227
1227–1241	,,	Gregory IX (Ugolino)	b. 1145?	d. 1241
1241	,,	Celestine IV		d. 1241
1243–1254	,,	Innocent IV (Fieschi)		d. 1254
1254–1261	,,	Alexander IV (Conti)		d. 1261
1261–1264	,,	Urban IV (Pantaléon)		d. 1264
1265–1268	,,	Clement IV (Foulques)		d. 1268
1271–1276	,,	Gregory X (Visconti)	b. 1210	d. 1276
1276	,,	Innocent V		d. 1276
1276	,,	Adrian V		d. 1276
1276–1277	,,	John XXI (Hispanus)		d. 1277
1277–1280	,,	Nicholas III (Orsini)	b. 1216?	d. 1280
1281–1285	,,	Martin IV (Brie)	b. 1210?	d. 1285
1285–1287	,,	Honorius IV (Savelli)	b. 1210?	d. 1287
1288–1292	,,	Nicholas IV		d. 1292
1294	,,	St. Celestine V (Murrone)	b. 1215	d. 1296
1294–1303	,,	Boniface VIII (Caetani)	b. 1235?	d. 1303
1303–1304	,,	Benedict XI		d. 1304
		(Papacy removed to Avignon from Rome)		
1305–1314	,,	Clement V (de Gouth)	b. 1264	d. 1314
1316–1334	,,	John XXII (d'Euse)	b. 1249	d. 1334
1328–1330	,,	Nicholas V (anti-pope)		
1334–1342	,,	Benedict XII		d. 1342
1342–1352	,,	Clement VI (Roger)	b. 1291	d. 1352
1352–1362	,,	Innocent VI (Aubert)		d. 1362
1362–1370	,,	Urban V (Grimoard)	b. 1310	d. 1370
1370–1378	,,	Gregory XI (de Beaufort)	b. 1331	d. 1378
		(Gregory returned to Rome in 1377)		
1378–1394	,,	Clement VII (anti-pope)	b. 1342?	d. 1394
		(Great Schism 1378–1417)		
1394–1423	,,	Benedict XIII (de Luna) (anti-pope)	b. 1328?	d. 1423?
		(Papacy returned to Rome)		
1378–1389	,,	Urban VI (Prignani)	b. 1318	d. 1389
1389–1404	,,	Boniface IX (Tomacelli)		d. 1404
1404–1406	,,	Innocent VII (Migliorati)	b. 1336?	d. 1406
1406–1415	,,	Gregory XII (Corrario)	b. 1327?	d. 1417
		(Papacy removed to Pisa)		
1409–1410	,,	Alexander V (Philargos)	b. 1340?	d. 1410
1410–1415	,,	John XXIII (anti-pope)	b. 1370?	d. 1419
		(Papacy returned to Rome)		
1417–1431	,,	Martin V (Colonna)	b. 1368	d. 1431
1424?–1429	,,	Clement VIII (anti-pope)	b. 1380?	d. 1446

(Left) Pope Julius II (1503–1513); (Middle) Pope Clement VII (1523–1534);
(Right) Pope Clement VIII (1592–1605).

1431–1447	Pope	Eugene IV (Condolmieri)	b. 1383	d. 1447
1439–1449	,,	Felix V of Savoy (last anti-pope; resigned his claim 1449)		d. 1451
1447–1455	,,	Nicholas V (Parentucelli)	b. 1397	d. 1455
1455–1458	,,	Calixtus or Callistus III (Borgia)	b. 1378	d. 1458
1458–1464	,,	Pius II (Piccolomini)	b. 1405	d. 1464
1464–1471	,,	Paul II (Barbo)	b. 1418	d. 1471
1471–1484	,,	Sixtus IV (Rovere)	b. 1414	d. 1484
1484–1492	,,	Innocent VIII (Cibò)	b. 1432	d. 1492
1492–1503	,,	Alexander VI (Borgia)	b. 1430	d. 1503
1503	,,	Pius III (Piccolomini)	b. 1439	d. 1503
1503–1513	,,	Julius II (Rovere)	b. 1443	d. 1513
1513–1521	,,	Leo X (Medici)	b. 1475	d. 1521
1522–1523	,,	Adrian VI (Dedel)	b. 1459	d. 1523
1523–1534	,,	Clement VII (Medici)	b. 1478?	d. 1534
1534–1549	,,	Paul III (Farnese)	b. 1468	d. 1549
1550–1555	,,	Julius III (Monte)	b. 1487	d. 1555
1555	,,	Marcellus II (Cervini)	b. 1501	d. 1555
1555–1559	,,	Paul IV (Caraffa)	b. 1476	d. 1559
1559–1565	,,	Pius IV (Medici)	b. 1499	d. 1565
1566–1572	,,	St. Pius V (Ghislieri)	b. 1504	d. 1572
1572–1585	,,	Gregory XIII (Buoncompagno)	b. 1502	d. 1585
1585–1590	,,	Sixtus V (Peretti)	b. 1521	d. 1590
1590	,,	Urban VII (Castagna)	b. 1521	d. 1590
1590–1591	,,	Gregory XIV (Sfondrati)	b. 1535	d. 1591
1591	,,	Innocent IX (Fachinetti)	b. 1519	d. 1591
1592–1605	,,	Clement VIII (Aldobrandini)	b. 1536?	d. 1605
1605	,,	Leo XI (Medici)	b. 1535	d. 1605
1605–1621	,,	Paul V (Borghese)	b. 1552	d. 1621
1621–1623	,,	Gregory XV (Ludovisi)	b. 1554	d. 1623
1623–1644	,,	Urban VIII (Barberini)	b. 1568	d. 1644
1644–1655	,,	Innocent X (Pamfili)	b. 1574	d. 1655
1655–1667	,,	Alexander VII (Chigi)	b. 1599	d. 1667
1667–1669	,,	Clement IX (Rospigliosi)	b. 1600	d. 1669

Pope Urban VIII (1623–1644).

Pope Innocent X (1644–1655), by
Velasquez.

Pope Alexander VII (1655–1667).

Pope Innocent XI (1676–1689).

(Left) Pope Alexander VIII (1689–1691); (Middle) Pope Clement XI (1700–1721); (Right) Pope Innocent XII (1691–1700).

Pope Pius VII (1800–1823), by Lawrence.

Pope Leo XII (1823–1829).

Pope Pius VIII (1829–1830).

1670–1676	Pope	Clement X (Altieri)	b. 1590	d. 1676
1676–1689	,,	Innocent XI (Odescalchi)	b. 1611	d. 1689
1689–1691	,,	Alexander VIII (Ottoboni)	b. 1610	d. 1691
1691–1700	,,	Innocent XII (Pignatelli)	b. 1615	d. 1700
1700–1721	,,	Clement XI (Albani)	b. 1649	d. 1721

Popes (continued)

1721–1724	Pope	Innocent XIII (Conti)	b. 1655	d. 1724
1724–1730	,,	Benedict XIII (Orsini)	b. 1649	d. 1730
1730–1740	,,	Clement XII (Corsini)	b. 1652	d. 1740
1740–1758	,,	Benedict XIV (Lambertini)	b. 1675	d. 1758
1758–1769	,,	Clement XIII (Rezzonico)	b. 1693	d. 1769
1769–1774	,,	Clement XIV (Ganganelli)	b. 1705	d. 1774
1775–1799	,,	Pius VI (Braschi)	b. 1717	d. 1799
1800–1823	,,	Pius VII (Chiaramonti)	b. 1742	d. 1823
1823–1829	,,	Leo XII (Della Genga)	b. 1760	d. 1829
1829–1830	,,	Pius VIII (Castiglioni)	b. 1761	d. 1830
1831–1846	,,	Gregory XVI (Cappellari)	b. 1765	d. 1846
1846–1878	,,	Pius IX (Mastai-Ferretti)	b. 1792	d. 1878

Pius IX (Mastai-Ferretti) was Pope for more than 31 years. His reign was the longest of any Pope in history. After an insurrection in 1848, he was forced to flee temporarily. He convened the Vatican Council which promulgated the dogma of papal infallibility.

(Left) Pope Pius IX (1846–1878); (Middle) Pope Pius XI (1922–1939); (Right) Pope Pius XII (1939–1958).

1878–1903	Pope	Leo XIII (Pecci)	b. 1810	d. 1903
1903–1914	,,	St. Pius X (Sarto)	b. 1835	d. 1914
1914–1922	,,	Benedict XV (della Chiesa)	b. 1854	d. 1922
1922–1939	,,	Pius XI (Ratti)	b. 1857	d. 1939
1939–1958	,,	Pius XII (Pacelli)	b. 1876	d. 1958
1958–1963	,,	John XXIII (Roncalli)	b. 1881	d. 1963
1963–	,,	Paul VI (Montini)	b. 1897	

Pope Paul VI (1963–   ).   *Pope John XXIII (1958–1963).*

John I, King of Portugal (1385–1433), entertains John of Gaunt of England (miniature from a 15th-century manuscript).

Portugal

(Portugal in ancient times was called Lusitania. It was under Roman and Moorish rule before emerging as an independent state)

HOUSE OF BURGUNDY

1094–1112	Count	Henry of Burgundy, grandson of Robert I of Burgundy	b. 1057	d. 1112
1112–1128	Regent	Teresa of Castile, consort of Henry of Burgundy		
1128–1140	Count	Alfonso I, son of Henry of Burgundy	b. 1094?	d. 1185
1140–1185	King	Alfonso I		

(Declared an independent Monarchy in 1140)

English versions of the names of rulers of Portuguese-speaking states are:

Charles–Carlos	Ferdinand–Fernando	John–João
Denis–Diniz	Henry–Enrique	Michael–Miguel
Edward–Duarte	James–Diogo	Peter–Pedro

A modern coin commemorates Alfonso I of Portugal (1128–1185).

1185–1211	King	Sancho I, son of Alfonso I	b. 1154	d. 1211
1211–1223	,,	Alfonso II (the Fat), son of Sancho I	b. 1186	d. 1223
1223–1245	,,	Sancho II, son of Alfonso II	b. 1210?	d. 1248
1245–1279	,,	Alfonso III, son of Alfonso II	b. 1210?	d. 1279

1279–1325	King	Diniz, son of Alfonso III	b. 1261	d. 1325
1325–1357	,,	Alfonso IV, son of Diniz	b. 1291	d. 1357
1357–1367	,,	Pedro I, son of Alfonso IV	b. 1320	d. 1367
1367–1383	,,	Ferdinand I, son of Pedro I	b. 1345	d. 1383
		(Internal conflicts, 1383–1385)		

HOUSE OF AVIZ

1385–1433	,,	John I, son of Peter of Burgundy	b. 1358	d. 1433
1433–1438	,,	Edward I, son of John 1	b. 1391	d. 1438
1438–1481	,,	Alfonso V (Africano), son of Edward I	b. 1432	d. 1481
1481–1495	,,	John II, son of Alfonso V	b. 1455	d. 1495

John II was known as "the Perfect" yet in the course of his struggles with the feudal nobles he executed the Duke of Braganza and murdered the Duke of Viseu. It was during his reign that Bartholomeu Diaz discovered the Cape of Good Hope, and by rounding it, opened the way to the East.

| 1495–1521 | King | Emanuel I, grandson of Alfonso V | b. 1469 | d. 1521 |

The reign of Emanuel I is significant for remarkable sea-voyages by Portuguese seamen: the opening of an all-sea route to India by Vasco da Gama, Cabral's landing in Brazil and Corte-Real's voyage to Labrador.

1521–1557	King	John III, son of Emanuel I	b. 1502	d. 1557
1557–1578	,,	Sebastian, grandson of John III	b. 1554	killed 1578
1578–1580	,,	Henry, brother of John III	b. 1512	d. 1580
1580	,,	Antonio, nephew of Henry	b. 1531	d. 1595
		(Ruled by Spain, 1580–1640)		

HOUSE OF BRAGANZA

1640–1656	,,	John IV, descendant of John I	b. 1604	d. 1656
1656–1667	,,	Alfonso VI, son of John IV	b. 1643	d. 1683
1667–1683	Regent	Pedro II, son of John IV	b. 1648	d. 1706
1683–1706	King	Pedro II		

On December 15, 1640, Duke John of Braganza was acclaimed King John IV of Portugal by the assembled nobles of the country.

Portugal (continued)

1706–1750	King	John V, son of Pedro II	b. 1689	d. 1750
1750–1777	„	Joseph Emanuel, son of John V	b. 1714	d. 1777
1777–1816	Queen	Maria I, daughter of Joseph Emanuel		b. 1734 d. 1816
1777–1786	Joint ruler	Pedro III, son of John V, husband of Maria I		b. 1717 d. 1786
1799–1816	Regent	John, son of Maria	b. 1767	d. 1826
1816–1826	King	John VI		
1826	„	Pedro IV, son of John VI abdicated 1826	b. 1798	d. 1834
1826–1828	Queen	Maria II, daughter of Pedro	b. 1819	d. 1853

(Left) Joseph Emanuel, King of Portugal (1750–1777).

(Right) Maria I, Queen of Portugal (1777–1816).

Maria II, Queen of Portugal (1826–1828, 1834–1853).

The usurper King Miguel of Portugal took the throne from his niece Maria II in 1828, but was overthrown in 1834.

1828–1834	King (usurper)	Miguel, uncle of Maria II abdicated 1834	b. 1802	d. 1866
1834–1853	Queen	Maria II		
1853–1861	King	Pedro V, son of Maria II	b. 1837	d. 1861
1861–1889	„	Louis I, son of Maria II	b. 1838	d. 1889
1889–1908	„	Carlos I, son of Louis I	b. 1863	assassinated 1908
1908–1910	„	Emanuel II, son of Carlos I abdicated 1910	b. 1888	d. 1932

(Left to right) Pedro V (1853–1861); Louis I (1861–1889); Carlos I (1889–1908); Emanuel II (1908–1910).

Francisco Craveiro Lopes, President of Portugal (1951–1958), greets Queen Elizabeth II of England.

REPUBLIC

(Proclaimed in 1910)

1910–1911	President (provisional)	Teófilo Braga	b. 1843	d. 1919
1911–1915	President	Manoel José de Arriaga	b. 1840	d. 1917
1915	,,	Teófilo Braga		
1915–1917	,,	Bernardino Luiz Machado Guimaraes	b. 1851	d. 1944
1917–1918	,,	Sidônio Bernadino Cardoso de Silva Paes	b. 1872	d. 1918
1918–1919	President (provisional)	João de Canto e Castro Silva Antunes	b. 1862	d. 1934
1919–1923	President	António José de Almeida	b. 1866	d. 1929
1923–1925	,,	Manoel Teixeira Gomes	b. 1860	d. 1914
1925–1926	,,	Bernardino Luiz Machado Guimaraes		
1926–1951	,,	Antonio Oscar de Fragoso Carmona	b. 1869	d. 1950
1951–1958	,,	Francisco Higino Craveiro Lopes	b. 1894	
1958–	,,	Américo Deus Rodrigues Tomás	b. 1894	

Statesmen

1505–1509	Viceroy	Francisco de Almeida	b. 1450?	killed 1510
1506–1515	,,	Afonso de Albuquerque	b. 1453?	d. 1515
1756–1777	Prime Minister	Sebastião José de Carvalho e Mello, Marquês de Pombal	b. 1699	d. 1782
1932–1968	Premier	António de Oliveira Salazar	b. 1889	
1968–	,,	Marcelo Caetano	b. 1906	

António de Oliveira Salazar, Premier of Portugal (1932–1968).

Américo Rodrigues Tomás, President of Portugal (1958–   ).

The Marquês de Pombal, Prime Minister of Portugal (1756–1777).

Puerto Rico

United States stamp issued for Puerto Rico before the establishment of the Commonwealth.

(Discovered by Christopher Columbus in 1493)			
1510	Spanish Governor	Juan Ponce de Léon	b. 1460? d. 1521
1511	„	Juan Cerón	
1512–1513	„	Rodrigo de Moscoso	
1513–1515	„	Cristóbal de Mendoza	
1515–1517	„	Juan Ponce de Léon	
1519–1521	„	Antonio de la Gama	
1521–1523	„	Pedro Moreno	
1523–1524	„	D. Alonso Manso	
1524–1529	„	Pedro Moreno	
		Antonio de la Gama	

1530–1536	Spanish Governor	Francisco Manuel de Lando
1536–1537	,,	Vasco de Tiedra
1537–1544	,,	Dos Alcaldes Ordinarios
1544–1545	,,	Gerónimo Lebrón
1545–1546	,,	Iñigo López Cervantes de Loaisa
1546–1548	,,	Diego de Caraza
1548–1550	,,	Dos Alcaldes Ordinarios
1550–1555	,,	Luis de Vallejo
1555	,,	Licenciado Esteves
1555–1561	,,	Diego de Caraza
1561–1564	,,	Antonio de la Llama Vallejo
1564–1568	,,	Francisco Bahamonde de Lugo
1568–1574	,,	Francisco de Solís
1575–1579	,,	Francisco de Obando y Mexia
1580	,,	Gerónimo de Aguero Campuzano
1580–1581	,,	Juan de Céspedes
1581–1582	,,	Juan López Melgarejo
1582–1593	,,	Diego Menéndez de Valdés
1593–1597	,,	Pedro Suárez
1597–1598	,,	Antonio de Mosquera
1598–1599	,,	Alonso de Mercado
1602–1608	,,	Sancho Ochoa de Castro
1608–1614	,,	Gabriel de Roxas
1613–1620	,,	Felipe de Beaumont y Navarra
1620–1625	,,	Juan de Vargas

La Fortaleza, Puerto Rico's executive mansion, has been the home of its governors for over 400 years. When it was built in 1533, it was intended as a fortress to guard the Bay of San Juan. Later it was found that the site was completely inadequate for defence and the building was turned into a residence for the island's governors.

1625–1630	Spanish Governor	Juan de Háro
1631–1635	,,	Enrique Enríquez de Sotomayor
1635–1641	,,	Iñigo de la Mota Sarmiento
1640–1641	,,	Agustín de Silva y Figueroa
1641–1642	,,	Juan de Bolaños

1642–1648	Spanish Governor	Fernando de la Riva Aguero
1649–1655	„	Diego de Aguilera y Gamboa
1655–1660	„	José Novoa y Moscoso
1660–1664	„	Juan Pérez de Guzmán
1664–1670	„	Gerónimo de Velasco
1670–1674	„	Gaspar de Arteaga
1674	„	Diego Robladillo
1675–1678	„	Alonso de Campos
1678–1683	„	Juan de Robles Lorenzana
1683–1685	„	Gaspar Martínez de Andino
1685–1690	„	Juan Francisco de Medina
1690–1695	„	Gaspar de Arredondo
1695–1697	„	Juan Francisco Medina
1697–1698	„	Tomás Franco
1698–1699	„	Antonio Robles
1700–1703	„	Gabriel Gutiérrez de Rivas
1703	„	Diego Villarán
1703	„	Francisco Sánchez
1704–1705	„	Pedro de Arroyo y Guerrero
1706	„	Juan Francisco Morla
1706–1708	„	Francisco Granados
1709–1714	„	Juan de Ribera
1716	„	José Carreño
1716–1720	„	Alonso Bertodano
1720–1724	„	Francisco Danio Granados
1724–1730	„	José Antonio de Mendizábal
1731–1743	„	Matías de Abadía
1743–1744	„	Domingo Pérez de Nandares
1744–1750	„	Juan José Colomo
1750–1751	„	Agustín de Parejas
1751–1753	„	Esteban Bravo de Rivero
1753–1757	„	Felipe Ramírez de Estenós
1757–1759	„	Esteban Bravo de Rivero
1759–1760	„	Mateo de Guazo Calderón
1760–1761	„	Esteban Bravo de Rivero
1761–1766	„	Ambrosio de Benavides
1766	„	Marcos de Vergara
1766–1770	„	José Trentor
1770–1776	„	Miguel de Muesas
1776–1783	„	José Dufresne
1783–1789	„	Juan Dabán
1789	„	Francisco Torralbo
1789–1792	„	Miguel Antonio de Ustariz
1792–1794	„	Francisco Torralbo
1794–1795	„	Enrique Grimarest
1795–1804	„	Ramón de Castro y Gutiérrez
1804–1809	„	Toribio de Montes
1809–1820	„	Salvador Meléndez y Ruíz
1820	„	Juan Vasco y Pascual
1820–1822	„	Gonzalo de Arostegui y Herrera
1822	„	José Navarro
1822	„	Francisco González de Linares
1822–1837	„	Miguel de la Torre
1837–1838	„	Francisco Moreda y Prieto
1838–1841	„	Miguel López de Baños
1841–1844	„	Santiago Méndez de Vigo
1844–1847	„	Rafael de Aristegui y Vélez
1847–1848	„	Juan Prim

1848–1851	Spanish Governor	Juan de la Pezuela Cevallos		
1851–1852	ʺ	Enrique de España y Taberner		
1852–1855	ʺ	Fernando de Norzagaray y Escudero		
1855	ʺ	Andrés Garcia Camba		
1855–1857	ʺ	José Lemery		
1860	ʺ	Fernando Cotoner y Chacón		
1860–1862	ʺ	Rafael Echague		
1862–1863	ʺ	Rafael Izquierdo		
1862–1865	ʺ	Félix María de Messina		
1865–1867	ʺ	José María Marchesi		
1867–1868	ʺ	Julión Juan Pavía		
1868–1870	ʺ	José Laureano Sanz y Posse		
1870–1873	ʺ	Gabriel Baldrich y Palau		
1872	ʺ	Ramón Gómez Pulido		
1872	ʺ	Simón de la Torre		
1872–1873	ʺ	Joaquín Eurile		
1873	ʺ	Juan Martínez Plowes		
1873–1874	ʺ	Rafael Primo de Rivera y Sobremonte		
1874–1875	ʺ	José Laureano Sanz y Posse		
1875–1877	ʺ	Segundo de la Portilla		
1877–1878	ʺ	Manuel de la Serna y Pinzón		
1878–1881	ʺ	Eulogio Despujols y Dussay		
1881–1883	ʺ	Segundo de la Portilla		
1883–1884	ʺ	Miguel de la Vega Inclán		
1884	ʺ	Ramón Fajardo		
1884–1887	ʺ	Luis Dabán y Ramírez de Arellano		
1887	ʺ	Romualdo Palacios		
1887–1888	ʺ	Juan Contreras		
1888–1890	ʺ	Pedro Ruíz Dana		
1890	ʺ	José Pascual Bonanza		
1890–1893	ʺ	José Lasso y Pérez		
1893–1895	ʺ	Antonio Dabán y Ramírez de Arellano		
1895–1896	ʺ	José Gamir		
1896	ʺ	Emilio March		
1896–1898	ʺ	Sabás Marín		
1898	ʺ	Ricardo Ortega		
1898	ʺ	Andrés González Muñoz		
1898	ʺ	Rocardo Ortega		
1898	ʺ	Manuel Macías Casado		
1898	ʺ	Ricardo Ortega		
		(ceded to the U.S.A. in 1898)		
1898	Military Governor	John Rutter Brooke	b. 1838	d. 1926
1898–1899	ʺ	Guy V. Henry		
1899–1900	ʺ	George Whitefield Davis	b. 1839	d. 1918
1900–1902	Civil Governor	Charles Herbert Allen	b. 1848	d. 1934
1902–1904	ʺ	William H. Hunt		
1904–1907	ʺ	Beekman Winthrop		
1907–1909	ʺ	Regis H. Post		
1909–1913	ʺ	George R. Colton		
1913–1921	ʺ	Arthur Yater		
1921–1923	ʺ	E. Montgomery Reilly		
1923–1929	ʺ	Horace Mann Towner		
1929–1932	ʺ	Theodore Roosevelt, Jr.	b. 1887	d. 1944
1932–1933	ʺ	James R. Beverly		
1933–1934	ʺ	Robert H. Gore		
1934–1939	ʺ	Blanton Winship		
1939–1940	ʺ	William Daniel Leahy	b. 1875	d. 1959
1941	ʺ	Guy J. Swope		

Luis Muñoz Marín, Governor of Puerto Rico (1949–1964).

Roberto Sánchez Vilella, Governor of Puerto Rico (1964–   ).

1941–1946	Civil Governor	Rexford G. Tugwell	b. 1891
1946–1949	,,	Jesús T. Piñero	
1949–1964	,,	Luis Muñoz Marín	
1964–	,,	Roberto Sánchez Vilella	b. 1913

(In 1952, Puerto Rico became a commonwealth associated with the United States, which retained control of the island's foreign affairs)

Qatar

(A sheikhdom under British protection)
–1960	Sheikh	Ali bin Abdullah Al Thani (abdicated)
1960–	,,	Ahmad

Rhodesia

Stamp of the colony of Southern Rhodesia.

(British colony of Southern Rhodesia, declared unilateral independence 1965)
1966–	Prime Minister	Ian Douglas Smith	b. 1919

Roman Empire

Octavian.

Julius Caesar.

(Traditional date of foundation was April 21, 753 B.C.)

B.C.

753– 716	Legendary King	Romulus, son of Rhea Silvia
716– 672	„	Numa Pompilius
672– 640	„	Tullus Hostilius
640– 616	„	Ancus Marcius, grandson of Numa Pompilius
616– 578	„	Lucius Tarquinius Priscus
578– 534	„	Servius Tullius, son-in-law of Tarquinius Priscus
534– 509	„	Lucius Tarquinius Superbus, son of Tarquinius Priscus
		(Republic, 509 – 31 B.C.)
60	First Triumvirate	Caesar, Pompey and Crassus
43–28	Second Triumvirate	Octavian, Antony and Lepidus
		Gaius Julius Caesar b. 100 B.C. assassinated 44 B.C.

Captured by pirates, Caesar threatened to crucify them—a promise he carried out faithfully as soon as possible after he was ransomed. Few dispute Caesar's military genius, but his role and achievements as statesman are still a subject of controversy, as they were more than 2,000 years ago.

Gnaeus Pompeius Magnus b. 106 B.C.   murdered 48 B.C.
Marcus Licinius Crassus   b. 115 B.C.? executed 53 B.C.
Octavian (Augustus), grand-nephew and
        adopted son of Julius Caesar   b. 63 B.C.   d. 14 A.D.
Antony (Marcus Antonius)   b. 83 B.C.? d. 30 B.C.
Marcus Aemilius Lepidus   d. 13 B.C.

Antony.

(Left) Augustus (the name assumed by Octavian on becoming Emperor) ; (Middle) Tiberius (with his mother, Livia, on the reverse of the coin) ; (Right) Caligula, whose cruel reign perhaps prompted an enemy to deface this coin.

CLAUDIAN DYNASTY

B.C.	A.D.			
27–	14	Emperor	Augustus (Octavian)	

First of the Roman emperors, Gaius Julius Caesar Octavianus was given the title of Augustus by the Roman senate in recognition of his outstanding services to the state. Despite his early crimes and cruelties, Augustus carried through reforms which united the Empire and secured peace. He ranks as one of the greatest statesmen of all time.

A.D.				
14–	37	Emperor	Tiberius, stepson of Augustus	b. 42 B.C. d. A.D. 37
37–	41	,,	Caligula (Gaius Caesar), grand-nephew of Tiberius	b. A.D. 12 assassinated A.D. 41
41–	54	,,	Claudius I, nephew of Tiberius	b. 10 B.C. poisoned A.D. 54
54–	68	,,	Nero, stepson of Claudius	b. A.D. 37 committed suicide A.D. 68

There can be little doubt that Nero was mad. He seized the throne, excluding the rightful heir, Britannicus, killed Britannicus and his own mother and wife, executed Seneca, and also killed his second wife Poppaea. In addition, he persecuted the Christians on a trumped-up charge of causing the burning of Rome.

				A.D.
68–	69	Emperor	Galba	b. 3 B.C. assassinated A.D. 69
69		,,	Otho	b. 32 committed suicide 69
69		,,	Vitellius	b. 15 murdered 69

(Left) Claudius I was poisoned by his niece, Agrippina.

(Right) Nero was declared an enemy of the state for his misdeeds and took his own life.

Titus, Roman Emperor (A.D. 79–81).

Vespasian, Roman Emperor (A.D. 69–79).

FLAVIAN DYNASTY

69–	79	Emperor	Vespasian	b. 9 d. 79
79–	81	,,	Titus, son of Vespasian	b. 41 ? d. 81
81–	96	,,	Domitian, son of Vespasian	b. 51 assassinated 96

Roman Empire (continued)

ANTONINE DYNASTY

96– 98	Emperor	Nerva	b. 35? d. 98
98– 117	,,	Trajan	b. 53? d. 117
117– 138	,,	Hadrian, nephew of Trajan	b. 76 d. 138

Hadrian visited Britain and was responsible for building a line of fortifications, Hadrian's Wall, from the Solway Firth to Wallsend on the mouth of the River Tyne. This line was intended to be a barrier against the Picts and Scots.

| 138– 161 | Emperor | Antoninus Pius | b. 86 d. 161 |

(Left) Nerva, Roman Emperor (A.D. 96–98); (Middle) Hadrian, Roman Emperor (A.D. 117–138); (Right) Trajan, Roman Emperor (A.D. 98–117).

(Left) Antoninus Pius, Roman Emperor (A.D. 138–161) appears on a coin of Roman Britain whose reverse design was revived in modern times on British coinage; (Right) Marcus Aurelius (161–180), Roman Emperor and Stoic philosopher, author of the "Meditations."

161– 180	Emperor	Marcus Aurelius, son-in-law of Antoninus Pius	b. 121 d. 180
161– 169	Co-regent	Lucius Aurelius Verus, adopted brother of Marcus Aurelius	b. 130 d. 169
180– 192	Emperor	Commodus, son of Marcus Aurelius	b. 161 murdered 192

AFRICAN AND SYRIAN EMPERORS

193	,,	Pertinax	b. 126 assassinated 193
193– 211	,,	Septimius Severus	b. 146 d. 211
193	Emperor (rival)	Didius Julianus	b. 133 murdered 193
193– 194	,, ,,	Pescennius Niger	
193– 197	,, ,,	Albinus	beheaded 197
211– 217	,,	Caracalla, son of Septimius Severus	b. 188 assassinated 217
211– 212	Co-regent	Geta, son of Septimius Severus	b. 189 murdered 212
217– 218	Emperor	Macrinus	b. 164 killed 218
218– 222	,,	Heliogabalus (Elagabalus)	b. 204 assassinated 222
222– 235	,,	Alexander Severus, cousin of Heliogabalus	b. 208? murdered 235
235– 238	,,	Maximinus Thrax	b. 173 murdered 238
238	Emperor (rival)	Gordianus I (Africanus)	b. 158 committed suicide 238
238	Co-regent	Gordianus II, son of Gordianus I	b. 192 killed 238
238	Emperor	Pupienus Maximus	murdered 238
238	Co-regent	Balbinus	murdered 238

238– 244	Emperor	Gordianus III, grandson of Gordianus I	b. 224? murdered 244
244– 249	”	Philip the Arabian	killed 249
249– 251	”	Decius	b. 201 killed 251
251– 253	”	Gallus	b. 205? murdered 253?
253	”	Aemilianus	b. 206? d. 253
253– 260	”	Valerian	d. 269?
260– 268	”	Gallienus, son of Valerian	assassinated 268

(Left to right) Caracalla, Roman Emperor (211–217); Heliogabalus, Roman Emperor (218–222); Alexander Severus, Roman Emperor (222–235); Philip the Arabian, Roman Emperor (244–249).

ILLYRIAN EMPERORS

268– 270	Emperor	Claudius II (Gothicus)	b. 214 d. 270
270– 275	”	Aurelian	b. 212 assassinated 275
275– 276	”	Tacitus	b. 200? murdered 276
276	”	Florian, brother of Tacitus	killed 276
276– 282	”	Probus	murdered 282
282– 283	”	Carus	b. 223? killed 283
283– 285	”	Carinus, son of Carus	murdered 285

Tacitus, Roman Emperor (275–276).   *Probus, Roman Emperor (276–282).*

LATER EMPERORS

(Before formal division of Empire into East and West, many emperors ruled simultaneously)

284– 305	Emperor	Diocletian	b. 245 d. 313

Diocletian is the Roman emperor associated with persecution of the Christians. In 303 he issued an edict against them and though he himself abdicated in 305 and retired to Dalmatia, the fierce persecutions he had begun lasted for 10 years.

285– 305	Emperor	Maximian	committed suicide 310
305– 306	”	Constantius I (Chlorus)	b. 250 d. 306
306– 311	”	Galerius	d. 311
306– 307	”	Severus	d. 307
307– 313	”	Maximinus, nephew of Galerius	d. 313
307– 337	”	Constantine I the Great, son of Constantius I	b. 288 d. 337
306– 312	”	Maxentius, son of Maximian	drowned 312
311– 324	”	Licinius, adopted son of Galerius	b. 270? executed 324
337– 340	”	Constantine II, son of Constantine I	b. 316? killed 340
337– 350	”	Constans I, son of Constantine I	b. 320 assassinated 350

337– 361	Emperor	Constantius II, son of Constantine I		b. 317	d. 361
361– 363	,,	Julian the Apostate, cousin of Constantius II		b. 331	killed 363
363– 364	,,	Jovian		b. 331	d. 364
		(Division of Empire, 364)			
364– 375	,, (West)	Valentinian I		b. 321	d. 375
364– 378	,, (East)	Valens, brother of Valentinian I	b. 328?		killed 378
375– 383	,, (West)	Gratian, son of Valentinian I	b. 359		assassinated 383
375– 392	,, (West)	Valentinian II, son of Valentinian I		b. 371	d. 392
379– 394	,, (East)	Theodosius I		b. 346	d. 395
383– 388	,, (West)	Maximus			executed 388
392– 394	,, (West)	Eugenius			killed 394
394– 395	,, (West)	Theodosius			

WESTERN ROMAN EMPIRE

395– 423	,,	Honorius, son of Theodosius I		b. 384	d. 423
425– 455	,,	Valentinian III, nephew of Honorius		b. 419	murdered 455
455	,,	Petronius Maximus			killed 455
455– 456	,,	Avitus			d. 456
457– 461	,,	Majorian			d. 461
461– 465	,,	Livius Severus			d. 465
467– 472	,,	Anthemius, son-in-law of Marcian			killed 472
472	,,	Olybrius, son-in-law of Valentinian III			
473– 474	,,	Glycerius			
474– 475	,,	Julius Nepos			assassinated 480?
475– 476	,,	Romulus Augustulus, son of Orestes		b. 461?	

(Western Roman Empire ended in 476, when Augustulus was defeated by Odoacer)

EASTERN ROMAN (BYZANTINE) EMPIRE
THEODOSIAN DYNASTY

| 395– 408 | ,, | Arcadius, son of Theodosius I | | b. 378? | d. 408 |
| 408– 450 | ,, | Theodosius II, son of Arcadius | | b. 401 | d. 450 |

(Left) Constantine I the Great, Roman Emperor (307–337); (Middle) Constantius II, Roman Emperor (337–361); (Right) Theodosius II, Eastern Roman Emperor (408–450).

THRACIAN DYNASTY

450– 457	Emperor	Marcianus, brother-in-law of Theodosius II	b. 392	d. 457
457– 474	,,	Leo I the Great	b. 400?	d. 474
474	,,	Leo II, grandson of Leo I the Great		d. 474
474– 491	,,	Zeno, father of Leo II	b. 426	d. 491
491– 518	,,	Anastasius I, son-in-law of Leo II	b. 430	d. 518

JUSTINIAN DYNASTY

| 518– 527 | ,, | Justin I | b. 450 | d. 527 |

With his code of Roman Law, the Emperor Justinian improved the conditions of slaves, codified and reformed the laws, and laid the foundations of the civil law of modern nations.

| 527– 565 | Emperor | Justinian I, nephew of Justin I | b. 483 | d. 565 |
| 565– 578 | ,, | Justin II, nephew of Justinian I | | d. 578 |

Justinian I, Eastern Roman Emperor (527–565) with his court.

578– 582	Emperor	Tiberius II Constantinus		d. 582
582– 602	„	Maurice, son-in-law of Tiberius II	b. 540	assassinated 602
602– 610	„	Phocas		beheaded 610

HERACLIAN DYNASTY

610– 641	„	Heraclius	b. 575?	d. 641
641	„	{ Constantine III, son of Heraclius	b. 612?	d. 641
641	Co-regent	{ Heracleonas, son of Heraclius	b. 614?	
641– 668	Emperor	Constans II, son of Constantine III	b. 630	murdered 668

Phocas, Eastern Roman Emperor (602–610).

Constans II, Eastern Roman Emperor (641–668) with his son, Constantine IV (668–685).

668– 685	Emperor	Constantine IV, son of Constans II	b. 648	d. 685
685– 695	„	Justinian II, son of Constantine IV	b. 669	assassinated 711
695– 698	„	Leontius		killed 705
698– 705	„	Tiberius III Apsimar		beheaded 705
705– 711	„	Justinian II		
711– 713	„	Philippicus		
713– 716	„	Anastasius II		executed 721
716– 717	„	Theodosius III		d. 718?

ISAURIAN DYNASTY

717– 741	„	Leo III the Isaurian	b. 680?	d. 741
741– 775	„	Constantine V, son of Leo III	b. 718	d. 775
775– 780	„	Leo IV, son of Constantine V	b. 750?	d. 780
780– 790	Empress (regent)	Irene, wife of Leo IV	b. 752	d. 803
780– 797	Emperor	Constantine VI, son of Irene	b. 770	murdered 797?
797– 802	Empress	Irene		
802– 811	Emperor	Nicephorus I		killed 811
811	„	Stauracius		
811– 813	„	Michael I, son-in-law of Nicephorus I		d. 845
813– 820	„	Leo V the Armenian		assassinated 820

AMORIAN DYNASTY

820– 829	„	Michael II		d. 829

829– 842	Emperor	Theophilus, son of Michael II	d. 842
842– 857	Empress (regent)	Theodora, mother of Michael III	d. 867?
842– 867	Emperor	Michael III, son of Theophilus	assassinated 867

MACEDONIAN DYNASTY

867– 886	,,	Basil I the Macedonian	b. 813? d. 886
886– 912	,,	Leo VI, son of Michael III	b. 866 d. 912
913– 919	,,	Constantine VII, son of Leo VI	b. 905 d. 959
919– 944	Emperor (regent)	Romanus I, stepfather of Constantine VII	d. 948
944– 959	Emperor	Constantine VII	
959– 963	,,	Romanus II, son of Constantine VII	b. 939 d. 963
963– 969	,,	Nicephorus II	b. 912? murdered 969
969– 976	,,	John I Zimisces	b. 925 d. 976
976–1025	,,	Basil II, son of Romanus II	b. 958? d. 1025
1025–1028	,,	Constantine VIII, son of Romanus II	b. 960? d. 1028
1028–1034	,,	Romanus III, son-in-law of Constantine VIII	b. 968? d. 1034
1034–1041	,,	Michael IV, son-in-law of Constantine VIII	d. 1041
1041–1042	,,	Michael V, nephew of Michael IV	
1042–1055	,,	Constantine IX, son-in-law of Constantine VIII	b. 1000? d. 1055
1055–1056	Empress	Theodora, daughter of Constantine VIII	b. 980 d. 1056
1056–1057	Emperor	Michael VI	
1057–1059	,,	Isaac I Comnenus	d. 1061

DUCAS DYNASTY

1059–1067	,,	Constantine X Ducas	b. 1007? d. 1067
1067–1071	,,	Romanus IV	murdered 1071
1071–1078	,,	Michael VII, son of Constantine X	
1078–1081	,,	Nicephorus III Botaniates	d. 1081

COMNENUS DYNASTY

1081–1118	,,	Alexius I Comnenus, nephew of Isaac I	b. 1048 d. 1118
1118–1143		John II Comnenus, son of Alexius I Comnenus	b. 1088 d. 1143
1143–1180	,,	Manuel I Comnenus, son of John II Comnenus	b. 1120 d. 1180
1180–1183	,,	Alexius II, son of Manuel I Comnenus	b. 1168? murdered 1183
1183–1185	,,	Andronicus I, grandson of Alexius I Comnenus	b. 1110? murdered 1185

ANGELUS DYNASTY

1185–1195	,,	Isaac II Angelus	executed 1204
1195–1203	,,	Alexius III, brother of Isaac II	d. 1210
1203–1204	,,	Alexius IV, son of Isaac II	executed 1204
1204	,,	Alexius V	executed 1204

*(Left) Romanus III, Eastern Roman Emperor
(1028–1034), being crowned by the Virgin Mary;
(Right) Michael VII, Eastern Roman Emperor
(1071–1078).*

John II Comnenus (1118–1143) and the Empress Irene bring gifts to the Virgin Mary and Jesus.

LATIN EMPERORS

1204–1205	Emperor	Baldwin I, son of Baldwin V, Count of Hainault	b. 1171	killed 1205?

A leader of the Fourth Crusade, Baldwin I was elected the first Latin emperor by the crusaders following their capture of Constantinople. The following year he was beaten, captured and killed by the Greeks and Bulgarians.

1205–1216	Emperor	Henry, brother of Baldwin I	b. 1174?	d. 1216
1216–1217	"	Peter, brother-in-law of Baldwin I		d. 1217
1217–1219	Empress (regent)	Yolande, wife of Peter		d. 1220?
1219–1228	Emperor	Robert, son of Peter		d. 1228
1228–1261	"	Baldwin II, brother of Robert	b. 1217	d. 1273

LASCARIS DYNASTY
(Empire of Nicaea)

1206–1222	Emperor	Theodore I Lascaris, son-in-law of Alexius III		d. 1222
1222–1254	"	John III Ducas, son-in-law of Theodore Lascaris	b. 1193	d. 1254
1254–1258	"	Theodore II Lascaris, son of John III Ducas	b. 1221	d. 1258
1258–1261	"	John IV Lascaris, son of Theodore II Lascaris	b. 1250	d. 1269
1259–1261	Regent	Michael Palaeologus	b. 1234	d. 1282

PALAEOLOGUS DYNASTY

1261–1282	Emperor	Michael VIII Palaeologus		
1282–1328	"	Andronicus II, son of Michael VIII	b. 1260	d. 1332
1328–1341	"	Andronicus III, grandson of Andronicus II	b. 1296	d. 1341
1341–1347	"	John V Palaeologus, son of Andronicus III	b. 1332	d. 1391
1347–1355	"	John VI Cantacuzene	b. 1292	d. 1383
1376–1379	Emperor (rival)	Andronicus IV, son of John V Palaeologus		d. 1385
1379–1391	Emperor	John V		
1391–1425	"	Manuel II Palaeologus, son of John V Palaeologus	b. 1350	d. 1425

1391–1412	Emperor	⎰ John VII, son of Andronicus IV	b. 1360	d. 1412
	Co-regent	⎱		
1425–1448	Emperor	John VIII, son of Manuel II		
		Palaeologus	b. 1390	d. 1448
1448–1453	„	Constantine XI, son of		
		Manuel II Palaeologus	b. 1403	killed 1453

Last Emperor of the Eastern Empire, Constantine XI Palaeologus fought bravely against the Turkish armies but he was killed in the last stages of the battle for Constantinople, at one of the gates of the city.

(The Eastern Empire ended with the capture of Constantinople by the Turks in 1453)

John VIII, Eastern Roman Emperor (1425–1448).

Ruanda, see Rwanda

Rumania

Karl Eitel Friedrich, Prince of Wallachia and Moldavia (1866–1881), ascended the throne of the new kingdom of Rumania as Carol I (1881–1914).

(Part of the Roman Empire in ancient times; overrun by barbarian tribes from the 6th to the 12th centuries; Wallachia founded in about 1290 and Moldavia founded in about 1340; Wallachia and Moldavia united in 1859)

1859–1866	Prince	Alexander John (Alexandru Ioan) I		
		(Cuza) of Moldavia	b. 1820	d. 1873
1866–1881	„	Karl Eitel Friedrich of		
		Hohenzollern-Sigmaringen	b. 1839	d. 1914

Second son of Karl Anton, Prince of Hohenzollern-Sigmaringen, Karl Eitel was elected ruler of Rumania by the assemblies of Moldavia and Wallachia. He was invested in Constantinople by the Sultan, who granted him the right to maintain an army of 30,000 men. The German prince's position was difficult during the Franco-German War, due to the Rumanian people's strong pro-French sympathies.

(Recognized as a Kingdom in 1881)

1881–1914	King	Carol I (Karl)		
1914–1927	„	Ferdinand I, nephew of Carol I	b. 1865	d. 1927

Ferdinand I, King of Rumania (1914–1927), and his consort, Queen Marie.

Michael I, King of Rumania, as a boy during his first reign (1927–1930).

Carol II, King of Rumania (1930–1940).

Michael I during his second reign (1940–1947).

1927–1930	King	Michael (Mihai), grandson of Ferdinand I	b. 1921	
1930–1940	„	Carol II, son of Ferdinand and father of Michael	b. 1893	d. 1953

King of Rumania from 1930 to 1940, Carol II was married to the daughter of King Constantine of the Hellenes, but it was his association with Madame Lupescu that attracted the world's attention during most of his life.

1940–1947	King	Michael

Coat-of-arms on a coin of the Rumanian People's Republic.

People's Republic

(Communist regime established 1948)

1948–1952	President	Constantin I. Parhon	b. 1874

Rumania (continued)

1952–1958	President	Petru Groza	b. 1884	d. 1958
1958–1961	Head of State	Ion Gheorghe Maurer	b. 1902	
1961–1965	Chairman of State Council	Gheorghe Gheorghiu-Dej	b. 1901	d. 1965
1965–1967	President	Chivu Stoica	b. 1908	
1961–	Chairman of Council of Ministers	Ion Gheorghe Maurer		
1967–	Chief of State	Nicolas Ceausescu	b. 1918	

The rulers of old Russia lived in citadels called "kremlins." The most famous of these is the Kremlin of Moscow, still the administrative headquarters of the Russian Government, shown here as it appeared in the 17th century.

Russia

(Norsemen, under Rurik, settled at Kiev in the 9th century; under his descendants Russia was divided into numerous independent principalities—said to number 64 between the 11th and 13th centuries)

GRAND DUKES OF KIEV

862– 879	Grand Duke	Rurik of Novgorod	d. 879
879– 912	„	Oleg (Helgi)	
912– 945	„	Igor, son of Rurik of Novgorod	
945– 955	Regent	St. Olga, wife of Igor	d. 969
955– 972	Grand Duke	Sviatoslav, son of Igor	
972– 977	„	Yaropolk, son of Sviatoslav	
977–1015	„	St. Vladimir, son of Sviatoslav	b. 956? d. 1015
1015–1019	„	Sviatopolk, son of St. Vladimir	
1019–1054	„	Yaroslav, son of St. Vladimir	d. 1054
1054–1073	„	Izhaslav (Isiaslav), son of Yaroslav	d. 1078
1073–1076	„	Sviatoslav, son of Yaroslav	
1078–1093	„	Vsevolod, son of Yaroslav	
1093–1113	„	Sviatopolk, son of Izhaslav	

1113–1125	Grand Duke	Vladimir Monomachus, son of Vsevolod	b. 1053	d. 1125
1125–1132	"	Mstislav, son of Vladimir Monomachus		
1132–1139	"	Yaropolk, brother of Mstislav		
1139–1146	"	Vsevolod, great-grandson of Yaroslav		
1146–1154	"	Izhaslav II, son of Mstislav		

(The title of Grand Duke passed from Kiev to Vladimir after 1154)

GRAND DUKES OF VLADIMIR

1154–1157	"	Yuri (George) Dolgoruki, son of Vladimir Monomachus		
1157–1175	"	Andrey Bogolyubski, son of Yuri Dolgoruki		
1176–1212	"	Vsevolod, son of Yuri Dolgoruki		
1212–1218	"	Konstantin, son of Vsevolod		
1218–1238	"	Yuri II, son of Vsevolod		
		(Invasion of Golden Horde, 1223)		
1238–1246	"	Yaroslav II, son of Vsevolod		
1246–1253	"	Andrey, son of Yaroslav II		
1253–1263	"	Aleksandr Nevsky, son of Yaroslav II	b. 1220?	d. 1263
1263–1272	"	Yaroslav of Tver, son of Yaroslav II		
1272–1276	"	Basil, son of Yaroslav II		
1276–1293	"	Demetrius, son of Aleksandr Nevsky		
1293–1304	"	Andrey, son of Aleksandr Nevsky		
1304–1318	"	Michael of Tver		
1318–1326	"	Yuri Danilovich of Moscow, grandson of Yaroslav II		
1326–1328	"	Alexander of Tver, son of Michael of Tver		

Aleksandr Nevsky, Grand Duke of Vladimir (1253-1263).

Ivan III the Great, Grand Duke of Moscow (1462-1505).

GRAND DUKES OF MOSCOW

1328–1341	"	Ivan I (Kalita), brother of Yuri Danilovich of Moscow		d. 1341
1341–1353	"	Simeon, son of Ivan I		
1353–1359	"	Ivan II, son of Ivan I		
1359–1389	"	Demetrius Donskoi, son of Ivan II	b. 1326	d. 1359
1389–1425	"	Basil I, son of Demetrius Donskoi	b. 1350	d. 1389
1425–1462	"	Basil II, son of Basil I	b. 1371	d. 1425
1462–1505	"	Ivan III the Great, son of Basil II	b. 1415	d. 1462
1505–1533	"	Basil III, son of Ivan the Great	b. 1440	d. 1505
			b. 1479	d. 1533

Ivan IV the Terrible, Tsar of all Russia (1533–1584).

Throne of Boris Godunov, Tsar of Russia (1598–1605).

1533–1584	"Tsar of all Russia" (from 1547)	Ivan IV the Terrible, son of Basil III	b. 1530	d. 1584

Ivan the Terrible was the first Russian ruler to use the title of tsar. The deaths of his wife and son Dmitri drove him mad, and he killed his eldest and best-loved son Ivan in a fit of rage. Remorse for this deed hastened his death. He wore the hood of a hermit and died as the "monk Jonah."

1584–1598	Tsar	Fedor I, son of Ivan IV	b. 1557	d. 1598
1598–1605	„	Boris Godunov, brother-in-law of Fedor I	b. 1552	d. 1605
1605	„	Fedor II, son of Boris Godunov	b. 1589	murdered 1605
1605–1606	Usurper	Dmitri (Demetrius I)		murdered 1606
1606–1610	Ruler	Basil IV Shuiski	b. 1552	d. 1612
1607–1610	Usurper	Demetrius II		killed 1610
1610–1612	Ruler	Ladislaus IV of Poland, son of Sigismund III	b. 1595	d. 1648

TSARS (EMPERORS)
HOUSE OF ROMANOV

1613–1645	Emperor	Michael I	b. 1596	d. 1645
1645–1676	„	Aleksei (Alexis), son of Michael	b. 1629	d. 1676
1676–1682	„	Fedor III, son of Aleksei	b. 1656	d. 1682
1682–1689	„	Ivan V, son of Aleksei deposed 1689	b. 1666	d. 1696
1682–1689	Regent	Sophia, daughter of Aleksei	b. 1657	d. 1704
1682–1725	Emperor	Peter I the Great, son of Aleksei	b. 1672	d. 1725
1725–1727	Empress	Catherine I, consort of Peter I the Great	b. 1684	d. 1727
1727–1730	Emperor	Peter II, grandson of Peter I the Great	b. 1715	d. 1730
1730–1740	Empress	Anna (Duchess of Courland), daughter of Ivan V	b. 1693	d. 1740
1740–1741	Emperor	Ivan VI, grand-nephew of Anna b. 1740		murdered 1764
1741–1762	Empress	Elizabeth Petrovna, daughter of Peter I the Great	b. 1709	d. 1762
1762	Emperor	Peter III, nephew of Elizabeth b. 1728		murdered 1762
1762–1796	Empress	Catherine II the Great, consort of Peter III	b. 1729	d. 1796

A Prussian-born princess, Catherine the Great, seized control of Russia from her husband, Peter III, and ruled Russia strongly for 34 years. Though she had numberless lovers, it was not a succession of her admirers who governed Russia, but she.

1796–1801	Emperor	Paul I, son of Peter III	b. 1754	murdered 1801

Catherine II, Empress of Russia (1762–1796).

Paul I, Emperor of Russia (1796–1801).

(Left) Alexander I, Emperor of Russia (1801–1825); (Middle) Nicholas I, Emperor of Russia (1825–1855); (Right) Nicholas II, last Russian Emperor (1894–1917) shown on a coin with the first Romanov Emperor, Michael I (1613–1645).

1801–1825	Emperor	Alexander I, son of Paul I	b. 1777	d. 1825
1825–1855	„	Nicholas I, son of Paul I	b. 1796	d. 1855
1855–1881	„	Alexander II, son of Nicholas I b. 1818	assassinated 1881	
1881–1894	„	Alexander III, son of Alexander II	b. 1845	d. 1894
1894–1917	„	Nicholas II, son of Alexander III		
		abdicated 1917	b. 1868	murdered 1918

STATESMEN

1696–1727	Leading minister	Prince Aleksandr Danilovich Menshikov	b. 1672	d. 1729
1730–1740	„	Ernst Johann Biron, Duke of Kurland	b. 1690	d. 1772
1721–1741	Foreign minister	Heinrich J. F. Ostermann		d. 1747
1732–1741	Field Marshal	Burkhard Christoph von Münnich	b. 1683	d. 1767
1762–1767	„	Burkhard Christoph von Münnich		
1762–1781	Leading minister	Nikita Ivanovich Panin	b. 1718	d. 1783
1774–1791	„	Grigori Aleksandrovich Potemkin	b. 1739	d. 1791
1809–1812	„	Mikhail Mikhailovich Speranski	b. 1772	d. 1839
1806–1825	Minister of War	Aleksei Andreevich Arakcheyev	b. 1769	d. 1834
1880–1881	Minister of Interior	Mikhail Tarielovich Loris-Melikov	b. 1825?	d. 1888
1880–1905	Procurator of the Holy Synod	Konstantin Petrovich Pobedonostsev	b. 1827	d. 1907

1856–1882	Foreign minister	Prince Aleksandr Mikhailovich Gorchakov	b. 1798	d. 1883
1882–1895	,,	Nikolai Karlovich de Giers	b. 1820	d. 1895
1895–1896	,,	Prince Aleksei Borisovich Lobanov-Rostovski	b. 1824	d. 1896
1897–1900	,,	Mikhail Nikolaevich Muraviev	b. 1845	d. 1900
1900–1906	,,	Vladimir Nikolaevich Lamsdorf	b. 1845	d. 1907
1906–1909	,,	Aleksandr Petrovich Izvolski	b. 1856	d. 1919
1892–1903	Minister of Finance	Sergei Yulievich Witte	b. 1849	d. 1915
1906–1911	Premier	Petr Arkadevich Stolypin	b. 1863	assassinated 1911
1917	,,	Prince Georgi Evgenievich Lvov	b. 1861	d. 1925
1917	,,	Aleksandr Feodorovich Kerenski	b. 1881	

(Revolutionary period, 1917–1922)

U.S.S.R. (UNION OF SOVIET SOCIALIST REPUBLICS)
(Formed in 1922)
Chairmen of the Presidium of the Supreme Soviet

1923–1946	President	Mikhail Ivanovich Kalinin	b. 1875	d. 1946
1946–1953	,,	Nikolai Mikhailovich Shvernik	b. 1888	
1953–1960	,,	Klimentiy Efremovich Voroshilov	b. 1881	
1960–1964	,,	Leonid Ilyich Brezhnev	b. 1906	
1964–1966	,,	Anastas Ivanovich Mikoyan	b. 1895	
1966–	,,	Nicolai Victorovich Podgorny	b. 1903	
1924–1953	Chairman	Joseph Stalin (Josif Vissarionovitch Dzhugashvili)	b. 1879	d. 1953

Chairmen of the Council of People's Commissars (Ministers)

1917–1924	Premier	Nikolai Lenin (Vladimir Ilich Ulyanov)	b. 1870	d. 1924

When Lenin was 20, his older brother was executed for a plot against the life of the tsar. As soon as news of revolutionary disturbances in Russia reached him in Switzerland in 1917 he sought to return to Russia and was allowed by the Germans to cross Germany in a sealed train. In Russia he took over leadership of the revolutionary movement. His embalmed body is still on public exhibition in a tomb in Red Square, Moscow.

Nikolai Lenin, Premier of Soviet Russia (1917–1924).

1924–1930	Premier	Aleksei Ivanovich Rykov	b. 1881	executed 1938
1930–1941	,,	Vyacheslav Mikhailovich Molotov (Skryabin)	b. 1890	
1941–1953	,,	Joseph Stalin		

Stalin ruled Russia with an iron hand for nearly 30 years. He expelled his rival, Trotsky, from the party and secured his banishment, in 1929. During his 1936–1937 purges of the Communist party and Soviet army millions of

Leon Trotsky, War Minister of the Soviet Union (1918–1925), reviews the troops.

Russians perished. In the Second World War he directed Russian military operations against Germany.

1953–1955	Premier	Georgi Maximilianovich Malenkov	b. 1901
1955–1958	,,	Nikolai Aleksandrovich Bulganin	b. 1895
1958–1964	,,	Nikita Sergeyevich Khrushchev	b. 1894
1964–	,,	Alexei Nikolaevich Kosygin	b. 1904
1917–1918	Foreign minister	Leon Trotsky (Lev Davydovich Bronstein)	b. 1879 murdered 1940

After the Revolution, Trotsky successfully organized both the red armies and industrial work battalions. In the struggle to succeed Lenin he was defeated by Stalin. He lived in Mexico until he was murdered—probably on Stalin's orders—in 1940. His biography of Stalin later became a best-seller.

1918–1925	War minister	Leon Trotsky (Lev Davydovich Bronstein)	
1918–1930	Foreign minister	Grigori Vasilievich Chicherin	b. 1872 d. 1936

Joseph Stalin, leader of the Soviet Union (1924–1953).

Nikita Khrushchev, Premier of the Soviet Union (1958–1964).

1930–1939	Foreign minister	Maksim Maksimovich Litvinov	b. 1876	d. 1951
1939–1949	„	Vyacheslav Mikhailovich Molotov		
1949–1953	„	Andrei Januaryevich Vyshinsky	b. 1883	d. 1954
1953–	„	Andrei A. Gromyko	b. 1909	

Stamp of Soviet Armenia.

MODERN ARMENIA

(The northern part of Armenia came under Russian rule in 1813. In 1917, Russian Armenia broke free and joined the Transcaucasian Republic with Georgia and Azerbaijan, then became a separate state in 1918)

1918–1920 Premier R. I. Kachaznuni
Foreign Minister A. I. Khatisian

(In 1920, Armenia was invaded by the Soviet Army and became a republic of the Soviet Union)

AZERBAIJAN

[Called Atropatene by the Greeks, the country was ruled by the Macedonians and Persians prior to the 7th century A.D. when it fell to the Byzantines, then the Arabs (642), Seljuks (11th century), Mongols (1236–1498), and Persians, until annexed by Russia in 1813; part of Transcaucasian Republic 1917–1918; declared independence 1918]

1918–1919 Chief of State Khan Khoiski   d. 1920
1919–1920   „   Nazim Beg Usubekov

(In 1920 conquered by Russian army and made a Soviet Republic)

BYELORUSSIA

(Prior to absorption by Lithuania in the 14th century, Byelorussia consisted of the independent duchies of Smolensk, Polotsk, and Turov. By the 18th century, most of Byelorussia was under Russian rule. Independent republic proclaimed 1918)

1918–1921 President Piotra Kreuceuski

(Following World War I, country partitioned between Poland and Russia, eastern part becoming Byelorussian Soviet Socialist Republic; western part regained following World War II)

GEORGIA

(Georgia corresponds to the ancient countries of Colchis and Iberia in the Caucasus. The history of the Christian kingdom of Georgia begins after the acceptance of Christianity by King Miriani of Iberia A.D. 300–362)

450– 503 King Vakhtang
562–   „   Guaram
c. 700 under Caliphate of the East
1008–1014 King Bagrat IV
1089–1125   „   David II
1184–1212 Queen Tamara
1236–   Under rule of Mongols
1314–1346 King Giorgi V
1360–1393   „   Bagrat V
1413–1443   „   Alexander

(Georgia divided into numerous kingdoms and principalities, some under Persian domination, others under Turkish. In the 18th century Taymurazi II assumed the throne of Kartlia and put his son on that of Kakhetia)

1744–1762	King of Kartlia	Taymurazi II	d. 1762
1744–1762	King of Khaketia	Irakli II	d. 1798
1762–1798	King of Kartlia and Khaketia Irakli II		
1798–1800	,,	Giorgi XII	d. 1800

(Russia annexed Kartlia and Khaketia 1801, and remaining Georgian principalities between 1810 and 1867)

Stamp of the Republic of Georgia.

Republic of Georgia

(Surrender of Russia to Germany led to creation in 1917 of short-lived Transcaucasian Republic, in which Georgia was linked with Armenia and Azerbaijan. Independent republic declared in 1918)

1918–1921	President Noe Jordania	b. 1869 d. ?
	Premier Akaki Chkhenkeli	

(In 1921 the Russian Army entered Georgia and the country became a Soviet Socialist Republic)

TRANSCAUCASIAN REPUBLIC

(After the collapse of Czarist Russia in 1917, the Russian possessions of Armenia, Azerbaijan, and Georgia established a federal republic which quickly collapsed)

1917–1918	President of Noe Jordania	b. 1869 d. ?
	Central Committee	

(In 1918 the Federation was dissolved)

UKRAINE

Stamp of the Republic of the Ukraine.

(In the Middle Ages, the Ukraine came under Polish and Lithuanian rule; by the end of the 18th century, it was largely under Russian rule; in 1917, an autonomous republic was declared, becoming independent in 1918)

1917	Chief Minister Vsevolod Holubovich	
1917	President Michael Hrushevsky	b. 1866 d. 1934
	(of Central Rada)	
1917	Prime Minister Volodymir Vinnichenko	b. 1880 d. 1951
1917	War Minister Simon Petlyura	b. 1879 assassinated 1926
1918	Chief of Directorate Volodymir Vinnichenko	
	(Under German occupation)	
1918	Hetman Paul Skoropadsky	
1918	Chief of Directorate Simon Petlyura	
	(Communist coup)	
1919	Chief of State Christian Rakovsky	b. 1873 d. ?

(1920 Soviet occupation; Ukraine becomes republic of Soviet Union)

Rwanda

(Under German rule until World War I, under Belgian administration thereafter, this republic, formerly known as Ruanda, became independent in 1962)

1961–   President   Grégoire Kayibanda   b. 1925

*Grégoire Kayibanda, President
of Rwanda (1961–   ).*

Salvador

*Alfonso Quiñónez Molina, President of
Salvador, appears on a coin with Pedro de
Alvarado, 16th-century Spanish explorer of
Central America.*

*José María Lemus, President of
Salvador (1956–1960).*

(Part of the Spanish vice-royalty of Guatemala, 1526–1821; joined the Central American Federation in 1821; independence obtained 1821; occupied by Mexico 1821–1823; period of anarchy until republic established in 1859)

1860–1863	President	Gerard Barrios	shot 1865
1863–1872	,,	Francis Dueñas	
1872–1876	,,	Gonzales	
1876–1885	,,	Rafael Zaldívar	
1885–1890	,,	Francisco Menéndez	d. 1890
1890–1894	President (provisional)	Carlos Ezeta	
1895–1899	President	Rafael Antonio Gutiérrez	
1899–1903	,,	Tomás Regalado	b. 1864
1903–1907	,,	Pedro José Escalón	
1907–1911	,,	Fernando Figueroa	
1911–1913	,,	Manuel Enrique Araújo	
1913–1914	President (acting)	Carlos Meléndez	
1914–1915	President (provisional)	Alfonso Quiñónez Molina	b. 1873 d. 1950
1915–1919	President	Carlos Meléndez	
1919–1923	,,	Jorge Meléndez	
1923–1927	,,	Alfonso Quiñónez Molina	
1927–1931	,,	Pio Romero Bosque	
1931	,,	Arturo Araújo	
1931–1934	,,	Maximiliano Hernández Martínez	b. 1882
1934–1935	President (acting)	Andrés Ignacio Menéndez	

1935–1944	President	Maximiliano Hernández Martínez	
1944	President (acting)	Andrés Ignacio Menéndez	
1944	President	Osmin Aguirre Salinas	
1945–1949	„	Salvador Castaneda Castro	
1949–1956	„	Oscar Osorio	
1956–1960	„	José María Lemus	
1960–1962	Head of Junta	Miguel Castillo	
1962	President (provisional)	Eusebio Rodolfo Cordon Cea	
1962–1967	President	Julio Adalberto Rivera	
1967–	„	Fidel Sánchez Fernández	b. 1918

Samoa, see Western Samoa

San Marino

Coat-of-arms of San Marino.

(San Marino is a republic governed by a Grand Council of 60 members, two of whom
serve as executives, Co-Regents, for six-month terms)

1966	Co-Regent	Leonida Luzzi Valli
1966	„	Stelio Montironi

Senegal

*Léopold Sédar Senghor, President
of Senegal (1960–   ), is also
known as a distinguished writer.*

(A former French Overseas Territory, Senegal became independent jointly with the
former French Sudan in 1960 in the Mali Federation. The Federation was dissolved
in the same year, Senegal retaining its own name, and the Sudanese Republic adopting
the name of Mali)

1960–	President	Léopold Sédar Senghor	b. 1907

Serbia, see Yugoslavia

Siam, see Thailand

Sierra Leone

Coin of Sierra Leone.

(A former British possession; became independent within the Commonwealth 1961)
1961–1967	Governor-General	Sir Henry Boston	
1961–1967	Prime Minister	Sir Albert Michael Margai	b. 1910
1967–	Head of military junta	Lt.-Col. Andrew Juxon-Smith	

Singapore
Also see Malaysia

(Part of Federation of Malaysia, 1963–1965; independent from 1965)
| 1965– | President | Yusof bin Ishak | |
| 1965– | Prime Minister | Lee Kuan Yew | b. 1923 |

Lee Kuan Yew, Prime Minister of Singapore (1965–   ).

Abdirizak Haji Hussein, Prime Minister of Somalia (1964–   ).

Somalia

(The Republic of Somalia came into being in 1960, through the union of the former colony of British Somaliland and the Italian trusteeship of Somalia)
1961–1967	President	Aden Abdulla Osman Daar	b. 1908
1967–	,,	Mohamed Ibrahim Egal	b. 1929
1964–	Prime Minister	Abdirizak Haji Hussein	b. 1920

South Africa

Cecil John Rhodes, Prime Minister of the Cape Colony (1890–1896), made a fortune in diamonds, a large part of which went towards the establishing of the famous Rhodes Scholarships at Oxford.

CAPE COLONY (OF GOOD HOPE)
(Settled by Dutch in mid-17th century; seized by Britain in 1795)

1797–1803	Governor	George Macartney, Earl Macartney	b. 1737	d. 1806
		(British military administration, 1806–14)		
1814–1826	,,	Lord Charles Somerset		
1828–1833	,,	Sir Galbraith Lowry Cale	b. 1772	d. 1842
1834–1838	,,	Sir Benjamin D'Urban	b. 1777	d. 1849
1838–1843	,,	Sir George Thomas Napier	b. 1784	d. 1855
1843–1844	,,	Sir Peregrine Maitland	b. 1777	d. 1854
1846–1847	,,	Sir Henry Pottinger	b. 1789	d. 1856
1847–1852	,,	Sir Harry Smith	b. 1787	d. 1860
1852–1854	,,	Sir George Cathcart	b. 1794	killed 1854
1854–1861	,,	Sir George Grey	b. 1812	d. 1898
1861–1869	,,	Sir Philip Edmond Wodehouse		
1870–1877	,,	Sir Henry Barkly	b. 1815	d. 1898
1877–1880	,,	Sir Henry Bartle Edward Frere	b. 1815	d. 1884
1880–1889	,,	Sir Hercules George Robert Robinson, Baron Rosmead	b. 1824	d. 1897
1889–1895	,,	Henry Brougham Loch, Baron Loch of Drylaw	b. 1827	d. 1900
1895–1897	,,	Sir Hercules George Robert Robinson, Baron Rosmead		
1897–1905	High Commissioner	Alfred Milner, Viscount Milner		
1905–1910	,,	William Waldegrave Palmer, Viscount Wolmer	b. 1859	d. 1942
1872–1878	Prime Minister	John Charles Molteno	b. 1814	d. 1886
1878–1881	,,	Sir John Gordon Sprigg	b. 1830	d. 1913
1881–1882		John Charles Molteno		
1886–1890	,,	Sir John Gordon Sprigg		
1890–1896	,,	Cecil John Rhodes	b. 1853	d. 1902

Rhodes made a fortune from the Kimberley diamond fields, obtained land north of Bechuanaland by cession from Lobengula, King of the Matabele, and tried to establish a South African British dominion. Following the failure of the Jameson Raid he was forced to resign as premier and afterwards devoted his energies to developing Rhodesia.

1896–1898	Prime Minister	Sir John Gordon Sprigg		
1900–1904	,,	Sir John Gordon Sprigg		
1904–1908	,,	Leander Starr Jameson	b. 1853	d. 1917
1908–1910	,,	John Xavier Merriman	b. 1841	d. 1926

TRANSVAAL REPUBLIC
(Recognized by Britain as independent in 1852)

1852–1853	Head of State	Andries Wilhelmus Jacobus Pretorius	b. 1799	d. 1853

1855–1871	President	Marthinus Wessels Pretorius	b. 1819	d. 1901
1872–1877	,,	Thomas Francois Burgers	b. 1834	d. 1881

(Transvaal annexed by England 1877–1880)

1883–1902	,,	Stefanus Johannes Paulus Kruger	b. 1825	d. 1904

As a boy, "Oom Paul" accompanied his family in the Great Trek of 1836–1840 and afterwards became a founder of the Transvaal state. A leader of the Boer rebellion of 1880, he tried in vain to obtain intervention of various European powers in the Boer War.

1902–1905	Governor	Alfred Milner, Viscount Milner

Stefanus Johannes Paulus Kruger, President of the Transvaal (1883–1902).

Viscount Milner, High Commissioner for South Africa (1897–1905).

1905–1910	Governor	William Waldegrave Palmer, Viscount Wolmer

ORANGE FREE STATE

(Recognized by Britain as independent in 1854)

1854–1855	President	Josias Philippus Hoffman	b. 1807	d. 1879
1855–1859	,,	Jacobus Nicolaas Boshoff	b. 1808	d. 1881
1859–1863	,,	Marthinus Wessel Pretorius	b. 1819	d. 1901
1864–1888	,,	Johannes Hendricus Brand	b. 1823	d. 1888
1888–1896	,,	Francis William Reitz	b. 1844	d. 1934
1896–1902	,,	Marthinus Theunis Steyn	b. 1857	d. 1916
1902–1905	Governor	Alfred Milner, Viscount Milner	b. 1854	d. 1925
1905–1910	,,	William Waldegrave Palmer, Viscount Wolmer	b. 1859	d. 1942

(Became a province of the Union in 1910)

NATAL

(Settled by the British in 1824)

1845–1849	Lieutenant-Governor	Martin Thomas West		d. 1849
1850–1855	,,	Benjamin Chilley Campbell Pine	b. 1813	d. 1891
1856–1864	,,	Sir John Scott	b. 1814	d. 1898

(Constituted a distinct British Colony in 1856)

1864–1865	,,	John Maclean	b. 1810	d. 1878
1867–1872	,,	Robert William Keate	b. 1814	d. 1873
1872–1873	,,	Anthony Musgrave	b. 1828	d. 1888
1873–1875	,,	Sir Benjamin Chilley Campbell Pine		
1875–1880	,,	Sir Henry Ernest Gascoigne Bulwer	b. 1836	d. 1914

1879–1880	Governor and High Commissioner for South East Africa	Sir Garnet Joseph Wolseley	b. 1833	d. 1913
1880–1881	,,	Sir George Pomeroy-Colley	b. 1835	killed 1881
1882–1885	Governor	Sir Henry Ernest Gascoigne Bulwer		
1886–1889	,,	Sir Arthur Elibank Havelock	b. 1844	d. 1908
1889–1893	,,	Sir Charles Bullen Hugh Mitchell	b. 1836	d. 1899
	(Achieved self-government in 1893)			
1893–1901	,,	Sir Walter Francis Hely-Hutchinson	b. 1849	d. 1913
1901–1907	,,	Sir Henry Edward McCallum	b. 1852	d. ?
1907–1909	,,	Sir Matthew Nathan	b. 1862	d. 1939
1910	,,	Paul Sanford Methuen, Baron Methuen	b. 1845	d. 1932

After fighting in the Ashanti, Egyptian and Boer Wars, and acting as a colonial governor, Baron Methuen ended a life of public service as Governor and Constable of the Tower of London.

Ernest George Jansen, Governor-General of the Union of South Africa (1951–1959).

Louis Botha, Prime Minister of the Union of South Africa (1910–1919).

1893–1897	Premier	Sir John Robinson	b. 1839	d. 1903
1897	,,	Sir Harry Escombe	b. 1838	d. 1899
1897–1899	,,	Sir Henry Binns	b. 1837	d. 1899
1899–1903	,,	Sir Albert Henry Hime	b. 1842	d. 1919
1903–1905	,,	Sir George Morris Sutton	b. 1834	d. 1913
1905–1906	,,	Charles John Smythe	b. 1852	d. 1918
1906–1910	,,	Frederick Robert Moor	b. 1853	d. 1927

(The self-governing colonies of the Cape of Good Hope, Natal, the Transvaal and the Orange River Colony united on May 31, 1910)

UNION OF SOUTH AFRICA

1910–1914	Governor-General	Herbert John Gladstone, Viscount Gladstone	b. 1854	d. 1930
1914–1920	,,	Sydney Charles Buxton, Earl Buxton	b. 1853	d. 1934

1920–1924	Governor-General	Prince Arthur Frederick Patrick Albert		
		of Connaught	b. 1883	d. 1938
1924–1931	„	Alexander Augustus Frederick William Alfred		
		George, Earl of Athlone	b. 1874	d. 1957
1931–1937	„	George Herbert Hyde Villiers,		
		Earl of Clarendon	b. 1877	d. 1955
1937–1943	„	Sir Patrick Duncan	b. 1870	d. 1943
1943–1945	Governor-General (acting)	Nicolas Jacobus De Wet	b. 1873	d. 1960
1946–1950	Governor-General	Gideon Brand van Zyl	b. 1873	d. 1956
1951–1959	„	Ernest George Jansen	b. 1881	d. 1959
1959–1961	„	Charles Robberts Swart	b. 1894	
1910–1919	Prime Minister	Louis Botha	b. 1862	d. 1919
1919–1924	„	Jan Christiaan Smuts	b. 1870	d. 1950
1924–1939	„	James Barry Munnik Hertzog	b. 1866	d. 1942
1939–1948	„	Jan Christiaan Smuts		

As a Commando leader, Field Marshal Smuts fought the British in the Boer War but he supported Britain in both World Wars, joining the Imperial War Cabinet in World War I and serving as Prime Minister during World War II.

1948–1954	Prime Minister	Daniel Francois Malan	b. 1874	d. 1959
1954–1958	„	Johannes Gerhardus Strijdom	b. 1873	d. 1958
1958–1961	„	Hendrik Frensch Verwoerd	b. 1901	assassinated 1966

(Became a Republic on May 31, 1961)

Johannes Gerhardus Strijdom, Prime Minister of the Union of South Africa (1954–1958).

Hendrik Frensch Verwoerd, South African Prime Minister (1958–1966), under whom South Africa became a republic.

Jan Christiaan Smuts, Prime Minister of the Union of South Africa (1919–1924, 1939–1948).

REPUBLIC OF SOUTH AFRICA

1961–1967	State President	Charles Robberts Swart		
1967–1968	„	Eben Donges	b. 1898	d. 1968
1968–	„	Jacobus Johannes Fouché		
1961–1966	Prime Minister	Hendrik Frensch Verwoerd		assassinated 1966
1966–	„	Balthazar John Vorster		b. 1915

Charles Robberts Swart, President of South Africa (1961–1967).

Balthazar John Vorster, Prime Minister of South Africa (1966–).

South Vietnam, *see* Vietnam

Southern Yemen

(The People's Republic of Southern Yemen was formed from the British Crown Colony of Aden and the British-protected Federation of South Arabia in 1967)
1967–   President   Qahtan al-Shaabi

Soviet Union, *see* Russia

Spain *(Sp. España)*

English versions of the names of rulers of Spanish-speaking states are:

Catherine–Catalina	Louis–Luis
Charles–Carlos	Peter–Pedro
Francis–Francisco	Philip–Felipe
James–Jaime, Diego	Raymond–Ramon
Joanna–Juana	Theobald–Teobaldo
John–Juan	

Ordoño III, King of Leon (951–956), in a 12th-century miniature.

(Spain was under Roman rule until conquered by the Visigoths)

VISIGOTHIC SPAIN

412– 415	King	Ataulfo (Ataulphus)	assassinated 415
419– 451	,,	Teodoredo (Theodoric)	

466– 484	King	Eurico (Euric)	
484– 507	,,	Alarico (Alaric)	
507– 532	,,	Amalarico (Amalaric)	
554– 567	,,	Atanagildo (Athanagild)	
572– 586	,,	Leovigildo (Leovigild)	
586– 601	,,	Recaredo (Reccared)	
612– 621	,,	Sisebuto (Sisebut)	
621– 631	,,	Suintila (Swintilla)	
642– 649	,,	Chindavinto (Chindaswinth)	
649– 672	,,	Recesvinto (Reccesswinth)	
672– 680	,,	Wamba	
680– 687	,,	Ervigio (Euric)	
709– 711	,,	Don Rodrigo (Roderic)	? killed 711

Suintila, King of Visigothic Spain (621–631).

FIRST MOORISH EMIRATE

711– 714	Emir	Tarik and Muza
714– 717	,,	Abdelaziz
718– 719	,,	Alhor
730– 732	,,	Abderraman el Gafeki

SECOND MOORISH EMIRATE

756– 788	Emir	Abd-er-Rahman I (Abderraman el Gafeki)	b. 731 d. 788
788– 796	,,	Hisham (Hixen) I, son of Abd-er-Rahman I	b. 757 d. 796
796– 822	,,	Hakam (Alhaken) I, son of Hisham I	d. 822
822– 852	,,	Abd-er-Rahman II, son of Hakam	b. 788 d. 852
852– 886	,,	Mohammed, son of Abd-er-Rahman II	
886– 888	,,	Mundhir, son of Mohammed	
888– 912	,,	Abdallah, son of Mohammed ·	
912– 929	,,	Abd-er-Rahman III, grandson of Abdallah	b. 891 d. 961

OMAYAD CALIPHATE of CORDOVA

929– 961	Caliph	Abd-er-Rahman III

Abd-er-Rahman III was the greatest prince of the Spanish Omayad dynasty. He subdued the Arab aristocrats, repulsed the North African Fatimites and proclaimed himself caliph.

961– 976	Caliph	Hakam (Alhaken) II, son of Abd-er-Rahman III	b. 913? d. 976
976–1009	,,	Hisham (Hixen) II, son of Hakam II	d. 1016?
1010–1016	,,	Hisham II	
		(internal conflicts and division after 1009)	
1027–1031	,,	Hisham (Hixen) II	d. 1031

[From 1031–1492, Moorish Spain was divided into numerous Kingdoms, known as "Taifas." The most important of these were Cordova, Toledo, Seville, Granada, Jaen, Murcia, Valencia, and Zaragoza. The last independent Moorish Kingdom was that of Granada, whose last king (1492) was Boabdil]

KINGDOM OF ASTURIAS

718– 737	King	Pelayo	
739– 757	,,	Alfonso I "the Catholic," son-in-law of Pelayo	
757– 791	,,	⎰ Fruela I	
	,,	Aurelio	
	,,	⎱ Silo	
	,,	Mauregato	
	,,	⎰ Bermudo I "the Deacon"	

(The above were known as "Reyes holgazanes," or "Lazy Kings" of Asturias)

791– 842	,,	Alfonso II "the Chaste"	d. 842
842– 850	,,	Ramiro I, son of Bermudo I	

850– 866	King	Ordoño I, son of Ramiro		
866– 909	,,	Alfonso III "the Great"	b. 848	d. 912

KINGDOM OF LEON

914– 924	,,	Ordoño II, son of Alfonso III		
931– 951	,,	Ramiro II		
951– 956	,,	Ordoño III, son of Ramiro II		
956– 966	,,	Sancho I "the Fat," brother of Ordoño III		
966– 982	,,	Ramiro III, son of Sancho		
	,,	Bermudo II, son of Ordoño III		
999–1027	,,	Alfonso V "the Noble"		
1027–1037	,,	Bermudo III		

COUNTY (CONDADO) OF CASTILE

860?	Count	Rodrigo	
	,,	Diego Rodriguez	
	,,	The Judges Nuño Rasura and Lain Calvo	
?923– 970?	,,	Fernan Gonzalez	
?970– 995	,,	Garci Fernández, son of Fernan Gonzalez	
995–1021	,,	Sancho García	
1021–1028	,,	García Sánchez	

KINGDOMS OF LEON AND CASTILE UNITED

1035–1065	King	Fernando I, son of Sancho III of Navarre, married to Doña Sancha de León, sister of Bermudo III of León	d. 1065
1065–1072	,,	Sancho II, son of Fernando	assassinated 1072
1072–1109	,,	Alfonso VI, brother of Sancho II	d. 1109

Alfonso VI is the hero of many stories in Spanish legend. The truth of some of these stories is perhaps doubtful, but there is no doubt that he was a strong and astute leader, protector of his Mohammedan subjects, and much respected by his Arab enemies.

1109–1126	Queen	Doña Urraca, daughter of Alfonso VI	b. 1081	d. 1126
1126–1157	King	Alfonso VII "the Emperor," son of Urraca		d. 1157

KINGDOM OF CASTILE

1157–1158	,,	Sancho III, son of Alfonso VII		d. 1158
1158–1214	,,	Alfonso VIII, son of Sancho III	b. 1155	d. 1214
1214–1217	,,	Enrique I, son of Alfonso	b. 1203?	d. 1217

KINGDOM OF LEON

1157–1188	,,	Fernando II, son of Alfonso VII
1188–1230	,,	Alfonso IX, son of Fernando II

KINGDOMS OF CASTILE AND LEON UNITED

1217–1252	,,	Fernando III "the Saint," son of Alfonso IX of Leon	b. 1199	d. 1252
1252–1284	,,	Alfonso X "the Wise," son of Fernando III	b. 1226?	d. 1284

Alfonso X encouraged astronomy and attempted to put the laws of his kingdoms in order. He tried to unite Spain in a crusade, but was opposed by his second son Sancho, who again opposed him when he made an ally of Morocco.

1284–1295	King	Sancho IV, son of Alfonso X	b. 1258	d. 1295
1295–1312	,,	Fernando IV, son of Sancho IV	b. 1285	d. 1312
1312–1350	,,	Alfonso XI, son of Fernando IV	b. 1310	d. 1350
1350–1369	,,	Pedro I "the Cruel," son of Alfonso XI	b. 1334	killed 1369

*Isabel I, Queen of Castile
(1474–1504).*

*Felipe I, King of Castile
(1504–1506).*

1369–1379	King	Enrique II, brother of Pedro	b. 1333	d. 1379
1379–1390	,,	Juan I, son of Enrique II	b. 1358	d. 1390
1390–1406	,,	Enrique III, son of Juan	b. 1379	d. 1406
1406–1454	,,	Juan II, son of Enrique III	b. 1405	d. 1454
1454–1474	,,	Enrique IV, son of Juan II	b. 1425	d. 1474
1474–1504	Queen	Isabel I, daughter of Juan II ("The Catholic" who married Fernando II of Aragon, thus uniting the Kingdoms of Castile and Aragon in 1479)		d. 1504
1504–1506	King	Felipe I, son-in-law of Isabel (Last separate Sovereign of Castile)	b. 1478	d. 1506

KINGDOM OF NAVARRE

840– 850?	King	Iñigo Arista
905– 925	,,	Sancho Garcés
925– 970	,,	García Sánchez
1000–1035	,,	Sancho "the Great"
1035–1054	,,	García I
1054–1076	,,	Sancho IV

KINGDOM OF ARAGON

1035–1063	,,	Ramiro I
1063–1094	,,	Sancho Ramírez

KINGDOMS OF NAVARRE AND ARAGON UNITED

1076–1094	King	Sancho Ramírez
1094–1104	,,	Pedro I
1104–1134	,,	Alfonso I "the Fighter"

KINGDOM OF NAVARRE

1134–1150	King	García Ramírez
1150–1194	,,	Sancho VI "the Wise"
1194–1234	,,	Sancho VII "the Strong"
1234–1253	,,	Teobaldo I
1253–1270	,,	Teobaldo II
1270–1274	,,	Enrique I
1274–1307	Queen	Juana I
		(Navarre belonged to France from 1284 to 1328)
1328–1349	Queen	Juana II
1349–1387	King	Carlos II "the Bad"
1387–1425	,,	Carlos III "the Noble"

1425–1441	Queen	Doña Blanca
1441–1446	King	Don Carlos de Viana
1461–1479	„	Juan II of Aragon
1479–1481	„	Francisco Febo
1481–1512	Queen	Catalina de Albret
		(Joined to Castile and Aragon 1512)

KINGDOM OF ARAGON

| 1134–1137 | King | Ramiro II "the Monk," brother of Alfonso I "the Fighter" |

MAJORCA (Sp. Mallorca)

(Majorca was detached from Aragon in 1276 and established as a separate kingdom)

1276–1311	King	Jaime I	b. 1243	d. 1311
1311–1324	„	Sancho		d. 1324
1324–1343	„	Jaime II	b. 1315	d. 1349

(Majorca was re-united with Aragon in 1343)

COUNTY (CONDADO) OF CATALONIA

874– 898	Count	Wifredo "the Hairy"
1035–1076	„	Ramón Berenguer I
1096–1131	„	Ramón Berenguer III
1131–1162	„	Ramón Berenguer IV

KINGDOM OF ARAGON UNITED TO CATALONIA

1162–1196	King	Alfonso II, son of Ramón Berenguer IV
1196–1213	„	Pedro II, son of Alfonso II
1213–1276	„	Jaime I "the Conqueror," son of Pedro II
1276–1285	„	Pedro III "the Great," son of Jaime I
1285–1291	„	Alfonso III, son of Pedro III

Alfonso III of Aragon was surnamed "the Great" because he succeeded in uniting his kingdom at the expense of the Moorish Omayad princes.

1291–1327	King	Jaime II, brother of Alfonso III
1327–1336	„	Alfonso IV
1336–1387	„	Pedro IV "the Ceremonious," son of Alfonso IV
1387–1395	„	Juan I, son of Pedro IV
1395–1410	„	Martin I "the Humane," brother of Juan I

(Throne vacant from 1410–1412, when Agreement of Caspe was held)

1412–1416	„	Fernando I, brother of Juan II of Castile
1416–1458	„	Alfonso V "the Magnanimous," son of Fernando
1479–(1516)	„	Fernando II "the Catholic" (Married Isabel of Castile, uniting the Kingdoms of Aragon and Castile)	b. 1452 d. 1516

Isabel I and Fernando II of Aragon, whose marriage and reign united Spain.

Charles I, King of Spain (1516–1556), became Holy Roman Emperor in 1519.

Fernando II of Aragon, on his marriage to Isabel of Castile, became joint sovereign as Fernando V.

KINGDOM OF SPAIN

1479–1504	"the Catholic Monarchs"	Isabel I and Fernando V (II of Aragon)		

Fernando V established his authority over all Spain and supported Columbus in his voyages—though he never shared Queen Isabel's enthusiasm for them. But Fernando broke his promises, deprived Columbus of the governorship of Hispaniola and had him shipped back to Spain in irons.

1505–1506	Regent	Felipe "the Handsome," husband of "Mad Joan," daughter of Isabel and Fernando	b. 1478	d. 1506
1506	„			
1507–1516	„	Fernando V		
1516–1517	„	Cardinal Cisneros		
1516–1556	King	Carlos I (or V of Holy Roman Empire)	b. 1500	d. 1558
1556–1598	„	Felipe II, son of Carlos	b. 1527	d. 1598

Felipe IV, King of Spain (1621–1665), in a portrait by Velasquez.

Felipe II, King of Spain (1556–1598), assumed the title of King of England on marrying Mary Tudor, a title not recognized by the English.

Carlos II, King of Spain (1665–1700), whose death touched off the War of the Spanish Succession.

Felipe V, King of Spain (1700–1724).

Fernando VI, King of Spain (1746–1759).

Carlos IV, King of Spain (1788–1808), with the Royal Family, in a painting by Goya.

1598–1621	King	Felipe III, son of Felipe II	b. 1578	d. 1621
1621–1665	,,	Felipe IV, son of Felipe III	b. 1605	d. 1665
1665–1700	,,	Carlos II, son of Felipe IV	b. 1661	d. 1700
1700–1724	,,	Felipe V of Bourbon, great-grandson of Felipe IV (abdicated 1724)	b. 1683	d. 1746
1724	,,	Luis I, son of Felipe V		d. 1724
1724–1746	,,	Felipe V		
1746–1759	,,	Fernando VI, son of Felipe V	b. 1713	d. 1759
1759–1788	,,	Carlos III, son of Felipe V	b. 1716	d. 1788
1788–1808	,,	Carlos IV, son of Carlos III (abdicated)	b. 1748	d. 1819
1808–1813	,,	Joseph Bonaparte (imposed by Napoleon)	b. 1768	d. 1844
1808–1833	,,	Fernando VII, son of Carlos IV	b. 1784	d. 1833
1833–1840	Regent	María Cristina, widow of Fernando VII	b. 1806	d. 1878
1840–1843	,,	Don Baldomero Espartero	b. 1792	d. 1879
1833–1868	Queen	Isabel II, daughter of Fernando VII (dethroned 1868, abdicated 1870)	b. 1830	d. 1904
1868–1870	Regent	Francisco Serrano	b. 1810	d. 1885
1870–1873	King	Amadeo of Savoy (abdicated)	b. 1845	d. 1890

Joseph Bonaparte, King of Spain (1808–1813).

Isabel II, Queen of Spain (1833–1868).

Fernando VII, King of Spain (1808–1833), as depicted by Goya.

(Left) Amadeo of Savoy, King of Spain (1870–1873).

(Right) Alfonso XIII, King of Spain (1886–1931).

1st Republic (which had four Presidents)

1873–1874	President	Estanislao Figueras, José Pi y Margall, Nicolas Salmerón and Emilio Castelar		
1874	Head of Provisional Government	Francisco Serrano		
1874–1885	King	Alfonso XII, son of Isabel II	b. 1857	d. 1885
1885–1902	Regent	María Cristina, widow of Alfonso XII	b. 1858	d. 1929
1886–1931	King	Alfonso XIII, son of Alfonso XII (dethroned)	b. 1886	d. 1941

Alfonso XIII was born a king, being proclaimed a sovereign at birth. On the day of his marriage in 1906 to a granddaughter of Queen Victoria a bomb was thrown at his carriage but he escaped injury. Outlawed by the Republicans, he fled the country and never returned to Spain, although reinstated as a citizen by Franco.

2nd Republic

1931–1936	President	Niceto Alcalá Zamora	b. 1877	d. 1949
1936	„	Manuel Azaña	b. 1880	d. 1940
		(Civil War 1936–1939)		
1936–	Chief of State	Francisco Franco	b. 1892	
	(Since 1947, Spain has officially been a Kingdom)			
1936–	Vice President	Agustin Muñoz Grandes		

STATESMEN

1621–1643	First Minister	Gaspar de Guzman, Count of Olivares	b. 1587	d. 1645
1715–1719	,,	Giulio Alberoni	b. 1664	d. 1752
1765–1773	,,	Pedro Pablo Abarca y Bolea, Count of Aranda	b. 1718	d. 1799
1777–1792	,,	José Moñino y Redondo, Count of Floridablanca	b. 1728	d. 1808
1792–1808	,,	Manuel de Godoy	b. 1767	d. 1851
1844–1868	,,	Ramón María Narváez, Duke of Valencia	b. 1800	d. 1868
1923–1930	Dictator	Miguel Primo de Rivera y Orbaneja	b. 1870	d. 1930

Agustin Muñoz Grandes, Vice President of Spain (1936–   ).

Francisco Franco, Spanish Chief of State (1936–   ).

States of the Church, see Popes

Sudan

(Administered by a Governor-General on behalf of Great Britain and Egypt, 1899–1956; an independent republic from 1956)

1956–1958	Prime Minister	Abdullah Khalil	
1958–1964	President	Ibrahim Abboud	
1964–1967	Chairman of Supreme Council of State	Ismail al-Azhari	b. 1900
1965–1966	Prime Minister	Muhammad Ahmed Mahgoub	b. 1908
1966–	,,	Sayed Sadikal-Mahdi	

Ibrahim Abboud, President of Sudan (1958–1964).

Muhammad Ahmed Mahgoub, Prime Minister of Sudan (1965–1966).

Swaziland

(A constitutional monarchy established in 1967 under British protection, became independent in September, 1968)

| 1967– | King | Sobhuza | b. 1899 |

Sweden *(Sw. Sverige)*

At Kalmar Castle in 1397 Queen Margaret of Norway united the crowns of Denmark, Norway, and Sweden.

(No authenticated information is available for the period prior to the 6th century; many petty Kingdoms existed from that time)

500	King	Egil
	"	Ottar, son of Egil
	"	Adils, son of Ottar
600	"	Osten, son of Adils
	"	Ingvar, son of Osten
	"	Anund, son of Ingvar

	King	Ingjald Illråde, son of Anund	
	,,	Olof Tratalja, son of Ingjald Illråde	
800	,,	Sigurd Ring	
	,,	Ragnar Lodbrok	
	,,	Bjorn Ironside, son of Ragnar Lodbrok	
850– 882	,,	Eric VI, son of Ragnar Lodbrok	
	,,	Bjorn, son of Eric VI	
	,,	Olof, son of Bjorn	
	,,	Emund Eriksson, son of Eric VI	
	,,	Eric VII, son of Bjorn	d. 994

(The Swedish Kingdom was established by Eric VII)

994–1022	,,	Olof Sköttkonung, son of Eric VI	d. 1022
1022–1050	,,	Anund Jakob, son of Olof Sköttkonung	d. 1050
1050–1060	,,	Emund the Old, brother of Anund Jakob	d. 1060
1060–1066	,,	Steinkel, son-in-law of Emund the Old	d. 1066

(Internal wars, 1066–1080)

1080–1110	King	{ Halstan, son of Steinkel	
1080–1112	Co-regent	{ Inge, son of Steinkel	
1112–1118	King	Philip, son of Halstan	
1112–1125	Co-regent	Inge, brother of Philip	

SVERKER AND ERIC DYNASTIES

1133–1156	King	Sverker	d. 1156
1150–1160	Rival king	Eric IX (St. Eric)	beheaded 1160
1160–1161	King	Magnus Henriksson, great-grandson of Inge	
1161–1167	,,	Charles VII, son of Sverker	assassinated 1167
1167–1195	,,	Knut Eriksson, son of Eric IX	
1195–1208	,,	Sverker Karlsson, son of Charles VII	d. 1210
1208–1216	,,	Eric X, son of Knut Eriksson	d. 1216
1216–1222	,,	John I Sverkersson, son of Sverker Karlsson	b. 1201? d. 1222
1222–1250	,,	Eric XI, son of Eric X	b. 1216 d. 1250
1229–1234	Rival king	Knut Lange, great-grandson of Eric IX	
1248–1266	Regent	Earl Birger, father of Waldemar I	d. 1266

FOLKUNG DYNASTY

1250–1275	King	Waldemar I, nephew of Eric XI	b. 1238? d. 1302?
1275–1290	,,	Magnus I Ladulås, brother of Waldemar	b. 1240 d. 1290
1290–1318	,,	Birger II, son of Magnus Ladulås	b. 1280 d. 1321

(UNION OF KALMAR between Sweden and Norway, 1319)

1319–1365	King	Magnus Eriksson II, grandson of Magnus Ladulås	b. 1316 d. 1374
1356–1359	Co-regent	Eric XII, son of Magnus Eriksson	b. 1339 d. 1359
1365–1389	King	Albert of Mecklenburg, nephew of Magnus	b. 1340? d. 1412
1389–1412	Regent	Margaret, consort of Hakan	b. 1353 d. 1412
1396–1439	King	Eric XIII of Pomerania (Eric VII of Denmark), grandnephew of Margaret	b. 1382 d. 1459

(Union of Kalmar between Sweden, Norway and Denmark, 1397)

1435–1436	Regent	Engelbrekt Engelbrektsson	murdered 1436
1438–1440	,,	Karl Knutsson	b. 1409 d. 1470
1440–1448	King	Christopher of Bavaria, nephew of Eric	b. 1418 d. 1448
1448–1457	,,	Charles VIII (Karl Knutsson)	
1457–1464	,,	Christian I of Denmark	b. 1426 d. 1481

Engelbrekt Engelbrektsson, Regent of Sweden (1435–1436), is regarded as the founder of the Swedish Parliament (statue by Carl Milles).

1464–1465	King	Charles VIII (Karl Knutsson)		
1465–1466	Regent	Jons Bengtsson Oxenstierna		d. 1467
1466–1467	,,	Erik Axelsson Tott		d. 1481
1467–1470	King	Charles VIII (Karl Knutsson)		
1470–1497	Regent	Sten Sture the Elder,		
		nephew of Charles VIII	b. 1440?	d. 1503
1497–1501	King	John (Hans) II of Denmark	b. 1455	d. 1513
1501–1503	Regent	Sten Sture		
1503–1512	,,	Svante Nilsson Sture		d. 1512
1512–1520	,,	Sten Sture the Younger,		
		son of Svante Nilsson Sture	b. 1492?	d. 1520
1520–1521	King	Christian II,		
		son of John II of Denmark	b. 1481	d. 1559

Earl Birger, Regent of Sweden (1248–1266), was the founder of Stockholm.

Gustavus Vasa, Regent of Sweden (1521–1523), ascended the throne as Gustavus I (1523–1560).

HOUSE OF VASA

1521–1523	Regent	Gustavus Eriksson Vasa	b. 1496	d. 1560
1523–1560	King	Gustavus I		

Gustavus fought against Christian II of Denmark and was captured and held as a hostage. Following his escape, Christian beheaded Gustavus' father and brother-in-law. Gustavus himself suffered great privations before beating the Danes and becoming King.

1560–1568	King	Eric XIV, son of Gustavus I	b. 1533	d. 1577
1568–1592	„	John III, son of Gustavus I	b. 1537	d. 1592
1592–1599	„	Sigismund, son of John III	b. 1566	d. 1632
1599–1604	Regent	Charles IX, son of Gustavus I	b. 1550	d. 1611
1604–1611	King	Charles IX		
1611–1632	„	Gustavus II Adolphus, son of Charles IX	b. 1594	killed 1632

Gustavus II, "Lion of the North," supported the Protestant cause against the Catholic League in the Thirty Years War. He saved Protestantism in Germany and won the Battle of Lützen against Wallenstein, but was mortally wounded in the hour of success.

1632–1654	Queen	Christina, daughter of Gustavus II abdicated 1654	b. 1626	d. 1689

PALATINATE DYNASTY

1654–1660	King	Charles X Gustavus, nephew of Gustavus II	b. 1622	d. 1660
1660–1697	„	Charles XI, son of Charles X	b. 1655	d. 1697
1697–1718	„	Charles XII, son of Charles XI	b. 1682	killed 1718
1718–1720	Queen	Ulrica Eleonora, sister of Charles XII abdicated 1720	b. 1688	d. 1741
1720–1751	King	Frederick I of Hesse, husband of Ulrica Eleonora	b. 1676	d. 1751

HOLSTEIN-GOTTORP DYNASTY

1751–1771	„	Adolphus Frederick	b. 1710	d. 1771
1771–1792	„	Gustavus III, son of Adolphus Frederick	b. 1746	assassinated 1792

Gustavus II Adolphus, King of Sweden (1611–1632).

Christina, Queen of Sweden (1632–1654).

Charles XII, King of Sweden (1697–1718).

Gustavus III, King of Sweden (1771–1792).

1792–1809	King	Gustavus IV Adolphus, son of Gustavus III abdicated 1809	b. 1778	d. 1837
1792–1796	Regent	Charles, son of Adolphus Frederick	b. 1748	d. 1818
1809–1818	King	Charles XIII		
		(Sweden united with Norway 1814–1905)		

BERNADOTTE DYNASTY

1818–1844	,,	Charles XIV John (Bernadotte)	b. 1763?	d. 1844
1844–1859	,,	Oscar I, son of Charles XIV	b. 1799	d. 1859
1859–1872	,,	Charles XV, son of Oscar I	b. 1826	d. 1872
1872–1907	,,	Oscar II, son of Oscar I	b. 1829	d. 1907
1907–1950	,,	Gustavus V, son of Oscar II	b. 1858	d. 1950
1950–	,,	Gustavus VI Adolf, son of Gustavus V	b. 1882	

STATESMEN

1290–1306	Marshal	Tyrgils Knutsson
1375–1386	,,	Bo Jonsson Grip

Charles XIV John, King of Sweden (1818–1844), was born Jean Bernadotte, became a Marshal of Napoleon, and was adopted by Charles XIII of Sweden.

Charles XV, King of Sweden (1859–1872), established the bicameral system in the Swedish Parliament.

1653–1660	President of Treasury Board	Herman Klasson Fleming		
1680–1685	,,	Klas Hermansson Fleming	b. 1649	d. 1685
1676–1680	Chief Counsellor	Johan Gyllenstierna	b. 1635	d. 1680
1685–1697	President of Estates Restitution Board	Fabian Wrede	b. 1641	d. 1712
1680–1702	Chancellor President	Bengt Gabrielsson Oxenstierna	b. 1623	shot 1702
1715–1718	Charles XII's Minister	Georg Henrik von Görtz	b. 1668	executed 1719
1710–1719	Prime Minister	Arvid Bernhard Horn	b. 1664	d. 1742
1719–1720	,,	Gustav Cronhjelm		d. 1737
1720–1738	,,	Arvid Bernhard Horn		
1739–1746	,,	Carl Gyllenborg	b. 1679	d. 1746
1747–1752	,,	Karl Gustav Tessin		d. 1770
1752–1761	,,	Anders Johan von Hopken		d. 1789
1761–1765	,,	Klas Ekeblad		d. 1771
1765–1768	,,	Karl Gustav Lowenhielm		d. 1768
1769–1771	,,	Klas Ekeblad		
1772	,,	Joachim von Duben		d. 1786
1772–1783	,,	Ulrik Scheffer	b. 1716	d. 1799
1783–1785	,,	Gustav Philip Creutz	b. 1731	d. 1785
1785–1787	,,	Emanuel De Geer		d. 1803
1787–1789	,,	Johan Gabriel Oxenstierna	b. 1750	d. 1818
1788–1790	,,	Carl Wilhelm von Duben		d. 1790
1792–1797	Chancellor	Frederick Sparre		d. 1803
1792–1796	Counsellor	Gustav Adolf Reuterholm	b. 1756	d. 1813
1801–1809	Chancellor President	Fredrik Vilhelm von Ehrenheim		d. 1828
1801–1810	Earl Marshal	Hans Axel von Fersen	b. 1755	murdered 1810
1834–1844	,,	Magnus Brahe		d. 1844
1858–1870	Chancellor	Louis Gerhard de Geer	b. 1818	d. 1896
1870–1874	,,	Axel Gustav Adlercreutz		d. 1880
1874–1875	,,	Edvard Henrik Carleson		d. 1884
1875–1876	,,	Louis Gerhard de Geer		
1876–1880	Prime Minister	Louis Gerhard de Geer		
1880–1883	,,	Arvid Rutger F. Posse		d. 1901
1883–1884	,,	Carl Johan Thyselius		d. 1891
1884–1888	,,	Oskar Robert Themptander		d. 1897

1888–1889	Prime Minister	Didrik A. G. Bildt		d. 1894
1889–1891	,,	Joh. Gustav N. S. Åkerhielm		d. 1900
1891–1900	,,	Erik Gustav Boström	b. 1842	d. 1907
1900–1902	,,	Fredrik Wilhelm von Otter		d. 1910
1902–1905	,,	Erik Gustav Boström		
1905	,,	Johan Olof Ramstedt	b. 1852	d. 1935
1905	,,	Christian Lundeberg	b. 1842	d. 1911
1905–1906	,,	Karl Albert Staaff	b. 1860	d. 1915
1906–1911	,,	Salomon Arvid Achates Lindman	b. 1862	d. 1936

Tage Erlander, Prime Minister of Sweden (1946–).

Gustav VI Adolf, King of Sweden (1950–).

Dag Hammarskjöld, Secretary-General of the United Nations (1953–1961).

1911–1914	,,	Karl Albert Staaff	b. 1860	d. 1915
1914–1917	,,	Knut Hjalmar Hammarskjöld	b. 1862	d. 1953

Prime Minister Hammarskjöld was the father of Dag Hammarskjöld the economist, who became secretary-general of the United Nations and who died tragically in a plane crash while on a peace-making trip to the Congo.

1917	Prime Minister	Carl Johan Gustav Swartz	b. 1858	d. 1926
1917–1920	,,	Nils Eden	b. 1871	d. 1945
1920	,,	Karl Hjalmar Branting	b. 1860	d. 1925
1920–1921	,,	Louis de Geer	b. 1854	d. 1935

1921	Prime Minister	Oskar Fredrik von Sydow	b. 1873	d. 1936
1921–1923	"	Karl Hjalmar Branting		
1923–1924	"	Ernst Trygger	b. 1857	d. 1943
1924–1925	"	Karl Hjalmar Branting		
1925–1926	"	Richard Johannes Sandler	b. 1884	d. 1965
1926–1928	"	Carl Gustav Ekman	b. 1872	d. 1945
1928–1930	"	Salomon Arvid Achates Lindman	b. 1862	d. 1936
1930–1932	"	Carl Gustav Ekman		
1932	"	Felix Teodor Hamrin	b. 1875	d. 1937
1932–1936	"	Per Albin Hansson	b. 1885	d. 1946
1936	"	Axel Alarik Pehrsson-Bramstorp	b. 1883	d. 1954
1936–1946	"	Per Albin Hansson	b. 1885	d. 1946
1946–	"	Tage Erlander	b. 1901	
1953–1961	Secretary-General of the United Nations	Dag Hammarskjöld	b. 1905	d. 1961

Philipp Etter, President of Switzerland (1939, 1942, 1947, 1953).

Switzerland (Fr. Suisse, Ger. Schweiz, It. Suizza)

(The Swiss Confederation was founded in 1291; a Federal Constitution was adopted in 1848)

Note: Switzerland's government is a collegiate body of 7 members called the Federal Council. There is no individual head of State. The Federal Councillors each take the Chair in turn for one year, during which period they hold the title of President of the Swiss Confederation, while at the same time discharging their normal duties.

1848–1849	President*	Jonas Furrer	b. 1805	d. 1861
1850	"	Daniel-Henri Druey	b. 1799	d. 1855
1851	"	Martin Joseph Munzinger	b. 1791	d. 1855
1852	"	Jonas Furrer		
1853	"	Wilhelm Mathias Naeff	b. 1802	d. 1881
1854	"	Friedrich Frey-Herosée	b. 1801	d. 1873
1855	"	Jonas Furrer		
1856	"	Jakob Stämpfli	b. 1820	d. 1879
1857	"	Charles-Emmanuel-Constant Fornerod	b. 1819	d. 1899
1858	"	Jonas Furrer		

* The President is elected in December of each year and holds office from January 1 until December 31.

1859	President	Jakob Stämpfli		
1860	"	Friedrich Frey-Herosee		
1861	"	Melchior Joseph Martin Knüsel	b. 1813	d. 1889
1862	"	Jakob Stämpfli		
1863	"	Charles-Emmanuel-Constant Fornerod		
1864	"	Jakob Dubs	b. 1822	d. 1879
1865	"	Karl Schenk	b. 1823	d. 1895
1866	"	Melchior Joseph Martin Knüsel		
1867	"	Charles-Emmanuel-Constant Fornerod		
1868	"	Jakob Dubs		
1869	"	Emil Welti	b. 1825	d. 1899
1870	"	Jakob Dubs		
1871	"	Karl Schenk		
1872	"	Emil Welti		
1873	"	Paul Ceresole	b. 1832	d. 1905
1874	"	Karl Schenk		
1875	"	Jakob Scherer	b. 1825	d. 1878
1876	"	Emil Welti		
1877	"	Joachim Heer	b. 1825	d. 1879
1878	"	Karl Schenk		
1879	"	Bernhard Hammer	b. 1822	d. 1907
1880	"	Emil Welti		
1881	"	Numa Droz	b. 1844	d. 1899
1882	"	Simeon Bavier	b. 1825	d. 1896
1883	"	Louis Ruchonnet	b. 1834	d. 1893
1884	"	Emil Welti		
1885	"	Karl Schenk		
1886	"	Adolf Deucher	b. 1831	d. 1912
1887	"	Numa Droz		
1888	"	Wilhelm Friedrich Hertenstein	b. 1825	d. 1888
1889	"	Bernhard Hammer		
1890	"	Louis Ruchonnet		
1891	"	Emil Welti		
1892	"	Walter Hauser	b. 1837	d. 1902
1893	"	Karl Schenk		
1894	"	Emil Frey	b. 1838	d. 1922
1895	"	Joseph Zemp	b. 1834	d. 1908
1896	"	Adrien Lachenal	b. 1849	d. 1918
1897	"	Adolf Deucher		
1898	"	Eugène Ruffy	b. 1854	d. 1919
1899	"	Eduard Müller	b. 1848	d. 1919
1900	"	Walter Hauser		
1901	"	Ernst Brenner	b. 1856	d. 1911
1902	"	Joseph Zemp	b. 1834	d. 1908

Max Petitpierre, President of Switzerland (1950, 1955, 1960).

1903	President	Adolf Deucher		
1904	"	Robert Comtesse	b. 1847	d. 1922
1905	"	Marc-Emile Ruchet	b. 1853	d. 1912
1906	"	Ludwig Forrer	b. 1845	d. 1921
1907	"	Eduard Müller		
1908	"	Ernst Brenner		
1909	"	Adolf Deucher		
1910	"	Robert Comtesse		
1911	"	Marc-Emile Ruchet		
1912	"	Ludwig Forrer		
1913	"	Eduard Müller		
1914	"	Arthur Hoffmann	b. 1857	d. 1927
1915	"	Giuseppe Motta	b. 1871	d. 1940
1916	"	Camille Decoppet	b. 1862	d. 1925
1917	"	Edmund Schulthess	b. 1868	d. 1944
1918	"	Felix Ludwig Calonder	b. 1863	d. 1952
1919	"	Gustave Ador	b. 1845	d. 1928
1920	"	Giuseppe Motta		
1921	"	Edmund Schulthess		
1922	"	Robert Haab	b. 1865	d. 1959
1923	"	Karl Scheurer	b. 1872	d. 1929
1924	"	Ernest Chuard	b. 1857	d. 1942
1925	"	Jean-Marie Musy	b. 1876	d. 1952
1926	"	Heinrich Häberlin	b. 1868	d. 1947
1927	"	Giuseppe Motta		
1928	"	Edmund Schulthess		
1929	"	Robert Haab		
1930	"	Jean-Marie Musy		
1931	"	Heinrich Häberlin		
1932	"	Giuseppe Motta		
1933	"	Edmund Schulthess		
1934	"	Marcel Pilet-Golaz	b. 1889	d. 1958
1935	"	Rudolf Minger	b. 1881	d. 1955
1936	"	Albert Meyer	b. 1870	d. 1953
1937	"	Giuseppe Motta		
1938	"	Johannes Baumann	b. 1874	d. 1953
1939	"	Philipp Etter	b. 1891	
1940	"	Marcel Pilet-Golaz		
1941	"	Ernst Wetter	b. 1877	
1942	"	Philipp Etter		
1943	"	Enrico Celio	b. 1889	

(Left)
Friedrich Wahlen,
President of
Switzerland (1961).

(Right)
Roger Bonvin, President
of Switzerland (1967).

1944	President	Walter Stämpfli	b. 1884	
1945	,,	Eduard von Steiger	b. 1881	d. 1962
1946	,,	Karl Kobelt	b. 1891	
1947	,,	Philipp Etter		
1948	,,	Enrico Celio	b. 1889	
1949	,,	Ernst Nobs	b. 1886	d. 1957
1950	,,	Max Petitpierre	b. 1899	
1951	,,	Eduard von Steiger		
1952	,,	Karl Kobelt		
1953	,,	Philipp Etter		
1954	,,	Rodolphe Rubattel	b. 1896	d. 1961
1955	,,	Max Petitpierre		
1956	,,	Markus Feldmann	b. 1897	d. 1958
1957	,,	Hans Streuli	b. 1892	
1958	,,	Thomas Holenstein	b. 1896	
1959	,,	Paul Chaudet	b. 1904	
1960	,,	Max Petitpierre		
1961	,,	Friedrich Wahlen	b. 1899	
1962	,,	Paul Chaudet		
1963	,,	Willy Spühler	b. 1902	
1964	,,	Ludwig von Moos	b. 1910	
1965	,,	Hans-Peter Tschudi	b. 1913	
1966	,,	Hans Schaffner	b. 1908	
1967	,,	Roger Bonvin		
1968	,,	Willy Spühler	b. 1902	

Syria
(Ancient)

*Seleucus I Nicator
(301–281 B.C.) with
his son Antiochus I
Soter (281–261 B.C.)
and wife Stratonice (in
a painting by Daniel
Seiter, courtesy of The
Art Gallery of Toronto).*

B.C.			B.C.
732– 605		Under Assyria	
605– 539		Under Babylonia	
539– 333		Under Persia	
333– 323	Conqueror	Alexander the Great	
		son of Philip II of Macedon	b. 356 d. 323
		(see Macedonia)	
323– 301	King	Antigonus I	b. 382 killed 301

SELEUCID DYNASTY

301– 281	King	Seleucus I Nicator	b. 356? assassinated 281
281– 261	,,	Antiochus I Soter, son of Seleucus I	b. 324 killed 261
261– 246	,,	Antiochus II Theos, son of Antiochus I	b. 286 d. 246
246– 226	,,	Seleucus II, son of Antiochus II	b. 247 d. 226

226– 223	King	Seleucus III, son of Seleucus II	assassinated 223
223– 187	,,	Antiochus III (the Great), son of Seleucus II	b. 242 d. 187
187– 176	,,	Seleucus IV, son of Antiochus III b. 217?	assassinated 176
175– 164	,,	Antiochus IV Epiphanes, son of Antiochus III	d. 164
164– 162	,,	Antiochus V Eupator, son of Antiochus IV	b. 173 killed 162
162– 150	,,	Demetrius I Soter, son of Seleucus IV	b. 187 killed 150
150– 145	,,	Alexander Balas	
145– 138	,,	Demetrius II Nicator, son of Demetrius I	killed 125
138– 129	,,	Antiochus VII, son of Demetrius I	b. 158? d. 129?
129– 125	,,	Demetrius II	
125– 96	,,	Antiochus VIII, son of Demetrius II	d. 96
96– 95	,,	Antiochus IX, son of Antiochus VII	d. 95
95– 94	,,	Antiochus X, son of Antiochus IX	d. 92
	,,	Demetrius III, cousin of Antiochus X	d. 88
69– 64	,,	Antiochus XIII, son of Antiochus X	
		(Syria became a Roman province in 64 B.C.)	

Syria (Modern)

(Ruled by Turks 1517–1918)

1831	Conqueror	Mehemet Ali	b. 1769	d. 1849
1878–1880	Governor-General	Midhat Pasha	b. 1822	d. 1884
		(French Mandate 1923–1946)		
1925–1927	High Commissioner	Henri de Jouvenel	b. 1876	d. 1935
1928	,,	Henri Ponsot		
1939	,,	Gabriel Puaux		
1940	,,	Jean Chiappe	b. 1878	killed 1940
1940	,,	Henri Dentz		
1941	President	Sheikh Taj-ed-Dine-el-Hassani		
1943–1950	,,	Shukri el-Kuwatli	b. 1891	d. 1967
1950–1951	,,	Hashim el-Atassi		
1951–1954	,,	Adib Shishakli		
1954–1955	,,	Hashim el-Atassi		
1955–1958	,,	Shukri el-Kuwatli		

(1958–1961 Syria linked with Egypt in the United Arab Republic)

1958–1961	President	Gamal Abdel Nasser	b. 1918
1961–1963	,,	Nazi M. el-Kudsi	
		(Army coup, 1963)	
1963–1966	,,	Amin al Hafiz	
1966–		Nureddin el- Atassi	b. 1928

Hashim el-Atassi, President of Syria
(1950–1951, 1954–1955).

Adib Shishakli, President of Syria
(1951–1954).

Tanzania

Julius Kambarage Nyerere, President of Tanganyika (1962–1964), President of Tanzania (1964–   ).

(Tanzania was created in 1964 by the union of Tanganyika and Zanzibar)

1964–	President	Julius Kambarage Nyerere	b. 1921
1964–	Vice-President	Abeid Amani Karume	b. 1906

TANGANYIKA
(Tanganyika was a German colony from 1885 until World War I, after which it became a British mandate under the League of Nations and a British trusteeship under the United Nations, until attaining independence in 1961)

1962–1964	President	Julius Kambarage Nyerere

ZANZIBAR
(Zanzibar, a sultanate under British protection until 1963, became a republic in 1964)

–1964	Sultan	Seyyid Jamshid bin Abdullah bin Khalifa (deposed)
1964–	President	Abeid Amani Karume

Coin of the Sultanate of Zanzibar.

Thailand (Siam)

Chula Chom Klao (Chulalongkorn), King of Thailand (1868–1910).

(Thailand broke away from the Khmer Empire and became a unified state *c.* A.D. 1350. Kings of the modern Thai dynasty are listed)

CHAKRI DYNASTY

1782–1809	King	Buddha Yod Fa	b. 1737	d. 1809
1809–1824	,,	Buddha Loes La Nabhalai, son of Yod Fa	b. 1768	d. 1824
1824–1851	,,	Nang Klao, son of Loes La Nabhala	b. 1788	d. 1851
1851–1868	,,	Chom Kloa (Mongkut), brother of Nang Klao	b. 1804	d. 1868
1868–1910	,,	Chula Chom Klao (Chulalongkorn), son of Chom Klao	b. 1853	d. 1910
1910–1925	,,	Mongkut Klao (Vajiravudh), son of Chula Chom Klao	b. 1881	d. 1925
1925–1935	,,	Prajadhipok (Phra Pok Klao), brother of Mongkut Klao abdicated 1935	b. 1893	d. 1941
1935–1946	,,	Ananda Mahidol, nephew of Prajadhipok b. 1925	assassinated 1946	

(Left) Mongkut Klao, King of Thailand (1910–1925); (Middle) Prajadhipok, King of Thailand (1925–1935); (Right) Ananda Mahidol, King of Thailand (1935–1946).

Bhumibol, King of Thailand (1946–   ) with Queen Sirikit.

1946–	King	Bhumibol Adulyadej, brother of Ananda	b. 1927

(The above Kings are also known as Rama I to IX respectively)

Togo

Coin issued by the French Government of Togo.

(The Republic of Togo is part of the former German colony of Togoland, mandated to France by the League of Nations after World War I, and held by France under a United Nations trusteeship from 1946 until 1960 when independence was achieved)

1961–1963	President	Sylvanus Olimpio	assassinated 1963
1963–1967	”	Nicolas Grunitsky	b. 1915
1967–	”	Etienne Eyadama	b. 1932

Transjordan, see Jordan

Trinidad and Tobago

Eric Williams, Prime Minister of Trinidad and Tobago (1962–   ) (at lower left).

(Became an independent state and a member of the British Commonwealth in 1962)

1962–	Governor-General	Sir Solomon Hochoy	b. 1905
1962–	Prime Minister	Eric Eustace Williams	b. 1911

Tripolitania, see Libya

Tunisia
Also see Carthage, Vandal Empire

Habib Ben Ali Bourguiba, President of Tunisia (1957–   ).

(French Protectorate, 1881–1956; independent sovereign state from 1956)
1957–   President   Habib Ben Ali Bourguiba   b. 1903

Turkey

Mohammed V, Sultan of Turkey (1909–1918), pictured on a stamp.

Seljuk Empire
(The Seljuk Empire was established by Turkic invaders from Central Asia and included much of what is now Turkey, Iran, Iraq and Syria)

1037–1063	Grand Sultan	Toghrul Beg
1063–1073	,,	Alp Arslan
1073–1092	,,	Malik Shah
1092–1104	,,	Barkiarok
1104–1116	,,	Mohammed
1116–1157	,,	Sandjar

(The Seljuk Empire was partitioned among four heirs. Of these successor states, that of Roum or Anatolia lasted the longest)

SELJUK EMPIRE (Sultans of Roum)

1092–1106	Sultan	Kilidy Arslan I
1107–1117	,,	Malik Shah
1117–1156	,,	Masoud I
1156–1193	,,	Kilidy Arslan II
1193–1211	,,	Khaikhosru II
1211–1222	,,	Azeddin Kaikus I
1222–1237	,,	Alaeddin Kaikobad
1247–1261	,,	Azeddin Kaikus II
1261–1267	,,	Kilidy Arslan III
1267–1276	,,	Kaikhosru III
1276–1283	,,	Masoud II
1283–1307	,,	Alaeddin

(Seljuk rule in Anatolia was replaced by that of the Ottomans)

OTTOMAN EMPIRE

1299–1326	Emir	Osman I (Othman)	b. 1259	d. 1326
1326–1359	Sultan	Orkhan, son of Osman	b. 1279	d. 1359
1359–1389	,,	Murad I (Amurath), son of Orkhan	b. 1319	killed 1389
1389–1403	,,	Bajazet I (Bayazid), son of Murad 1	b. 1347	d. 1403
1403–1411	,,	Suleiman (Solyman), son of Bajazet I		d. 1411
1411–1413	,,	Prince Musa		
1413–1421	,,	Mohammed I, son of Bajazet I	b. 1387	d. 1421
1421–1451	,,	Murad II, son of Mohammed I	b. 1403 ?	d. 1451
1451–1481	,,	Mohammed II, son of Murad II	b. 1430	d. 1481

Mohammed II, Sultan of Turkey (1451–1481).

Selim I, Sultan of Turkey (1512–1520).

Suleiman I, Sultan of Turkey (1520–1566).

1481–1512	Sultan	Bajazet II (Bayazid), son of Mohammed II	b. 1447	d. 1513
1512–1520	,,	Selim I, son of Bajazet II	b. 1467	d. 1520
1520–1566	,,	Suleiman I (or II), son of Selim I	b. 1496 ?	d. 1566

Turkey reached the apex of its power during the reign of Suleiman "the Magnificent", who added greatly to the Turkish territories, conquering Belgrade, Budapest, Rhodes, Tabriz, Baghdad, Aden and Algiers. He reorganized the country's administration, encouraged arts and sciences, and improved the conditions of his Christian subjects.

1566–1574	Sultan	Selim II, son of Suleiman I	b. 1524?	d. 1574
1574–1595	,,	Murad III, son of Selim II	b. 1546	d. 1595
1595–1603	,,	Mohammed III, son of Murad III	b. 1566	d. 1603
1603–1617	,,	Ahmed I (Achmet), son of Mohammed III	b. 1589	d. 1617
1617–1618	,,	Mustafa I (Mustapha), son of Ahmed I	b. 1591	d. 1639
1618–1622	,,	Osman II, brother of Mustafa I	b. 1604	murdered 1622
1622–1623	,,	Mustafa I		abdicated 1623
1623–1640	,,	Murad IV, nephew of Mustafa I	b. 1609	d. 1640
1640–1648	,,	Ibrahim I, brother of Murad IV	b. 1615	murdered 1648
1648–1687	,,	Mohammed IV, son of Ibrahim	b. 1641	d. 1691
1687–1691	,,	Suleiman II (or III), brother of Mohammed IV	b. 1641	d. 1691
1691–1695	,,	Ahmed II, brother of Suleiman II	b. 1642	d. 1695
1695–1703	,,	Mustafa II, brother of Ahmed II	b. 1664	d. 1704
1703–1730	,,	Ahmed III, brother of Mustafa II	b. 1673	d. 1736
1730–1754	,,	Mahmud I (Mahmoud), nephew of Ahmed III	b. 1696	d. 1754
1754–1757	,,	Osman III, brother of Mahmud I	b. 1696	d. 1757
1757–1773	,,	Mustafa III	b. 1717	d. 1773
1773–1789	,,	Abdul-Hamid I, brother of Mustafa III	b. 1725	d. 1789
1789–1807	,,	Selim III, nephew of Abdul-Hamid I	b. 1761	murdered 1808
1807–1808	,,	Mustafa IV	b. 1779	assassinated 1808
1808–1839	,,	Mahmud II, brother of Mustafa IV	b. 1785	d. 1839
1839–1861	,,	Abdul-Medjid I, son of Mahmud II	b. 1823	d. 1861
1861–1876	,,	Abdul-Aziz, son of Mahmud II	b. 1830	d. 1876
1876	,,	Murad V, son of Abdul-Medjid	b. 1840	d. 1904
1876–1909	,,	Abdul-Hamid II, son of Abdul-Medjid	b. 1842	d. 1918
1909–1918	,,	Mohammed V (Mehmed), brother of Abdul-Hamid II	b. 1844	d. 1918
1918–1922	,,	Mohammed VI, brother of Mohammed V	b. 1861	d. 1926

(Sultanate abolished, 1922; Republic proclaimed, 1923)

Kemal Atatürk, President of Turkey (1923–1938).

REPUBLIC

1923–1938 President Kemal Atatürk (Mustafa Kemal Pasha)   b. 1881 d. 1938

Although he ran away from his first school, after he entered military college the future "Father of Turkey" received the prophetic name of Kemal,

Cemal Gürsel, President of Turkey (1960– 1966).

Ismet Inonü, President of Turkey (1938–1950).

meaning "perfection." After resisting the Greek army's occupation of Turkey and defeating the Greeks, he became the first president of the Turkish Republic.

1938–1950	President	Ismet Inonü	b. 1884	
1950–1960	,,	Celal Bayar	b. 1884	
1960–1966	,,	Cemal Gürsel	b. 1895	d. 1966
1966–	,,	Cevdet Sunay	b. 1900	

Ubangi-Shari, see Central African Republic

Uganda

(Uganda, a former British Protectorate, became an independent republic in 1963)

1963–1966	President	Sir Edward Mutesa II	b. 1924
1966–	,,	Apollo Milton Obote	b. 1924

Apollo Milton Obote, President of Uganda (1966–   ).

George Washington, President of the United States (1789–1797), with his family, in a portrait by Edward Savage (courtesy of National Gallery of Art, Washington, D.C.).

United States of America

PRESIDENTS

F—Federalist	D—Democratic	W—Whig
D/R—Republican party, later Democratic		R—Republican

1789–1797	President	George Washington (F)	b. 1732 d. 1799
1797–1801	,,	John Adams (F)	b. 1735 d. 1826
1801–1809	,,	Thomas Jefferson (D/R)	b. 1743 d. 1826
1809–1817	,,	James Madison (D/R)	b. 1751 d. 1836

Thomas Jefferson, President of the United States (1801–1809), is depicted leaving for his inauguration.

John Adams, President of the United States (1797–1801).

Andrew Jackson, President of the United States (1829–1837).

1817–1825	President	James Monroe (D/R)	b. 1759	d. 1831
1825–1829	,,	John Quincy Adams (D/R)	b. 1767	d. 1848
1829–1837	,,	Andrew Jackson (D)	b. 1767	d. 1845
1837–1841	,,	Martin Van Buren (D)	b. 1782	d. 1862
1841 (31 days)	,,	William Henry Harrison (W)	b. 1773	d. 1841
1841–1845	,,	John Tyler (W)	b. 1790	d. 1862
1845–1849	,,	James Knox Polk (D)	b. 1795	d. 1849
1849–1850	,,	Zachary Taylor (W)	b. 1784	d. 1850

William Henry Harrison, President of the United States (1841).

James Knox Polk, President of the United States (1845–1849).

Zachary Taylor, President of the United States (1849–1850).

Franklin Pierce, President of the United States (1853–1857).

1850–1853	President	Millard Fillmore (W)		b. 1800 d. 1874
1853–1857	,,	Franklin Pierce (D)		b. 1804 d. 1869
1857–1861	,,	James Buchanan (D)		b. 1791 d. 1868
1861–1865	,,	Abraham Lincoln (R)	b. 1809	assassinated 1865
1865–1869	,,	Andrew Johnson (R)		b. 1808 d. 1875
1869–1877	,,	Ulysses Simpson Grant (R)		b. 1822 d. 1885
1877–1881	,,	Rutherford Birchard Hayes (R)		b. 1822 d. 1893
1881 (6 mths.)	,,	James Abram Garfield (R)	b. 1831	assassinated 1881
1881–1885	,,	Chester Alan Arthur (R)		b. 1830 d. 1886
1885–1889	,,	Stephen Grover Cleveland (D)		b. 1837 d. 1908

Abraham Lincoln, President of the United States (1861–1865), enters Richmond to the acclaim of the emancipated slaves.

Ulysses Simpson Grant, President of the United States (1869–1877), visited China where he posed with Li Hung Chang in the Viceregal Palace in Tien Tsin.

The body of James Abram Garfield, President of the United States (1881), lies in state in the Capitol after his assassination.

Stephen Grover Cleveland, President of the United States (1885–1889, 1893–1897).

Rutherford Birchard Hayes, President of the United States (1877–1881).

Benjamin Harrison, President of the United States (1889–1893).

William McKinley (at left), President of the United States (1897–1901), with his Vice President, Theodore Roosevelt, who succeeded him (1901–1909).

William Howard Taft (at left), President of the United States (1909–1913), takes a drive with his family.

1889–1893	President	Benjamin Harrison (R)	b. 1833	d. 1901
1893–1897	,,	Stephen Grover Cleveland (D)		
1897–1901	,,	William McKinley (R)	b. 1843	assassinated 1901
1901–1909	,,	Theodore Roosevelt (R)		b. 1858 d. 1919
1909–1913	,,	William Howard Taft (R)		b. 1857 d. 1930
1913–1921	,,	Thomas Woodrow Wilson (D)		b. 1856 d. 1924
1921–1923	,,	Warren Gamaliel Harding (R)		b. 1865 d. 1923
1923–1929	,,	Calvin Coolidge (R)		b. 1872 d. 1933
1929–1933	,,	Herbert Clark Hoover (R)		b. 1874 d. 1964
1933–1945	,,	Franklin Delano Roosevelt (D)		b. 1882 d. 1945
1945–1953	,,	Harry S. Truman (D)		b. 1884
1953–1961	,,	Dwight David Eisenhower (R)		b. 1890 d. 1969
1961–1963	,,	John Fitzgerald Kennedy (D)	b. 1917	assassinated 1963
1963–1969	,,	Lyndon Baines Johnson (D)		b. 1908
1969–	,,	Richard M. Nixon (R)		b. 1913

Thomas Woodrow Wilson, President of the United States (1913–1921), was instrumental in creating the League of Nations.

Herbert Clark Hoover, President of the United States (1929–1933).

Warren Gamaliel Harding, President of the United States (1921–1923).

Franklin Delano Roosevelt, President of the United States (1933–1945), confers with Winston Churchill during World War II.

Harry S. Truman, President of the United States (1945–1953), emerged from obscurity to become a strong leader following the death of Franklin Roosevelt.

Dwight David Eisenhower, President of the United States (1953–1961), led the Allied forces to victory in World War II.

John Fitzgerald Kennedy, President of the
United States (1961–1963), at 43 was the
youngest man to be elected President.

Lyndon Baines Johnson, President of the
United States (1963–1969), began his
career as a schoolteacher.

VICE PRESIDENTS

1789–1797	Vice President	John Adams (F)	b. 1735	d. 1826
1797–1801	,,	Thomas Jefferson (D/R)	b. 1743	d. 1826
1801–1805	,,	Aaron Burr (D/R)	b. 1756	d. 1836
1805–1812	,,	George Clinton (D/R)	b. 1739	d. 1812
1813–1814	,,	Elbridge Gerry (D/R)	b. 1744	d. 1814
1817–1825	,,	Daniel Tompkins (D/R)	b. 1744	d. 1825

Millard Fillmore, Vice President
of the United States (1849–1850), succeeded Zachary Taylor as President
(1850–1853).

John Tyler, Vice President (1841),
following the death of William Henry
Harrison became President (1841–1845).

1825–1832	Vice President	John C. Calhoun (D/R)	b. 1782	d. 1850
1833–1837	„	Martin Van Buren (D)	b. 1782	d. 1862
1837–1841	„	Richard M. Johnson (D)	b. 1780	d. 1850
1841	„	John Tyler (W)	b. 1790	d. 1862
1845–1849	„	George M. Dallas (D)	b. 1792	d. 1864
1849–1850	„	Millard Fillmore (W)	b. 1800	d. 1874
1853	„	William R. King (D)	b. 1786	d. 1853
1857–1861	„	John C. Breckinridge (D)	b. 1821	d. 1875
1861–1865	„	Hannibal Hamlin (R)	b. 1809	d. 1891
1865	„	Andrew Johnson (R)	b. 1808	d. 1875

Andrew Johnson, although a Democrat, was elected Vice President on the Republican ticket (1864) and served as President (1865–1869) after the assassination of Lincoln.

Chester Alan Arthur, Vice President of the United States (1881), assumed the presidency (1881–1885) after the fatal shooting of President Garfield.

1869–1873	Vice President	Schuyler Colfax (R)	b. 1823	d. 1885
1873–1875	„	Henry Wilson (R)	b. 1812	d. 1875
1877–1881	„	William A. Wheeler (R)	b. 1819	d. 1887
1881	„	Chester Alan Arthur (R)	b. 1830	d. 1886
1885	„	Thomas A. Hendricks (D)	b. 1819	d. 1885
1889–1893	„	Levi P. Morton (R)	b. 1824	d. 1920
1893–1897	„	Adlai E. Stevenson (D)	b. 1835	d. 1914
1897–1899	„	Garret A. Hobart (R)	b. 1844	d. 1899
1901	„	Theodore Roosevelt (R)	b. 1858	d. 1919
1905–1909	„	Charles W. Fairbanks (R)	b. 1852	d. 1918
1909–1912	„	James S. Sherman (R)	b. 1855	d. 1912
1913–1921	„	Thomas R. Marshall (D)	b. 1854	d. 1925
1921–1923	„	Calvin Coolidge (R)	b. 1872	d. 1933
1925–1929	„	Charles G. Dawes (R)	b. 1865	d. 1951
1929–1933	„	Charles Curtis (R)	b. 1860	d. 1936
1933–1941	„	John Nance Garner (D)	b. 1868	d. 1967

Calvin Coolidge was Vice President (1921–1923) under Harding. When the latter died in office, Coolidge became President in his place, and was later elected to that office serving altogether from 1923 till 1929.

1941–1945	Vice President	Henry A. Wallace (D)	b. 1888	d. 1965
1945	”	Harry S. Truman (D)	b. 1884	
1949–1953	”	Alben W. Barkley (D)	b. 1877	d. 1956
1953–1961	”	Richard M. Nixon (R)	b. 1913	
1961–1963	”	Lyndon Baines Johnson (D)	b. 1908	
1965–1969	”	Hubert H. Humphrey (D)	b. 1911	

STATESMEN
Secretaries of State

1784–1789	Secretary of State	John Jay	b. 1745	d. 1829
1789–1793	”	Thomas Jefferson	b. 1743	d. 1826
1794–1795	”	Edmund Randolph	b. 1753	d. 1813
1795–1800	”	Timothy Pickering	b. 1745	d. 1829
1800–1801	”	John Marshall	b. 1755	d. 1835
1801–1809	”	James Madison	b. 1751	d. 1836
1809–1811	”	Robert Smith	b. 1757	d. 1842
1811–1817	”	James Monroe	b. 1758	d. 1831
1817	”	Richard Rush	b. 1780	d. 1859
1817–1825	”	John Quincy Adams	b. 1767	d. 1848
1825–1829	”	Henry Clay	b. 1777	d. 1852
1829–1831	”	Martin Van Buren	b. 1782	d. 1862
1831–1833	”	Edward Livingston	b. 1764	d. 1836
1833–1834	”	Louis McLane	b. 1786	d. 1857
1834–1841	”	John Forsyth	b. 1780	d. 1841
1841–1843	”	Daniel Webster	b. 1782	d. 1852
1843–1844	”	Abel Parker Upshur	b. 1791	d. 1844
1844–1845	”	John Caldwell Calhoun	b. 1782	d. 1850
1845–1849	”	James Buchanan	b. 1791	d. 1868
1849–1850	”	John Middleton Clayton	b. 1796	d. 1856
1850–1852	”	Daniel Webster		
1852–1853	”	Edward Everett	b. 1794	d. 1865
1853–1857	”	William Learned Marcy	b. 1786	d. 1857
1857–1860	”	Lewis Cass	b. 1782	d. 1866
1860–1861	”	Jeremiah Sullivan Black	b. 1810	d. 1883
1861–1869	”	William Henry Seward	b. 1801	d. 1872
1869	”	Elihu Benjamin Washburne	b. 1816	d. 1887

1869–1877 Secretary of State	Hamilton Fish		b. 1808	d. 1893
1877–1881	„	William Maxwell Evarts	b. 1818	d. 1901
1881	„	James Gillespie Blaine	b. 1830	d. 1893
1881–1885	„	Frederick Theodore Frelinghuysen	b. 1817	d. 1885
1885–1889	„	Thomas Francis Bayard	b. 1828	d. 1898
1889–1892	„	James Gillespie Blaine		
1892–1893	„	John Watson Foster	b. 1836	d. 1917

James Madison, President of the United States (1809–1817), served first as Secretary of State (1801–1809).

Martin Van Buren, President of the United States (1837–1841), also served as Secretary of State (1829–1831).

James Monroe, Secretary of State (1811–1817), enunciated the Monroe Doctrine during his Presidency (1817–1825).

William Henry Seward, Secretary of State (1861–1869), negotiated the purchase of Alaska from Russia. Opponents of the transaction dubbed Alaska "Seward's Folly."

James Buchanan was also a Secretary of State (1845–1849) before becoming President of the United States (1857–1861).

(Left) Charles Evans Hughes, remembered as Chief Justice of the United States Supreme Court, served as Secretary of State (1921–1925).

(Right) Cordell Hull, Secretary of State (1933–1944).

1893–1895 Secretary of State	Walter Quintin Gresham	b. 1832	d. 1895
1895–1897	"	Richard Olney	b. 1835	d. 1917
1897–1898	"	John Sherman	b. 1823	d. 1900
1898	"	William Rufus Day	b. 1849	d. 1923
1898–1905	"	John Milton Hay	b. 1838	d. 1905
1905–1909	"	Elihu Root	b. 1845	d. 1937
1909	"	Robert Bacon	b. 1860	d. 1919
1909–1913	"	Philander Chase Knox	b. 1853	d. 1921

Dean G. Acheson (right), Secretary of State (1949–1953), confers with Warren Austin, United States Ambassador to the United Nations (1946–1953).

John Foster Dulles, Secretary of State (1953–1959), is seen here at the 38th Parallel just before the outbreak of the Korean War.

1913–1915	Secretary of State	William Jennings Bryan	b 1860	d. 1925
1915–1920	,,	Robert Lansing	b. 1864	d. 1928
1920–1921	,,	Bainbridge Colby	b. 1869	d. 1950
1921–1925	,,	Charles Evans Hughes	b. 1862	d. 1948
1925–1929	,,	Frank Billings Kellogg	b. 1856	d. 1937
1929–1933	,,	Henry Lewis Stimson	b. 1867	d. 1950
1933–1944	,,	Cordell Hull	b. 1871	d. 1955
1944–1945	,,	Edward Reilley Stettinius, Jr.	b. 1900	d. 1949
1945–1947	,,	James Francis Byrnes	b. 1879	
1947–1949	,,	George Catlett Marshall	b. 1880	d. 1959
1949–1953	,,	Dean G. Acheson	b. 1893	
1953–1959	,,	John Foster Dulles	b. 1888	d. 1959
1959–1961	,,	Christian Archibald Herter	b. 1895	
1961–	,,	Dean Rusk	b. 1909	

Secretaries of the Treasury

1789–1795	Secretary of the Treasury	Alexander Hamilton	b. 1755	d. 1804
1795–1801	,,	Oliver Wolcott	b. 1760	d. 1833
1801	,,	Samuel Dexter	b. 1761	d. 1816
1801–1814	,,	Albert Gallatin	b. 1761	d. 1849

(Left) Alexander Hamilton, first United States Secretary of the Treasury (1789–1795); (Middle) Carter Glass, Secretary of the Treasury (1918–1920); (Right) Andrew William Mellon, Secretary of the Treasury (1921–1932), donated the National Gallery of Art in Washington, D.C.

1814	Secretary of the Treasury	George Washington Campbell	b. 1769	d. 1848
1814–1816	,,	Alexander James Dallas	b. 1759	d. 1817
1816–1825	,,	William Harris Crawford	b. 1772	d. 1834
1825–1829	,,	Richard Rush	b. 1780	d. 1859
1829–1831	,,	Samuel Delucenna Ingham	b. 1779	d. 1860
1831–1833	,,	Louis McLane	b. 1786	d. 1857
1833	,,	William John Duane	b. 1780	d. 1865
1833–1834	,,	Roger Brooke Taney	b. 1777	d. 1864
1834–1841	,,	Levi Woodbury	b. 1789	d. 1851
1841	,,	Thomas Ewing	b. 1789	d. 1871
1841–1843	,,	Walter Forward	b. 1786	d. 1852
1843–1844	,,	John Canfield Spencer	b. 1788	d. 1855
1844–1845	,,	Goerge Mortimer Bibb	b. 1776	d. 1859
1845–1849	,,	Robert John (or James) Walker	b. 1801	d. 1869
1849–1850	,,	William Morris Meredith	b. 1799	d. 1873
1850–1853	,,	Thomas Corwin	b. 1794	d. 1865
1853–1857	,,	James Guthrie	b. 1792	d. 1869
1857–1860	,,	Howell Cobb	b. 1815	d. 1868
1860–1861	,,	Philip F. Thomas		
1861	,,	John Adams Dix	b. 1798	d. 1879
1861–1864	,,	Salmon Portland Chase	b. 1808	d. 1873
1864–1865	,,	William Pitt Fessenden	b. 1806	d. 1869
1865–1869	,,	Hugh McCulloch	b. 1808	d. 1895
1869–1873	,,	George Sewall Boutwell	b. 1818	d. 1905
1873–1874	,,	William A. Richardson		
1874–1876	,,	Benjamin Helm Bristow	b. 1832	d. 1896
1876–1877	,,	Lot Myrick Morrill	b. 1812	d. 1883
1877–1881	,,	John Sherman	b. 1823	d. 1900
1881	,,	William Windom	b. 1827	d. 1891
1881–1884	,,	Charles James Folger	b. 1818	d. 1884
1884	,,	Walter Quintin Gresham	b. 1832	d. 1895
1884–1885	,,	Hugh McCulloch		
1885–1887	,,	Daniel Manning	b. 1831	d. 1887
1887–1889	,,	Charles Stebbins Fairchild	b. 1842	d. 1924
1889–1891	,,	William Windom		
1891–1893	,,	Charles Foster	b. 1828	d. 1904
1893–1897	,,	John Griffin Carlisle	b. 1835	d. 1910
1897–1902	,,	Lyman Judson Gage	b. 1836	d. 1927
1902–1907	,,	Leslie Mortier Shaw	b. 1848	d. 1932
1907–1909	,,	George Bruce Cortelyou	b. 1862	d. 1940
1909–1913	,,	Franklin MacVeagh	b. 1837	d. 1934
1913–1918	,,	William Gibbs McAdoo	b. 1863	d. 1941
1918–1920	,,	Carter Glass	b. 1858	d. 1946
1920–1921	,,	David Franklin Houston	b. 1866	d. 1940
1921–1932	,,	Andrew William Mellon	b. 1855	d. 1937
1932–1933	,,	Ogden Livingston Mills	b. 1884	d. 1937
1933–1934	,,	William Hartman Woodin	b. 1868	d. 1934
1934–1945	,,	Henry Morgenthau, Jr.	b. 1891	
1945–1946	,,	Frederick Moore Vinson	b. 1890	d. 1953
1946–1953	,,	John Wesley Snyder	b. 1895	
1953–1957	,,	George M. Humphrey		
1957–1961	,,	Robert B. Anderson		
1961–1965	,,	C. Douglas Dillon		
1965–	,,	Henry H. Fowler		

Other Statesmen

1776–1785	Ambassador to France	Benjamin Franklin	b. 1706	d. 1790
1842–1846	Minister to Spain	Washington Irving	b. 1783	d. 1859

Benjamin Franklin, United States Ambassador to France (1776–1785), is remembered as a scientist, inventor, and author.

Carl Schurz, Secretary of the Interior (1877–1881), was a political refugee from Germany who fought in the American Civil War and rose to high office in his adopted country.

Washington Irving, United States Minister to Spain (1842–1846), is best known as the author of beguiling tales of colonial New York.

1877–1881	Secretary of the Interior	Carl Schurz	b. 1829	d. 1906
1918–1946	Presidential Adviser	Bernard Baruch	b. 1870	d. 1965
1924–1925	Attorney General	Harlan Fiske Stone	b. 1872	d. 1946
1933–1936	Ambassador to Russia	William Christian Bullitt	b. 1891	d. 1967
1936–1941	Ambassador to France	William Christian Bullitt		
1941–1942	Ambassador-at-Large	William Christian Bullitt		
1939–1950	Personal representative of President to the Vatican	Myron Charles Taylor	b. 1874	d. 1959
1945–1953	Delegate to United Nations	Anna Eleanor Roosevelt	b. 1884	d. 1962
1961	,,	Anna Eleanor Roosevelt		
1946–1953	Ambassador to United Nations	Warren Austin	b. 1877	d. 1962
1952	Ambassador to Russia	George Frost Kennan	b. 1904	
1953–1960	Ambassador to United Nations	Henry Cabot Lodge	b. 1902	

1958–	United Nations Undersecretary for Special Political Affairs	Ralph Johnson Bunche	b. 1904
1961–1965	Ambassador to United Nations	Adlai E. Stevenson (grandson of Vice President of the same name)	b. 1900 d. 1965
1965–1968	,,	Arthur J. Goldberg	b. 1908

Anna Eleanor Roosevelt, widow of Franklin Roosevelt, and niece of Theodore Roosevelt, represented the United States in the United Nations (1945–1953, 1961).

Adlai E. Stevenson, grandson of the Vice President of the same name, was United States Ambassador to the United Nations (1961–1965).

Arthur J. Goldberg, Ambassador of the United States to the United Nations (1965–1968).

Ralph Johnson Bunche, United Nations Undersecretary for Special Political Affairs (1958–   ), was awarded the 1950 Nobel Peace Prize for his role in mediating the Arab-Israeli truce.

ALASKA
(Discovered by Vitus Bering in 1741)

1790–1818	Russian Governor	Alexander Adreevich Baranof	b. 1747	d. 1819
1818	,,	Leonti Andreanovich Hagemeister		
1818–1820	,,	Simeon Ivanovich Yanovsky		
1820–1825	,,	Matvei Ivanovich Muravief		
1825–1830	,,	Peter Egorovich Christiakof		
1830–1835	,,	Ferdinant von Wrangel	b. 1794	d. 1870
1835–1840	,,	Ivan Antonovich Kuprianof		
1840–1845	,,	Adolph Karlovich Etolin		
1845–1850	,,	Michael Dmitrievich Tebenkof		d. 1872
1850–1853	,,	Nicholai Yakovlevich Rosenberg		d. 1872
1853–1854	,,	Alexander Ilich Rudakof		
1854–1859	,,	Stephen Vasili Voevodsky		
1859–1863	,,	Ivan Vasilivich Furulelm		
1863–1867	,,	Dimitri Maksoutof		

(Purchased from Russia by the U.S.A. in 1867; Military rule 1867–1884)

1884–1885	American Governor	John H. Kinkead (R)	b. 1826	d. 1904
1885–1889	,,	Alfred P. Swineford (D)	b. 1834	d. 1909
1889–1893	,,	Lyman E. Knapp (R)	b. 1837	d. 1904
1893–1897	,,	James Sheakley (D)	b. 1827	d. 1917
1897–1906	,,	John G. Brady (R)	b. 1848	d. 1918
1906–1909	,,	Wilford B. Hoggatt (R)	b. 1865	d. 1938
1909–1912	,,	Walter E. Clark (R)	b. 1869	d. 1950

(Incorporated as a Territory in 1912)

1912–1913	Territorial Governor	Walter E. Clark (R)		
1913–1918	,,	John F. A. Strong (D)	b. ?	d. 1929
1918–1921	,,	Thomas Riggs (D)	b. 1873	d. 1945
1921–1925	,,	Scott C. Bone (R)	b. 1860	d. 1936
1925–1933	,,	George A. Parks (R)	b. 1883	
1933–1939	,,	John W. Troy (D)	b. 1868	d. 1942
1939–1953	,,	Ernest Gruening (D)	b. 1887	
1953–1957	,,	B. Frank Heintzleman (R)	b. 1888	
1957	,, (acting)	Waine E. Hendrickson (R)	b. 1896	
1957–1959	,,	Mike Stepovich (R)	b. 1919	

(Became the 49th U.S. State in 1959)

1959–1966	State Governor	William A. Egan (D)	b. 1914
1966–	,,	Walter J. Hickel (R)	

CONFEDERATE STATES OF AMERICA

1861–1865   President Jefferson Davis   b. 1808   d. 1889
(The Confederate States consisted of 11 states that seceded from the United States of
America in 1861; reconquered by the United States at the conclusion of the Civil War in
1865)

GUAM

(Following the Spanish-American War, Guam was annexed to the United States in
1899, and was governed by United States Naval officers until 1949)

(Civilian Governors)

1949	Governor	Carlton Skinner
1953	Governor (acting)	R. S. Herman
1953	Governor	Ford Q. Elvidge
1956	Governor (acting)	William T. Corbett
1956–1959	Governor	Richard Barrett Lowe
1960–1961	,,	Joseph Flores
1961–1963	,,	Bill Daniel
1963–	,,	Manual F. L. Guerrero

King Kamehameha I of
Hawaii (1810–1819)
united the main islands of
Hawaii into a single
kingdom after a series of
successful wars.

HAWAII

(An independent kingdom and republic before annexation to the United States)

1810–1819	King	Kamehameha I	b. 1758	d. 1819
1819–1824	,,	Kamehameha II (Liholiho)	b. 1797	d. 1824
1824–1854	,,	Kamehameha III (Kauikeaouli)	b. 1814	d. 1854

1855–1863	King	Kamehameha IV (Alexander Liholiho)	b. 1834	d. 18
1863–1872	,,	Kamehameha V (Lot Kamehameha)	b. 1830	d. 18
1872–1874	,,	Lunalilo (William Charles)	b. 1835	d. 18
1874–1891	,,	Kalakaua (David)	b. 1836	d. 18
1891–1893	Queen	Liliuokalani (Lydia)	b. 1838	d. 19
1893–1900	President	Sanford Ballard Dole	b. 1844	d. 19

TERRITORIAL GOVERNORS OF HAWAII (Appointed by the President
the U.S.)

1900–1903	Governor	Sanford Ballard Dole		
1903–1907	,,	George Robert Carter	b. 1866	d. 19
1907–1913	,,	Walter Francies Frear	b. 1863	d. 19
1913–1918	,,	Lucius Eugene Pinkham	b. 1850	d. 192
1918–1921	,,	Charles James McCarthy	b. 1861	d. 192
1921–1929	,,	Wallace Rider Farrington	b. 1871	d. 19
1929–1934	,,	Lawrence McCully Judd	b. 1887	
1934–1938	,,	Joseph Boyd Poindexter	b. 1869	d. 195
1942–1951	,,	Ingram Macklin Stainback	b. 1883	d. 196
1951–1953	,,	Oren Ethelbirt Long	b. 1889	
1953–1957	,,	Samuel Wilder King	b. 1886	d. 195
1957–1962	,,	William Francis Quinn	b. 1919	
1962–	,,	John A. Burns	b. 1909	
		(Hawaii achieved statehood in 1960)		

REPUBLIC OF TEXAS

(Seceded from Mexico 1836; independent republic 1836–1845; joined the Unite
States 1845)

1836–1838	President	Sam Houston	b. 1793	d. 186
1838–1841	,,	Mirabeau B. Lamar	b. 1798	d. 185
1841–1844	,,	Sam Houston		
1844–1846	,,	Anson Jones	b. 1798	d. 185
		(President Jones formally handed over power to the U.S. in
February, 1846)		

Sam Houston, President of Texas (1836–1838, 1841–1844), hero of the Texan War for Independence from Mexico, later served as Governor of the State of Texas but was removed from office when he refused to take the oath of allegiance to the Government of the Confederate States.

pper Volta
(Fr. Haute-Volta)

Maurice Yaméogo, President of
Upper Volta (1959–1966).

pper Volta, a former Overseas Territory of France, became autonomous in 1958,
and an independent republic in 1960)

59–1966	President	Maurice Yaméogo	b. 1920
	Foreign Minister	Lompolo Kane	
66–	Chief of State	Lt.-Col. Sangoule Lamizana	

Uruguay

José Gervasio Artigas,
Protector of Uruguay
(1813–1820).

Uruguay gained independence from Spain in 1811, along with Argentina; the struggle to
sist Argentine domination led to Brazilian occupation 1820–1827; constitutional
government achieved 1830)

813–1820	Protector	José Gervasio Artigas	b. 1764	d. 1850
830–1835	President	José Fructuoso Rivera	b. 1789	d. 1854
835–1838	„	Manuel Oribe	b. 1790	d. 1857
838–1842	„	José Fructuoso Rivera		
843–1852	„	Joaquin Suarel		
852–1853	„	Juan Francisco Giró	b. 1781	d. 1863
854–1855	„	Venancio Flores	b. 1808	d. 1868
855–1856	President (provisional)	Manuel B. Bustamante	b. 1785	d. 1863
856–1860	President	Gabriel Antonio Pereira	b. 1794	d. 1861
860–1864	„	Bernardo Prudencio Berro	b. 1803	d. 1868
864–1865	President (provisional)	Atanasio Cruz Aguirre	b. 1801	d. 1875
865–1868	President	Venancio Flores		
868	President (acting)	Pedro Varela	b. 1837	
868–1872	President	Lorenzo Batlle	b. 1810	d. 1887
872–1873	President (acting)	Tomás Gomensoro	b. 1810	d. 1900
873–1875	President	José Ellauri	b. 1839	d. 1897
875–1876	„	Pedro Varela	b. 1837	
876–1880	„	Lorenzo Latorre	b. 1844	d. 1916
880–1882	„	Francisco A. Vidal	b. 1827	d. 1889
882–1886	„	Máximo Santos	b. 1847	d. 1889
886–1890	„	Máximo Tajes	b. 1852	d. 1912
890–1894	„	Julio Herrera y Obes	b. 1876	d. 1912

1894–1897	President	Juan Idiarte Borda	b. 1844	d. 18
1897–1903	,,	Juan Lindolfo Cuestas	b. 1837	d. 19
1903–1907	,,	José Batlle y Ordóñez	b. 1856	d. 19
1907–1911	,,	Claudio Williman	b. 1863	d. 19
1911–1915	,,	José Batlle y Ordóñez		
1915–1919	,,	Feliciano Viera	b. 1870	d. 19
1919–1923	,,	Baltasar Brum	b. 1883	d. 19
1923–1927	,,	José Serrato		
1927–1931	,,	Juan Campisteguy	b. 1859	d. 19
1931–1938	,,	Gabriel Terra		d. 19
1938–1943	,,	Alfredo Baldomir	b. 1884	d. 19
1943–1947	,,	Juan José Amézaga		
1947–1947	,,	Tomas Berreta	b. 1875	d. 19
1947–1951	,,	Luis Batlle Berres		
1951–1955	,,	Andres Martinez Trueba		
1955	Council of Government	Luis Batlle Berres		
1956	,,	Alberto Zubiria		
1957	,,	Arturo Lezama		
1958	,,	Carlos Z. Fisher		
1959	,,	Martin R. Echegoyen		
1960	,,	Benito Nardone		
1961	,,	Eduardo Victor Haedo		
1962	,,	Faustino Harrison		
1963	,,	Daniel Fernandez Crespo		
1964	,,	Washington Beltram		
1965	,,	Carlos Maria Penades		
1966	,,	Alberto Heber		
1967	President	Oscar Daniel Gestido	b. 1901	d. 19
1967–	,,	Jorge Pacheco Areco		

Urundi, see Burundi

U.S.S.R., see Russia

Vandal Empire

(In 409, the Vandals entered Spain from Gaul, and in 428, the entire Vandal natio
migrated from Spain to Africa)

| 428– 477 | King | Genseric (Gaiseric) | d. 4 |

Genseric conquered Carthage, the city destroyed by Scipio the Younger
nearly 6 centuries earlier and made it the Vandal capital. When he sacked
Rome in A.D. 455 it was as if the ancient Carthaginians were being revenged.

477– 484	,,	Hunneric, son of Genseric	d. 4
484– 496	,,	Gunthamund, cousin of Hunneric	
496– 523	,,	Thrasamund, brother of Gunthamund	d. 5
523– 531	,,	Hilderic, son of Hunneric	murdered 5
531– 534	,,	Gelimer, nephew of Thrasamund	

(Belisarius conquered the Vandal Empire, which became a province of the Byzanti
Empire in 534)

Vatican, see Popes

Venezuela

Simón Bolívar, President of Greater Colombia which included Venezuela.

(Venezuela became independent from Spain in 1811, as part of Greater Colombia, under the presidency of Simón Bolívar. In 1830, Venezuela seceded and became a separate nation)

1830–1846	President	José Antonio Paez	b. 1790	d. 1873
1846–1851	"	José Tadeo Mónagas	b. 1784	d. 1868
1851–1855	"	José Gregorio Mónagas, brother of José Tadeo Mónagas	b. 1795	d. 1858
		(Civil War 1858 to 1863)		
1863–1868	"	Juan Crisóstomo Falcón	b. 1820	d. 1870
1868–1870	"	José Ruperto Mónagas, son of José Tadeo Mónagas		
1870–1889	"	Antonio Guzman Blanco	b. 1829	d. 1899
1888–1890	President (provisional)	José Pablo Rojas Paul		
1890–1892	President	Raimundo Andueza Palacio		
1892–1898	"	Joaquín Crespo	b. 1845	killed 1898
1898–1899	"	Ignacio Andrade		
1899–1908	"	Cipriano Castro	b. 1858?	d. 1924
1908–1914	"	Juan Vicente Gómez	b. 1857?	d. 1935
1915–1922	President (provisional)	Victorio Marquez Bustillos		
1922–1929	President	Juan Vicente Gómez		
1929–1931	President (provisional)	Juan Bautista Pérez		
1931–1935	President	Juan Vicente Gómez		
1935–1941	"	Elcazar Lopez Contreras		
1941–1945	"	Isaías Medina Angarita	b. 1897	d. 1945

Rómulo Betancourt, President of Venezuela (1959–1964).

Raúl Leoní, President of Venezuela (1964–   ).

1945–1947	President	Rómulo Betancourt	
1948	,,	Rómulo Gallegos	b. 1884
1948–1950	Military Junta	Carlos Delgado Chalbaud (assassinated)	
1950–1952	Government Junta	G. Suarez Flamerich	
1953–1958	President	Marcos Pérez Jiménez	b. 1914
1958	,,	Wolfgang Larrazabal Ugueto	
1958–1959	,,	Edgard Sanabria	
1959–1964	,,	Rómulo Betancourt	
1964–	,,	Raúl Leoní	b. 1905

Venice, see Italy

Khai Dinh, Emperor of Annam (1916–1926), visits Paris with members of the Royal Family.

Vietnam

(Under Chinese rule from 3rd century B.C. to 15th century A.D.; came under French administration in 19th century as part of French Indo-China. Monarchs of French colonial period are listed below)

ANNAM

1889–1914	Emperor	Than Thoi
1914–1916	,,	Duy Than
1916–1926	,,	Khai Dinh
1926–1940	,,	Bao Dai
	(1940–1945 Japanese occupation)	

*Duong Van Minh, President of
South Vietnam (1963–1964).*

*Nguyen Cao Ky, Prime Minister of
South Vietnam (1965–1967).*

(Vietnam, composed of the former French possessions of Cochin-China, Annam, and Tonkin, came into being as an Associated State of Indo-China in 1949, French rule ended in 1954, and the country was partitioned along the line of the 17th parallel into South and North Vietnam)

Southern Zone

1949–1955	Head of State	Bao Dai	b. 1913
1955–1963	President	Ngo Dinh Diem	b. 1901 murdered 1963
1963–1964	,,	Duong Van Minh	
1964–1965	,,	Nguyen Khanh	b. 1927
1965–1967	Chief of State	Nguyen Van Thieu	
1967–	President	Nguyen Van Thieu	
1948–1949	Prime Minister	Nguyen Van Xuan	
1950	,,	Nguyen Phan Long	
1950–1952	,,	Tran Van Huu	
1952–1953	,,	Nguyen Van Tam	
1953–1954	,,	Buu Loc	
1954–1955	,,	Ngo Dinh Diem	
1963–1964	,,	Nguyen Ngoc Tho	b. 1908
1964–1965	,,	Nguyen Khanh	
1965–1967	,,	Nguyen Cao Ky	
1967–1968	,,	Nguyen Van Loc	b. 1922
1968–	,,	Tran Van Huong	b. 1903

Ngo Dinh Diem.

Northern Zone

1945–	President	Ho Chi-Minh	b. 1890
1954–	Prime Minister	Pham van Dong	b. 1906

Western Samoa

(Formerly administered by Germany and New Zealand; became the first Polynesian state to regain independence, 1962)

1962–	Head of State	Malietoa Tanumafili II	b. 1913
1962–	Prime Minister	Hon Fiame Mata'afa Faumuina Mulinu'u II	

Yemen

The reign of Ahmed, Imam of Yemen (1949–1962), was terminated by revolution and a republic was declared.

(In ancient times, home of the Minaean and Sabaean Kingdoms; Anglo-Turkish boundary fixed, 1902–1904)

1904–1948	Imam	Yahya Hamied Alddien	b. 1871	murdered 1948
1949–1962	„	Ahmed, son of Yahya Hamied Alddien	b. 1898	d. 1962
1962–	„	Muhammed al Badr, son of Ahmed Hamied Alddien	b. 1928	

(Revolutionary government set up, 1962; Republican regime recognized by United Nations and most countries)

1962–1965	President	Abdullah Al Sallal	b. 1917
1965–1967	Chairman of Presidential Council	Abdullah Al Sallal	
1967–	„	Abdul Rahman al-Iryani	b. 1912

Yugoslavia

(Kingdom proclaimed on December 1, 1918)

1919–1921	King	Peter I (of Serbia)	b. 1844	d. 1921
1918–1921	Regent	Alexander, son of Peter I	b. 1888	assassinated 1934
1921–1934	King	Alexander I		

Alexander I, King of the Serbs, Croats and Slovenes, served with distinction in the Balkan War and held the position of commander-in-chief of the Serbian army when World War I began. He succeeded his father as King, 6 weeks after an attempt on his life, and on a visit to France 13 years later, was killed by a Croat assassin at Marseilles.

1934–1941	Regent	Paul, cousin of Alexander I	b. 1893
1934–1945	King	Peter II, son of Alexander I	b. 1923

(Communist republican regime since 1945)

1945–1953	President	Ivan Ribar	b. 1881
1953–	„	Josip Broz Tito	b. 1892

STATESMEN

1912–1918	Prime Minister	Nikola Pasic	b. 1846	d. 1926
1921–1924	„	Nikola Pasic		
1924–1926	„	Nikola Pasic		

President Tito addresses the Federal Executive Council of Yugoslavia on the anniversary of the Republic.

1945–1963 President of Federal   Josip Broz Tito
          Executive Council
   Tito began life as a metal worker, and during World War II he led the partisans in their successful fight against the German Nazi occupation. By following a political line independent of Moscow after the war he estranged himself and his country from other Communist regimes.

1963–   President of Federal   Petar Stambolic   b. 1912
          Executive Council

Peter II, King of Yugoslavia (1934–1945).

Alexander I, King of Yugoslavia (1921–1934).

Ivan Ribar, President of Yugoslavia (1945–1953), stands beside Josip Broz Tito, President since 1953, in the days when they led Yugoslav resistance during World War II.

Petar Stambolic, President of Federal Executive Council of Yugoslavia (1963–   ).

BOSNIA AND HERZEGOVINA

(Occupied by Austria in 1878)

1878	Governor	Freiherr Josef von Philippovich		
		Philippsberg	b. 1819	d. 1889
1878–1881	,,	Wilhelm Nikolaus, Herzog von Württemberg	b. 1828	d. 1896
1881–1882	,,	Freiherr Hermann Dahlen-Orlaburg	b. 1828	d. 1887
1882–1903	,,	Freiherr Johann von Appel	b. 1826	d. 1906
1903–1907	,,	Freiherr Eugen von Albori	b. 1838	d. 1915
1907–1909	,,	Freiherr Anton von Winzor	b. 1844	d. 1910
		(Annexed by Austria-Hungary in 1908)		
1909–1911	,,	Freiherr Marian von Varesanin-Vares	b. 1847	d. 1917
1911–1914	,,	Oskar Potiorek	b. 1853	d. 1933
1915–1918	,,	Freiherr Stefan von Sarkotic-Lovcen	b. 1858	d. 1939
		(Part of Yugoslavia since 1918)		

Coin of the puppet Kingdom of Croatia.

CROATIA

(Under Hungary from 1091; under Turkey from 1526; 1809–1813 part of France; under Austria-Hungary until 1918, when it became part of Yugoslavia; Croatia declared independent 1941)

1941–1944 Dictator Ante Pavelich	b. 1889	d. 1959

(Kingdom created by Italians)

1941–1943   King   Aimone of Spoleto   abdicated
(Croatia under Germans until reunited with Yugoslavia after World War II)

MONTENEGRO

(No information is available regarding the earliest rulers; Montenegro was independent from the 14th Century)

1697–1737 Prince-Bishop Danilo Petrović	b. 1677	d. 1737
1737–? ,, Sava		d. 1782

Nicholas I, Prince and later King, of Montenegro (1860–1918).

? –1766	Prince-Bishop	Vasili	d. 1766
1766–1774	,,	Stephen the Little	murdered 1774
1774–1782	,,	Sava	
1782–1830	,,	Peter I, nephew of Sava	b. 1760? d. 1830

Yugoslavia (continued)

1830–1851	Prince-Bishop	Peter II, nephew of Peter I	b. 1812	d. 1851
1851–1860	Lord	Danilo II	b. 1826	assassinated 1860
1860–1910	Prince	Nicholas I, nephew of Danilo II	b. 1841	d. 1921
1910–1918	King	Nicholas I abdicated 1918		

Nicholas I obtained recognition of Montenegro's independence from the European powers in 1878—an independence his country had defended since 1389. When Austria-Hungary attacked Serbia in 1914 he immediately went to Serbia's aid.

(Occupied by Austria, 1916–1918; incorporated with Yugoslavia from 1918)

SERBIA

(Established in the 7th century by emigrants from the Carpathian Mountains; ruled by Turkey, 1459–1829)

1804–1813	National Leader	Karageorge (George Petrović)	b. 1766?	d. 1817

Karageorge ("Black George") was the founder of Serbian independence. Supplanted as Serbian national leader by Miloš Obrenović, Karageorge was murdered in his sleep and his head sent to Constantinople. This act led to a long feud between the two rival dynasties.

1817–1839	Prince	Miloš Obrenović	b. 1780	d. 1860
1839	„	Milan, son of Miloš Obrenović	b. 1819	d. 1839
1839–1842	„	Michael, son of Miloš Obrenović	b. 1823	assassinated 1868
1842–1858	„	Alexander Karadjordjević, son of Karageorge	b. 1806	d. 1885
1858–1860	„	Miloš Obrenović		
1860–1868	„	Michael, son of Miloš Obrenović		
1868–1882	„	Milan, grand-nephew of Miloš Obrenović	b. 1854	d. 1901

Karageorge, early 19th-century leader of Serbian nationalism.

(Left) Michael, Prince of Serbia (1839–1942, 1860–1868); (Right) Milan I, Prince and later King, of Serbia (1868–1889).

(In 1882 Prince Milan assumed the title of King)

1882–1889	King	Milan I		abdicated 1889
1889–1903	„	Alexander I, son of Milan I	b. 1876	assassinated 1903
1903–1921	„	Peter I Karadjordjević, son of Alexander	b. 1844	d. 1921

(Occupied by Austria, 1915–1918; part of Yugoslavia since 1918)

Zambia

Kenneth David Kaunda, President of Zambia (1964–   ).

(Zambia, formerly the British Protectorate of Northern Rhodesia, became an independent republic in 1964)

| 1964– | President | Kenneth David Kaunda | b. 1924 |

Picture Credits

The publishers wish to thank the following for the use of illustrations in this book: A.C.L., Brussels; Agentstvo Pechagi Novosti, Moscow; American Swedish News Exchange, New York; Anefo, Amsterdam, Holland; Annan Photgraphers, Glasgow, Scotland; Argentine Embassy, London; Argentine National Ministry Directory; Art Gallery of Toronto; Australian News and Information Bureau, New York; Edgar Barvoix, Ghent; Baron Studios, London; Belga, Brussels; Belgian Institute of Information and Documentation, Brussels; Bergne Portrait Studio, Stockholm; British Information Services, New York; British Museum, London; British Overseas Airways Corporation, London; British Travel, New York; Canada House, London; Central Directory of Information, Vietnam; Central Art Gallery, Manchester; Central Office of Information, London; Codex Monacensis; A. C. Cooper and Sons Ltd., London; Wm. Harold Cox, Luton, England; Crescente, Rome; Djambatan International Educational Publishing House, Amsterdam; East African Office, London; Enosis Photographic Service, Athens; European Picture Union, Oslo, Norway; European Press Photo Agencies Union, Oslo, Norway; Felici Photographers, Rome; Finnish Tourist Association, Helsinki, Finland; French Embassy, London; German Information Center, New York; Grechs Studio, Valletta, Malta; Greek Photo News, Athens; Herrnried Photo, Stockholm; Hungarian News Agency, Budapest; Imperial Ethiopian Embassy, London; Imperial Iranian Embassy, London; Imperial War Museum, London; Information Service of India, India House, London; Institute of Pacific Relations, New York; Irish Press, Dublin; Israel Information, New York; Italian Center of Information, New York; Italian Cultural Institute, New York; Jamaican Tourist Board, Kingston; R. Kayaert, Brussels; Eduoard Kutter and Fils Photograph Agency, Luxembourg; Lehtikuva Oy, Helsinki; Lensmen Photographic Agency, Dublin; Luxembourg Consulate, New York; Megalokonomou Bros. Photo Service, Athens; Mexican Embassy, London; Moroccan Secretariat of Information, Rabat; Museum of Fine Arts, Ghent; National Film Board, Ottawa; National Gallery of Art, Washington; National Galleries of Scotland, Edinburgh; National Information Service of Ecuador; National Portrait Gallery, London; National Publicity Studios, Wellington, New Zealand; Netherlands Government Information Service; New York Public Library; New Zealand Consulate, New York; Ontario Dept. of Tourism and Information; Penoptaz; Photo Information of the Ivory Coast; Photographic Information Service, Rome; Photopress Zurich, Switzerland; Picture Archives of the Eastern National Library; The Picture Archives of the National Library; R. S. W. Prasa, Central Photograph Agency, Warsaw; Prentice-Hall, Inc., New Jersey; Press Information Bureau, Government of India, New Delhi; Public Archives of Canada; Public Relations Dept., Bangkok; Puerto Rico News Service, New York; Queens Portrait Gallery, Buckingham Palace, London; Reading Museum and Art Gallery; Greig Royle, Wellington, New Zealand; Royal Danish Ministry for Foreign Affairs, Copenhagen; El Salvador Embassy, London; Scandinavia House, New York; Simonis;

South African Information Service, New York; Sudan Government Ministry of Information; Victor Sumathipala, Dept. of Information, Ceylon; Swedish National Travel Office, New York; Tanjug Photo, Belgrade; Petur Thomsen; Tunisian Embassy, London; Turkish Embassy, London; United Nations, New York; Universal Photos, London; Venezuelan Embassy, London; A. Verviris, Athens; Vietnam Cong-Hoa Bo Thong-Tin Tam-Ly Chien; Walter Wachter Vaduz, Liechtenstein; Wide World Photos, Wiener Press, Bilddienst, Vienna.

Acknowledgments

The editors and publishers particularly thank the following for their co-operation and helpful assistance in supplying information for this volume: Argentine Embassy, London; Belgian Government Information Center, New York; Ceylon Embassy, Washington, D.C.; Ceylon Mission to United Nations, New York; Consulate General of Australia, New York; Consulate General of Canada, New York; Consulate General of Jamaica, New York; Consulate General of South Africa, New York; Ethiopian Embassy, London; Finnish Embassy, London; French Embassy, London; Iranian Embassy, London; Irish Information Center, New York; Malaysian Mission to United Nations, New York; Mexican Embassy, London; Netherlands Embassy, London; Polish Embassy, London; Puerto Rican Information Office, New York; Salvador Embassy, New York; Singapore Mission to United Nations, New York; Spanish Embassy, London; Swiss Information Center, New York; Syrian Mission to United Nations, New York; Togo Mission to United Nations, New York; Tunisian Embassy, London; Turkish Embassy, London; United Kingdom Mission to United Nations, New York; United Nations Information Bureau, New York; Venezuelan Embassy, London; and Burton Hobson for photographs from various coin books written and edited by him, including the "Catalogue of the World's Most Popular Coins."